MAKING NEW PEOPLE

MAKING NEW PEOPLE

Politics, Cinema, and Liberation in Burkina Faso, 1983–1987

James E. Genova

MICHIGAN STATE UNIVERSITY PRESS | *East Lansing*

Copyright © 2023 by James E. Genova

Michigan State University Press
East Lansing, Michigan 48823-5245

Library of Congress Cataloging-in-Publication Data
Names: Genova, James Eskridge, author.
Title: Making new people : politics, cinema, and liberation in Burkina Faso, 1983-1987 / James E. Genova.
Other titles: Politics, cinema, and liberation in Burkina Faso, 1983-1987
Description: East Lansing : Michigan State University Press, [2023] | Includes bibliographical references and index.
Identifiers: LCCN 2022001639 | ISBN 9781611864397 (paperback) | ISBN 9781609177096 (pdf) | ISBN 9781628954777 (epub) | ISBN 9781628964714 (Kindle)
Subjects: LCSH: Burkina Faso—Politics and government—20th century. | Burkina Faso—History—Coup d'état, 1987. | Motion pictures—Burkina Faso. | Revolutions in motion pictures.
Classification: LCC DT555.835 .G46 2022 | DDC 966.25053—dc23/eng/20220113
LC record available at https://lccn.loc.gov/2022001639

Cover design by Shaun Allshouse, www.sallshouse.com

Cover photo: President Thomas Sankara (*left*) and Blaise Compaoré (*right*) meeting on an airport tarmac on an unknown date in Burkina Faso.

Visit Michigan State University Press at *www.msupress.org*

To my wife Stephanie, daughter Eva, and son-in-law Nick

Contents

- ix   **PREFACE**
- xxv   **ACKNOWLEDGMENTS**
- xxvii   **LIST OF ABBREVIATIONS**

- 1   **CHAPTER 1**
  Politics and Culture in Upper Volta
  (1960s–1982)

- 33   **CHAPTER 2**
  Dual Power and the Triumph of the Burkinabè Revolution
  (1982–1983)

- 61   **CHAPTER 3**
  Building Revolutionary Structures and Making New People
  (1983–1984)

- 89   **CHAPTER 4**
  Cultural Revolution, Economic Reform, and Global Engagement
  (1984–1985)

- 121   **CHAPTER 5**
  Recalibration of the Burkinabè Revolution
  (1985–1986)

- 151   **CHAPTER 6**
  Twilight of the Revolution and Sankara's Murder
  (1986–1987)

- 183   **CONCLUSION**
- 195   **NOTES**
- 239   **BIBLIOGRAPHY**
- 247   **INDEX**

Preface

"A Sad Day for Africa," read an *Africa Report* headline on 1 November 1987, referencing events that transpired in Ouagadougou, Burkina Faso, on 15 October 1987. The article began, "Capt. Thomas Sankara and 13 of his close associates were murdered in mid-October when Capt. Blaise Compaoré, the late president's number-two and former minister of state in the National Council of the Revolution (Conseil national de la révolution, CNR), seized power in a bloody coup d'état that left up to 100 people dead."[1] Just over twenty-seven years later, on 31 October 2014, Blaise Compaoré was forced from power and fled to neighboring Côte d'Ivoire. During the mass protests demanding that Compaoré step down youths flooded the streets of Ouagadougou wearing T-shirts emblazoned with Sankara's image. His sayings adorned signs hoisted by the jubilant and defiant crowds. As one student interviewed by *Al Jazeera America* put it, "Sankara was not just fighting imperialism for the sake of politics, but he wanted the Burkinabe [sic] people to develop themselves and their land and rely essentially on themselves instead of the West."[2] One year later elements loyal to Compaoré attempted a military coup to stop the transition to a new civilian government but were thwarted by hundreds of thousands of Burkinabè citizens, who took to the streets and once again invoked Sankara's name and memory. As the *Guardian* put it, "Wearing T-shirts bearing the image of the legendary former Burkina Faso leader, Thomas Sankara, they [the residents of Ouagadougou] chanted the slogan of his government: 'La patrie ou la mort, nous vaincrons!' . . . A few days later, leaders of the coup, loyal to former president Blaise Compaoré, were forced to back down and the country's interim leadership was restored."[3] Despite lasting for just four years and having been overturned more than thirty years earlier, the ideals, aspirations, and accomplishments of the Burkinabè Revolution, as testified to by the protesters quoted above, continues to inspire the country's population as well as people across Africa and around the world.

This book looks at Burkina Faso's revolutionary government as a window into a critical transition period in modern African history between the closing of the era of the fight for national liberation and the dawning of new forces around neoliberal capitalist globalization that threatened the achievements of the first post-independence decades. The Burkinabè Revolution (1983–1987) transpired when the International Monetary Fund (IMF) was pushing Structural Adjustment Programs (SAPs) that aimed to remake the world economy based on a radical free market system, undercutting the victories of the anti-colonial movements, and sabotaging the socioeconomic and cultural development realized by many postcolonial African states. Sankara's government refused to accept the SAP urged on his country by the IMF and instead pursued a policy of self-directed development structured around the resources available within the country and the people's most urgent needs.[4] The field of cultural production was a critical arena through which the revolution sought to mobilize the population as well empower them to express their aspirations while fulfilling the goals of economic and political development. Therefore, this book focuses on the regime's cultural politics and specifically the importance the revolutionaries attached to the cinema as a mechanism for social change. Film presented models to be emulated by the people as well as a means of expression for the masses as they developed their own creativity.

When the revolutionary government took power on 4 August 1983 the new administration committed itself to the development of Upper Volta (as the country was then known) in a manner that emphasized its independence and claimed an equal place in the international arena with all other sovereign countries. In the Cold War context, the revolutionary regime charted its own path toward social, economic, cultural, and political development based on the real conditions found within the country. The new leaders exuded a fearlessness and authenticity that inspired hope among the populace. Led by Captain Thomas Sankara, a coalition of radical military officers, communist activists from a variety of parties, labor leaders, and militant students coalesced in the months prior to the revolution and provided the rich ideological and experiential basis that framed the new government's objectives. It also generated a remarkable political openness that favored experimentation and debate. Those forces included, among the military, Captain Blaise Compaoré, Major Jean-Baptiste Boukary Lingani, Captain Henri Zongo, and Captain Pierre Ouédraogo, all committed Marxists who became friends in the mid-1970s and constituted a core of communist officers working to promote revolution from within the ranks of the armed forces. Those radical soldiers were joined by prominent communist activists from the country's pro-Soviet African Independence Party (Parti africain de l'indépendence, PAI) including Philippe Ouédraogo and Adama Touré and the Maoist-oriented Union of Communist Struggle (Union de Lutte Communiste, ULC) led by Valère Somé, a close personal friend of Sankara's who emerged from the expatriate student movement in Paris. It also encompassed other unaffiliated Marxists, student organizers, and labor leaders including Babou Paulin Bamouni who would become the chief ideologue of the revolutionary government, and Soumane Touré, the country's most prominent labor leader as well as a member of the PAI.

The vitality of the revolutionaries was not solely derived from their remarkable youth (Sankara was only thirty-three and Compaoré thirty-two at the time of the revolution), but from the freshness of their ideas. The breadth of the revolutionary coalition meant that the government was not bound to a strict dogma or beholden to external interests, a circumstance that produced passionate debate and even conflict among the revolutionaries. This openness contrasted with the seeming tiredness of the Cold War ideological pronouncements coming from the Soviet Union and the United States that did not appear to produce much enthusiasm from their peoples or inspire others around the world. Such ideological ferment and the energy exhibited by the Burkinabè people in carrying out the revolution's policies aroused the attention of conservative leaders in the region as well as the former imperial power, France. It also generated considerable confusion and frustration among officials in Washington, Moscow, Paris, and Tripoli who sought to define the new regime according to rigid categories of geopolitical alignment. Consequently, one thread of this story is the unlikely assortment of forces inside and outside the country with which the Burkinabè revolutionaries had to contend and the treacherous international waters they had to navigate.[5]

The main paths of the narrative, though, are the remarkable and at times prescient aspects of policy that elucidate the ideological nature of the revolution.[6] The revolutionary government was one of the earliest in the world to identify climate change (global warming and desertification), international debt, and gender inequality as critical inhibitors to the aspirations that drove the movement for independence in the 1950s. The CNR launched literacy programs, vaccination campaigns, and reform of local administrative structures, all hallmarks of the era of national liberation. The Sankara-led administration also engaged in reforestation programs, promoted women's rights and empowerment at all levels of society, and pointed to the crushing structural debt that beset many of the world's former colonies as signal injustices that thwarted any meaningful social change in what was once called the Third World. The revolutionary regime pointed to food imports as a source of external control over the people as well as an indignity that undermined the confidence of the society in its own capacity for development. The CNR directly confronted the IMF over its policies of using debt to force ideological change on poor countries. Moreover, Sankara called out his fellow African leaders for not standing up to external financiers and the former colonial powers in defense of their own people and their countries' sovereignty.

Finally, the revolutionary government deployed significant resources as well as used its rhetorical powers to animate the cultural arena as a critical vector through which it would forge the capacity to transform the country's social and political structures by changing the people's mentality. Within that field the CNR developed, used, and promoted the cinema as a vehicle to spread the regime's message and facilitate Burkina Faso's and Africa's economic and social growth through the transformation of the person. The nation was already host to the continent's major biennial film festival FESPACO (Festival Panafricain de Cinéma et de Télévision de Ouagadougou) and led the charge to take control of African countries' motion picture distribution networks.[7] However, the advocacy and public support (financial, rhetorical, and institutional) furnished to the cinema industrial complex by the revolutionary government was unprecedented and was critical to African film's revival and growth in subsequent decades. It indelibly placed Burkina Faso at the center of African cinema and as a player in the global film arena.[8]

One of the most enduring and significant aspects of the Democratic and Popular Revolution (La Révolution démocratique et populaire, RDP) led by the CNR was its promotion of film as a vehicle for raising the people's consciousness, inspiring their efforts at social transformation, and articulating a new self-generated image of Africa and the African that was aimed at overturning the negative tropes that persisted from colonialism.[9] This involved the expansion of the theater system in Burkina Faso that enabled African films to reach a broader audience as well as building out the educational infrastructure to train more Burkinabè and others from throughout Africa in the many facets of filmmaking.[10] Moreover, the revolutionary government cultivated close relationships with African cineastes through the Pan-African Federation of Filmmakers (Fédération Panafricaine des Cinéastes, FEPACI).[11] Consequently, many African filmmakers embraced the Burkinabè Revolution, and it became one of the mechanisms that facilitated Burkina Faso's remarkable influence on the world stage during the revolutionary period. The CNR reciprocated that global embrace by initiating lasting transformations to the nature of FESPACO, opening it to filmmakers from beyond Africa and redefining it as an international festival with an African core. Moreover, the Burkinabè Revolution impacted the trajectory and influence of African cinema within and beyond the continent. Foregrounding film—and more broadly the Democratic and Popular Revolution's policies in the field of culture—provides a more deeply nuanced understanding of the reasons behind the revolution's enduring influence throughout Africa and the world beyond the 1980s.

The history of the Burkinabè Revolution, especially through a focus on its cultural politics, provides an exemplary framework for exploring the emergent forces that restructured global relations, the international economy, and the nature of the state in the transition to the age of neoliberal capitalist globalization. The revolutionary government found itself confronted by newly empowered financial institutions that sought to leverage debt into socioeconomic and political reform that would open the countries of the global south to the market interests of multinational corporations without the need for direct military intervention. Even the nature of funding for African film production generally and FESPACO specifically was impacted by those global financial pressures and the revolutionary government responded by finding alternative bases for carrying on the work of the festival.[12] The mounting threat from neoliberalism complicated the traditional program of national liberation that constituted the initial foundation for the new government's domestic and international policies. The revolution's leadership was aware of those difficulties and sought to adapt the politics of national liberation to the era of neoliberal globalization, presaging many of the issues that came to the fore in subsequent decades. Moreover, the Democratic and Popular Revolution sought to avoid the pitfalls of Cold War international entanglements even as Sankara's government pointed to a post–Cold War global politics that was based on multipolarity and global cooperation.

Theoretical Foundations of the Revolution

At its core, this analysis reveals a revolutionary process formed around concepts of the formation of a new and complete person, presented by the CNR as essential to the success of the revolution. Renaming the country from Upper Volta to Burkina Faso (Land of the Dignified People) speaks to the importance of human transformation to the revolutionary project.[13] In philosophy the concept of "making new people" derives from an interrogation of "alienation" as a debilitating factor in the realization of the full potential of the person, or the actualization of their essential human selves. Sankara and his comrades were well-versed in some of the major radical political philosophers of the previous century. Moreover, he and his comrades came of age in the immediate aftermath of the struggles for independence from European rule that ended formal colonial power across much of Africa in the 1960s. Many of those movements were inspired by the theories of Karl Marx, the French existentialists, Frantz Fanon, Mao Zedong, and Amilcar Cabral. In addition to philosophical systems, there were plenty of contemporary examples of revolutions that offered models of social reform to the future leaders of Burkina Faso. Cuba, led by Fidel Castro, was a strong influence on Sankara and his associates' political formation as was Mao's China, Muammar Qaddafi's Libya, and, shortly before the 4 August

1983 Revolution, Jerry Rawlings in Ghana. The Burkinabè revolutionaries viewed those experiences as examples of possible social change that offered useful insights into political strategies, policies, and the difficulties confronting progressively oriented states. Burkina Faso's leaders nevertheless insisted that their country had to chart its own unique path forward rather than copy a model from the outside. Importantly, the formation of "new people" within the experiences and efforts of the Burkinabè people was the foundation of any possible national belonging or development. Thus, the notion of nationalism associated with the CNR emphasized matching practice with circumstance within the limits of the possible in Burkinabè society rather than being anchored to any essentialist ethnic or identity politics.[14]

The idea of alienation informed many of the policies implemented by the government of the CNR. It also reflected the revolutionary leaders' own generational experience as shaped by the upheavals that gripped countries around the world in the 1960s when many of them were students, as Pierre Englebert demonstrates in his history of the Burkinabè Revolution.[15] Specifically, I argue that one of the most significant intellectual influences on Sankara and his associates was the anti-colonial revolutionary theorist Frantz Fanon. For Fanon, the struggle against imperialism had to involve a material confrontation with the imperial power, as well as an existential war to recover (or invent) the sense of self that was destroyed by the colonial experience. That is, by engaging in the struggle for liberation, a person is reinvented, and a new person emerges that is prepared to build the postcolonial society.[16] This is a battle to annihilate the alienation at the foundation of racism and colonialism. Fanon argues the alienation attendant upon racist imperialism is "never wholly successful." It does, however, have the effect of causing the targeted group to blame itself for all its problems and to believe that they stem directly from its inherent "racial and cultural characteristics." The initial reaction of the colonized to the discovery of their alienation is to passionately embrace the colonialist-constructed imagination of the culture of the oppressed and invert the value system through a radical embracement of that imaginary as their true essence. Fanon explains, "Rediscovering tradition, living it as a defense mechanism, as a symbol of purity, of salvation," the colonized embraces an "archaic" notion of identity that no longer corresponds to the modern reality or accounts for all that has changed with the experience of racism and imperialism. Fanon concludes, "The culture put into capsules, which has vegetated since the foreign domination, is revalorized." He argues that this inaugural phase of awakening must move toward a rejection of that "paradoxical" notion of culture and engage in the "fight against all forms of exploitation and of [the] alienation of man." This leads to the "struggle of the inferiorized [being] situated on a markedly more human level."[17]

Critically for the Burkinabè revolutionaries in following Fanon's analysis of the liberation process, what begins as a cultural program resolves in an economic and social plan of action for the development of society and the person. Fanon's nationalism is the coming-to-be of a new community based on the shared experience of the war (physical and psychological) for liberation not an essentialist or cultural understanding of some pre-formed exclusive society.[18] As Fanon writes, "After the conflict there is not only the disappearance of colonialism but also the disappearance of the colonized man. The new humanity cannot do otherwise than define a new humanism both for itself and for others. . . . The value of this type of conflict is that it supplies the maximum of conditions necessary for the development and aims of culture." In the end, "the existence of a new type of man is revealed to the public." However, "if you really wish your country to avoid regression, or at best halts and uncertainties, a rapid step must be taken from national consciousness to political and social consciousness." In the end, it is the material conditions of life for the people that are the basis for political action and the elaboration of a new community of belonging.[19]

For the leaders of the Burkinabè Revolution, the idea that a new person would be forged through struggle hinged on a claim that the (post)colonial subject was an alienated being, transformed by (neo)colonialism into a thing external to the self so that it could be exploited by the foreign power and the capitalist ruling class. Overcoming the colonial legacy entailed a process of realizing the person as a fully conscious and expressive being. Fanon and the leaders of the Burkinabè Revolution shared an understanding of alienation derived from Karl Marx's writings about the conditions of the worker under industrial capitalism. Marx observes that the capitalist "changes the worker into an insensible being lacking all needs, just as he changes his activity into a pure abstraction from all activity." The person is continually degraded, being reduced to specific categories of usefulness for production. The estrangement of the self from the person renders the worker a thing, a commodity to be exploited for profit by the capitalist class. Marx writes, "The less you *are*, the less you express your own life, the greater is your *alienated* life, the more you *have*, the greater is the store of your estranged being." As with Fanon, the remedy of this condition is a fight for liberation of the self and society against those material and psychological structures that produce the alienated subject. The goal of this process is nothing less than "the actual realization for man of man's essence and of his essence as something real."[20]

The last point grounds the ideal of the person in the material conditions of their existence. This provides the link between liberation and development that was foundational for the Burkinabè Revolution. As Marx put it, "Man is not lost in his object only when the object becomes for him a *human* object or objective man. This is possible only when the object becomes for him a *social* object, he himself for himself a social being, just as society becomes a being for him in this object."[21] Following from that philosophical trajectory, the Burkinabè revolutionaries did not frame development policies around the attainment of particular numerical targets or the acquisition of specific tools of production. Rather, progress was reinterpreted as a social project where the mentality of the person and structure of society should be transformed in ways that restored dignity to the people and unleashed the community's creative capacity. This explains the importance of the cultural arena generally and cinema specifically as essential vectors through which the entire revolutionary project would be realized. It also allows the revolution to be read through a Fanonian theoretical lens following his notions of alienation, liberation, and the formation of new people that would forge a new world.[22]

Sources, Methodology, and Historiography

This book is based on research in France and West Africa, examination of published sources from around the world, media accounts of the period and subsequently, official documents from the revolutionary government, as well as a synthesis and rereading of the published works on the Burkinabè Revolution. It is not a biography, although Sankara's personality looms large in any analysis of the revolution. Histories of events such as the Burkinabè Revolution, especially when guided by high-profile and charismatic personalities, risk overemphasizing the role of a single person in historical processes. Sankara was a product of his time and society while also playing a part in shaping both. He did not accede to power with a pre-formed political ideology, and the nature of his government was above all characterized by flexibility and showed a capacity to adapt to changing domestic and international circumstances. Therefore, this study provides a reconstruction from the ground up of a revolutionary regime and process that remains part of the present and of which Sankara was one element, but not the sole driver of the regime or its outcomes. The analysis builds upon the existing studies of Sankara and the Burkinabè Revolution in a manner that moves the conversation beyond a debate over Sankara as a person or the ideological divisions of the Cold War.

Many published works on Sankara and the Burkinabè Revolution include a debate over the nature of the regime, specifically whether it was a real revolution or another in a lineage of military coups that plagued many African countries during the 1980s. Pierre Englebert produced perhaps the earliest scholarly study of the revolution, written in its midst. He sought to uncover the nature of the events roiling Burkina Faso and insisted that the revolution be taken seriously by policymakers, political activists, and researchers outside the country. Based on his initial analysis, with the caveat that it was still very early in the new government, Englebert concludes that while the regime had the façade of a typical military regime, "the army did not take power alone." Combined with popular movements to which elements of the officer corps had connections, the new regime was a mix of military and radical civilian forces. "It is this [the social agitation prior to the coup and the military links with it]," according to Englebert, "that marks a fundamental difference with the preceding regimes where the directing organ was always exclusively [the] military."[23]

Englebert's study is nuanced and explores the successes as well as the contradictions that characterized the revolution. He outlines the development of new institutions meant to carry out the revolutionary agenda as well as craft it, but also hints at growing disaffection among key sectors of society because of those very structures and policies. Moreover, Englebert ties the internal unfolding of the Burkinabè Revolution to the wider world, showing how some of the inhibiting factors and potential threats to the revolution derive from international elements. The combination of internal rifts and external opposition, Englebert warns, could be the source of the revolution's undoing. The key to its durability, he notes, will be the government's ability to deal effectively with those threats. If it does so, "the original character of the Burkinabè Revolution could be preserved and the hope that emanates from it will continue along side of it."[24]

In the immediate aftermath of Sankara's assassination in 1987, scholars, journalists, and political activists sought to make sense of what had just happened.

Such early analyses followed the political divide around the Burkinabè Revolution, arguing either in favor of Sankara's government and producing a defense of its policies, or explaining its limitation and how its demise was in some ways at least predictable if not inevitable. That division is aptly reflected in two books published in 1989, one by Ludo Martens and another by Bruno Jaffré, both of whom went on to author several more studies of Sankara, Burkina Faso, and the Burkinabè Revolution and its aftermath. Martens wrote a critical assessment of the revolution, *Sankara, Compaoré et la révolution Burkinabè*, which reads as a justification of the 1987 coup that ushered in Compaoré's long rule of Burkina Faso. Contrary to Englebert, Martens sees Sankara's government as fundamentally a military junta centered on the mystical personhood of the head of state. This, according to Martens, is the fundamental flaw that spawned the misguided or poorly implemented policies of the Burkinabè Revolution, as well as led to the regime's demise. Sankara's government gradually descended into personal rule based on contradictory and empty declarations that only confused the masses and alienated the governing inner circle. Martens paints a portrait of a country sliding into chaos, fractured from top to bottom. For Martens, the Sankara regime was delegitimized from the start by the very process of its coming-to-be. Since it was not based on a mass revolutionary upheaval organized by a vanguard political force, it does not deserve the characterization as a "revolution" and the government's efforts to portray the regime as such merely sowed discord, bewilderment, and undermined the real potential revolutionary forces operating within Burkinabè society. Martens identified the real revolution as a force that was present and building throughout Burkina Faso before 4 August 1983, continued independent from and at times opposed to the Sankara regime, and persisted after his fall.[25]

Jaffré, on the other hand, offers a positive assessment of the CNR and a more critical approach to the successor regime. He presents an overview of the country's attitude in the tumultuous last days of Sankara's life, followed by a detailed analysis of some of the government's central campaigns and reforms. For Jaffré, the Burkinabè Revolution was genuine from the start and marked a notable departure not only from the country's previous governments but also from other progressive regimes throughout Africa. He asserts that, "The Burkinabè [people have] discovered hope since 1983." And, despite all the contradictions and challenges buffeting the country, during the period of Sankara's rule, Burkina Faso "advanced considerably." Most significantly, according to

Jaffré, "Sankara's contribution at the head of that [revolutionary process] was of primary importance."²⁶ In subsequent work, Jaffré offers a more strident defense of Sankara, his legacy, and the policies of the revolutionary government in his biography of the revolutionary leader, *Biographie de Thomas Sankara: La patrie ou la mort*. In this work, he provides insight into the formation of Sankara's personality and style of work as well as his political development. Jaffré asserts that the future leader of Burkina Faso diligently studied the major theoretical works of thinkers such as Frantz Fanon, Karl Marx, and Amilcar Cabral while cultivating personal relationships with radicals within Upper Volta and around the world, especially in Madagascar.²⁷

Until recently there was not much scholarship about the Burkinabè Revolution or its leader in English. In terms of biographies, Harsch's short sketch of Sankara's life was a welcome opening gesture that offers a brief analysis of many facets of revolutionary policy in Burkina Faso under Sankara.²⁸ However, Brian Peterson's biography of Sankara vastly expands that narrative and provides an in-depth examination of Sankara that reaches back into his family's history to situate the CNR leader in the context of his country's experience in the twentieth century. It incorporates valuable oral testimonials from those close to the Burkinabè leader as well as figures from within the government. He presents a portrait of a "highly moralistic" person who "placed far too much trust in others." Moreover, Peterson shows that Sankara's political philosophy was deeply touched by "his Catholic faith and liberation theology," dimensions often missing from other analyses that center on his Marxist influences. He situates Sankara's personal development in the context of the Cold War as African states emerged and had to grapple with the bipolar world. Peterson paints a portrait of a flawed politician who always had the best intentions and expected that others around him operated the same way. Consequently, there is a naivety to Sankara that contributed to his eventual isolation within the revolutionary government and made his assassination a nearly preordained act of martyrdom. Peterson's book provides a strong background to Sankara's upbringing, the formation of his circle of friends of whom many entered the CNR, and the importance of his personal life in shaping Sankara's public persona and eventual mythologization.²⁹

In the revolution's immediate aftermath, several studies offer glimpses into broader aspects of the regime and its policies.³⁰ From the economic perspective, the most significant work to date is that produced by Apollinaire J. Kyélem de Tambèla who furnishes a comprehensive analysis of the motivations, policies, and impacts of the Burkinabè Revolution on the country's society. Drawing on government publications and data gathered by international agencies, Kyélem de Tambèla presents a detailed exposition of the socioeconomic transformation wrought under Sankara's leadership and builds a persuasive case in defense the revolution's programs in terms of their material benefit to the population. Moreover, he contextualizes those acts in the international environment, linking the domestic changes to the global situation in which they responded and to which they adapted.[31]

In addition, there are collections of essays that highlight aspects of Burkina Faso's revolutionary period, either exploring why Sankara was overthrown, and the virtues of the government led by Blaise Compaoré after 1987, or offering support for the murdered Burkinabè president in an effort to keep his legacy alive for future generations.[32] Recent studies of Burkina Faso by Englebert and Harsch furnish some overview of the revolutionary period, but they do so in the context of a general history of the country from precolonial times to the present.[33] In the field of cultural politics and the cinema, Colin Dupré's excellent history of FESPACO is a comprehensive study of the festival and gives due prominence to Sankara's role in shaping its trajectory. Dupré demonstrates how what started as a showcase for African films became a matter of state importance to the governments of Upper Volta/Burkina Faso from the early 1970s into the twenty-first century. Consequently, FESPACO became intricately connected to and dependent upon relations with the various administrations ruling the country as well as critical to those governments' international relations. Dupré illuminates the benefits and well as the complexities that arose from that partnership and produces a detailed history of Africa's premier film festival from its origins to the second decade of the twenty-first century.[34]

Building on existing scholarship, this book offers a history of the revolution that foregrounds its cultural politics and analyzes the importance of the cinema industrial complex as revelatory of the philosophical framework that structured the CNR's policies as well as its global interactions.[35] It argues that through film and other creative endeavors, the revolution aimed to effect a transformation of the person, transcending their alienation to realize a new society and with it a new world. Fanon's theories of the colonized mentality, nature of the liberation struggle, and objectives of the conquest of true independence permeated the revolutionaries' rhetoric, framing of programs, and interpretation of history. Even changing the name of the country from Upper Volta to Burkina Faso

(Land of Dignified People) can be read as a Fanonian gesture and pointed to the aspiration to realize the authentic self as no longer separated into an objective "thing" opposing and oppressing the being-in-itself. It is an assertion of the universality of value and worth in all people as well as the inherent fluidity of cultural expression and development that is essential to the very existence and survival of humanity.[36] To gain a nuanced understanding of the effectiveness, limitations, and durability of the CNR's actions on the cultural terrain, this study situates the Burkinabè Revolution at a critical historical crossroads between the period of national liberation and decolonization and the emergent epoch of neoliberal capitalist globalization. Buffeted by those powerful international currents, the Burkinabè revolutionaries adapted their domestic and international strategies while also causing external actors to react to the CNR's moves. What emerged was a stunning context wherein Burkina Faso became one of the most important forces on the world stage, and it caught the attention of a motley assortment of global powers and external actors, many of which felt threatened by the revolution's very existence. At the nexus of it all stood culture and the cinema as a major arena of struggle among the contending forces within and without the revolution.

The book is divided into six chapters followed by a conclusion. The first chapter presents an overview of the political, economic, and social history of Burkina Faso before the Revolution of 4 August 1983. It introduces some of the political forces that played key roles in the revolution as well as the social dynamics that drove the radicalization and polarization of the country's politics. At that time, Upper Volta also emerged as an important force in the development of African cinema. Finally, chapter 1 discusses the shifting international situation as new forces emerged in the West while the socialist bloc entered a period of economic crisis. That fracturing of the Cold War stasis opened the door to the expanded influence of international institutions such as the IMF and World Bank in shaping the global environment.

The second chapter focuses on the events immediately preceding the revolution, specifically the political chaos that engulfed Upper Volta from late 1982 into the summer of 1983. It details how the revolutionary circle, including Sankara, navigated the shifting and treacherous waters of Voltaic politics. Chapter 3 explores the first year of the new revolutionary government as it consolidated power and defined its nature through its first domestic and international policies. This chapter examines the political movements, parties, and organizations that participated in the new government, or chose to stand aside, hoping to prod it in more radical directions from the outside. This first year was critical to forging the context for understanding the Burkinabè Revolution as well as laying the groundwork for some of the elements that would eventually turn against it from the inside and outside. The period from August 1983 to the summer of 1984 also illuminates the efforts of the government to construct a new kind of state by reforming the system and institutions of governance, remake Burkinabè society by taking on archaic social practices and structures, and to forge a basis for equal and solidarity-based interaction among truly sovereign nations. It is in this context that the regime's cultural politics became more clearly elaborated and focused with the cinema as a prominent element within that arena of engagement.

Chapter 4 follows the revolution from 1984 through 1985. It covers the period of the "clarification" that marked the first anniversary of Sankara's accession to leadership through the unfolding of the Popular Plan for Development (Plan populaire de développement, PPD). The PPD inaugurated the revolution in the countryside and built out the fundamental aspects of the cultural dimension of the revolutionary process tying it to economic and social programs launched at the same time. The earliest successes of the CNR became manifest during that year and it spurred the administration to move faster and on a broader front to transform the country as well as its position in world affairs. Sankara made his historic speech before the United Nations in October 1984 that brought him and the government he headed into the center of the still tense Cold War standoff between the United States and the Soviet Union. In 1985 Sankara hosted FESPACO for the first time as president and ushered in radical changes to the nature of the festival, introduced new measures to promote domestic filmmaking, and broadened the international impact of African cinema.

The fifth chapter takes the narrative from late 1985 to early 1987. During that period, the revolutionary government moderated some of its policies and sought to broaden the revolution's social base. The shock of the war with Mali at the end of 1985 caused Sankara and some of his comrades to rethink aspects of the Burkinabè Revolution and create a space for consolidating the gains of the previous two years. New mass organizations emerged, former political opponents were rehabilitated, and the country made overtures to rivals on the world stage. On the economic front, 1986 witnessed the launch of Burkina Faso's first Five-Year Plan for Development that focused on self-sufficiency and self-directed structural adjustment. Chapter 6 covers the final year of the Burkinabè Revolution from late 1986 until its overthrow on 15 October 1987. The CNR continued to implement the social reforms at the heart of the revolution as defined in the Five-Year Plan, introduced further projects to broaden the social base of the revolutionary movement with a strong impetus toward the mobilization of the peasantry, and Burkina Faso hosted the 1987 FESPACO, wherein Sankara and his allies deepened and expanded the changes to the festival initiated two years earlier. The CNR emphasized cancellation of the debt and solidarity with those still struggling for liberation, especially the people of South Africa and its neighboring countries subject to repeated attacks from the apartheid regime, as integral to its foreign policy.

The conclusion explores how the ideas and policies associated with the Burkinabè Revolution have remained relevant to today. It highlights the CNR's foregrounding of cultural politics and the cinema industrial complex as an important vector for realizing the revolution's objectives. Sankara and his comrades believed that through self-directed development and engagement in struggle a new person would emerge who would build a society based on human dignity and happiness. The cinema was a critical space where the people's creativity could be discovered, enhanced, and contribute to the wider growth of humanity. The conclusion presents the Burkinabè Revolution as a window into a moment of historical transition from the era of decolonization to the issues that have defined the world's conversation from the late twentieth and early twenty-first centuries. Those include the crisis of climate change, the debilitating effects of international debt, and the ongoing oppression of women through the persistence of entrenched patriarchal power structures and archaic traditions. Many of these themes subsequently found expression in some of the most important works of African filmmaking, a clear indication of the important changes wrought by the Burkinabè Revolution. Burkina Faso's revolutionary experiment raised vital questions that still desperately call for answers today. To get there, our story begins with the emergence of those people and circumstances that made the Burkinabè Revolution thinkable and possible in the first place.

Acknowledgments

THIS BOOK IS A RESULT OF MY LONGSTANDING INTEREST IN THE BURKINABÈ Revolution. As a student, I enthusiastically followed the developments that transpired in Burkina Faso under the leadership of Thomas Sankara. The remarkable accomplishments, daring experiments, and audacity of independence on the world stage was captivating and inspiring. I am grateful to have had the support and opportunity to write its history. The book has benefited from the countless conversations and exchanges with people who have expressed support for this project and provided encouragement all along the way. I wish to thank Herman Lebovics, Olufemi Vaughan, Ousman Kobo, and Ahmad Sikainga for their keen insights, support, and critical interventions as the concept for this project took shape. They helped to clarify and inspire important aspects of this book. They also provided encouragement to complete the project.

This work is the result of research conducted over many years in locations around the world. I received invaluable assistance from the personnel at Le Centre Georges Pompidou and La Cinémathèque Française in Paris. Each has critical records (print, audio, and visual) that were essential to completing this study. In addition, Bruno Jaffré and Mr. X maintain thomassankara.net, one of the most comprehensive and critically important repositories of materials relating to the Burkinabè Revolution, its aftermath, and legacy. Those materials are vital to any understanding of the revolution. The anonymous managers of capitainethomassankara.net also provided rare and essential video and audio materials as well as press of the period without which this book could not have been written.

In addition, I have benefited from the financial support of Ohio State University, especially from the Marion Campus. I received several professional development grants from the Marion Campus of Ohio State University as well as research support from the History Department. Those funds enabled travel overseas to gather the raw materials for this project and were indispensable to its completion. I especially thank Dean Greg Rose and Associate Dean Bishun Pandey on the Marion Campus for their unflagging support of and interest in this project. I am also deeply grateful for the interest, encouragement, and important critiques provided by my editor at Michigan State University Press, Caitlin Tyler-Richards. Her enthusiasm for this project and vital interventions on the manuscript provided the drive and energy for me to revise and refine this book, finally bringing it to life. She has vastly improved the final product.

Finally, I express my deepest thanks to my wife and colleague, Stephanie Smith. Her important work on the intersection of art, culture, and politics have been a formative influence on my own approach to the Burkinabè Revolution. Her analysis of the role played by culture in giving form to and influencing revolutionary processes helped to shape the arguments of this project. Moreover, her transnational approach to her research on the Mexican Revolution helped me to situate the narrative of the Burkinabè Revolution in a global context. Most importantly, my life would not be what it is without her. Our conversations, travels around the world, and the exciting experiences we have shared have made me the person that I am and provide new inspiration to me every day. I can't wait for all the adventures we will share in the coming years.

List of Abbreviations

CDR	Comités de défense de la révolution
CIDC	Consortium Interafricain de Distribution Cinématographique
CIPROFILM	Centre Interafricain de Production de Films
CMRPN	Comité Militaire de Redressement pour le Progrès National
CNR	Conseil national de la révolution
CSB	Confédération Syndicale Burkinabè
CSP	Conseil de Salut du Peuple
CSV	Confédération Syndicale Voltaïque
FEPACI	Fédération Panafricaine des Cinéastes
FESPACO	Festival Panafricain de Cinéma et de Télévision de Ouagadougou
FIMATS	Force d'Intervention du Ministère de l'Administration Territoriale et de la Sécurité
GCB	Groupe Communiste Burkinabè
INAFEC	Institut Africain d'Éducation Cinématographique

LIPAD	Ligue patriotique pour le développement
MLN	Mouvement de Libération National
OCV	Organization Communiste Voltaïque
OMR	Organisation Militaire Révolutionnaire
PAI	Parti africain de l'indépendence
PCRV	Parti Communiste Révolutionnaire Voltaïque
PMK	Prytanée Militaire de Kadiogo
PPD	Plan Populaire de développement
PQDP	Plan quinquennal de développement populaire
RDA	Rassemblement Démocratique Africain
RDP	Révolution démocratique et populaire
ROC	Rassemblement des Officiers Communistes
SGN	Secrétaire Général National (des CDR)
SNEAHV	Syndicat National des Enseignements Africains de Haute-Volta
SUVESS	Syndicat Unifié Voltaïque des Enseignants du Secondaire et du Supérieur
TPR	Tribunaux Populaires de la Révolution
UCB	Union des Communistes Burkinabè
ULC	Union de Lutte Communiste
ULC–*La Flamme*	Union de Lutte Communiste–*La Flamme*
ULCR	Union de Lutte Communiste–Reconstruite

1

Politics and Culture in Upper Volta

(1960s–1982)

ON 5 AUGUST 1960, JOYOUS CROWDS CELEBRATED UPPER VOLTA'S INDEpendence from France. Part of the larger colonial federation of French West Africa since its conquest in 1898, the territory had long served as a reservoir of labor for other zones of France's empire. In 1932 it was dissolved and partitioned among other colonies only to be restored on 4 September 1947 as an "overseas territory." By then anti-colonial political parties and growing organized labor movements had begun to challenge French authority in the region. A wave of strikes and demonstrations reflected an upsurge of militancy that aligned with the socialist and communist left in France in the years following the Second World War. Workers from what had been Upper Volta were among those at the forefront of the burgeoning radical agitation in the federation and in large numbers they joined the Rassemblement Démocratique Africain (RDA) after its formation in 1946. Jaffré argues that a motive for reestablishing Upper Volta as a separate territory was France's desire to "counterbalance the [growing] influence" of that party in a struggle by the metropole to reassert its authority in the empire.[1] Moreover, the RDA was allied with the French Communist Party (Parti

Communiste Français, PCF) at a time when the wartime resistance coalition in France frayed, culminating in the expulsion of the PCF from the government in May 1947. Consequently, the emergence of Cold War political divisions was also reflected in the French government's maneuvers in the overseas territories. Peterson adds that pressure from the conservative Mossi chiefs was a significant factor in France's decision to reconstitute Upper Volta. That also aligned with France's aim to counter the growth of radical political groups in West Africa. Over the next decade, the momentum toward political independence gathered steam and resulted in the entire federation achieving political sovereignty by 1960. In that process, the French government largely managed the transition, even bringing the main elements of the RDA into association with its policies in the region. That left France in a strong position to influence the policies of the new governments that came to power in countries like Upper Volta at independence.[2] As Babou Paulin Bamouni, one of Sankara's future advisors and a leading figure in the Burkinabè Revolution, wrote, "Without capitulating, colonialism turned into neocolonialism to continue its exploitation and domination of the African masses," and he surmised that, "neocolonialism would prove to be more dangerous and more cynical than colonialism."[3]

During the 1940s and 1950s in Upper Volta, political groups formed, prominent personalities emerged, and the fault lines of ideological division arose that produced the framework for the state's policies and popular reaction to them. It was also in this context that those who later directed the Burkinabè Revolution were born and grew up. Consequently, they were deeply imprinted with the issues and influences that defined Upper Volta's existence as a country. In their youth, that generation witnessed the optimism attendant upon independence from France as well as the fierce debates over what independence meant and how to realize the people's aspirations for a better life. Those disputes ranged from advocates for a return to sources (most closely associated with the *négritude* philosophy articulated by Senegal's new president, Léopold Sédar Senghor), to those like Fanon who insisted that a much more radical destruction of the colonial system was required to clear a path to real sovereignty and meaningful development. That clash of ideas dominated meetings of cultural and political activists from Africa in the late 1950s that carried over into the 1960s.[4] Moreover, they entered adulthood as the cultural politics within the struggle for decolonization took sharper form in the early postcolonial period, especially with the foundation of African cinema and its rapid growth in the late 1960s. At that moment, Upper Volta became the epicenter of a struggle for control over the cinema industrial complex through a dispute over control of the movie theater infrastructure and distribution system up to then dominated by French-based monopolies in league with France. [5]

This chapter charts the emergence of the forces that shaped Voltaic politics as well as the development of social movements that became radicalized in response to the failures of the early postcolonial governments to deliver on the expectations aroused with the achievement of independence. By the mid-1970s, several militant groups, labor federations, and student groups had emerged that sought to radically restructure Voltaic society. In addition, a circle of junior officers coalesced and became radicalized in the wake of a wasteful war with Mali. After that conflict, Sankara, Compaoré, Boukary Lingani, and Zongo created an underground group within the military that connected with the civilian radical groups. Simultaneously and in parallel with the developments on the political front, Upper Volta became a center of activity for the emergence of African cinema as well as the incipient convergence of interests between filmmakers and the state during the 1970s. The continent's premier film festival was founded in Ouagadougou in 1969. At that time, Upper Volta became the first country to nationalize the cinematic infrastructure in a fight over control of revenue that escalated into a symbolic struggle to further realize a complete decolonization from France. This drew the attention of revolutionary African filmmakers to the state and prepared the foundation for a closer collaboration between the cineastes and government policy in Upper Volta in the coming years. Consequently, the revolutionary forces that formed in that period embraced the possibility of deploying the cinema as an instrument through which the restructuring of Voltaic society and culture could be accomplished as well as a vector for unleashing the creative capacity of the people in making the new society.

Politics and Decolonization

For the first several decades of Upper Volta's history, the RDA was the dominant political party. Initially, its official posture was radical and embraced an uncompromising demand for complete independence from France. However, the RDA was structurally a loose organization with real power centered in the sections based in each territory that reflected the political orientation of local leadership. For example, Sékou Touré and the organized labor movement dominated the RDA in Guinea, infusing that branch with a strong revolutionary Marxist politics that was closely aligned with the Soviet Union in the global Cold War division. Modibo Keïta in Mali tended to associate with France's socialist party and social democracy. And Félix Houphouët-Boigny, leader of the RDA in Côte d'Ivoire, was more conservative, increasingly embraced the French political center, and often endorsed France's policies regarding the overseas territories. Despite its administrative separation, Upper Volta's section of the RDA was effectively controlled by its more powerful and prosperous neighbor during the 1940s and 1950s. Following the brutal repression of the RDA in 1949–1950 by French authorities, Houphouët-Boigny sought to break the party's isolation. He abandoned the alliance with French communists and affected a rapprochement with France's political elite. That included France's minister for the overseas territories, François Mitterrand. The result was the RDA's realignment with the French political center, including the Christian Democratic MRP and Mitterrand's UDSR.[6]

One consequence of that political shift was that the RDA supported France's decision, embodied in the 1956 Loi Cadre, to split the Federation into its eight constituent parts, a move echoed by the party as well. In Upper Volta, the section was renamed the Voltaic Democratic Union–RDA (UDV–RDA). To prepare for the 31 March 1957 elections to constitute new governments for each of the separate territories, the UDV–RDA (under Ouezzin Coulibaly) formed a coalition with another smaller party (led by Joseph Conombo) to create the Unified Democratic Party (PDU). Their main rivals were the progressives who had broken with the RDA and formed the Voltaic Democratic Movement (Mouvement Démocratique Voltaïque, MDV) in 1955 under Gérard Kango Ouédraogo, which included among its leaders Maurice Yaméogo. After the elections, a unity government formed that made Coulibaly vice president under the French governor. However, Conombo withdrew his party from the partnership with the UDV–RDA, joined the MDV and the pro-French MPA in a new alignment and demanded Coulibaly's ouster. That maneuver failed when some deputies, including Yaméogo, sided with Coulibaly.[7]

With the fall of France's Fourth Republic in 1958 due to political divisions resulting from Algeria's liberation war, Charles de Gaulle returned as president and called a referendum to back his new constitution of the Fifth French

Republic. In the meantime, Coulibaly resigned for health reasons and was succeeded by Yaméogo as president of Upper Volta. Neither the RDA nor the opposition PRA (Parti du régroupement Africain) opposed the referendum, so in October 1958, Upper Volta voted overwhelmingly to remain in the newly constituted French community. According to the historian Englebert, Yaméogo wanted to consolidate absolute power in his hands and maneuvered the Mossi emperor into proclaiming his ambition to establish a monarchy in Upper Volta. The Mossi emperor's declaration, including a request for assistance from the French government, eliminated that constituency from standing in Yaméogo's path since it implied collaboration with the imperial power. Then Yaméogo went after the PRA. His opportunity came in the wake of the 1959 legislative elections, largely contested on the question of whether Upper Volta would join the proposed Mali Federation, merging several West African territories into a single country. The RDA opposed the union and secured sixty-nine out of seventy-five seats in the vote. The results led the PRA to drop its opposition to Yaméogo's government to secure for it a role in the soon-to-be independent state. Shortly before Upper Volta's independence on 5 August 1960, it merged into the RDA essentially creating a one-party state led by Yaméogo. By 1961, he had banned the remaining opposition as well.[8]

The one potential site for the emergence of a movement in opposition to Yaméogo's administration was organized labor. Despite having fewer than five million people at independence, the overwhelming majority of whom were peasants working the land and living in rural areas, Upper Volta was home to a vibrant if fractured working class with a history of political activism. Partly that circumstance derived from the country's use by France as a repository for labor deployed in other colonies throughout the region. Upper Volta dispatched thousands of workers to Côte d'Ivoire, Niger, Benin (Dahomey), Mali, and elsewhere in West Africa throughout the period of French rule. Those laborers forged networks of social solidarity to support their existence and to defend themselves against local prejudices and the abuses of the imperial power. The transitory nature of their work (mainly on agricultural plantations, in mines, or on railroads) meant there was a continuous movement of Voltaic workers back and forth. That migration facilitated the exchange of ideas, networking, and ultimately the formation of organized unions. Consequently, Upper Volta had a conscious working class enmeshed in the struggles for power unfolding in the late colonial and early postcolonial period.[9]

By the 1960s the country had three major labor federations roughly corresponding to the major groupings in the French workers' movement: l'Union Syndicale des Travailleurs Voltaïques (USTV, inclined toward the communists); la Confédération Africaine des Travailleurs Croyants (CATC, allied with the Christian Democrats); and l'Union Nationale des Syndicates des Travailleurs de Haute-Volta (UNSTHV, associated with the anti-communist left). After Yaméogo eliminated the political opposition in the early 1960s, the working-class organizations became the site for resistance. Joseph Ki-Zerbo, leader of the banned pan-Africanist and socialist Mouvement de Libération National (MLN), led his followers into the USTV, while Joseph Ouédraogo, a former supporter of Ouézzin Coulibaly and ex-mayor of the capital Ouagadougou, became the leader of the CATC. Despite their small membership, the unions were well-organized and disciplined. Upper Volta's president sought to isolate, control, and defang the unions by coopting them into the government and transforming them into agents of the regime. In 1962 the RDA called for the unification of the labor movement into a single federation allied to the ruling party for the purpose of facilitating the "development of the national economy."[10] In other words, the unions would become enforcers of Yaméogo's will within the working class, serving as blunt instruments against opposition to his rule. By casting them as key agents in economic development, however, Yaméogo inadvertently positioned organized labor as the primary mechanism whereby Upper Volta's economic development and social progress could be realized.

However, Yaméogo's increasing reliance on France for support and the subjugation of Upper Volta's economy to foreign and regional interests undermined the regime's legitimacy, especially among organized labor. By 1965, Upper Volta was significantly in debt and the economy had not achieved any meaningful level of development.[11] Moreover, the corruption that riddled the government became more apparent, with Yaméogo appointing members of his family to cabinet posts, who became ostentatiously wealthy. At the same time, he responded to pressures from foreign lenders and regional powerbrokers, foremost among them Houphouët-Boigny, and imposed austerity measures that targeted government workers, the mainstay of the urban working class. Yaméogo drastically reduced their pay, cut allowances for their families, and signed a bilateral deal with Côte d'Ivoire allowing for dual citizenship for Voltaic workers, the vast majority of whom worked in there to the benefit of that territory and its international trade in cocoa. The last act reestablished the colonial practice of using Upper Volta's people as a reserve of labor for the region.[12]

The unions resisted the new measures and Joseph Ouédraogo emerged as a prominent figure among the opposition to Yaméogo's regime. On 29 December 1965, the USTV and CATC formed a united front to counter the austerity measures. They called for demonstrations and demanded the draconian fiscal actions be rescinded. Yaméogo was out of the country negotiating the bilateral deal with Houphouët-Boigny mentioned above. Upon his return, the president called a meeting of the unions with the government ostensibly to reach some accord to head off a larger political crisis. In fact, it was a trap designed to expose the opposition and destroy it. On 31 December 1965, the police attacked and dispersed the unions. Yaméogo reached into the Cold War playbook and declared that the tumult resulted from "communist subversion" directed by Joseph Ouédraogo (CATC). The president declared that Joseph Ouédraogo wanted to deliver Upper Volta "into the hands of Ghana" (led by the pan-Africanist Kwame Nkrumah) "and the People's Republic of China" (under the stewardship of Mao Zedong). The government declared a state of emergency, which thrust the military onto the political scene. To this point, Upper Volta's military had been outside of the debates roiling the country. It was a small, largely under-equipped force that preserved much of its structure and command from the days of French rule. In fact, as in so many other independent African states, the military remained closely associated with the former colonial power, receiving the bulk of its equipment and training via that source. It was not uncommon for African military officers to be deployed to other former French African colonies or even France for further instruction.

In response to the emergency declaration, the unions called a general strike and mass mobilization on 3 January 1966. Yaméogo banned the strike and ordered suppression of the demonstrations. That day tens of thousands of people massed in Ouagadougou. A tense encounter followed. The military was deployed in the main square, directed by Colonel Sangoulé Lamizana. In a sign of Yaméogo's weakened position and the military's ambivalence toward the state, Lamizana did not order his troops to quell the unrest. Instead, the union leaders opened negotiations with the officers and chants of "the army to power" rippled through the assembled masses. By all accounts, Lamizana did not seek to take power that day and there had not been any pre-planning for a military coup. What transpired was a spontaneous uprising of the people and the abandonment of the military's loyalty to Yaméogo's government. At 10:00 p.m., Lamizana announced an agreement with the protest leaders, principal among them Joseph Ouédraogo, that as head of the military Lamizana was taking "charge of the responsibilities of the head of state until a new order could be established."[13]

Lamizana's unintentional coup brought the military to the fore of Voltaic politics, transforming it into a site of political contestation. With Yaméogo deposed, opposition parties resurfaced and hoped to play a role in the transition. Ki-Zerbo's MLN along with the refounded PRA and even the reconstituted RDA (minus Yaméogo who was put under house arrest) entered conversations with Lamizana about the formation of a new transitional government. By June 1966, the state of emergency had been lifted, and it appeared that normal political life was resuming. With the reemergence of political activity, the unions were pushed to the sidelines by the party leaders who jockeyed for places in the new administrative order. Lamizana took advantage of the changed dynamics on the ground and got the labor movement to accede to the very austerity measures they had opposed in December 1965, including significant pay cuts for civil servants. The political parties, however, soon fell out and clashes erupted in several parts of Upper Volta between supporters of the deposed president and the MLN. On that pretext, Lamizana ordered the suspension of all parties on 12 December 1966 and reorganized the military leadership into the Council of the Voltaic Armed Forces (CFAV). He declared that the military would have to remain in power for the next four years as it guided the country back to stability and fiscal solvency.[14]

Still, rather than repress the civilian political movements, Lamizana sought to coopt them. By late December 1966, he announced a new government that included representatives from the three major parties—RDA, MLN, and PRA—as well as military officers. Within the governing coalition, the military kept control through appointing officers to a majority (seven out of twelve) of the posts in the new administration. But even this majority was calculated to give the impression of a partnership with all the parties, in essence, a true national unity government. The state imbricated party politics with the military and injected the armed forces into the calculations of civilian movements. Left by the roadside were the unions and other mass organizations that led the uprising of 3 January 1966.

The Emergence of a Revolutionary Movement and the Politics of Culture

Just at this moment, Sankara confronted a critical choice in his own life. Born on 21 December 1949, he turned seventeen as Lamizana's new government took shape. Soon after seizing power, Lamizana founded the Prytanée Militaire de Kadiogo (PMK) to train officers for the country's military. This was a gesture toward some of the more radical protesters who helped Lamizana to power since they wanted a cleaner break from France and Yaméogo's discredited policies. The new institution would be nominally independent of France and produce officers within the country for the first time rather than have them exclusively trained in the former imperial power and by implication beholden to its interests. Sankara decided to attend the new school in the fall of 1966 and, as Jaffré notes, his enrollment at the PMK was decisive in his and his cohort of revolutionaries' early political development.[15] Many young people throughout Upper Volta were inspired by the promise of a new and better day following the momentous events of 3 January 1966 and believed the army was a force for good that could realize the country's aspirations for national development. Peterson writes that the more prosaic aspects of the military such as the uniforms, the access to food, and even enhanced dating prospects also attracted people of Sankara's age to the service.[16]

What made the PMK experience ideologically significant for Sankara, Boukary Lingani, Compaoré, and other future radical officers was the presence there of Adama Touré, a leading member of the African Independence Party (Parti africain de l'indépendence, PAI). Adama Touré taught history and geography at the PMK and served as its academic director until 1981 (except 1969–1971). The PAI was a pro-Soviet communist party founded in 1963. Until the coup of 1966, it had not played a major role in Upper Volta's politics. However, the change in regime accompanied by the mass mobilization that brought it about opened the door for more radical movements to become active in the country's politics, even if surreptitiously. While the PAI remained banned by Lamizana's government, its cadres used the fluidity of the transition from Yaméogo's regime to gain influence within the existing student, labor, and opposition movements. Their role in the upheaval of January 1966 brought some PAI leaders to the attention of the new government. Some were appointed to important roles in lower administration, educational institutions, and at the PMK even though their political affiliation remained secret as in the case of Adama Touré. While at the PMK, he used his position to introduce young students like Sankara to Marxism, analyses of imperialism, and fired them with a passion for the struggle of the oppressed in pursuit of a better life. Adama Touré regularly invited a select handful of students including Sankara to his home for lively discussions on politics, economics, culture, and the world situation as it pertained to the Cold War and imperialism's ongoing assaults on the Third World. Those encounters certainly influenced the young officer-in-training and encouraged Sankara to view the military as a potential vehicle for the achievement of the deepest aspirations and needs of the people.[17] Fidèle Toé, a key participant in the Burkinabè Revolution, told the historian Peterson years later, "Adama Touré was sort of Thomas' revolutionary father" and through his influence the PMK exposed many officers of that generation to the revolutionary ideas circulating in the late 1960s through the 1970s.[18]

After Sankara graduated from the PMK in 1969, he remained in close contact with Adama Touré. Moreover, Adama Touré continued to influence other young officers as they passed through the training institute during those critical years. His analysis of neocolonialism as the systemic force oppressing Upper Volta and other newly independent African countries created a deep impression. It provided an analytical framework for understanding the failures of postcolonial governments to fulfill the promises of decolonization. Adama Touré went beyond instruction in the classroom and created a space for political networking that permitted former and current students to bond, work through ideas, and formulate plans for political action in the future. He was also a vector enabling young officers to gain access to the underground revolutionary movement in the country and create a link between radical soldiers and their civilian counterparts. Adama Touré's political work laid the foundation for a broad coalition of revolutionary forces that would include critical elements from within the military like Sankara, Compaoré, Boukary Lingani, and Zongo.[19]

Upper Volta and African Cinema

The year of Sankara's graduation from the PMK in 1969, Upper Volta became the accidental site for the battle between the pioneer generation of African filmmakers and France for control of the cinema industrial complex. Throughout the decolonization era cultural activists including Paulin Soumanou Vieyra (Benin/Senegal) and Ousmane Sembène (Senegal) had sought to deploy film as an essential tool to counter the cultural alienation produced by the colonial condition as a preliminary step toward "all development in Africa, economic, social, or political."[20] With independence African filmmakers were finally able to make their own motion pictures, including Sembène's historic productions after he completed his training in the Soviet Union in 1963. In addition, African directors attended international cultural conferences, formed networks with others in the field, and tenaciously fought to carve out an independent space to explore their creativity and present a new image of Africa and the African to continental and global audiences. As Fanon writes, "For these individuals, the demand of a national culture and the affirmation of the existence of such a culture represent a special battlefield." In fact, the fight in the cultural field is the sine qua non of national liberation through which the new person is formed giving rise to a new humanism that is truly universal.[21]

By the late 1960s, an independent African cinema was well on the path to development and several films had already made their mark as substantial contributions to the global cinematic field. Motion pictures such as Sembène's *La noire de . . .* (1966) and *Mandabi* (1968) as well as Med Hondo's *Soleil Ô* (1969) were stridently anti-racist and anti-imperialist in imagery and messaging. From their first productions, African filmmakers inserted radical political messages meant to challenge and subvert the colonialist paradigms that produced the alienated colonized subject. That project took on new, more experimental forms after 1968 with the articulation of Third Cinema theory. It advocated a guerrilla style of film politics that wanted to demolish the cultural and psychological foundations that sustained neocolonial capitalist hegemony and precluded true liberation. That was a clear echo of Fanon's arguments, which Third Cinema theorists frequently cited, about the nature of imperialism and the form of resistance needed to transcend its deleterious impact on African mentalities and societies. This militant approach also was manifested in the material confrontations with financiers and those who controlled the technical aspects of filmmaking, such as France's Ministry of Cooperation through its Cinema Bureau. For African filmmakers like Sembène and Hondo, the mere making of a motion picture was a revolutionary act in the neocolonial global environment.[22] Above all, however, early African films sought to raise consciousness among the people to arm them to struggle against the sources of their alienation and oppression. As Sembène told Teshome Gabriel in a later interview, "I had no belief that after people saw [*Mandabi*] they would go out and make a revolution. . . . people liked the film and talked about it. . . . I participated in their awareness."[23]

African filmmakers made films outside the parameters controlled by the former imperial powers and created alternative, empowering images and messages that inspired Africans to jettison their colonialist-generated inferiority complexes and emerge bristling with power to forge their own destinies.[24] They also formed networks and built movements that magnified the impact cinema could have in changing their societies and the world. Beginning with the *Festival Mondial des Arts Nègres de Dakar* (1966), for which Vieyra was one of the principle organizers, African cineastes attended a series of gatherings where they worked through some of the fundamental questions about the role of film in the liberation struggle, what defined the nature of an African cinema, and techniques for reaching their target audience to effect the change they desired. The Dakar event (1–24 April 1966) inspired Tahar Cheriaa to hold the first major film festival on the African continent in Tunis, Tunisia, in December 1966. The momentum from the Journées Cinématographiques de Carthage (JCC) carried into the Havana Cultural Congress in Cuba (4–11 January 1968) at which African filmmakers received encouragement, assistance, and inspiration. Moreover, they forged connections with revolutionary directors from throughout Latin America and the rest of the global south. Fidel Castro's revolutionary government provided the space and material support to facilitate ongoing communication and coordination. Coming out of Havana, Sembène, Hondo, and others agreed to convene a conference in Algiers, Algeria, in 1969 to further explore the establishment of a formal association of African filmmakers. They even discussed the possibility of creating an exclusively African film festival where they could showcase their work and provide access to wider African audiences.[25]

In reaction to those developments France sought to protect its position more aggressively in the African cinematic field and head off any potential threats that might come from African directors or other state actors like Cuba.[26] Surprisingly, Upper Volta found itself at the center of the intensifying struggle between African filmmakers and France for control of the cinematic field in Africa. In 1968, Claude Prieux, director of the Franco-Voltaic Cultural Center (CCFV), one of many such institutions in West Africa financed largely by the French government to maintain its cultural influence in the former colonies, hit upon the idea of hosting a film screening event. As the film scholar Dupré observes, most of the movies chosen were American, French, or Indian productions. However, there was a thirst among the students and other cinephiles within the group to view African motion pictures. Conversations between Prieux and the French ambassador to Upper Volta led the group to purchase African films and convene a "Festival of African Cinema," which would be distinguished from the JCC that screened pictures from throughout the Mediterranean and Middle East, by showing only African productions. In this manner, France could pose as the sponsor of the one true African film festival. Such was the origin of the first "Week of African Cinema" held in Ouagadougou 1–15 February 1969.[27]

The escalating struggle for control over the cinema industrial complex between France and West African filmmakers continued along parallel paths throughout 1969. *Présence Africaine*, the leading anti-colonial journal from the 1950s which also served as an organizer and promoter of cultural activism, sponsored the Algiers Cultural Festival on 21 July–1 August 1969. It was attended by Sembène, Hondo, Souleymane Cissé (Mali), Gaston Kaboré (Upper Volta), and other progenitors of African cinema. They all contributed to the formulation of the manifesto released at its conclusion partly in response to France's continued efforts at controlling the African cinematic field. Echoing Fanon, the manifesto opens with the assertion that "culture begins with the people who are its creator, and which transforms their lives." The statement outlines the process of alienation instantiated in Africa through colonial rule, argues that those structures have persisted into the postcolonial period, and demands that a war be waged in the arena of culture as an essential precondition to the liberation of Africa's people. The result of this decisive battle must be nothing less than "the conversion of mentalities," or in Fanon's language, the making of new people.[28] The filmmakers present in Algiers resolved to meet again 11–18 October 1970, at the third JCC and form their own organization, FEPACI.[29]

While Lamizana's government did not express any overt interest in cultural politics, it did seek to address the fiscal crisis plaguing the country in part by extracting more revenue from its cinema industry. In the decades after 1945, the audience for motion pictures grew significantly in Upper Volta as it did across West Africa. That was one of the reasons France invested significantly in the distribution of its films to the region in the last years of colonial rule. It also increased its regulation of movie theaters to produce added revenue by taxing the box office receipts and controlling the licensure of the establishments. Those arrangements promoting the distribution of French motion pictures and support for the colonial-era theater monopolies (COMACICO and SECMA) persisted into the postcolonial era.[30] In 1969, Lamizana raised taxes on movie tickets and demanded greater profit sharing with COMACICO and SECMA. In response, the companies, backed by France, declared a boycott on importing films to Upper Volta. Lamizana reacted by nationalizing the theaters, and he created a government entity to run them, SONAVOCI, on 5 January 1970.[31] Subsequent negotiations allowed COMACICO and SECMA to continue importing films to the country, but they relinquished control of the buildings. By 1972 the Voltaic government had also assumed control over the film festival inaugurated three years earlier as the Week of African Cinema, officially establishing the FESPACO, which has continued to be held biennially since 1979.[32] Those actions burnished Lamizana's nationalist credentials, shored up his flagging support among the population, and even attracted the accolades of African filmmakers who pointed to Upper Volta as a leader in the fight against neocolonial domination of Africa's culture.[33] This favor was reciprocated when FEPACI garnered a leading role in selecting prize winners at the festival as well as having a hand in choosing the entries for the competition.[34] By 1972, Upper Volta had an emerging generation of revolutionaries, was home to Africa's film festival, and was a locus of struggle in the cinematic field between radical cultural activists and France.

Political Paralysis and Economic Crisis

Despite the imposition of austerity in 1966 and Lamizana's efforts to derive more capital from the cinema and other foreign-owned industries, Upper Volta's debt continued to mount. That crisis worsened as the global economy slowed then began to fall in 1972 and 1973, fatally punctured with the onset of the oil embargo imposed by Organization of Petroleum Exporting Countries (OPEC) on the Western world for its support of Israel during the October 1973 Yom Kippur War. According to the World Bank, Upper Volta's external debt jumped over 55 percent in 1973, or from $20 million to over $31 million in 2019 values.[35] At roughly the same time, the country faced a massive ecological crisis with severe drought accompanied by the expansion of the Sahara Desert into the northern portion of the country. The combination of mounting costs associated with global inflation, declining prices for domestically produced agricultural goods, and the urgency of the climate catastrophe brought Upper Volta to its knees. Lamizana made feeble appeals for national development to reclaim the nationalist mantle and salvage his political project.[36] However, it was too late, and the crisis worsened.

In January 1973, the teachers called a general strike, demanding improved conditions and better housing. Led by the Syndicat National des Enseignements Africains de Haute-Volta (SNEAHV), of which Adama Touré was a leading member, the walkout continued into the spring of 1973. The police attempted to crush it, leading the MLN and PRA to call people into the streets to support the teachers. This isolated the RDA within the administration and caused it to fall back on the military to maintain the status quo. However, the shifting political sands brought into the open a split at the top of the RDA between the nominal head of the party and leader of the National Assembly, Joseph Ouédraogo, and the prime minister, Gérard Ouédraogo. Joseph Ouédraogo was still the head of the CATC labor federation giving him a potential mass base of support outside of the RDA and government institutions. Despite that reserve of power, Joseph Ouédraogo would not call out his union in support of the teachers. However, he was prepared to use his influence within the RDA and position as president of the National Assembly to isolate the prime minister and extract reforms from Lamizana. Under pressure, the government opened negotiations with the teachers leading to a settlement of the strikes.[37]

The teachers' strikes combined with the ongoing economic and ecological crises led to further political radicalization. In September 1973, the PAI formed a legal mass front organization to broaden the struggle against the Lamizana/RDA government, the Ligue patriotique pour le développement (LIPAD) led by Arba Diallo. Its most important section was in Ouagadougou, which was directed by Soumane Touré, who also led the PAI-dominated CSV (Confédération Syndicale Voltaïque) formed in September 1974. Adama Touré also continued his political work among the military's future officers at the PMK. With the collapse and fracturing of the government coalition, the newly founded LIPAD and other PAI-associated groups were well-positioned to lead popular discontent and provide a clear ideology to sustain the struggle.[38]

It was in this tumultuous environment that Sankara returned to Upper Volta after a three-year posting in Madagascar for additional training. The scholar Jaffré provides a detailed and insightful exposition of Sankara's years in Madagascar, much of which is also reproduced by the journalist Harsch and the historian Peterson in their biographies. Most significantly in this period, Jaffré notes that the sociologist Théophile Andrianoelisoa had a major intellectual influence on Sankara and exposed him to a veritable library of research on methodologies for reaching into the countryside to effect social change and development among the peasants. Andrianoelisoa approached the subject from a Marxist perspective tinged with doctrines of Third World revolution wherein the project of national liberation was intrinsically linked to societal transformation, each dependent upon the other.[39] The practices Sankara witnessed and participated in during his posting in Madagascar also placed the emphasis on the peasantry as the motor force for social change.[40]

In Madagascar, Sankara also observed firsthand the translation of thought into action.[41] The Malagasy army had a special division, the Green Berets, whose mission was to assist in rural development projects. They were meant to be agents of economic growth and to provide a link to the countryside where they would project the power of the state and tie the peasants to the policies of the government. Sankara often joined those units during deployments and, in fact, stayed longer in Madagascar so that he could learn more about this unique relationship between the military and the people.[42] During his last year in the country, Madagascar experienced significant social unrest. Protests and strikes erupted in early 1972 during which the students emerged as a decisive element. They were incensed by the prevalence of French teachers at all levels of Malagasy education and demanded an end to cultural imperialism.[43] On 18 May 1972, the military took power. The new government embarked on increasingly radical social reforms, expanded development programs aimed at the rural population, and promoted closer collaboration between the armed forces and civilians. Sankara returned to Upper Volta in October 1973 and was posted to Bobo-Dioulasso to lead the training of new recruits for the Voltaic army. Inspired by his sojourn in Madagascar, Sankara reformed the methods of instruction and introduced new curricula emphasizing the civic responsibilities of the military and its role in the development of the country. He insisted that "a soldier must also be an enlightened citizen." This earned Sankara the respect and support of the young soldiers as well as the attention of his superiors.[44]

In the meantime, Upper Volta's state had essentially ceased to function, gripped by deepening economic crisis and ongoing political paralysis.[45] A general strike shut down the country on 22 January 1974. On 2 February 1974 organized labor petitioned Lamizana to unblock the system. Recognizing his precarious situation, Lamizana dismissed the government, suspended the constitution, and assumed total powers. The newly declared Government of National Renewal (GNR) followed a familiar formula in that it consisted of a majority of twelve appointed military officers, along with a minority of four handpicked civilian politicians.[46] In addition to the paralysis at the level of government, tensions also escalated between Upper Volta and its neighbor Mali. Ostensibly the conflict centered on a disputed border zone known as the Agacher Strip. Both sides believed the region contained valuable natural resources vital to raise capital on the international markets needed to service their mounting debts. The border between the two countries had been vaguely defined by the French during the colonial period and obfuscated further by France's decision to dissolve Upper Volta between 1932 and 1947. By 1974, both countries were ruled by unpopular military dictators, with Moussa Traoré of Mali notorious for his brutality and corruption. He came to power in 1968 after ousting the independence leader and socialist Modibo Keïta. By late November 1974, skirmishes erupted between the two countries' border guards, which escalated by mid-December 1974 into a larger armed conflict resulting in hundreds of deaths. Regional leaders and the OAU mediated a truce and both sides submitted to arbitration of the border dispute.[47]

The Agacher Strip War was a turning point for Sankara and sparked the growth of the circle that eventually directed the Burkinabè Revolution. He was deployed to the front where the young officer acquitted himself well. More importantly he witnessed firsthand the suffering of the people living on the northern frontier directly impacted by the relentless drought and expansion of the Sahara Desert. Sankara also experienced the corruption of Upper Volta's military and its poor state of preparedness. He was appalled by the theft and abuse of power conducted by higher officers as well as their indifference, even hostility toward the local population. By all accounts Sankara emerged from the war with Mali committed to the transformation of his country and, moreover, convinced of the urgency of such a project. Finally, it was during his deployment to the frontier that Sankara met Blaise Compaoré, another young officer who believed Upper Volta needed radical social change, and who quickly became one of Sankara's closest friends and confidantes. In the months following the Agacher Strip War that group grew to include Boukary Lingani and Zongo who also served in the conflict.[48]

The war further exposed the weakness and ineffectiveness of the Lamizana regime. In its aftermath the unions mobilized strikes and demonstrations demanding political reform. At the same time, scandals that involved the syphoning of international aid earmarked for drought relief rocked the country. Mysterious proclamations appeared in the streets of Upper Volta's major cities and in the country's military barracks. These tracts named intimates of the president and leading businesspeople as complicit in the scandals, indicating that they emanated from knowledgeable sources. The leaflets were signed by a previously unknown group calling itself the Rassemblement des Officiers Communistes (ROC). In a later interview, Jean-Baptiste Boukary Lingani revealed that he and Sankara were behind the ROC publications. They were joined by Henri Zongo and Compaoré as constituting the core of the underground organization.[49]

Lamizana for the first time faced the prospect of dissent from within the ranks. To countervail that threat and recreate something akin to the mixed military/civilian administration he had used in the past to mollify discontent, Lamizana decided to form a political party of his own. On 29 November 1975, he announced the creation of National Renewal Movement (Mouvement National pour le Renouveau, MNR). In response, the unions called a general strike on 17–18 December 1975. Among the participants in the mobilization was the LIPAD as well as the PAI-directed CSV. The ROC established links with the PAI and its mass organizations through Adama Touré and Soumane Touré. Responding to the pressure, Lamizana abandoned his plan for a single-party state and again dissolved the government on 29 January 1976. The new administration returned to the old formula of a majority (ten) civilian leaders checked by a minority (five) of military officers and pledged a swift transition to a multiparty political system.[50]

Lamizana introduced a new constitution in 1977 that allowed the return of multiparty elections. The RDA backed Lamizana while a dissident faction of the RDA led by Joseph Ouédraogo broke away and contested the presidential elections. Ki-Zerbo resurfaced having renamed the MLN as the Union Progressiste Voltaïque (UPV) and the PRA revived as well. One new party did appear on the scene called the Union Nationale pour la Défense de la Démocratie (UNDD) that was a vehicle for the return to power of the deposed president, Maurice Yaméogo. In the legislative elections of 30 April 1978, the RDA placed first followed by the UNDD and then the UPV. In the presidential elections, the RDA split its vote as Joseph Ouédraogo refused to back Lamizana. That caused a runoff between Lamizana and the UNDD candidate Macaire Ouédraogo. Lamizana won and remained president of Upper Volta. The country's politics resembled a game of musical chairs.[51]

All the while the country's crises deepened. In 1977, Upper Volta's foreign debt jumped an eye-popping 92.5 percent to over $164 million compared to $31 million in 1973. The next year the country's debt rocketed to $263 million, reaching $330 million by 1980.[52] In the same period, Upper Volta's GDP increased more slowly from $675 million in 1973 to $1.9 billion in 1980.[53] In other words, the economy was three times larger in 1980 (an increase of 181 percent) while the foreign debt was ten times greater (an expansion of 964 percent), vastly outstripping the rate of economic expansion and revealing a profound structural crisis that precluded any possibility of development or the alleviation of poverty. And yet Upper Volta's political establishment remained paralyzed. By 1980, Bamouni describes a society plunging into the depths of crisis as its leaders directed their gaze outside seeking to please foreign lenders, international investors, and to satiate the demands of their own domestic clients. They agreed to even more loans and the increasingly stringent conditions attached to those lines of credit by the IMF and World Bank.[54] Per capita income grew from a paltry $110 to a meager $300 over the period 1973 to 1980, an increase of only 173 percent, less than the expansion of the country's GDP.[55] Even that elevation of per capita income does not paint the entire picture as much of the gain was eaten away by mounting inflation and the increases were concentrated at the top in any event, exacerbating the gap between the rich and the poor. A social crisis was brewing in a context where the institutions of the state had no possibility of being responsive to the desperation of the people.[56]

The Consolidation of a Revolutionary Political Movement

From 1976 to 1980, Sankara served as commander of the National Training Center for Commandos (CNC) in the city of Pô, just south of Ouagadougou. He continued to meet with his closest confidantes—Compaoré, Zongo, and Boukary Lingani—as well as key members of the PAI and its affiliated organizations of LIPAD and CSV, such as Adama Touré and Soumane Touré.[57] The coordination between the pro-Soviet communist party and the ROC became more regular, facilitating the imbrication of military and civilian activists committed to the project of revolutionary national development and social transformation. During this period, Sankara and his expanding circle of comrades immersed themselves in radical theory, studying Mao's *Little Red Book*, Qaddafi's *Green Book*, and the publications of liberation theologians. Sankara was especially impressed by China's successes in eliminating hunger in the countryside, the role that leaders could play in directly reaching the people, and the concept of collective sacrifice for the greater good.[58] Sankara's posting at Pô confirmed his view that the military also needed reform. It was often used as a blunt instrument to suppress mass discontent and was viewed, as Jaffré notes, as "an army of occupation" rather than a partner with the civilian population. Sankara and others in the ROC were convinced that the army could be a revolutionary force, but only if its members viewed themselves as part of the population, sharing in their struggles and assisting them in their needs.[59]

While some elements within Upper Volta's military became more radicalized, the civilian revolutionary left became better organized and more diversified. One of the groups founded in this period was the Organization Communiste Voltaïque (OCV). It was launched in August 1977 among Voltaic intellectuals largely based in France with some connections in their home country. One of its leaders, Valère Somé, became a close friend and ideological advisor to Sankara in the late 1970s. They first encountered one another during a visit to France when Sankara (along with Compaoré) was posted to Rabat, Morocco, for further training between January and May 1978. Valère Somé was the same age as Compaoré and less than a year younger than Sankara. He was a student during the upheavals of the late 1960s to early 1970s and was strongly influenced by the New Left and its ideas of alienation. Moreover, for Valère Somé and his cohort, the fight against imperialism formed the primary point of struggle in the world. However, the relative isolation of the students and expatriates based in France fueled their drift into ultra-leftist fractious positions. They focused much of their energy on disputes over which model of socialism was the purest, making that distinction a more urgent question than the unfolding social crisis in Upper Volta.[60] Sankara's encounter with Valère Somé and the OCV opened the possibility of broadening the constellation of revolutionary forces forming against the Lamizana government to include those who were based outside Upper Volta but were connected to the student movement in country. Moreover, for the OCV links with the radical officers afforded the opportunity to become more firmly grounded in the emergent political crisis unfolding in their country. Shortly after those initial encounters, though, the OCV split into rival parties—the pro-Albanian Voltaic Revolutionary Communist Party (Parti Communiste Révolutionnaire Voltaïque, PCRV) founded on 1 October 1978 and the pro-Chinese Union of Communist Struggle (Union de Lutte Communiste, ULC) formed 12–14 October 1979 and led by Valère Somé.

Radicalization within African Cinema

As the revolutionary forces became better organized in Upper Volta during the 1970s, African filmmakers continued to fight for the centrality of the cultural question and cinema specifically in the struggle against imperialism and for African liberation as well as the transformation of the person. As early as the 1969 Pan-African Cultural Festival, African filmmakers identified "alienation sustained by colonialism" as a significant inhibitor to social development and called for a "cultural revolution" to defeat imperialism and achieve true liberation.[61] Following FEPACI's founding in 1970, the group was one of the main organizers of the Meeting of Third World Filmmakers in Algiers, Algeria, 5–14 December 1973. The attendees focused on devising strategies to "combat imperialism and neocolonialism" as primary threats to the achievement of the goals central to the liberation struggles of the previous two decades. Pointedly, the resolution released at the meeting's end declared that "action must be taken to seize from imperialism the means to influence ideologically.... This implies control by the people's state of all cultural activities and, in respect to cinema, nationalization in the interest of the masses of people: production, distribution, and commercialization."[62] By then the revolutionary concepts of Third Cinema had gained strong influence among directors such as Sembène, Hondo, and Cissé. Continuing a pattern established in the 1960s, Cuba also played a key role at the 1973 meeting followed by additional pledges of support in the areas of communication and the exchange of technology. Symbolic of the growing cooperation between Cuba and African filmmakers, FEPACI decided at the end of the conference to establish a permanent secretariat in Havana, Cuba. Those relationships carried into the period of the Burkinabè Revolution when the Sankara government integrated Cuba into FESPACO and partnered with Castro's regime to facilitate the expansion of the cinema infrastructure in Burkina Faso.[63]

In January 1975, FEPACI convened its Second Congress in Algiers, Algeria, and produced one of the most important documents in the history of African filmmaking, "The Algiers Charter on African Cinema." The "Algiers Charter" begins with an analysis of the state of the world in the mid-1970s that asserted African countries remained dominated by the imperialist world from which they were ostensibly freed through decolonization. FEPACI noted, "Cultural domination, which is all the more dangerous for being insidious, imposes on our peoples models of behavior and systems of values whose essential function is to buttress the ideological and economic ascendancy of the imperialist powers." Cultural oppression enables economic exploitation and fuels political corruption. The filmmakers declared that cinema "has a vital part to play" in the liberation struggle "because it is a means of education, information and consciousness raising, as well as a stimulus to creativity." In conclusion, the cineastes affirmed that international solidarity was critical to the realization of victory in their fight and once more positioned the state as a vital partner in assisting the filmmakers in building a truly independent and progressive cinema industrial complex in Africa. "The state," the charter declared, "must take the leading role in building a national cinema free of the shackles of censorship or any other form of coercion likely to diminish the filmmakers' creative scope and the democratic and responsible exercise of their profession."[64]

Once more Upper Volta was at the center of implementing the vision outlined by African filmmakers. Following its successful nationalization of the theater system in 1970, other African countries took control of the motion picture viewing spaces in their countries during the early 1970s.[65] That set the stage for the creation of the CIDC (Consortium Interafricain de Distribution Cinématographique) in 1974, headquartered in Ouagadougou. Initially fourteen African countries joined CIDC, which was designed to be a sovereign distribution network for films throughout the continent. The CIDC pooled resources, procured films, and subsidized their dissemination to the national theater agencies among the member states. That was followed with the establishment of INAFEC (Institut Africain d'Éducation Cinématographique) in Ouagadougou in 1976. This was the first institution in Africa for training the continent's people in the multiple aspects of making motion pictures. Partially funded by UNESCO, INAFEC became a mecca for aspiring African filmmakers over the next decade as it offered a space independent from the Western powers for the cultivation of the skills essential to the cinema industry. The next year Gaston Kaboré was tapped to head the newly formed CNC (Centre National du Cinéma) in Upper Volta. That was the state institution that directed all aspects of the cinema industrial complex and was tasked with the expansion and promotion of Upper Volta's domestic film production. Finally, in 1979, Ouagadougou became the home for CIPROFILM (Centre Interafricain de Production de Films). This expanded upon the work of INAFEC and looped the CNC into a pan-African agency aimed at maximizing the effectiveness of training filmmakers as well as assisting the completion of individual films. The formation of CIPROFILM for the first time permitted the possibility of editing and postproduction in Africa, avoiding the often contentious and frequently debilitating reliance on facilities operated through France's Ministry of Cooperation and other institutions in the imperialist countries.[66] All of those developments aligned with the goals FEPACI outlined through its statements from 1969 to 1975 and once more positioned the Lamizana regime and more specifically Upper Volta at the center of the African cinematic field.

However, the institutional success of African cineastes was counterbalanced by escalating conflict between the directors and their own governments during the 1970s. Increasingly, Sembène, Cissé, Djibril-Diop Mambèty (Senegal), and others focused their work on exposing the corruption and ineffectiveness of African states. They also took aim at archaic traditions and the use of imaginary constructs of the precolonial past as weapons to blunt the progressive development of African societies. This is evident in films like Sembène's *Xala* (1974) and *Ceddo* (1976), Cissé's *cinq jours d'une vie* (1972) and *Den Muso* (1975), and Mambèty's *Touki-bouki* (1973). Cissé's *Den Muso* landed him in prison, and Sembène suffered censorship and prohibition of some of his films.[67] Consequently, African filmmakers were in an ambiguous position of witnessing success in the material arena as African governments created the institutions necessary for the cinema's further development while also having their messages constrained or blocked by those same states. This produced a divergence between the materialism of the cinema industrial complex and its representational aspect, precluding the primary objective of transforming mentalities and fostering a cultural revolution in the project of achieving liberation and social development.[68] The blockage experienced by the social movements in Upper Volta was also experienced by African filmmakers by the late 1970s, further escalating tensions as well as intensifying the sense of urgency to resolve the fundamental problems afflicting people's lives. Those stresses were compounded by the crushing economic crisis of the late 1970s and early 1980s. In 1979, even France massively slashed its funding for African filmmaking, and Dupré notes that CIDC and CIPROFILM had become largely ineffective and dysfunctional by 1980.[69] This contributed to the more defensive tone struck by FEPACI at its Third Congress in Niamey, Niger, 1–4 March 1982, that produced the Niamey Manifesto. Much of the document focused on the material aspects of the cinema industrial complex and called for partnership with African governments in the realization of filmmakers' creative works. Moreover, FEPACI called on its members to tamp down some of the criticism directed at those upon whom they relied for their craft. It obliquely concluded that "filmmakers should maintain a sense of responsibility and morality in dealing with their governments and others they have dealings with." The manifesto once more asserted, "There cannot be any viable cinema without the involvement of African states."[70] However, that support was increasingly absent by the early 1980s and several states including Upper Volta entered a period of extreme crisis politically and economically.

The Saye Zerbo Coup

A new wave of strikes paralyzed Upper Volta in late 1979 that included rural workers on a significant scale for the first time.[71] The boiling political turmoil escalated in the summer of 1980 when the government enacted new laws that slashed the benefits of teachers and constrained their political activities. The SNEAHV launched an indefinite general strike on 1 October 1980.[72] Within weeks other labor federations joined the strike. Lamizana blamed the disturbances on an international communist conspiracy, reprising the rhetoric of Maurice Yaméogo shortly before his ouster in 1966. While the strikes abated in November 1980, tensions remained high throughout the country and especially within the military at the core of the government. Some high-ranking officers had become convinced that Lamizana's time had passed, and a new regime was needed to prevent the more radical forces behind the strikes and demonstrations of the previous year from taking power.[73] Consequently, the people of Upper Volta awoke on the morning of 25 November 1980 to the sight of tanks moving through the streets of Ouagadougou. The elite special forces of the Régiment Inter-Armes d'Appui (RIA) commanded by Colonel Saye Zerbo had taken control. He dismissed the government, abolished political parties, and suspended the constitution. The Comité Militaire de Redressement pour le Progrès National (CMRPN) declared a state of emergency.[74] As René Odou, correspondent for *Afrique Nouvelle*, put it, "The military putsch, in sum, came to put an end to a gerontocracy that had not known how to counteract the effects of the social crisis."[75] The CMRPN government received declarations of support from the chieftaincies and the Catholic clergy who viewed Saye Zerbo's accession to power as "an act of God." Even the previously ousted president Maurice Yaméogo embraced the new government. However, the real power behind the new administration was Joseph Ki-Zerbo and his FPV. He had been an informal advisor to the new military ruler and rallied those that had opposed the Lamizana governments to Saye Zerbo's side in the immediate aftermath of the coup.[76]

The Burkinabè revolutionary Bamouni characterizes the CMRPN as a "fascist-type" government. It imprisoned former political officials and suppressed their parties, formed a new special force trained by Belgian officers to attack the revolutionary parties of the left, and promoted factions within the armed forces to manipulate that institution and preclude the possibility of organized resistance in the ranks.[77] One of the mantras of the CMRPN regime was the restoration of order, including a pledge to root out corruption. Certainly, the chaos of the late 1970s and the early 1980s had eroded the legitimacy of the state and contributed to the general sense of insecurity in society. However, Saye Zerbo also deployed some of the left's rhetoric to diffuse the potential resistance of organized labor and the radical parties to his administration. On 1 May 1981, the CMRPN issued a declaration that pledged to "unite all Voltaïcs in order to develop the country." Such a project would be "based on the elimination of all exterior domination and the exploitation of man by man" with the goal of benefiting all those classes that have previously been oppressed.[78]

Despite the rhetoric of the 1 May 1981 pronouncement, the government moved quickly to suppress the organized parties and unions of the left, such as the CSV, LIPAD, PCRV, and ULC, before they could mobilize. The CMRPN's task was made easier because of the fractious nature of the revolutionary forces. Only the most tentative steps had been taken toward unity, most of which were prompted by the work of the officers in the ROC. They had connections with the PAI/LIPAD/CSV as well as with Valère Somé's ULC. Since the military had seized power overtly and concentrated all authority in its hands, the ROC was vulnerable to exposure and destruction. Saye Zerbo was determined to maintain complete adherence to the regime within the military's ranks. That meant organized political work within the barracks became more difficult and any opposition to the military junta would be dealt with severely. Consequently, the oppressive measures put in place by Saye Zerbo forced the ROC into hiatus; the revolutionary officers limited their contacts with other radical and leftist organizations. For its part, the PCRV was cautious and viewed the recent events as part of an as-yet-incomplete bourgeois revolution that would end with true independence for Upper Volta. To the PCRV, the new government was nothing more than a continuation of that process and did not require a shift in tactics.[79]

The left paid a heavy and near fatal price in the first months of Saye Zerbo's tenure in power. One example of the disarray that afflicted the revolutionary parties was the unexpected demise of Valère Somé's ULC. The pro-Chinese party formed in 1979 out of a schism within the OCV had been riven with internal dissention from its inception. After Saye Zerbo's tanks rolled into the streets, the tenuous links that held the ULC together came untethered. Valère Somé took the extraordinary step of dissolving the ULC at a special congress held 15–16 February 1981. The political theorist Martens describes the circumstances surrounding the disappearance of the ULC as being clouded in mystery. Valère Somé claimed that the Central Committee of the Party met and formally terminated the organization due to the factionalism that made the group's functioning impossible. However, dissidents within the ULC asserted that no such meeting took place and Valère Somé made the decision on his own. They argued, in Martens's words, that "it was the search for an easy life and the fear of repression launched by the colonels of the CMRPN that led Valère Somé to betray communist principles." Adding to the confusion, Valère Somé later said the organization went underground and continued its work in preparation for the day when revolutionary politics could again resurface in Upper Volta.[80] Then, years after that, Valère Somé told Peterson he "had come to believe that 'communism was failing'" and he wanted "'to convince [the revolutionary officers of the ROC] that the solution was not communism.'"[81] Regardless of the truth, the elimination of the ULC signaled a weakened revolutionary left.

Nevertheless, by the summer and fall of 1981, opposition to the regime mounted as the CMRPN failed to address Upper Volta's multiplying fiscal, social, and ecological disasters. Saye Zerbo's government embraced deflationary policies to tackle the problem of inflation. That meant slashed funding for social services, reducing the public service payroll by replacing civilian administrators with soldiers, and cutting wages. Those actions temporarily reduced inflation in Upper Volta from over 12 percent in 1980 to 7.5 percent in 1981, only to see it rise again to 12 percent in 1982. The country's GDP, however, peaked in 1980 at just under $2 billion and fell to $1.75 billion by 1982. Upper Volta's national debt moderated, but continued to climb reaching $352 million by 1982, up from $330 million when Saye Zerbo took power.[82] The figures reveal a country plunging into economic crisis with a contracting economy, declining per capita income, unsustainable debt, and a widening gap between rich and poor.

By October 1981, Soumane Touré's CSV called a general strike against the CMRPN. It was the most potent labor federation in the country with a well-disciplined and experienced cadre of organizers throughout the country. In response, the government abolished the right to strike on 1 November 1981. Soumane Touré countered by scheduling the general strike for 8–9 December 1981. In turn, Saye Zerbo banned the CSV on 24 November 1981 and issued an arrest warrant for Soumane Touré. The teachers' union (SNEAHV), controlled by Ki-Zerbo's PFV, disaffiliated from the CSV and pledged its support for the military dictatorship. Despite those repressive measures, the CSV appealed for new strike action in early 1982.[83] The CSV's determination gave it a measure of authority in the workers' movement and throughout the society, such that Soumane Touré became one of the most popular figures in the country.

In response, Saye Zerbo sought to harness popular figures from within the military to the CMRPN. His attention turned to the thirty-one-year-old, recently promoted Captain Thomas Sankara as a potential ally and offered him a post in the government. Sankara accepted and became minister of information for the CMRPN.[84] Sankara did not want a post in the new government, a fact confirmed by several scholars and close friends.[85] However, he was also loyal to the institution of the armed forces of Upper Volta, respected the hierarchy of command, and felt responsible for assisting his own family members due to his fortuitous position as an officer. Sankara sought the counsel of his closest ideological friends, specifically Soumane Touré and Adama Touré from the PAI, and Valère Somé from the now-dissolved ULC. Each offered opposing advice on what Sankara should do. According to Sankara's biographer Jaffré, the PAI urged Sankara to not be coopted into the CMRPN. Their logic was that the posting was not part of the normal responsibilities of the military and could be refused without violating any sense of institutional loyalty. Moreover, they thought that the revolutionary forces needed to take a distinct and resistant position regarding the state. Valère Somé, however, believed Sankara should take advantage of Saye Zerbo's apparent weakness and enter the government. Valère Somé argued, according to Jaffré, that it was "too early to engage [the CMRPN government] when the balance of forces was clearly against" the revolutionaries. Consequently, to avoid being exposed and eliminated, Valère Somé urged Sankara to accept the invitation and erode the dictatorship from the inside.[86]

Sankara audaciously negotiated the terms of his appointment. He demanded that his friend and confidante Compaoré replace him at the command center in Pô and that his own appointment last for only two months until a more suitable candidate could be found. These demands, if accepted, would enable Sankara and his associates in the ROC to maintain effective command over and influence within the critical military division at Pô in the event of a subsequent coup or an effort by Saye Zerbo to crush opposition within the armed forces.[87] The CMRPN accepted Sankara's conditions and on 13 September 1981, he entered the government as minister of information. In a letter from Sankara to his superiors dated 23 December 1981 and reproduced by Bamouni, Sankara repeatedly emphasizes that his decision was the result only of his sense of institutional loyalty to the military and service to the country.[88]

One way Sankara made his new position work in favor of the radical officers' agenda was to exploit the CMRPN's pledge to stamp out corruption. From his command of the press, he urged reporters to conduct investigations into malfeasance by public officials. As the military dictatorship clamped down on the CSV and waged war against the labor unions throughout November and December 1981, Sankara's Ministry of Information promoted press revelations of the embezzlement of state funds by high-ranking officials. Saye Zerbo's agents sought to muzzle those reports, but Sankara consistently defended the right of the press to expose wrongdoing and encouraged reporters to continue doing their jobs.[89]

Sankara's foray into public affairs was a significant moment in the consolidation of revolutionary forces. He assembled a team at the Ministry of Information made up of figures who later became some of his most trusted and loyal advisors during the revolution. This included long-time friend Fidèle Toé. They had known one another for nearly twenty years, and, in Toé's words, he felt like he was part of the family. Toé described Sankara's approach to his job as minister of information as providing the means to bring the world in "real time to the people" and to furnish them with useful information so that "they could realize their aspirations."⁹⁰ Another figure with whom Sankara became associated by virtue of his new role was Watamou Lamien. He was head of Upper Volta's national radio and a clandestine member of the PCRV.⁹¹ By early 1982, a broad network of revolutionary activists was gelling inside and outside of the military government. The officers of the ROC led by Sankara; the PAI through Soumane Touré, Adama Touré, and Philippe Ouédraogo; the former members of the ULC directed by Valère Somé; and even loosely affiliated members of the PCRV like Watamou Lamien converged into a potent oppositional force preparing to ride a wave of popular discontent against the CMRPN. They met at the Ministry of Information within the government, held meetings at friends' homes away from the barracks, and encountered each other at press conferences and other meetings organized as part of Sankara's government work.

In February 1982, prominent newspapers in Upper Volta published a series of damning exposés on government corruption. The CMRPN responded by arresting several members of the press, holding them for extended periods of questioning without charges. In a letter dated 4 March 1982 to the Ministry of the Interior, Sankara "strongly protested the manner and circumstance" of the arrests. He assailed the prejudicial attitude of the state toward the press and specifically his ministry. Sankara argued it was in the government's best interest to allow the Ministry of Information to fulfill its core mission since the dissemination of true and exact news would "clarify public opinion to the detriment [of the power] of sordid and harmful rumors."⁹²

Meanwhile, the country's economic calamity worsened. As part of the deflationary policies pushed by Ronald Reagan in the United States and Margaret Thatcher in the United Kingdom, global interest rates on debt held by the global south spiked to apocalyptic levels in 1981. For example, in June 1981, President Reagan authorized Paul Volcker, chairman of the U.S. Federal Reserve System, to increase the prime lending rate to 20 percent (peaking at 21.5 percent shortly thereafter). Only two years earlier, the rate had been just over 11 percent. Countries across Latin America, Africa, and Asia could no longer even service their existing obligations since their interest rates were benchmarked to the U.S. prime rate. Moreover, by early 1982, even the most developed capitalist states had plunged into the worst economic crisis since the Great Depression of the 1930s. The explosive growth in the value of the U.S. dollar by 1982 also meant that prices for exports from Upper Volta crashed, cutting foreign capital earnings, and further undermining the country's budget. For a country like

Upper Volta, this constituted a mortal blow to an already tottering state. It had to procure new loans to service existing obligations, which only compounded the situation. After peaking at $300 in 1980–1981, Upper Volta's per capita income fell to $280 in 1982.[93]

Jaffré and Harsch surmise that the anti-CMRPN forces believed the moment was propitious to strike at the regime and the people would rally to their cause. They intimate that a break from Saye Zerbo done in a public, spectacular fashion would energize the people and provide a popular basis for a new administration to take power. Consequently, the worsening economic crisis combined with intensified political repression led Sankara to quit the government. On 12 April 1982, he submitted his resignation citing the "class basis" of the regime as expressed through its relentless crackdown on the labor movement, specifically its effort to arrest Soumane Touré who was Sankara's friend and political ally. Before his resignation took effect, Sankara used his post as minister of information to do a live broadcast during a meeting of officials from CIDC and CIPROFILM hosted by Saye Zerbo to denounce the dictatorship. The representatives of the CIDC and CIPROFILM were meeting to begin preparations for the forthcoming 1983 FESPACO. It was, therefore, one of the most important organizational meetings of officials directly connected to the organization of African filmmakers (FEPACI) as well as to the entire cinema industrial complex within Upper Volta and Africa as a whole. Sankara's address connected his role as minister of information in the government with the important role film played in the broader project of social change. He proclaimed, "There can be no cinema without freedom of expression, and there is no freedom of expression without liberty in general. . . . Woe to those who would gag their people."[94] After his broadcast, Sankara was arrested, imprisoned for six months, demoted in rank, and dispatched to a remote posting. Compaoré and Zongo suffered similar fates, sending the ROC into disarray. Soumane Touré was captured and imprisoned on 10 September 1982. The unions staged some strikes, but they had already been weakened in the previous year's battles with Saye Zerbo's dictatorship. The regime appeared to have weathered the storm.[95]

To further consolidate its hold on the country and further isolate the revolutionary forces from the masses, the junta called for an internal review of the state and recommendations for a path forward in the transition to civilian leadership. Saye Zerbo appointed Jean-Baptiste Ouédraogo as head of the commission. Unbeknownst to the CMRPN, the revolutionary officers had already connected with Jean-Baptiste Ouédraogo (an officer and doctor) and were convinced he would assist them against the dictatorship. Jean-Baptiste Ouédraogo's commission delivered a highly critical report to the CMRPN in which it recommended democratic debate be reinstated at the highest levels of government, a real struggle against corruption, the removal of unpopular officials, the appointment of new leaders who could reinstate discipline in the army, and the lifting of the restrictive measures directed at the labor movement. The dictatorship rejected all the proposals signaling to opposition elements within the military that they had to move against Saye Zerbo's regime.[96]

On the morning of 7 November 1982, the people of Upper Volta awoke once more to the sight of tanks rolling through the streets of Ouagadougou and soldiers positioned at strategic points across the country. A coup removed the reviled CMRPN from power and instantiated a new regime that called itself the Council for the Salvation of the People (Conseil de Salut du Peuple, CSP). The primary instigators of the putsch included the commander of Upper Volta's armed forces Gabriel Somé Yorian, Fidèle Guébré, and Jean-Baptiste Ouédraogo. The troika reflected a range of political perspectives. Somé Yorian was close to ex-president Maurice Yaméogo, while Guébré supported the former ruler Sangoulé Lamizana. Jean-Baptiste Ouédraogo had contacts with the progressive officers in Sankara's circle but was a centrist whose ambition was to restore unity within the armed forces and stability in the country. The primary loser in the upheaval of 7 November 1982 was Ki-Zerbo's UPV.

Within days the new government announced Jean-Baptiste Ouédraogo as president. The new regime restored Sankara, Compaoré, and Zongo to rank and their previous posts. According to Jaffré and confirmed by Jean-Baptiste Ouédraogo, the CSP offered Sankara the post of president, but he refused on the grounds that the political orientation of the country's new rulers was not clear, and the new junta included many conservative elements whose interests were diametrically opposed to those of the ROC and its allies. The conservative officers backed Somé Yorian for the top post. After two days of wrangling, Jean-Baptiste Ouédraogo was named leader of the CSP on 9 November 1982.[97] A tenuous balance had been struck between forces of the old order and the reinvigorated revolutionary groups. Upper Volta entered 1983 on a knife's edge.

2

Dual Power and the Triumph of the Burkinabè Revolution

(1982–1983)

Upon taking power on 7 November 1982, the CSP explained the reasons behind Upper Volta's latest military coup. It denounced the "mismanagement, corruption, and illicit enrichment" of the CMRPN that "aggravated the economic slump" in which the country found itself. It decried the "unjustified repression of workers and students" and the "elimination of fundamental freedoms, individual and collective." The CSP pledged that once they had decided on a political program and made it public the soldiers would resign, handing power to a civilian government.[1] The coup originated entirely within the military and was not connected to any mass movement in the streets or strike wave as in previous changes of administration. However, the junta did include progressive officers associated with the ROC. Partly that was made possible precisely because of the exile imposed on Sankara, Compaoré, and Zongo. In their absence, other members of the ROC like Pierre Ouédraogo, Laurent Sédogo, and Jean-Claude Kamboulé continued to network, maintained the group's coherence, and had linked with Jean-Baptiste Ouédraogo before he was appointed to head Saye

Zerbo's reform commission. Most important among them was Pierre Ouédraogo who had contacts with the conservative officers who planned the coup.²

Sankara's future advisor Bamouni outlines the four ideological currents that came together in an alliance of convenience through their opposition to the Saye Zerbo regime. The first was the "conservatives" represented by Marc Garango (a former minister for Lamizana) and Fidèle Guébré, a military officer and member of the CSP. Their aim was the restoration of the personnel and policies of the Lamizana era. They desired a moderate dictatorial state with generally pro-capitalist and pro-imperialist policies that included a measure of civil liberties and civilian involvement in the management of the state. The second element, also conservative, was directed by Somé Yorian, leader of the coup and potential candidate for president of the CSP. Many supported the restoration of Maurice Yaméogo to the presidency, but fundamentally their economic and foreign policies did not diverge from the other conservatives. Bamouni labels the third current "nationalists of a certain type." They differed from the conservatives mostly in foreign policy and desired a greater assertion of sovereignty for Upper Volta. This translated into more emphasis on domestic economic development. The trend was directed by Jean-Baptiste Ouédraogo, the president of the CSP. The key element that was critical to the potential survival of the new regime was the inclusion of the fourth group, called by Bamouni "patriotic progressives." That group was led by the ROC under Sankara, Compaoré, Boukary Lingani, and Zongo, military officers with connections to the revolutionary left, specifically the PAI (LIPAD/CSV) and the group around Valère Somé and the now-dissolved ULC. It also had contact with the PCRV through Watamou Lamien. Their policies called for the complete assertion of Upper Volta's sovereignty on the world stage, solidarity with socialist and progressive countries, support for Third World liberation, and the economic development and cultural transformation of Upper Volta.³

While it had been agreed that Jean-Baptiste Ouédraogo would be the face of the new regime during the transition to civilian rule, Jean-Claude Kamboulé pushed for Sankara, as the most popular and widely known of the ROC officers, to take charge. But others among the radicals believed it was too soon to take power and begin a revolution. Moreover, in *Thomas Sankara et la Révolution au Burkina Faso*, Kyélem de Tambèla explains that the peasantry remained supportive of the ousted regime because of its folkloric policies and emphasis on tradition.⁴ For his part, Sankara's biographer Jaffré writes that the captain was prepared to exploit the CSP's need for the support of the progressive officers, but he was wary of too close an affiliation with the junta lest the ROC lose its credibility among the revolutionary forces in society and the people more broadly. Sankara called for a compromise wherein the ROC would participate in the CSP while pushing the agenda further to the left and mobilizing the population behind that more progressive orientation.⁵ After much discussion within their ranks, the ROC agreed to enter the new government and backed Jean-Baptiste Ouédraogo as president in a vote on 13 November 1982. At a subsequent meeting of the CSP (22–26 November 1982), Boukary Lingani (ROC) was named secretary general of the new National Assembly, seconded by another ROC member, Kilimité Hien. Compaoré was also added to the CSP. For the first time elements of the PAI/LIPAD as well as Valère Somé's former ULC entered the government.⁶

The influence of the progressive officers was evident in the public pronouncements of the CSP as well as its first official acts. It pledged to "liberate the people" through promoting "social justice, freedom of the press, freedom of expression, popular democracy, empowerment of the masses, and progressive nationalism aimed at freeing the country from all imperialist servitude and its neocolonial corollary."⁷ The aims of the new government echoed Sankara's rhetoric as minister of information and his public resignation speech the previous spring. In its first month, the CSP overturned many of the most repressive laws of the CMRPN, lifted the ban on strikes, legalized the CSV while releasing from prison its leader, Soumane Touré, and opened the press to permit a wide-ranging public debate about the country's future.⁸

However, the majority of the CSP derived from conservative forces within the military, the business elite, and even supporters of previous Voltaic governments under Lamizana. The ROC and its civilian allies among the revolutionary left occupied an uneasy and potentially vulnerable space in the new regime. This chapter analyzes how that uneasy coalition of forces attempted to work together and ultimately fell apart. By the spring of 1983, the government was poised to split as competing centers of power emerged in society that threatened to plunge Upper Volta into civil war. Foreign powers such as France, Côte d'Ivoire, and Libya intervened in that crisis to shape its outcome. By the late summer of 1983, a showdown neared between the radicals supported by Libya and Ghana, and the conservatives sustained by France and Côte d'Ivoire. In that context, the revolutionary officers in the ROC decided the time was ripe to strike and inaugurate what became the Burkinabè Revolution.

Consolidation of Revolutionary Forces within the CSP

To mark the revival of labor activity, Sankara made a major speech on 10 December 1982 before the XI Congress of SUVESS (Syndicat Unifié Voltaïque des Enseignants du Secondaire et du Supérieur) the most powerful teachers' union in the country. During his presentation, Sankara explained the rationale for the coup that had brought the CSP to power. He acknowledged that in the past the military had taken power with the promise to break the chains of exploitation and improve the lives of their people, only to betray those pronouncements. Sankara said those failures arose because "the Voltaïc army had within it the same contradictions as the Voltaïc people." Within the military there were conservative elements who derived from the elite of the country and served to advance their interests. However, there were also soldiers who came from the peasantry and working class who had different expectations for the country and were open to a progressive agenda of social reform. Thus, there was often a struggle within the armed forces between reactionaries and revolutionaries that in the past was won by those on the right who preserved the status quo and betrayed the hopes of the people. He urged SUVESS to play a leading role in guaranteeing there would not be disappointment this time. Their actions through demonstrations, strikes, and protests whenever the government failed to live up to their expectations would make sure that the previous trend toward abandonment of the progressive aspirations of the people would not be repeated. The unions had to be constant and vigilant watchdogs over the government applying pressure in the streets when necessary to keep the regime on the path of making a real improvement in people's lives. Sankara even asserted that the CSP intended to support the expansion of organized labor as essential to improving society. He wrapped up his address by calling for an "open and frank dialogue between [the government] and the unions" and declared "long live the working class . . . long live democracy for the welfare of the people."[9]

In the first weeks after the coup, Sankara frequently met with his associates in the PAI as well as with Valère Somé (former ULC) to strategize about how to use their positions from within the government to realize their progressive agenda in the face of anticipated resistance from the conservatives in the CSP. In addition, the ROC formally met on 21 December 1982, to clarify its own position going forward, perhaps the first time it had convened as such. Sankara, Compaoré, Boukary Lingani, and Zongo were there along with other key members of the group, such as Pierre Ouédraogo and Jean-Claude Kamboulé. According to interviews with Compaoré conducted much later (our only source of information on this encounter), they decided to formally constitute the Organisation Militaire Révolutionnaire (OMR) to replace the amorphous ROC. They made their first objective to create a post of prime minister and push Sankara as the only acceptable candidate. The OMR would present the proposal as a necessary step toward the transition to civilian rule and suggest only Sankara had the public credibility to lead that process. Moreover, the OMR agreed to support the candidacy of PAI members to cabinet posts as well as Valère Somé.[10]

At an extraordinary meeting of the CSP in early January 1983 the OMR presented its demands. The resolution to create the post of prime minister asserted that it would be independent of the president's authority and not answerable to the CSP Assembly. The prime minister was to be a free agent equal in power to the president and the CSP.[11] Jean-Baptiste Ouédraogo was inclined to accept the OMR's proposals, if only to harness Sankara's name to the government. The conservatives opposed the proposition. After a contentious debate, the OMR won the day. On 11 January 1983, Sankara became prime minister. He added two members of the PAI (Ibrahima Koné and Dadjouari Emmanuel) and Eugène Dondassé, a former member of the ULC, as part of his cabinet.[12]

Bamouni describes the CSP as a dual power situation. The politicians of the right (led by President Jean-Baptiste Ouédraogo) favored capitalism, good relations with France and the other imperialist states of the West, and cooperation with likeminded regional leaders such as Houphouët-Boigny in Côte d'Ivoire. They also represented the interests of the old guard of Upper Volta's political establishment including supporters of the former presidents Yaméogo and Lamizana. On the other hand, the progressive military officers led by Prime Minister Sankara pushed socialist-oriented development plans, sought to integrate organized labor into the management of the state, raise the people's political consciousness, and break the neocolonial control of the imperialist world over Upper Volta. In regional politics, the progressives sought closer relations with radical governments in Africa, such as Mozambique, Angola, and Libya, while also developing ties with Cuba, North Korea, and the socialist world more broadly. Bamouni concludes, "In this race against the clock for the control of power by each of the two tendencies, the ideological divergences had become too apparent not to lead to a breakup" at some point in the not-too-distant future.[13]

Upon being invested as prime minister of Upper Volta, Sankara delivered a brief speech outlining his policies. He provided a background to the current situation and argued that the main force behind the latest change in government stemmed from the "profound aspiration of the Voltaïc people for independence and liberty." Those desires included a government that would free the country from "all humiliating tutelage and all exploitative dependence. . . . restore to the Voltaïc people their confidence that they have the capacity to change their own destiny. . . . unleash the creative capacity of the Voltaïc people to give them the means to feed the people, to provide them with clean drinking water, clothes to wear, education, and healthcare." In foreign policy, Sankara called for closer relations with the African people and non-alignment in the Cold War. Regarding the relationship between the state and the people, he asserted that the government served the people, but he warned that while the people were entitled to liberty that did not include the right to exploit others or engage in corruption. The work of the CSP included efforts to impart confidence among the people that they could understand and formulate what was in their own best interests and that they had the capacity to build a better society through their own efforts. He then called on the CSP to provide the means for the masses to participate in the creation of a new way of life. Sankara turned to the members of the CSP in the audience and said, "You must give respect to the people, respect their competence, their work, and the worker. . . . You must show this respect through your rigorous morality, honesty, and the justice of your comportment [in public]. . . . Because you are, day and night, in Upper Volta and outside [the country], at all times and in all places the charges of the permanent mission of the Voltaïc people." He wrapped up his investiture speech proclaiming, "Our commitment must be total, based from the start on an anti-imperialist position, a determination to liquidate neocolonialism and the irreversibility of our march toward a really democratic society armed to build a society of a new type that will bury the [capitalist] past. Anything less than that, we will not tolerate. . . . Long live the people of Upper Volta who we serve!"[14]

The CSP and the Nigerian Migrant Crisis

Shortly after Sankara became prime minister, the CSP confronted its first serious foreign policy crisis centered on migrant rights in Nigeria. That country's government, led by Shehu Shagari, was suffering a severe economic decline that had been exacerbated by the sharp fall in world oil prices after 1981 (oil constituted a significant portion of Nigeria's export earnings). As his popularity declined and rumors of yet another military coup spread, on 17 January 1983, Shagari expelled African migrants from neighboring African states, including those from Upper Volta. The Shagari regime claimed that the "illegal" immigrants were criminals who brought disorder to the country while taking jobs away from deserving Nigerians. In fact, many of the migrants now slated for immediate mass deportation had come to Nigeria because of the oil boom of the late 1970s when jobs were plentiful. One of the reasons behind the expulsion was Shagari's animosity toward the government of Jerry Rawlings in Ghana since he had come to power overthrowing Hilla Limann on 31 December 1981. Shagari had developed a positive relationship with Limann and was angered by Rawlings's return to power. Upward of two million migrants were to be forcibly expelled from the country by mid-February 1983, the vast majority from Ghana which lent the operation its ugly name, "Ghana Must Go."[15] The government made the announcement suddenly and without warning to its neighbors and gave a deadline of about two weeks for all migrants in Nigeria without proper paperwork to leave. Shagari also passively permitted vigilantism against migrants or anyone identified as foreign. Over the ensuing weeks there were widespread attacks on migrants. The roads were clogged, possessions strewn along the sides of highways, and property abandoned.[16] The crisis was exacerbated when neighboring countries, including Ghana, Benin, and Niger closed their borders to their own citizens since they did not want to be flooded with large numbers of unemployed thereby undermining their own economies.[17]

Sankara chose to suspend the right of free migration enjoyed by his own people to transit to other countries in the region, effectively closing Upper Volta's borders. While this was intended as retaliation against Nigeria's actions, it also hit other countries like Côte d'Ivoire that were much more prominent destinations for its citizens. His argument was that this would deny Nigeria (and other countries) the ability to exploit the cheap labor of the Voltaic people and show that Upper Volta would no longer serve as a human reservoir for the region.[18] However, Sankara did not prevent Voltaic citizens from returning, unlike Ghana and Benin whose people were then trapped in a no man's land at the border.[19]

Sankara's suspension of the right of migration confused people in Upper Volta and others within the CSP. The measure appeared to punish the Voltaic people by restricting their right to movement. Sankara's associates within the CSP expressed concern that the peasants' anger would boil over and destabilize the government. That worry was compounded by pressure from other regional leaders, foremost among them Côte d'Ivoire's Houphouët-Boigny, who relied on the steady influx of workers from Upper Volta to labor on his country's cocoa plantations. However, President Jean-Baptiste Ouédraogo and the conservatives within they junta also could not appear as if they simply acquiesced to Nigeria's draconian actions. The CSP made a more robust assertion of Upper Volta's sovereignty one of its cornerstone positions. Sankara's move put them in an awkward position that compelled the conservatives aligned with Jean-Baptiste Ouédraogo to associate with Sankara's tough stance while assuaging the concerns of regional allies like Houphouët-Boigny and mollifying the discontent of Upper Volta's peasants and business community.

Houphouët-Boigny fortuitously furnished a way out for the CSP's conservatives when he called an emergency meeting of the Conseil de l'Entênte, a regional association of former French colonies—Côte d'Ivoire, Burkina Faso, Niger, Benin, and Togo—in early February 1983 to address the brewing crisis and coordinate a regional response to Nigeria's actions. The group was forged in the dying days of colonialism in 1959 at the urging of Houphouët-Boigny as a counter to the proposed creation of the Mali Federation. Consequently, from its inception it was conservative in politics, pro-French in foreign policy, and emphasized the separation of the newly formed nation-states coming out of the imperial federations.[20] The emergency meeting sought to de-escalate tensions with Nigeria while standing firmly against the action. The final communique was largely influenced by Upper Volta's President Jean-Baptiste Ouédraogo, according to a reporter from *Carrefour Africain* present at the meeting.[21] It condemned Nigeria's expulsion of undocumented immigrants "as contrary to the spirit of African hospitality and various international agreements" but did not offer any remedies.[22] The expulsion order stood but Shagari's xenophobic policies did not save him. Before the year was out, the military had once more taken power in Nigeria ushering in decades of brutal dictatorial rule.

Sankara and Revolutionary Cinema at FESPACO 1983

During the migrant crisis, Sankara hosted Africa's major film festival, FESPACO, in Ouagadougou (5–13 February 1983). It was Sankara's first prominent role at the event, and it came at a time when African cinema was in a state of crisis. In the early 1980s, the organization of African filmmakers, FEPACI, nearly split over a dispute about the nature of African cinema. A younger generation organized as Le Collectif l'Oeil Vert pushed for a greater emphasis on the entertainment function of motion pictures rather than the political didacticism that characterized the works of Ousmane Sembène, Med Hondo, and Souleymane Cissé in the 1960s and 1970s.[23] That aesthetic dispute was exacerbated by the increased material difficulties in making motion pictures. France had drastically cut its funding for African filmmaking in 1979, and the general economic crisis of the late 1970s and 1980s led to escalating costs in all aspects of the industry. To reconcile the dispute, FEPACI convened the First International Conference on Cinema Production in Africa in Niamey, Niger (1–4 March 1982). The "Niamey Manifesto of African Filmmakers" that resulted from the meeting signaled a retreat from the explicit militantism and optimistic tone of the 1975 "Algiers Charter." Much of the document focused on the material and technical aspects of filmmaking. Several sections laid out detailed recommendations for the creation of training institutes in Africa, the provision of cinema technology to African filmmakers, and the establishment of marketing and distribution agencies to promote the dissemination of African movies. It also laid out a detailed set of recommendations for how cineastes could partner with governments and the private sector to realize their creative work.[24] Just one month after that meeting (April 1982), Sankara delivered his speech resigning as minister of information in the CMRPN government during the planning meeting for the 1983 FESPACO. At that gathering, the recommendations of FEPACI from its conference in Niamey were discussed as the basis for the festival's programming.[25]

The film scholar Dupré observes that with the 1983 FESPACO a new era arrived largely because of Sankara's intervention in the cinematic field. Beginning with the 1982 planning conference, Sankara publicly associated the cinema with the project of social transformation and elevated it to a level of critical importance as an instrument that both reflected the creative aspirations of the people and provided guidance in raising their consciousness. For example, in an unprecedented gesture, the prime minister chose to personally award

FESPACO's grand prize, the Étalon de Yennenga, to Cissé for his film *Finyé*. Normally, politicians did not take an active role in the festival's business. In making the presentation to Cissé, Sankara highlighted the significance of the motion picture's theme. He said, "Through their actions, two students, Bah and Batrou, resist the established order and are arrested. During their imprisonment they suffer physical abuse and mental humiliation. This only gave them more strength to fight."[26] Cissé, one of the pioneers of African cinema, a graduate of a Soviet film school, had been persecuted for calling out corruption and tyrannical invocations of tradition in Mali; he was identified with the revolutionary forces within FEPACI. Sankara's decision to present Cissé with the trophy and his speech aligned the prime minister's political objectives with those of the radical filmmakers who had laid the groundwork for African cinema over the previous two decades. It also enhanced cinema's importance as an element to advance the government's progressive agenda. Moreover, *Finyé*'s theme of resisting persecution in the pursuit of a better life fit with the CSP's more radical stated objectives.[27]

The historian Lindiwe Dovey writes, "Sankara is also one of the very few [leaders] who have seen the value inherent in a *film festival*." As Sankara explained at a press conference two years later, "If Burkina is attached to FESPACO, it is because we are aware that the purification of cinema is a requirement of our struggle.... We are also aware that the screen, the camera, the film, and the messages carried there constitute a cultural universe, a cultural space that we must occupy under pain of letting it be occupied by others... to broadcast messages that go in the direction of [those others'] interests."[28] At the 1983 FESPACO, Sankara also announced the formation of the Marché International du Cinéma Africain (MICA), a demonstration of his awareness of "the economic dimensions of African film."[29] MICA was designed as a space for the exchange of film stock and generic footage that could be used by other filmmakers to complete their works, similar to the practice in Hollywood of using filler scenes to bridge a film's main action. This would facilitate a continental market to promote the further development and expansion of African cinema by lowering the cost of making motion pictures and thereby opening the field to new entrants. The festival strongly emphasized the commercial dimension of African cinema, and the CSP's provision of resources for MICA demonstrated its support for the recommendations put forward in the Niamey Manifesto the previous year. While the markets were well-attended, they did not generate significant revenue in

1983.³⁰ Regardless, FEPACI and the attendees at the 1983 FESPACO took note of Sankara's high profile during the festivities and his insertion into the festival's proceedings as an indication of support for African cinema in general as well as an endorsement of the work of the more radically oriented filmmakers. Accordingly, the film scholar Ukadike argues that Sankara's commitment to African filmmaking and the enhancement of FESPACO beginning with his role as prime minister in 1983 was "exemplary" and revealed his "strong vision for Africa and its culture and for black African films."³¹

Global Alignments and International Intrigue

Shortly after FESPACO's conclusion, on 24 February 1983, Sankara left for his first official foreign trip. The prime minister traveled first to Niger in transit to Libya, led by the mercurial Muammar Qaddafi, whose *Green Book* Sankara and his comrades in the ROC, including Compaoré, read in the mid-1970s. In Niger, Sankara met with the country's leader Seyni Kountché who had overthrown Niger's independence leader Hamani Diori in 1974. In January 1983, Kountché began a transition to civilian rule that included the creation of a commission to draft a new constitution. The notion of managing a transition from military to civilian rule intrigued Sankara since the pretext for his becoming prime minister was that he would direct a similar handover in Upper Volta. After those meetings, Sankara moved on to Libya. Qaddafi had extended repeated invitations to Sankara that were refused. Sankara's biographer Jaffré suggests that one of the reasons the prime minister eventually took the Libyan leader up on his offer was his curiosity about the level of progress made in economic development by a country that was among the most isolated in the world, therefore being forced to rely upon its own resources. For his part, Qaddafi was keen to impress the young captain and staged massive military parades, provided extensive tours of development projects and communes, and entertained him lavishly. Qaddafi sought to court Sankara as a regional ally since the Libyan leader was at that time deeply embroiled in an intractable conflict with Chad and supported a variety of militias and organizations whose work subverted governments in Egypt, Niger, Liberia, Central African Republic, Uganda, and others. However, Jaffré believes Sankara was "more impressed with the meetings [he held] with technical experts" and the promises of economic and military aid made to assist Upper Volta. After Libya, Sankara journeyed to North Korea (Democratic People's Republic of Korea), holding a summit with its leader Kim Il-Sung, although not much information has been made available regarding the details of the encounter.[32]

While Sankara was out of the country, dramatic events unfolded in Upper Volta. On 28 February 1983, officers close to the deposed dictator Saye Zerbo attempted a coup. Units loyal to the former ruler hoped to capture the entire CSP in one place and massacre them. However, the plotters bungled the operation and were arrested. Jean-Baptiste Ouédraogo seized on the attempted takeover, as well as Sankara being out of the country, to bolster his status within the CSP vis-à-vis the progressives aligned with the prime minister. He pledged to establish "order and security," describing the country as being in a state of "total anarchy" fueled by corruption and fraud. Jean-Baptiste Ouédraogo also pledged to Upper Volta's business community that it would remain the "primary motor of the country's economic activity," a response to growing concerns among the capitalist class over Sankara's public alignment with organized labor and his ongoing visits to Libya, then North Korea.[33] Those apprehensions seemed to be confirmed upon Sankara's return to Upper Volta in early March 1983, which was followed by the arrival of a Libyan military transport plane. This gave Jean-Baptiste Ouédraogo and the conservatives within the CSP an angle from which to further wrest some authority from the prime minister by painting him as Qaddafi's puppet. Anonymous broadsides circulated that slandered the progressives within the government as tools of foreign subversion and agents who undermined Upper Volta's sovereignty, an attempt to appropriate the nationalist mantle for the conservatives in the CSP. As Sankara's biographer Peterson relates, the arrival of the Libyan plane led the Reagan Administration to categorize the prime minister "as a pro-Libyan acolyte and suspected of planning a communist takeover of Upper Volta."[34]

Such perceptions were amplified a few weeks later when Sankara again left the country, this time heading to New Delhi, India, for a meeting of the Non-Aligned Movement. The conference presented the first opportunity for Sankara to meet many of his sources of inspiration and to make a mark on the world stage. At that meeting from 7–12 March 1983, Sankara had encounters with Fidel Castro (Cuba), Daniel Ortega (Nicaragua), Mathieu Kérékou (Benin), Jerry Rawlings (Ghana), Indira Gandhi (India), Chali Benjedid (Algeria), and Julius Nyerere (Tanzania). The prime minister held long conversations with many of them, resolutely impressed by their strong anti-imperialist stance. He sought to have Upper Volta join in that coalition on the global stage.[35] He developed a particularly close relationship with Castro, becoming especially enamored of the effective use Cuba made of the cinema to promote and bring about the revolution in that country as well as its commitment to Third World filmmaking. The Cuban government's dedication to both the material and representational aspects of the cinema industrial complex and its steadfast anti-imperialist internationalism was precisely the project of the Third Cinema movement within FEPACI that Sankara and his allies in Upper Volta also shared.[36]

At the summit, Sankara delivered a speech that outlined his vision of the world and Upper Volta's place in it. Sankara offered strong praise for Fidel Castro, particularly for his work in strengthening the dignity and credibility of the developing countries. Sankara walked the audience through the litany of constraints imposed on the global south by imperialism and the neocolonial armature of the world system. He insisted that each people had the right to choose their own path of development and challenged the efforts by the Western world to impose a simplistic definition of non-alignment on the organization. Instead, Sankara asserted that nonalignment did not mean that they would not stand up against racism, injustice, imperialist aggression, and exploitation. As examples, Sankara denounced Israel's invasion of Lebanon and massacres of Palestinians at Sabra and Shatila in Beirut, lauded Nicaragua's resistance to U.S. interference in that country's internal affairs, praised the communist FMLN rebels in El Salvador for their struggle for national liberation, and highlighted SWAPO's (Southwest Africa People's Organization) fight for their freedom from rule by apartheid South Africa and the campaign to end that "odious racist system."[37] At the summit, Sankara also took aim at some of the regional leaders in West Africa and the conservatives in the CSP, telling the director of the journal *Afrique Asie* that the CSP was plagued with intrigue and rumors of plots, and that "everything is guided from the exterior from Côte d'Ivoire, Togo, at the instigation of the big neocolonial interests of diverse countries in Upper Volta among them, of course [is] France."[38]

Crisis of Dual Power within the CSP

Upon his return to Upper Volta, Sankara indeed found the country in a state of ferment. The coup plot had unnerved the CSP; arrests continued, and Jean-Baptiste Ouédraogo toured the country to reassure the conservative elements of society that the recent pronouncements of his prime minister at the Non-Aligned Summit did not reflect a radical turn in the government. As a gesture to show that the CSP remained unified and committed to the broad program it had outlined following the November 1982 coup, the government organized a demonstration in Ouagadougou for 26 March 1983 at which all the major figures in the regime would appear together. They would present a united front that constrained the progressives' agenda within the larger approach to administration of the country by the junta. The spokesperson for the CSP, Kilimité Hien, a member of the OMR, announced the event and took charge of its organization.[39]

As the crowd of tens of thousands pressed into the Place du 3 Janvier, the leaders of the CSP took the stage to address the people. Boukary Lingani (OMR) made the introductory remarks as secretary general of the CSP. He set the tone with a denunciation of imperialism and exploiters.[40] Then Sankara (OMR) took the dais and started with the rhetorical question, "Who are the enemies of the people?" The prime minister launched into an impassioned and electric speech that became a turning point in the country's politics and catapulted Sankara to immense popularity. He declared, "The enemies of the people are in the interior and exterior [to the country]. . . . The interior enemies are those who enrich themselves in an illicit manner, profiting from their social position, profiting from their bureaucratic position." Sankara turned to those lurking outside Upper Volta who sought to exploit, denigrate, and constrain the people. Specifically, he highlighted neocolonialism and imperialism as malevolent forces undermining the development and sovereignty of the country. The prime minister reassured the masses that countries such as Libya and North Korea were friends of Upper Volta, and he denounced all intimations that his visits to those countries signaled submission to foreign ideologies or control. If Upper Volta wants to trade with Libya, Sankara asserted, it had every right to do so. He offered praise for Qaddafi saying that his policies were resulting in economic development and putting the country's resources at the disposal of its people. Finally, Sankara explained that what was being attacked in the malicious red-baiting tracts circulating throughout the country was the liberty of the people, their right to development, and their sovereignty. The prime minister dismissed all labels as a diversion to play on people's fears and emotions. If the enemies want to say it is communism to provide benefits to the workers, improve the lives of the people, and develop the country then let them, it does not matter, he said.[41]

When Sankara concluded, Jean-Baptiste Ouédraogo took the stage. By all accounts he was rattled, clearly unprepared for the kind of address his prime minister had just unleashed and presented a poor study in contrast to the agitated crowds. His speech was moderate in both tone and substance. In fact, according to the political economist Kyélem de Tambèla and other scholars, the people started to disperse as the president was speaking. In somber cadence, Jean-Baptiste Ouédraogo denied that there were any differences within the CSP and outlined his vision of an orderly transition to civilian rule and a normal constitutional life.[42] In fact, Sankara's biographer Jaffré describes the president's address as being in the classic tradition of nationalism that seemed almost quaint in comparison with Sankara's fiery denunciation of imperialism and assertion of people's power.[43] Rather than dispel the rumors of a deep split within the ruling junta, the "Meeting of Truth," as the gathering was called, laid bare the dual power conflict that was rending the CSP government.

From late March 1983, the CSP entered a period of terminal crisis. The communist-leaning forces behind Sankara continued to push the government in progressive directions domestically and in foreign policy. The centrist and conservative elements grouped around Jean-Baptiste Ouédraogo and Gabriel Somé Yorian now viewed Sankara as a threat to their survival and began to plot his removal. Jaffré relates an unrecorded meeting between Jean-Baptiste Ouédraogo and Jean-Claude Kamboulé, Gen. Somé Yorian's nephew and member of the OMR, in which they discussed the need "to put an end" to Sankara.[44] While their exact meaning was unclear, it portended an ominous showdown between the competing powers in the government as well as an effort to split the radical officers' group. In a seeming counter to Sankara's global travels, Jean-Baptiste Ouédraogo set off on his own tour (18–26 April 1983) and visited Togo, Ghana, Benin, and Niger. Moreover, he desired a meeting with Houphouët-Boigny in Côte d'Ivoire, but the latter refused, sending a signal to Upper Volta's president that something should be done about Sankara and his allies.

As Jean-Baptiste Ouédraogo wrapped up his tour, Qaddafi was in the area on a state visit to Benin, headed by the communist Mathieu Kérékou. While

Qaddafi was there, Sankara dispatched an envoy to Benin to invite the Libyan leader to visit Upper Volta upon his journey back home.[45] Qaddafi accepted and arrived in Ouagadougou on 30 April 1983, staying until 1 May 1983. There was a "veritable panic within the CSP" upon the Libyan leader's arrival. Englebert writes, "The visit appeared as a provocation and resulted in confirming in their opinion those who saw [Sankara] as a pawn of the Libyan colonel."[46] The political theorist Martens also highlights Qaddafi's visit as a watershed moment in the war between the president and prime minister of Upper Volta. He notes that between 26 March 1983 and 14 May 1983, Sankara "openly defied the authority of President Jean-Baptiste Ouédraogo" in meeting after meeting.[47] In addition to conferencing with Sankara, Qaddafi spoke with other intimates of the OMR, including Compaoré, who purportedly had a copy of Qaddafi's *Green Book* with him at the airport upon the latter's arrival in Ouagadougou.[48] The final communiqué released by the offices of both countries affirmed their lasting friendship and made pledges for closer economic cooperation. It also proclaimed the solidarity of the socialist revolution in Libya with the ongoing "revolution of the Voltaïc people."[49]

To head off a collision that would sunder the CSP, the junta decided to call another mass meeting on 14 May 1983, this time in Bobo-Dioulasso, the country's second largest city. Specifically, the CSP invited representatives of the students' movements and other youth groups to attend the assembly. Sankara reprised the themes from his speech before the crowds in Ouagadougou in March 1983. He declared, "The enemy is at our gates" and implored the youth to take the offensive against those enemies. Using call and response, Sankara got the crowd to affirm each of his statements concerning their willingness to use force to repel the enemy, to fight them whether they were internal or external to the country. The prime minister said the youth had to mobilize through public debate, the cinema, theater, conferences, popular gatherings, ideological education, and any other public avenue. The prime minister demanded the construction of new schools, roads and infrastructure, infirmaries, and other "concrete acts, to say nothing of the physical acts" of developing the country. Commenting on the foreign debt, Sankara called for self-directed development, which is "true liberation . . . taking control of one's own destiny." The captain again addressed the accusations that he was a puppet of Libya and North Korea, saying that he had negotiated aid packages with both countries and, "comrades, it is with these countries that we are beginning to see the first results."[50] Through that speech,

Sankara outlined the broad agenda of the revolutionary elements within the CSP and cornered the conservatives allied to Jean-Baptiste Ouédraogo. They either must adhere to the prime minister's policy objectives, which aligned with the CSP's official statements of principle, or betray their pronouncements. In so doing, it would confirm Sankara's description of previous governments that wound up betraying the people's aspirations as sketched in his speech to the teachers' union in December 1982.

Evidence suggests that, at least from the time of the 14 May 1983 meeting if not earlier, Jean-Baptiste Ouédraogo conspired with Somé Yorian (supported by France) to orchestrate Sankara's removal from office. As the leaders of the CSP dispersed on 15 May 1983 from the mass meeting in Bobo-Dioulasso, the president met with his military leaders to arrange their next move.[51] The following day, 16 May 1983, Guy Penne, director of African Affairs for France's President François Mitterrand, suddenly arrived in Ouagadougou. The Burkinabè revolutionary Bamouni writes, "The coup d'état was prepared and executed by Colonel Yoryan [sic] Gabriel Somé, head of the military, with the complicity of France. France's ambassador to Burkina, Gaston Boyer, was particularly active in this coup." He adds, "Yoryan [sic] was the principal author of the event because President Jean-Baptiste Ouédraogo was only a strawman." Penne's arrival in Upper Volta was unannounced, covered in secrecy, and took place in the dead of night, at approximately 11:50 p.m. that Monday. The press was prohibited from going to the airport to greet him. Penne even eschewed the residence reserved for foreign dignitaries and instead "spent the night at the home of France's ambassador."[52] The historian Guy Martin, citing an observer of the events that night, describes what unfolded as "one of the most audacious neocolonial interventions in postcolonial African history." He relates a meeting at the ambassador's residence between Penne and Colonel Somé Yorian at which they jointly took the decision to move against Sankara and arrest him along with all his allies within the CSP.[53]

The "Coup" of 17 May 1983 and the Split in the CSP

Bamouni writes, "At 2:00 in the morning of 17 May 1983, the armored vehicles commanded by Jean-Claude Kamboulé began to move under the instructions of the military commander, Colonel [Gabriel Somé Yorian]. Shortly afterward, the home of the prime minister was surrounded by five tanks." Sankara ordered his guards not to attack and instead walked out and surrendered. In addition to Sankara, Boukary Lingani, general secretary of the CSP, was also arrested. Zongo was trapped at CNEC in Pô and surrendered later in the day, while Compaoré escaped and was holed up with commandos and Valère Somé at Pô. Even the ambassador from Libya was surrounded and ordered to depart the country within forty-eight hours.[54] By late afternoon, the coup was mostly complete. Jean-Baptiste Ouédraogo was brought in by the plotters and pledged his loyalty to a reconfigured CSP government devoid of the progressive officers and members of the radical left parties. He issued a statement in which the government reaffirmed its commitment to the original principles of the CSP, in particular "to restore the confidence [of power] to the Voltaïc people with the goal of freely returning to them the structures of the interior [political] life with a delay of two years, outside of partisan quarrels and all demagogic and irresponsible actions." The president concluded with an "appeal for calm and vigilance of the populations in our cities and countryside, of our armed forces, military, and para-military."[55]

The plotters did not mask France's involvement. The CSP leaders hosted Mitterrand's African Affairs advisor, Guy Penne, for lunch where the visiting dignitary showered the government with praise, pledged France's enduring partnership with Upper Volta, and announced a new aid package. France also promised military assistance for Jean-Baptiste Ouédraogo's government. The historian of the Burkinabè Revolution Kyélem de Tambèla observes that, "Guy Penne seem[ed] therefore to have been at the center of the events of 17 May 1983, which resulted in the fall of the CSP I" government.[56] The rightists within the CSP exuded confidence that they had finally dealt with their troublesome prime minister, eliminated the radical left as a threat, and assured France (and others in the neighborhood) of their loyalty in the Cold War international alignment. France was particularly keen to keep Upper Volta so oriented because of its ongoing conflict with Libya in Chad.[57]

Among scholars there is a debate about the events of the 17 May 1983 coup regarding the seeming ease with which the conservatives in the CSP were able to isolate and remove the progressives with French complicity. On the surface, it appears as if the OMR and its allies in the PAI and former members of the ULC had made no contingency plans for a possible move against them even though it was a recurring theme in many of Sankara's, Boukary Lingani's, and Ibrahima

Koné's speeches during the spring of 1983. For example, the anthropologist and former U.S. ambassador to Upper Volta Elliot Skinner argues, "At this stage of his career, Sankara had obviously miscalculated the conjunction of political forces arrayed against him."[58] However, the prime minister's biographer Jaffré points to the assiduous work Sankara and his associates had done within the CSP to win broad popular and institutional support. In fact, Jaffré suggests that the OMR had a majority within the CSP by the time of the coup.[59] While Sankara later told a reporter that he and his comrades "were naïve and gave them the means to arrest us," he also expressed the belief that the Voltaic people would not let this stand. He pointed to the work the OMR and other revolutionaries had done in the preceding months to energize the people, draw them into the affairs of state, and even the ideological preparation done within the ranks of the military as reservoirs of support that would resist any move to derail the unfolding revolution.[60]

Sankara's assertion about the shifting alignments within the country's armed forces seemed to be born out within hours of the coup when Compaoré proclaimed an open rebellion against the reconfigured CSP government. In a message to Jean-Baptiste Ouédraogo, the OMR leader wrote, "Given the fact that the CSP's Charter does not allow the President to imprison his Prime Minister we are at odds." Compaoré erected a sign outside the military camp proclaiming "The Republic of Pô" and university students, labor activists, and supporters of the revolutionary left made the trek there to join the resistance. Libya and Ghana denounced the coup and endorsed Compaoré's actions, supplying weapons to the hold out garrison.[61] Ironically, the coup against Sankara precipitated a level of unity among Upper Volta's communist forces that had long been elusive. The pro-Soviet PAI (LIPAD/CSV) went into action immediately, taking direction from officials still in the CSP government, including Ibrahima Koné, minister of youth and sports who had convened the mass rally in Bobo-Dioulasso on 14 May 1983. Ibrahima Koné called on the student organizations and other youth groups to prepare mass demonstrations in support of Sankara and to denounce the putschists. Philippe Ouédraogo, leader of the PAI, mobilized his forces from the underground. Former members of Valère Somé's ULC rallied their forces as well. The PAI and former adherents of the ULC issued joint declarations calling themselves the "commandos of the revolution." The propaganda work of the revolutionaries brought together Philippe Ouédraogo (PAI/LIPAD), Adama Touré (PAI), Ibrahima Koné (PAI), Valère Somé (of the former ULC), Basile Guissou (of the former ULC), and others in a coalition anchored by the OMR around Sankara.⁶² On the left, only the PCRV remained ambivalent and interpreted the upheavals within the CSP as an internal dispute of the "petit bourgeois" elements.⁶³

The political commentator Diallo writes, "In the days that followed, great demonstrations flared up in Ouagadougou, where the slogan 'Free Sankara!' rang out."⁶⁴ On 20 May 1983, tens of thousands of students flooded the capital's streets in one of the largest demonstrations in Upper Volta's history. They proclaimed an indefinite general strike until Sankara and his comrades were freed. The next day the schools remained empty, shops closed, and workers stayed home. Pro-socialist and pro-communist tracts circulated widely among the protesters, many leaflets calling for the overthrow of Jean-Baptiste Ouédraogo's government and the installation of a truly revolutionary regime. The demonstrators urged unity of action with the rebels at Pô. Rather than terminate the situation of dual power, the move by rightists in the CSP had exploded it into the streets of Upper Volta and sundered the state in two.⁶⁵

The CSP called a counter-demonstration on 22 May 1983. Jean-Baptiste Ouédraogo dismissed the protests of 20–21 May 1983 as a small group of students who were being exploited by a bunch of troublemakers playing on their innocence. He claimed the gatherings were not spontaneous but had been planned for a long time by Sankara and his supporters as part of a plot to overthrow the state when they realized their message could not win the day. He had confidence that "the young people who, naïvely, allowed themselves to be manipulated" would eventually adhere to their obligations. He then appealed "to the parents to fulfill their responsibilities to control their children." The president added, "The CSP is not the property of anyone, it will not bow to the will of anyone." As the crowds gathered on 22 May 1983 under banners reading "Down with Communism!" it was clear they lacked energy and commitment. In fact, the communist left infiltrated the pro-government march, leading to scuffles between partisans of the ousted prime minister and the president.⁶⁶ The remaining CSP leadership had hitched its identity to a clumsy Cold War anti-communism that failed to resonate among the people. As Jean-Baptiste Ouédraogo later told a press conference, "The eviction of Sankara is a problem of ideology. The PAI put itself at the service of Sankara and [Boukary] Lingani to advance their own ideology. We were on the path of little by little following the program of the PAI and its program must have ended with [the establishment] of a communist society."⁶⁷

Within the CSP, deep divisions arose over its next steps. The president wanted a peaceful resolution and hoped that a public display of support would mollify critics at home and abroad over the arrest of his prime minister. Others around Somé Yorian, Jean-Claude Kamboulé, and Fidèle Guébré wanted a more aggressive approach that would crush the progressive forces, restore order, and preserve their power. On 23 May 1983, Jean-Baptiste Ouédraogo called an emergency meeting of the junta. The president survived a vote of confidence with nearly half the remaining CSP delegates abstaining. Somé Yorian then moved to have the government declare its opposition to communism. He was persuaded to drop the motion and instead backed a proclamation that the government remained committed to the original program of the CSP. Another act to support Sankara's arrest and dissolve the post of prime minister obtained only a handful of votes and failed. The president considered resigning at the meeting but was dissuaded by the pleas of France's ambassador to Upper Volta, Gaston Boyer.⁶⁸ To save his government and diffuse the explosive situation in Upper Volta, Jean-Baptiste Ouédraogo announced in an address to the people on 27 May 1983 that the government was dissolved and replaced by the CSP II. In the interim he dismissed Somé Yorian as commander of the military (25 May 1983). In his speech, the president also ordered the army back to the barracks, the immediate release of all soldiers and civilians arrested for political reasons, and proclaimed a six-month timetable for the writing of a new constitution and the return to civilian rule. Days later, on 30 May 1983, Sankara and Boukary Lingani were released, as were the former presidents (Maurice Yaméogo, Lamizana, and Saye Zerbo). All of this was done at the urging of France's ambassador as a strategy to create a mood of reconciliation that would lead to deradicalization.⁶⁹

Jean-Baptiste Ouédraogo then opened negotiations with Sankara to resolve the mounting political crisis. The ousted prime minister was permitted to join his comrade Compaoré at Pô to persuade the renegade captain to come back into the fold and end his state of rebellion. However, days later, in another twist that confirmed the confused direction of the CSP II government, Sankara, Boukary Lingani, and Zongo were rearrested under orders from the deposed army chief of staff Somé Yorian. This prompted a meeting of military officers on 13 June 1983 to head off the possibility of civil war. Compaoré sent a letter to that meeting from his rebel base at Pô in which he lambasted the arrests of his comrades and claimed, "patriots have taken up arms and are preparing to confront the mercenaries and other foreign legionnaires."[70] Compaoré threatened to march on the capital, whereupon the OMR prisoners were freed once more on 16 June 1983. This time the deal leading to the release of the progressive officers called for their redeployment throughout the country and beyond. Sankara was to be posted to France by the fall, isolating him from political developments in Upper Volta.[71]

In the meantime, the rebels refused to stand down. Compaoré formed his forces into the National Liberation Army and received regular supplies from Libya via Ghana and Ghana as well. According to the commander at Pô, he warned Rawlings that if the Ghanaian leader "did not back him, Ghana would have to face Togo and Côte d'Ivoire . . . all alone." In addition to the military assistance, the revolutionaries received propaganda aid in the distribution of leaflets calling on the people to resist the CSP II.[72] The PAI/LIPAD ran weapons to the garrison at Pô and mobilized its militants throughout the country. At this time, a new radio station, *La Voix de la Révolution voltaïque*, "began broadcasting from Bardaï in the north of Chad directed toward Upper Volta." This was territory under the control of Libya and its proxies.[73] Somé Yorian's forces mobilized as well in June 1983, surreptitiously being supplied with weapons from France. The colonel and his supporters plotted several attacks against the garrison at Pô and even to assassinate Sankara. Somé Yorian wanted to use the BIA, the elite battalion stationed at the airport, to march on Compaoré's National Liberation Army. However, morale was atrocious within the armed forces. In addition, the PAI had successfully infiltrated both the BIA and the presidential guard. Several explosions had already rocked munitions depots on 31 May 1983 and again on 16 June 1983, purportedly set off by agents of the resistance. Somé Yorian could not even get his own forces to muster in practice drills for the march against Pô that he plotted for late June 1983. And, adding insult to injury, several of Jean-Baptiste Ouédraogo's own personal guards defected to Ghana around that time. The president even offered the post of head of the military (essentially chief of staff) to at least two officers both of whom declined the offer.[74]

As the political drama played out, the country's economy crumbled. Over the course of 1983, Upper Volta's external debt jumped another 13 percent to nearly $398 million, the largest percentage increase since 1979. Its GDP slumped to $1.6 billion after peaking at $1.929 billion in 1980. The decline in 1983 amounted to an 8.8 percent contraction in the size of Upper Volta's economy. The IMF reports that in 1983 real GDP contacted at an annualized rate of 1.2 percent, while inflation remained at 8.3 percent. The inflation rate only dropped moderately from the previous year and remained elevated at levels going back ten years. Finally, GNI per capita income levels slipped to $240, a second straight yearly drop since peaking in 1980–1981 at $300. In other words, the average purchasing power for the country's people had collapsed by 20 percent in just two years.[75] The collapse of Upper Volta's economy poured fuel on the government crisis and contributed to a surge in popular support for Sankara's restoration as prime minister and for the rebels based at Pô.

The Democratic and Popular Revolution

Sensing the moment was ripe to strike a mortal blow at the crumbing administration and to forestall potential intervention from abroad, the revolutionaries accelerated plans for a takeover. On 15 July 1983, the communist forces of the OMR, PAI, former ULC members, and the National Liberation Army united in a "Left Front." Other loosely organized Marxist-Leninists allied with the Left Front, including Etienne Traoré, Amidou Diallo, Keita Soumaïla, Watamou Lamien (now formerly of the PCRV), and Guillaume Sessouma. They shortly coalesced into another communist faction known as the Union of Burkinabè Communists (Union des Communistes Burkinabè, UCB). Finally, within the PCRV, a schism grew between those, such as Jean-Marc Palm and Issa Konaté, who wanted to support the insurrection and the leadership of the party that abstained from the drama. Eventually the party split with the pro-revolution elements forming yet another communist organization called the Burkinabè Communist Group (Groupe Communiste Burkinabè, GCB).[76]

On 16 July 1983, the OMR and its political allies worked out a strategy to seize power. The plan's timing hinged on any hint of a provocative act by the CSP II. Unlike 17 May 1983, the revolutionaries would not be caught off guard. In addition, Sankara's posting to France began on 1 September 1983, which could not be allowed. With Compaoré leading, the revolutionaries drew up operational plans based on an assessment of which units in the military were prepared to move against the CSP II, which could be counted on to remain neutral, and those that were likely to resist. The BAI was viewed as a threat as it was under the influence of Somé Yorian and the far-right. Moreover, they had demonstrated their independence from the government by their rogue actions on 9 June 1983 when they rearrested Sankara and his associates. The Left Front formed a command staff, organized signals for communication, and delegated responsibility for preparing to take power. By 20 July 1983, the Left Front had agreed on a political program to be inaugurated with the success of the revolution. The program would establish a revolutionary state based on popular sovereignty and action, directed toward the building of a truly independent socialist society. A further strategy session took place at Pô between the OMR and the PAI on 25 July 1983 to clarify specific tasks to be carried out on the day of the insurrection and to organize a government. Each party of the Left Front was asked to submit the names of individuals who would represent them in the new administration. The OMR would retain overall direction of the state, but the communist parties would be brought in as partners apportioned according to their relative strength in society and their participation in taking power.[77]

In fact, Sankara signaled to the French government what was in the offing. The captain gave a message to a friend that was forwarded to Jean-Christophe Mitterrand, the French president's son. The only account of this message is produced by Jaffré in his biography of Sankara. There he writes that the captain informed his friend to get a message to France's president in which he warned the former colonial power that, if it continued to impose its will on Upper Volta, "we will be obliged, the Voltaïc nationalists, to take matters in our own hands. And the French are not going to be able to say that the communists or the Libyans or the Soviets are behind us. No one is behind us."[78] Sankara explained that the revolutionaries opposed the transition to civilian rule as it was being orchestrated by the CSP II because it maintained the "distinction between civilians and the military in the exercise of power and in the construction of our people's destiny." The former prime minister concluded that the military and civilian population had to work in tandem since "we all are made from the same people and [forged] through the same struggles."[79]

The Left Front fixed 1 August 1983 as the day for the uprising. However, due to ongoing planning and preparation, the date was pushed back to 3 August 1983, then 4 August 1983. The urgency with which the revolutionaries made their move was based on the belief that a new plot was being hatched by Somé Yorian with the connivance of France to assassinate Sankara and storm the barracks at Pô. In addition, the recently freed officers under Saye Zerbo's CMRPN were plotting their own coup for 6 August 1983. Bamouni claims that France knew about Somé Yorian's plot and was fully behind it. He says that Upper Volta's foreign minister had already signed a "military cooperation agreement" with France in anticipation of the elimination of the revolutionaries. "These accords," Bamouni writes, "permitted France to intervene militarily in the internal affairs of diverse states to maintain by force the neocolonial regimes already in place, and to change those that menaced the imperialists' interests."[80] They thought that the pretext for such an attack would be the country's independence celebrations on 5 August 1983. At first the revolutionaries wanted to strike before the military units assembled in the capital for the celebration. However, they decided that it would be better to use the distraction of the festivities to pre-position forces and move when the government did not expect it.

Consequently, as the sun rose over Upper Volta on 4 August 1983, Compaoré and his officers of the National Liberation Army held their regular morning briefing at Pô with updates on the preparation for the day's official festivities as well as for the insurrection. Bamouni notes that at noon the mood changed at Pô. Rumors circulated that Somé Yorian and Fidèle Guebré were moving forces in an irregular manner indicating they might strike at the rebel stronghold. However, the garrisons under Somé Yorian had been infiltrated by loyalists of the revolutionaries, so they passed information to the rebels based at Pô. At 3:00 p.m., the revolutionaries crossed the Rubicon. Compaoré gave orders for the National Liberation Army to seize the city of Pô and secure it as a base of operations as other military units moved across the country. Within thirty minutes all key parts of the city were in the hands of the revolutionaries, and they began to distribute arms to the people who had gathered outside the military base. The rebels commandeered fifty trucks from a Canadian construction company to transport the revolutionaries commanded by Compaoré to the capital.[81]

As the columns of rebel soldiers moved north to the capital, the official celebrations got underway. Jean-Baptiste Ouédraogo gave a speech outlining the next steps in the transition to constitutional rule, he warned about the politicization of the armed forces, and reassured the people that the old politicians would be prohibited from running for office. The president called for "patriots [and] new men with a sense of responsibility and national realities" to take the reins and held out a special warning for the youth not to be "contaminated with party politics."[82] Since communications had been cut with Pô, there was no hint in the CSP II of what was transpiring as the president gave his speech.

Compaoré had organized his forces into five subgroups each with specific operational objectives upon arrival in the capital. The five groups were to hit the typical targets—presidential palace, national radio, the police headquarters, the Republican Security Guard, and the BIA. After rumbling north for several hours, the rebels arrived in Ouagadougou shortly before 8:00 p.m. They quickly branched off into their zones of responsibility. At that moment, PAI and activists of the former ULC cut communications and the power throughout the major cities of Upper Volta. That was the signal to the revolutionary soldiers and their civilian allies to strike. One village after another fell into rebel hands as most military units declared their adhesion to the forces commanded by Compaoré. Moreover, the labor movement and underground network directed by the PAI mobilized their members to take control of strategic roads and other vital nodes of administration, such as the police, radio, and telephone. All this was coordinated by walkie-talkie and the secure communications system directed by Compaoré and other officers in the OMR. In dramatic fashion, Bamouni describes how "Compaoré demanded that the advance accelerate even faster [and even] surveyed the action by helicopter." Jean-Baptiste Ouédraogo finished his speech at about 8:30 p.m., and at 9:25 p.m., the rebels moved. Exchanges of gunfire were heard throughout the city. However, the operation had been carried off with total surprise, the main objectives achieved within minutes, and the president was arrested. The last holdout was the BAI. The National Liberation Army poured fire into the base with "rocket launchers and anti-tank grenades... destroying two tanks." Captain Jean-Claude Kamboulé, a renegade from the OMR, abandoned his troops and tried to escape. Somé Yorian's house was surrounded, but he was not home. He was found two days later, then executed along with Fidèle Guébré on 9 August 1983 for attempting to foment counterrevolution. The garrison surrendered in the early morning hours of 5 August 1983.[83]

At 10:00 p.m. on 4 August 1983, the national radio of Upper Volta went back on the air with a special announcement. Bamouni writes, "At 22 hours Captain Thomas Sankara in the uniform of a commando, red beret [on his head], Kalashnikov in his hand, with firm voice and slightly moved, interrupted the radio broadcast and read the Proclamation of the historic night of 4 August 1983."[84] Sankara's declaration began with a justification of the move against the CSP II. He noted that the ideals of the coup of 7 November 1982 had been betrayed by the events of 17 May 1983 conducted by "reactionary conservative forces who know to do nothing other than serve the interests of the enemies of the people, the interests of foreign domination, of neocolonialism." The captain continued, "To realize the objectives of the honor, the dignity, the true independence, and progress for Upper Volta and for its people, the current movement of Voltaïc armed forces . . . constitute this day, 4 August 1983, the National Council of the Revolution." Then he called on the people of Upper Volta "to mobilize in active and vigilant support" of the revolution. "The National Council of the Revolution invites the Voltaïc people to constitute Committees in Defense of the Revolution (Comités de défense de la révolution, CDR) to participate in the great patriotic struggle of the CNR and to prevent the interior and exterior enemies from doing harm to our people." Sankara announced that all parties were dissolved and affirmed Upper Volta's commitments to all existing treaties and organizations. "The National Council of the Revolution," the proclamation continued, "is not directed against any country, against any state, or people. It proclaims its solidarity with all the peoples, its will to live in peace, and good friendship with all the countries and notably with all the countries neighboring Upper Volta." Sankara concluded, "The fundamental reason and objective of the National Council of the Revolution is the defense of the interests of the Voltaïc people, the realization of their profound aspirations for liberty, true independence, and economic and social progress. Country or death, we will win!"[85]

The *New York Times* printed a story from the Associated Press declaring that "a pro-Libyan paratroop captain . . . seized power in [Upper Volta] today in a coup that left 13 people dead and 15 wounded . . . six of the wounded were French nationals." The report noted, "Captain Sankara is said to be particularly popular among young Upper Voltans." Then came the crux of the story, "Captain Sankara's takeover, coupled with Libyan involvement in Chad's civil war and Colonel Kadaffi's [sic] open ambitions to extend his influence in Africa, was expected to fuel fears in Western-oriented African capitals," although the article claimed that American and French diplomats expressed no concern about the upheaval of 4 August 1983 in Upper Volta.[86] While taking power was relatively easy, the real question was holding it and implementing a revolutionary plan of action to alleviate the myriad crises that had produced the revolutionary context in the first place. That would also provide the test of whether the Western powers had reason to be concerned about developments in Upper Volta.

3

Building Revolutionary Structures and Making New People

(1983–1984)

On 5 August 1983, the anniversary of Upper Volta's independence from France, thousands of people poured into the streets in celebration and excited conversation over the events of the previous night. Sankara's close advisor Bamouni writes, "On 5 August [1983] in the morning there was a general mobilization in the capital shaken by an explosion of insane joy. Through monster parades the people gave their active support to the National Council of the Revolution."[1] Despite the heavy presence of the armed forces on the streets, there was no sign of apprehension among the populace. Rather, wild scenes of civilians and soldiers embracing each other characterized the first momentous day of the revolution. The new government had not yet been announced, and little information about the new regime had been released. However, the fact that Sankara had read the CNR's proclamation and appeared to be at the helm of the previous day's dramatic political upheaval was enough to reassure and encourage the assembled masses, many of whom has been engaged in the demonstrations, strikes, and mobilizations throughout the summer as the CSP II government crumbled. The parties of the revolutionary left had played their role and their militants were conspicuous among the people in the streets that day despite the declaration that all parties were now abolished. It took several days to bring some renegade military units under control, and other opponents of the new regime fled abroad to escape imprisonment.

Despite the mass demonstration of support on 5 August 1983, followed by a second even larger display of enthusiasm across the country on 7 August 1983, not even all the revolutionary left supported the CNR. From the start, the PCRV officially declared its opposition to the CNR and worked to undermine the new government. That position provoked some opposition within the party, and they coalesced around Jean-Marc Palm in a faction known as the "Communist Group." They took a positive approach to the CNR, in part a result of previous work with the ROC/OMR when Sankara was minister of information and prime minister. Eventually, they split out of the PCRV and joined the revolutionary government.[2] Within the OMR, there was also disagreement over what kind of revolution they intended to bring about in the country and who should lead it. Compaoré's supporters claim that he was the real moving force of the revolution and that he intended to be (or should have been) president upon the overthrow of Jean-Baptiste Ouédraogo's government. Ernest Nongma Ouédraogo, minister of security in the revolutionary government, years later gave a radio interview in which he claimed there was no preset notion of who would take charge should the uprising be successful. At a meeting of the CNR shortly after taking power, Compaoré offered himself as president for the new government. He had led the commandos from Pô, freed Sankara from house arrest, and organized the military aspects of the takeover. Compaoré, therefore, felt that he was the leader of the movement and believed Sankara would be reinstalled as prime minister. However, Ernest Nongma Ouédraogo asserts that Compaoré's candidacy was vehemently opposed by the communist groups—the PAI and Valère Somé's supporters of the former ULC—that formed the other legs of the three-part coalition that engineered the conquest of power. They demanded Sankara be made president. According to the former security minister, Compaoré "understood that his time had not yet arrived. He therefore decided to take a low profile."[3] Sankara's biographer Jaffré also intimates that there was some ambiguity as to the leadership of the revolution in its initial hours.[4]

Regardless, Sankara was identified as "president" of the CNR, and he read the statement announcing its formation on 4 August 1983. Out of an abundance of caution, the composition of the CNR was initially kept secret although Sankara, Compaoré, Zongo and Boukary Lingani, also referred to as the "Four Historic Leaders of the Revolution," were known to be among them. Sankara asked the PAI/LIPAD and Valère Somé as representative of the former ULC to give the names of those they wanted to nominate to be part of the new cabinet. In a strategic move, the PAI did not nominate Soumane Touré, leader of the PAI-controlled CSV labor federation, as one of its candidates for membership in the emerging administration. The pro-Soviet party wanted him to remain as labor leader and to turn the CSV into a potent force for mass mobilization independent of the CNR. In the transitional period when the revolutionary state was being formed, it would serve as a pressure group to move the CNR in a more explicitly communist direction in emulation of the Soviet Union. Moreover, the PAI requested that the position of secretary general of the CDR be elected by the members of the CDR in a National Congress. The CDR were conceived to be the base of revolutionary governance and the primary instruments for carrying out the state's policies. Control of them would translate into ultimate control over the direction of the revolution as it unfolded. The PAI's hope was that Soumane Touré would win the election as leader of the CDR in any popular vote.[5] While not dismissed out of hand, the idea of holding elections for general secretary of the CDR was shelved by the country's new rulers as they confronted more urgent tasks in the process of securing control throughout the country and creating new structures through which to govern.

The CNR focused its activities in three areas that it identified as critical to make changes that would guarantee the survival and success of the revolution. First was a radical restructuring of the state and the system of governance in the country. The revolutionaries created the CNR as the paramount center of power and defined its role in relation to other organs of the administration also formed in that period, the most important of which were the CDR and the Popular Tribunals of the Revolution (Tribunaux Populaires de la Révolution, TPR) that gradually supplanted the established courts. The CNR provided ideological guidance and formulated policies that the CDR, as grassroots organizations, would implement. The TPR were designed to facilitate swift justice for those accused of hampering the revolutionary process as well as to provide retribution from those who had previously committed acts that harmed the people, such as engaging in corruption. As public events, the TPR were also devised to facilitate the direct involvement of the people in the judicial system and rectify the injustices of the past. Kyélem de Tambèla argues that "colonial exploitation has [produced] ... the pauperization of the population" that resulted in developmental "regression" and encouraged the people to "abandon the territory" to the benefit of building other colonies' economies. The pattern of out-migration and impoverishment persisted after colonial rule ended.[6] Those objective conditions, according to Sennen Andriamirado, resulted in "an economic desert, peopled by beggars."[7] The CDR and TPR aimed to correct that history and set the country on a new course of self-directed development.

Critical to the successful economic growth of the country was the CNR's second axis of activity, which was the extension of the revolutionary process to the countryside. The entrenched power of traditional chieftaincies presented a potential obstacle to the durability of the revolutionary government. Consequently, the CNR moved quickly to strip them of their special legal status, deprive them of access to labor, and have the land nationalized. Sankara's administration relied heavily upon the deployment of cinema in the countryside to bring film to the people and encouraged their engagement with motion pictures as an industry and expressive form. The revolutionaries believed that would raise the peasants' consciousness and empower them to overturn the oppressive social structures that benefited the chiefs. Already Africa's radical filmmakers had defined their role in precisely that manner, and Sankara had demonstrated his affinity for their perspective at the 1983 FESPACO during his tenure as prime minister. Med Hondo, the revolutionary director from Mauritania, describes the "alienation disseminated through the image" as "all the more dangerous for being insidious, uncontroversial, 'accepted,' seemingly inoffensive and neutral." He insists on the vital "role of the cinema in the construction of peoples' consciousnesses."[8] African filmmakers organized in FEPACI had made their core mission the construction of a liberated culture through consciousness raising and political engagement to make new people. This would be accomplished, according to Third Cinema theory, through "the destruction of ... the old image shaped by colonialism and neocolonialism, and the creation of a new cinema" based on the lived realities and the aspirations of the unalienated person in society.[9] Moreover, the CNR cultivated relationships with African filmmakers through FEPACI and FESPACO to broaden the reach of the revolution to the wider world as well as involving them in the domestic revolutionary process. According to Dupré, "The cultural field was among those which was the most affected, because for the first time the country adopted a real cultural policy with concrete and motivated objectives."[10]

That connected with the third area of major activity for the CNR, which was the field of international relations. The revolutionary government set out to redefine its relationship with France while also building friendships with progressive and socialist countries and movements. The CNR's vigorous foreign policy aimed to insulate the new government from counterrevolutionary pressures from the imperialist world and buy the regime time to implement its policies to change the society. In the first days after 4 August 1983, that was an urgent consideration as France was directly implicated in the coup of 17 May 1983 that had removed Sankara as prime minister, and the now deposed government of Jean-Baptiste Ouédraogo had signed security agreements with the former imperial power that included provisions for the deployment of French troops in Upper Volta to assist in maintaining order. Moreover, Côte d'Ivoire's leader Houphouët-Boigny had expressed his displeasure with Sankara's actions as prime minister earlier in the year while the Reagan Administration in the United States had voiced concerns that the new CNR president was a "puppet" of Libya's Qaddafi.[11]

This chapter explores the process whereby the revolutionaries who took power on 4 August 1983 put in place the institutional structures through which their project of personal and social transformation could be realized. As they moved forward to bring about those changes, the first serious fissures within the ruling coalition emerged. What began as disputes over how fast and how hard to push the changes envisioned by the CNR devolved into a contest for partisan and personal power. Those disagreements often thrust Sankara to the center as a mediator among the factions, which both enhanced his prominence within the revolutionary government and made him vulnerable to attack from multiple angles. As Sankara's biographer Peterson asserts, "[Sankara] was far and away the centerpiece of the revolution, its chief symbol." But he "was a complex individual," and there has been an ineluctable tendency to "over-personalize the revolution, highlighting Sankara and playing down other political actors."[12] In part, that resulted from the multiple times that the president was called upon to bring the warring factions together and keep the revolutionary process on track. Regardless, the first year of the revolution also produced tangible results in stabilizing the economy and engaging the people to directly participate in carrying out the changes to their lives.

Organizing the Apparatus of Government

On 19 August 1983, the CNR convened to determine the new government, and on 24 August 1983, the new cabinet was announced. The CNR retained ultimate power, but the business of government was conducted by a cabinet of twenty members. Five seats were reserved for the military (the OMR dissolved itself at this point), five seats were given to the pro-Soviet PAI/LIPAD (including Adama Touré as minister of information, Arba Diallo as foreign minister, and Philippe Ouédraogo as minister of equipment and communication), three seats were given to Valère Somé's former comrades within the ULC (including Basile Guissou as minister of the environment and tourism and Train Raymond Pooda as minister of justice), and the remaining seven were given to unaffiliated civilians deemed trustworthy and loyal to the revolution including Fidèle Toé as minister of labor and social security, and elements of the Communist Group from within the PCRV. Sankara was named president, Compaoré minister of state, Boukary Lingani minister of defense, and Zongo minister in charge of state agencies. Other leaders of the CNR, but not part of the government, included Valère Somé and Paulin Bamouni.[13] Pierre Ouédraogo (a leading member of the OMR and part of the emerging UCB) was appointed as secretary general of the CDR.[14]

While the CNR and cabinet occupied the center of political power, the CDR constituted the institution through which the people asserted authority and direction over the policies that shaped the Democratic and Popular Revolution. The CDR were voluntary organizations formed by people in their workplaces and neighborhoods whose purpose was to defend the revolution from internal and external enemies as well as mobilize resources (material and human) to carry out the government's programs. In addition, the CDR, which formed spontaneously after the CNR's proclamation of 4 August 1983, became local watchdogs, at times even operating as an unofficial police force to ensure conformity with the revolution's ideological positions. It was through the CDR that the armed forces and the people would be structurally connected since many CDR leaders were soldiers and the armed forces supplied them with weapons. Moreover, they had a practical purpose given the international and regional context. As Sankara explained, "We will give them some military training so that, if the need arises, they can defend their homeland and the people's power. The slogan 'The fatherland or death, we will overcome' will not be a hollow phrase, void of all meaning. The slogan is very good, but above all things must be done to make it a reality. Hence the need for military training that will be undertaken at the appropriate time. Upper Volta will not be Chile."[15] This last statement was a reference to the tragic events of 11 September 1973 when a U.S.-engineered coup overthrew the democratically elected Marxist president of Chile, Salvador Allende, and installed a brutal military junta directed by General Augusto Pinochet, still in power at the time of the Burkinabè Revolution.

Already by 6 August 1983, the first CDR had formed in the capital, and over the subsequent days, more sprouted in the country's major cities. The armed forces remained on highest alert for any potential counterrevolutionary action or foreign intervention that might reverse the CNR's accession to power.[16] The CDR were unprecedented in Upper Volta's history and were modeled on the experiences of other revolutionary countries, especially Cuba from which even the name was borrowed. Kyélem de Tambèla writes, "Contrary to preceding regimes which sought to use to their advantage preexisting social and political institutions, with the CDR the CNR created its own political networks [that were] new and independent." The new government also redrew the administrative map of the country on 15 August 1984 to break the authority of entrenched local powerbrokers by eliminating their offices and areas of jurisdiction. They would be replaced by CDR that were entrusted as the new agencies through which government power was exercised on the local level.[17] The structures of the CDR corresponded roughly to villages, neighborhoods (in larger cities), places of employment or economic sectors, military units, and schools. The local CDR were grouped into larger CDR of a department, garrison, or national enterprise. A provincial council oversaw those CDR below it, and finally the National Congress of the CDR represented its highest body. Membership in the CDR was limited to those who "adhered to the political line established by the CNR in the Discourse of Political Orientation of 2 October 1983."[18]

In the first months after the revolution, the CDR formed on an improvised basis, which allowed the contending groups within the revolutionary movement to jockey for position. The PAI took the offensive through its mass organization LIPAD to push the revolution in the direction it wanted it to go. On 13 September 1983, LIPAD activists took control of the national electric company and deposed its director, replacing it with a committee under its leadership. On 16 September 1983, LIPAD moved on the director of the national television station who was accused of not being sufficiently revolutionary. Finally, on 22 September 1983, LIPAD organized a march on the mayor of Ouagadougou to depose him, though it was thwarted by Pierre Ouédraogo, the head of the CDR. Moreover, the PAI used its extensive network of labor and student activists to secure dominance over most of the local CDR in the major cities. As Martens observes, "At the beginning of 1984, the PAI controlled the majority of the CDR in the capital and proved its capacity to mobilize by itself the masses."[19]

To bring order to the work of the CDR and clarify the chain of command under the new government, the CNR promulgated the *Statut Général des Comités de Défense de la Révolution* (General statutes of the CDR) on 17 May 1984 that largely confirmed the structures that had already formed throughout the country. The statutes reaffirmed the nature of the revolution of 4 August 1983 as "the result of the spontaneous movement of the masses," which "embodie[d] the pursuit and the development at a higher level of the great popular struggles" going back to 1966. The preamble declared that each upheaval of the people introduced a new stage in the fight for true liberation and the realization of the aspirations of the population. Every iteration of popular revolt in the country's history had sharpened the class struggle and reached a critical point in the lead up to the CNR taking power. According to the statutes, the CDR were created to provide the organized cadre and the structural means to achieve the aspirations embodied in the revolution. The statutes make clear that the CDR emanate from the CNR and are, therefore, juridically subordinate to it. However, "[The CDR] are the instrument forged by the people to become the sovereign masters of their destiny." The primary purpose of the CDR is to defend the Revolution and realize its programs. Through that process, the CDR will also contribute to "the ideological formation of the people" and facilitate "the diffusion of revolutionary ideas." In its function, the CDR will be based on the strictest discipline, according to the "principles of democratic centralism."[20]

The National General Secretariat (Secrétaire Général National, SGN) of the CDR constituted the ultimate leadership of the new institution and was elected at a National Congress. This was a provision aimed at appeasing the PAI, which from the start advocated that the leadership of the CDR be determined by popular vote. The National Congress was comprised of elected delegates from all the CDR throughout the country. According to the rules of democratic centralism, the congress formulated the broad policies of the CDR, which were then enforced through the management of the SGN. It was the responsibility of each CDR to carry out the policies as established by the National Congress as interpreted by the SGN. Below the SGN was a General Assembly that met periodically and was responsible for electing the Executive Bureau of the CDR.[21] While explicitly stating that the CDR was not a political party, it closely approximated the structures of communist parties around the world and functioned according to the same principle.

Framing the Revolution's Ideology

LIPAD's success in gaining control over many CDR during September 1983 brought to the fore the divergent conceptions of the revolution and its pace. According to Jaffré, the PAI fiercely defended its autonomy and resisted suggestions that it dissolve or merge into a larger united organization. It conceived of itself as the vanguard of the working class, had a long institutional history going back to its founding in 1963, and envisioned creating a Soviet-style society in Upper Volta. Valère Somé was deeply and personally devoted to Sankara and had spent most of his political life isolated from the major struggles in the country. Since the demise of the ULC in early 1981, he lacked an organization and his influence derived mostly from his relationship with the new CNR president and his connections to former members of the ULC. When confronted with the PAI's successes in the early weeks of the revolution, Valère Somé conceived the idea of reviving his party, which he formally committed to in November 1983. He even wrote to Sankara explaining his decision and stated that it was necessary to reestablish the party to counterbalance the power of the PAI. His organization (known after its formal creation in March 1984 as the Union de Lutte Communiste–Reconstruite, ULCR) was ostensibly pro-China in its orientation within the multipolar Cold War framework, pushed a Third Worldist and pan-Africanist approach in foreign policy, and advocated self-directed development in domestic policy, loosely consistent with Maoism. However, it lacked the mass base of the PAI.[22] Finally, there were others within the CNR who were grounded in Marxism but did not belong to an organization, including Sankara. Their desire was to build a new type of state in Upper Volta based on popular power, integrate the military and civilians as one people, steer the country toward economic development, and maintain aggressive neutrality on the world stage. Sankara, Bamouni, and others embraced Fanon's idea of true decolonization that entailed a radical transformation of society and international relations. They wanted unity among the revolutionary forces, not necessarily conformity, and hoped that the organizations that adhered to the revolution would voluntarily work toward unifying into a single party.[23]

To establish the basis for cooperation among the groups and provide clear guidance to the people as to the goals of the CNR, Sankara appointed an informal committee of advisors that included Philippe Ouédraogo (PAI), Kader Cissé (former member of the ULC), and Valère Somé (former leader of the ULC) to draft a statement of principles. The result was the *Discours d'Orientation Politique* (Discourse of political orientation), which was read over radio and television on 2 October 1983. Martens asserts that "Sankara took responsibility [for the process] by himself. The document [that was] so important was not examined or adopted by the CNR."[24] However, the evidence indicates that, while there was not a formal vote of the CNR on the *Discours d'Orientation Politique*, it did have the imprimatur of the CNR's approval and articulated the ideas shared by the entire revolutionary government. This is indicated by the fact that it was read while Sankara was out of the country (he left for France that morning to attend the Tenth Conference of the Heads of State of Africa and France) and the broadcast at 8:00 p.m. that night was officially released by the Ministry of Information, headed by Adama Touré of the PAI. Moreover, the CDR mobilized its members and the broader population in mass demonstrations planned for the day after the address as a validation of popular support for the declared principles of the revolutionary government. As Harsch writes, "Sankara and those who looked to his leadership tended to place greater stress on ways to involve broader layers of the population, particularly rural villagers, in the country's political life. . . . One of the most notable features of Burkina's August 1983 revolution was the seriousness with which the question of popular participation was addressed."[25] Martin adds, "The notion of the 'people' as the most important actor and primary beneficiary of the Revolution is at the heart of Sankara's political thought."[26]

The *Discours d'Orientation Politique* presents a comprehensive overview of the revolution, a restated rationale for taking power, and describes the nature of the regime. It is directed internally, to mobilize the masses for the work of revolutionary construction to be undertaken, and externally as a statement of the government's view of the world and the rights of its people among all humanity. The *Discours d'Orientation Politique* recalls the events of dual power that defined the struggle throughout 1983 in Upper Volta. The termination of dual power was brought about, according to the statement, through the triumph of the people on 4 August 1983 behind the CNR whose shared goal is to build "a new society freed from social injustice, freed from the domination and secular exploitation of international imperialism." The speech that was subsequently published as a declaration is structured by a Marxist and Third Worldist theoretical framework that draws a clear link between "international imperialism and its domestic allies" and revisits Sankara's denunciation of the enemies of the people from his speech on 26 March 1983. The *Discours d'Orientation Politique* restates the significance of the alliance between the progressive officers in the armed forces and the organized masses who brought about the revolution and traces a lineage of popular mobilization against oppression and neocolonialism that culminated on 4 August 1983. The critical moment, it asserts, was 17 May 1983 "which opened the eyes of the Voltaïc people" to the "brutal and cruel" nature of the imperialist system of oppression. It laid bare the class contradictions within society that could not be resolved by compromise solutions.[27]

The *Discours d'Orientation Politique* shifts to a longer-term analysis of neocolonialism that has "maintained our country in a situation of poverty and economic and cultural backwardness." The key to the success of France's strategy of neocolonial domination was its alliance with the reactionary forces in Upper Volta, including the political elite, traditional rulers, religious leaders, and comprador capitalists. The result was the economic, social, and environmental crisis in which Upper Volta found itself, where an honest salary could not sustain a person let alone a family. The solution to every economic slump, according to the *Discours d'Orientation Politique*, was to take more away from the poor and working people to enrich the elite and their foreign masters. The external debt, inflation, and lack of economic development were all intended results of the neocolonial imperialist system. For the people, this pushed them towards a catastrophe. The statement then warns the people that their triumph is not permanent. There are forces at work who want to reverse the revolution. Specifically, the "parasitical classes" want to turn back the clock "because they are attached by an umbilical cord to international imperialism." The *Discours d'Orientation Politique* then produces a catalogue of "enemies of the people" including the Voltaic bourgeoisie and the "retrograde forces" like traditional chieftaincies and religious leaders.[28]

Opposed to those forces were the revolutionary social elements, including the working class, the petit-bourgeoisie, the peasantry, and the lumpen-proletariat. Those forces united to provide the revolution of 4 August 1983 with its present historical character, defined as "a democratic and popular revolution." The immediate tasks in this stage of history were the "liquidation of imperialist domination and exploitation, [and] the purging of all obstacles from the countryside, economic and cultural, which maintain it in a backward state." To achieve those objectives, it was essential "to know how to link revolutionary theory and practice [since] that will be the decisive criteria that permits" the identification of true revolutionaries from those opportunists who hitch their wagons to the revolutionary train. That was why the CNR created the CDR. They would not only enable local interests to be advanced but also concentrate the people's energies toward the realization of collective goals. The CDR, using terminology that echoed Fanon, were conceived as a means for the creation of "new people," the condition sine qua non of true decolonization. The work of those in the CDR had to be done with the utmost integrity so that they became revolutionary examples to the broader population.[29]

The *Discours d'Orientation Politique* outlines three fundamental areas that required a radical restructuring to realize the aspirations of the people and the full development of the society. These are the military, the place of women, and economic growth. The military's role was redefined as not only the defender of the country from internal and external enemies but also a participant in national production by working with the people to achieve their needs, thereby changing each soldier into a militant revolutionary. Regarding women, the declaration called for breaking the domination of men over women, most blatantly sustained by traditional beliefs and forms of social organization. It states, "This is not an act of charity or a humanist gesture to speak of the emancipation of women. It is a fundamental necessity for the triumph of the Revolution." This entailed a radical change of mentalities among men and women. Structurally, it required the elevation of women to positions of responsibility throughout society and their integration into all aspects of the revolutionary struggle and development projects. "This should not be understood as a mechanical equality between men and women," according to the *Discours d'Orientation Politique*. It must be a true, visceral equality that was naturalized throughout society in all relations between men and women. In the realm of economic development, the statement called for an "independent, self-sufficient, and planned [economy] in the service of a democratic and popular society." Some of the programs outlined in the discourse, included agrarian reform, administrative changes, educational innovation, and cultural edification. The result would be the formation of a new culture. Writers, filmmakers, artists, and others were called upon to play their role in the regeneration of the country, a call familiar to those activists in the 1950s and 1960s, who advanced a cultural revolution as concomitant with political sovereignty.[30]

The *Discours d'Orientation Politique* outlines some immediate practical programs that can get the revolutionary transformations started, including the provision of maternal and natal care, immunization campaigns, hygienic education, termination of speculation in the rental market, affordable housing programs, breaking down ethnic and linguistic barriers in society, and balanced economic development across the entire country. The revolution was not an isolated event, according to the declaration, it was part of a process of world revolution. Upper Volta must insert itself into world affairs as an equal and sovereign country. To that end, the CNR through the *Discours d'Orientation Politique* declared its solidarity with those actively fighting for their independence including SWAPO in Namibia, the Sahrawi resisting Moroccan aggression, and the Palestinians in their struggle against Israel.[31]

Of note in the *Discours d'Orientation Politique* was the primacy of place given to cultural politics to implementing the revolution and realizing the overarching objectives expressed by the CNR. It described how the "colonial school was substituted by a neocolonial school that pursued the same goals of the alienation of children from their country and the reproduction of a society essentially at the service of the imperialists' interests." One of the CNR's main tasks was to "destroy the old order and put in its place a society of a new type." Echoing Fanon, the statement proclaims as a central objective "the creation of a new Voltaïc, with an exemplary morality and social comportment that inspires admiration and the confidence of the masses. Neocolonial domination has placed in our society a rotting such that we must use these next years to purify it." Repeatedly, the *Discours d'Orientation Politique* discusses the need for a comprehensive transformation of the person through a cultural revolution that forms new people. It reads, "The Democratic and Popular Revolution will create the propitious conditions for the hatching of a new culture." Sankara had already demonstrated his commitment to the cinema industrial complex as an important vehicle for achieving just those results.[32]

The language and theoretical framework of the *Discours d'Orientation Politique*, which became the central document that expressed the CNR's ideology and guided the formulation of its policies, confirms the benefit of reading the

Burkinabè Revolution through a Fanonian lens and reveals how deeply his theories had been absorbed by those who now directed the government. As Fanon explains, the experience of imperial domination produced an important change in the colonized subject that generated a class of intellectuals steeped in the colonial value system and its rendering of the African past. Since force alone could not sustain the foreign power, it waged war on the cultural front to empty "the native's brain of all form and content," substituting an ossified and alienated imaginary of the colonized subject's culture and past. Only through successive stages of struggle does consciousness emerge of the sources of oppression. Finally, a new class of intelligentsia forms that breaks with the colonial mentality and becomes "the mouthpiece of a new reality in action." That element cultivates a national culture that "is the whole body of efforts made by a people in the sphere of thought to describe, justify, and praise the action through which that people has created itself and keeps itself in existence." The culmination of this process is "not only the disappearance of colonialism but also the disappearance of the colonized [subject]. This new humanity cannot do otherwise than define a new humanism."[33] Through the *Discours d'Orientation Politique* the CNR declared its intention to fulfill that objective and place Upper Volta at the service of a global transformation of values and social relations.

The *Discours d'Orientation Politique* set Upper Volta explicitly on the path of socialist development albeit at a pace and in a manner that the people would decide based on the real conditions in the country and its traditions. The declaration described the country as a people's democracy that was an intermediate form of governance based on the alliance of workers, peasants, the indigent poor, and petit-bourgeoisie as they eliminated capitalist forms of production and social relations. Only later could the state advance to socialist construction. The statement's authors were inspired by the experience of revolutions around the world, including the Soviet Union, China, Cuba, Angola, Algeria, Libya, and Vietnam, but did not commit to explicitly emulate any of them.[34] On 3 October 1983, hundreds of thousands of people, organized by local CDR, descended into the streets of Ouagadougou to express their support for the *Discours d'Orientation Politique*. Since Sankara was out of the country, Compaoré greeted the masses as they reached the presidential palace.[35]

Threats to the Revolution and the Role of the Tribunaux Populaires de la Révolution

However, as the *Discours d'Orientation Politique* warned, not everyone was on board with transforming Upper Volta into a revolutionary socialist society. For instance, on 5 August 1983, the SNEAHV teachers' union at the direction of Joseph Ki-Zerbo's FPV denounced the new government and called for organized resistance. However, when no popular support for his pronouncement took shape, Joseph Ki-Zerbo went into exile.[36] More seriously, on 11 October 1983, the government uncovered a plot by a coalition of conservative parties associated with previous administrations to overthrow the revolutionary government. The CNR imprisoned thirteen former political leaders and charged them with treason and counterrevolution. They had been accumulating weapons and contracted with foreign mercenaries to launch an armed uprising against Sankara's government. On 28 October 1983, President Sankara held an urgent press conference at which he claimed that there was "an imminent [act of] aggression" planned against the revolution. Sankara explained that his security forces had uncovered a new plot involving Joseph Ki-Zerbo and the FPV, who had been smuggling weapons into Upper Volta since at least 20 October 1983 and had formed a command structure led by the renegade Jean-Claude Kamboulé. He and a group of mercenaries were to be parachuted into Upper Volta with the assistance of a Cuban exile funded by the CIA. The operation was being financed, Sankara claimed, by the bank account of an unnamed "leader of a neighboring state."[37] Sankara appealed to the CDR and people of the country to mobilize for the defense of the revolution. On 29 October 1983, a hint was dropped as to who might have been the mysterious foreign leader of whom the CNR leader referred. Sankara traveled to Niamey, Niger, to attend the Summit of West African States. Prior to that meeting he had made a gesture of friendship to Mali by lifting Upper Volta's veto of that country's membership in the group.[38] According to the rules of the regional association, Upper Volta was to have assumed the largely symbolic presidency giving it the right to host the next summit and control its agenda. However, Houphouët-Boigny moved to suspend the rules and nominated the just-admitted Mali to leadership of the group. This public snub signaled Côte d'Ivoire's opposition to the new regime. Ironically, as that rebuff took place on 1 November 1983, Upper Volta was elected as one of the rotating member states of the United Nations' Security Council.[39]

To counterbalance the external threat, the CNR cultivated its friendship with Ghana and its president, Jerry Rawlings. Upper Volta and Ghana conducted joint military exercises along the border of the two countries 4–8 November 1983. At the conclusion of the demonstration, Rawlings joined the four historic leaders of the Burkinabè Revolution at Pô for a celebration and declarations of friendship.[40]

Concerned that the forces of reaction were getting better organized within the country as well, the revolutionaries issued an ordinance on 19 October 1983 creating Tribunaux Populaires de la Révolution (TPR). Their intention was to create an expedited framework outside the traditional judicial system for dealing with imminent threats to the revolution. Many in the CNR believed that the courts were still filled with adherents to former regimes who would use their position to thwart the revolutionary government's objectives and protect the regime's enemies.[41] The TPR were formed to deal with crimes "against the internal and external security of the state." The definition of criminal acts was expanded in this new institution to include corruption, which undermined the general welfare of the people.[42]

The date of the first TPR on 3 January 1984 coincided with the anniversary of the popular uprising in 1966 that led to the overthrow of the country's first president, Maurice Yaméogo. Sankara gave the opening address to the TPR and used the opportunity to further elaborate its mission. According to his speech, he envisioned the TPR to empower the people that was not possible within the traditional courts. Sankara said the TPR was founded on "the principles of the effective participation of the working and exploited classes in the administration and direction of the affairs of the state." The president explained that the judges would be "chosen from within the working classes and the sole mission of those workers is to carry out the will of the people." The judges were to be guided "in the absence of codified texts" by the principle of "rejecting the laws of neocolonial society." The TPR justices were to function as hammers smashing the bureaucratic aspects of the state inherited from the past. Their purpose was to deal specifically with "political and social crimes against the people." Finally, they were also part of the process of educating the population as to its power and role in building the new revolutionary society.[43]

The precise nature of the TPR was malleable since the CDR had the authority to initiate charges, and public participation in the process meant that the precise order of business was never consistent from one instance to another. Moreover, the TPR were not permanent courts. They were formed at specific times to try individual cases and then dissolved when their work was done. The proceedings of the TPR were always public, filmed, broadcast over the radio, and accessible to anyone who wanted to attend. As a rule, no lawyers were permitted. Instead, the accused were arrayed across from the tribunal usually composed of a soldier, a judge "who is always the one to ask the questions," and five members of the CDR with jurisdiction over the affair. The entire process was supposed to be completed expeditiously, usually within an hour or so, although sometimes a case could take several days to complete. All documents and evidence gathered by the CDR or made available by the defendants was to be assembled and presented to the judges beforehand.[44] According to Compaoré, the TPR were designed to permit the state "in a short amount of time, to educate, politicize, [and] raise the consciousness of all the people."[45] These were not show trials or extrajudicial means to eliminate political opponents: in the first case, Lamizana was acquitted of charges of corruption and embezzlement. Most of those found guilty were levied fines, forced to make restitution, or served brief prison terms. In August 1985, the TPR were expanded to completely replace customary courts controlled by the chieftaincies and the regular courts, which were suppressed by decree that month.[46]

Fissures in the Ruling Coalition and the Shift to Revolutionize the Countryside

Even as the CNR contended with potential foreign adversaries and opposition from those it had displaced from power, disagreements within the coalition that made up the revolutionary government continued to plague the implementation of its policies. On 18 November 1983, a group of armed workers directed by LIPAD invaded the headquarters of the Office of Posts and Telecommunications (OPT) and took its director hostage. The workers declared themselves a TPR as per the decree of the previous month and began impromptu proceedings against the OPT management. Sankara denounced the actions as anarchistic and without foundation in justice. Other leading members of the CNR also expressed their disapproval, specifically the military officers and the former members of the ULC. Eventually the PAI distanced itself from the action, causing it to fall apart. Some among the PAI even suggested that Soumane Touré was preparing a coup, and this represented an intolerable adventurism as it broke the discipline of the pro-Soviet party.⁴⁷

Valère Somé appears to have been the most agitated over the incident. In a letter to Sankara, dated the same day of the LIPAD action at the OPT, Valère Somé explained that he was "reviving his organization" so as "to serve our goals (in the sense of our common ideal)." He then launched into an unprecedented attack on the PAI/LIPAD. First, he suggested that the revolution could not succeed without a unified single party to guide it, and said he was open to PAI and the former members of the ULC merging into one guiding force that would include the former OMR. However, absent the willingness of the PAI to dissolve, it would be necessary to cut all ties with the party. Valère Somé explained to the president, "You have to persuade yourself that the sooner we are done with this organization (PAI) and its annex (LIPAD), the better it will be for the revolution."⁴⁸

The internal crisis continued to boil into December 1983 when Valère Somé revived his idea to create a Democratic and Popular Union (UDR) as a mass organization like the PAI's LIPAD. Adama Touré (PAI), as minister of information, refused to issue a press release announcing the new front organization, which precipitated a major crisis within the government. Sankara convened a meeting of the CNR to bring the three groups to the table to hash out their differences and reestablish a consensus on how to move forward. The PAI members of the CNR denounced Valère Somé's project for creating the UDR since it was aimed explicitly at LIPAD, one of the main forces that brought about the revolution. Sankara pushed back stating that it would be unjust to deny Valère Somé's emerging ULCR their own mass organization so long as the PAI maintained LIPAD. As the political theorist Martens relates, Sankara said that "the best solution would be to dissolve all the organizations and unite them."⁴⁹ Outside the CNR, Soumane Touré continued his public campaign to position himself at the head of the CSV/LIPAD as the main revolutionary force in Upper Volta. He claimed that he was following the will of the workers in their imperative to sustain the present revolution.⁵⁰

One thing the various organizations still agreed on was the need to begin implementing social reforms to rescue the country from its economic crisis. On 9 November 1983, the CNR decreed the establishment of the Caisse de Solidarité Revolutonnaire (CSR) to receive voluntary donations from the population to aid the people in the north of Upper Volta suffering from drought and desertification. While not compulsory, the CSR did establish a sliding scale of donations among the salaried workers that would go directly into the fund. The CSV expressed its enthusiasm for the program and framed the contributions in terms of building support for the revolution. Soumane Touré's labor federation also supported the decree in January 1984 that lowered public employees' salaries to address the mounting debt. For the CNR, the new fund and the reduction in public sector salaries were part of building a foundation for economic development that would be directed from within the country and sustained by what was available in Upper Volta in terms of its human, material, and fiscal capacity. This was consistent with the policies outlined in the *Discours d'Orientation Politique*. As an additional benefit, the work of social assistance and revolutionary solidarity would heal the divisions among the political parties within the CNR.[51]

The prospective beneficiaries of the revolution's first social reforms were the peasants. Money would be extracted from urban areas through the CSR and transferred to rural communities where over 90 percent of the country's population lived. This reversed the traditional practice of socialist construction wherein wealth was squeezed from the countryside to fuel the industrialization of the cities. To guarantee those funds improved the lives of those who most urgently needed assistance, it was necessary to bring about a social revolution in the countryside. The target of that transformation was the traditional chieftaincies, which had been identified in the *Discours d'Orientation Politique* as one of the major obstacles to the realization of the revolution's goals. In that statement, the CNR proclaimed that one of the most critical aspects to the improvement of the agricultural sector was "the abolition of all the obstacles inherent in the traditional socioeconomic structures which oppress the peasants." The CNR pledged that "there would be a struggle against all the starvers of the people, speculators and agricultural capitalists of all types." Moreover, the *Discours d'Orientation Politique*'s analysis argued that capitalist modes of production had "penetrated" the countryside, introducing its attendant social forms. The traditional chieftaincy was regarded as a rural capitalist class that retained many of the privileges of an aristocracy. Until the CNR took power, the peasants still owed forms of labor and other services to rural chiefs. They also were subject to traditional courts presided over by chiefs and other tribal elders until their replacement by the TPR. The revolution must, the CNR argued, be extended to the countryside, and would succeed or fail in the degree to which the peasants could be mobilized to carry out their own liberation.⁵² By the time the CNR took power, the chiefs were also deeply unpopular.

The first step in the war on chieftaincy was to abolish their legal status as a class. On 30 December 1983, the CNR issued an ordinance that "abrogated all texts that codified the political and administrative attributions, the remunerations, and the advantages of the tribal leaders."⁵³ One of the most despised legacies of the colonial period was the extension of the power of the chieftaincy to urban centers. This was the product of a rethinking of imperial practice after the First World War, the aim of which was to defang the emerging power of Western-educated urban elites and empower a more pliable social class with roots in the precolonial period.⁵⁴ To break that power on 7 January 1984, the CNR decreed a reorganization of the physical administrative space of the cities in Upper Volta. Instead of the old quarters governed by customary rulers, Ouagadougou, Bobo-Dioulasso, and the other major urban centers of the country were divided into sectors that intentionally had no relation to the previously extant zones. The CNR delegated the local CDR as the authorities in the newly created administrative districts.⁵⁵

Then in February 1984, the CNR abolished all mandatory labor and other services provided to chiefs. This destroyed their economic power. One of the core objectives of the CNR as presented in the *Discours d'Orientation Politique* was to "increase labor productivity by a better organization of the peasants and the introduction to the rural world the techniques of modern agriculture." That would "make agriculture the fulcrum for the development of industry."⁵⁶ Cued and empowered by the CNR, the CDR began to implement this vision. On 9 April 1984, some of the committees began to distribute land to the peasants in the recently formed sectors of cities and large villages.⁵⁷ On 8 August 1984, the CNR issued an ordinance that "nationalized all customary land and transferred control to all those who had a real social need [for it], without distinction of sex or status."⁵⁸ The ordinance asserted, from that date all the "soil and sub-soil [of the country was the] exclusive Burkinabè property of the Revolutionary State the exploitation of which [must] conform to the interests of the Burkinabè people."⁵⁹ The management of that land passed into the hands of government ministries (such as environment, economics, and peasantry) as well as the CDR, who were the boots on the ground that organized the peasants to take full advantage of their changed socioeconomic and juridical status. The same agrarian reform also stripped the customary rulers of any judicial authority. The CDR subsequently founded their own tribunals to handle matters of justice in rural areas. According to the political economist Kyélem de Tambèla, "Deprived of their ability to collect the head tax, of its authority over the land, of the power to legislate in the area of their traditional domains of competence, and to render justice, the customary chieftaincy effectively did not hold any further influence among themselves."[60]

Revolutionary Diplomacy and Global Solidarity

One of the rationales behind mobilizing the peasantry was that it reduced the revolution's vulnerability to external pressures. The *Discours d'Orientation Politique* identified the peasantry as a force that had to be liberated from the imperialist constraints imposed on them so as to transform them into a reservoir of support for reactionary forces inside and outside the country. In more basic terms, self-sufficiency in food production would eliminate it as a weapon in the hands of the imperialists, who had used it to hold the country hostage and subvert its revolutionary aspirations.[61]

One of the most entrenched and debilitating foreign relationships the Upper Volta had was with its former colonizer, France. In September 1983, Christian Nucci, France's minister of cooperation, visited for three days to reassure the revolutionary government that France would not interfere in Upper Volta's internal affairs. However, the Ministry of Cooperation was France's primary vector for projecting its cultural influence throughout the world and maintaining its dominant position in the cinematic field in the former colonies. It was through that agency that France funded African filmmakers, controlled post-production processes and facilities, and promoted French-made films across its former empire. Sembène, Hondo, and other African filmmakers had a long and bitter history with the Cooperation that fueled their passion to create a truly independent African cinema that reflected its peoples' needs while also stimulating them to take power in their own societies.[62]

The CNR made the renegotiation of Upper Volta's relationship with France a top priority and upon Nucci's arrival informed him that the existing treaties had to be completely redone based on real equality between the two countries. That set off a protracted period of negotiations that would not conclude with a new treaty until 4 February 1986. In the meantime, on 2 October 1983, Sankara travelled to France for the Tenth Franco-African Summit of Heads of State. Upon his arrival, Guy Penne, Mitterrand's director of African affairs and the architect of Sankara's overthrow in May 1983, greeted the CNR president at the airport. Sankara was furious and regarded it as a deliberate insult. Consequently, on 3 October 1983, Sankara refused to attend the official dinner sponsored by President Mitterrand. Instead, he convened an alternative dinner of activists from Africa, who supported the Democratic and Popular Revolution unfolding in Upper Volta.[63] The following day, 4 October 1983, President Sankara faced the international press who had gathered to cover the summit. He reiterated themes by then familiar to audiences in Upper Volta, such as the need to struggle against the enemies of the people inside and outside the country. Sankara described those broadly as international capitalism that exploits the human and material resources of the nation. In that context, he argued it was necessary to renegotiate the cooperation agreements with France since they derived from neocolonial origins and perpetuated the inequality of peoples. Sankara also signaled the orientation of the CNR's development strategy when he insisted that Upper Volta specifically and Africa generally had sufficient resources and markets for its own economic and social growth. Consequently, the revolutionary government would not rely on external support for its existence. The CNR leader explained that his country would henceforward defend its sovereignty on the world stage and actively engage in the struggles of those still fighting for liberation. He highlighted the heroic fight against apartheid on all fronts as an example of one area the revolutionary government would be on the frontlines rendering any support in its capacity.[64]

Confronting France was a bold move for the newly installed government and posed a serious political and economic risk. France had a military presence in neighboring Côte d'Ivoire as well as in Chad, the conflict that had been the center of discussion at the Franco-African Summit. Consequently, the CNR moved quickly to resolve some regional disputes that had festered for years. It also built alliances with progressive and socialist forces around the world as a matter of self-preservation as well as part of the revolutionary government's objective to reorient the country's foreign policy. One source of tension that threatened Upper Volta's security was the ongoing dispute with Mali over the Agacher Strip. To resolve that problem, Sankara traveled to Mali on 16 September 1983 where he reached an agreement with Moussa Traoré to submit the territorial dispute to international mediation and form a mixed commission to explore further lines of cooperation. Part of that deal included Sankara's commitment to lift Upper Volta's veto on Mali's application for membership in the West African Monetary Union (Union Monétaire Ouest Africaine, UMOA) and allow it to join the Community of West African States (Comunauté des États d'Afrique de l'Ouest, CEAO).[65] Sankara then went to Niger. While the two countries did not announce any major new agreements, the visit helped to solidify the relationship between Niger and Upper Volta. The CNR had alarmed some leaders in the region who feared the new government sought to export its revolution. Therefore, Sankara's visit to Niger in September 1983 was meant to reassure its neighbor that "Upper Volta does not want to be a springboard for destabilization, there is no reason to fear."[66]

In addition to Niger, the CNR sought to smooth relations with Houphouët-Boigny. However, it was not until 28 May 1984 that President Sankara made his first official state visit to Côte d'Ivoire. After lengthy negotiations on the agenda for the summit, the two sides had a falling out just as Sankara was prepared to begin his journey. On arrival, the CNR leader was confined to the capital city Yamoussoukro and restricted in his activities. Originally, Sankara wanted to travel to Abidjan and hold a meeting with the large Voltaic population living there. Houphouët-Boigny feared that such a meeting would radicalize them and create a potential base of opposition to the Ivoirian president. The Ivoirian leader prohibited the meeting thereby thwarting Sankara's efforts to connect with expatriates from his country. The trip did not yield any notable results and underscored the tension between the two states.[67]

If Côte d'Ivoire represented a state potentially hostile to the CNR government, Rawlings's regime in Ghana was one of its closest allies. During an official visit to Ghana on 14 November 1983, Defense Minister Boukary Lingani announced that the Voltaic "armed forces will assure the defense of Ghana in the event of any aggression."[68] After those early encounters, the two countries moved toward closer cooperation on all fronts including the establishment of connections between the CDR of each country and a gesture toward eventual political union.[69] In addition to Ghana, the CNR found a friend in Benin's Mathieu Kérékou. Sankara paid his first state visit to that country on 21 January 1984 where the two governments signed cooperation agreements including one that permitted Upper Volta to use the port of Cotonou for trade. However, the two never became as close as it appeared likely, given their shared commitment to socialism. Sankara viewed Kérékou as not sincere in following through on his revolutionary rhetoric and therefore never pursued as tight a relationship with that country as he and the CNR leadership did with others.[70] Outside Africa, Cuba was one of the first countries to bond with the CNR government in Upper Volta. On 21 December 1983, the two countries signed a scientific, economic, and technical cooperation agreement, the first major treaty of the sort agreed to by the CNR. The most significant part of that deal was a cultural exchange that prepared the foundation for ongoing projects in the fields of cinema, the plastic arts, literature, and music.[71]

The agreement with Cuba was struck as the CNR conducted the first "National Week of Culture," which symbolically tied the regime's foreign policy to its aspirations to transform the mentality of its people. The festivities opened on 20 December 1983 and were organized to democratize culture by providing direct access to the people of the creative works of musicians, artists, writers, filmmakers, and artisans, and to facilitate the participants' ability to create their own culture. This was integral to the Democratic and Popular Revolution's objective of "transforming the manner of being and thinking of the Burkinabè ... [that would] contribute to the decolonization and liberation of mentalities." To finance those activities as well as ongoing creativity in subsequent years, the revolutionary government systematized the procurement and dispensation of capital when it instituted the BBDA (Bureau burkinabè du droit d'auteur) "to raise taxes on the sale of literary and artistic works to provide financial assistance to writers and artists." In the cinematic field, the CNR also founded the SOCI-B (Société du cinéma du Burkina) that funneled financial and material aid to filmmakers while also organizing mobile film units to disperse throughout the country bringing movie culture to the masses. Already in the early months of the revolution, the new government allocated funds for building more film theaters, acquisition of film stock, and offered increased scholarships to attend INAFEC, the film training institute established in 1976. The CNR aimed to forge a culture that enriched and further developed humanity rather than a nationalist culture. Consequently, the CNR invited cultural workers from throughout the world to participate in the first National Week of Culture as well as all subsequent events so that the creative energies of the global community could stimulate one another. Representatives from Cuba, the USSR, North Korea, China, and elsewhere were prominent visitors at the first National Week of Culture. In fact, one aspect of the agreement struck between Upper Volta and Cuba during that event was the formation of grants for Burkinabè students to study in Cuba and the provision of Cuban volunteers to assist in building Upper Volta's motion picture theaters, stages, and other cultural infrastructure.[72]

One of the most important dignitaries to attend the first National Week of Culture was President Eduardo dos Santos of Angola. Dos Santos's country was at that time embroiled in a bitter Cold War proxy fight with rebels backed by apartheid South Africa and the United States. The CNR's invitation to Angola's president reflected the revolutionary government's declared opposition to apartheid and support for all those fighting to eliminate it. It was also part of the strategy to align Upper Volta's foreign policy with those states and movements identified as anti-imperialist. That included directly challenging the United States and its allies when they engaged in imperialistic actions or oppressed people as they were in southern Africa. As a further example, two months earlier, in October 1983, the United States invaded Grenada and overthrew its Marxist government. Upper Volta immediately withdrew its ambassador to Washington in protest. In a speech on 11 February 1984, Sankara explained the CNR's decision and the basis for its approach to international relations. He said, "We recalled our ambassador to the U.S. to transmit a message to President Reagan: it is necessary for the U.S. to withdraw all its troops from Grenada, in fulfillment of Upper Volta's responsibilities, we condemn [the invasion].... The Americans wanted to dictate to Upper Volta its position at the Security Council of the United Nations. We will not accept this blackmail." Sankara added that if the United States wanted to cancel aid to Upper Volta "so be it." Upper Volta would not be "servile." This did not, however, constitute an uncritical alignment with the Soviet Union as the other pole in the Cold War global arena. Sankara said his government "will continue to agree with Moscow (the Soviet Union) in its positions" with regard to the world situation as long as they are just, "but the day when Moscow's positions are no longer just, we will separate ourselves from them and condemn them."[73]

The CNR also waded into other global conflicts and struck a stridently independent position regardless of whether the participants were allies or foes of the revolutionary government. This was evident in its relations with Qaddafi's Libya. Qaddafi posed as a supporter of anti-colonial liberation movements and a promoter of pan-Africanism as well as pan-Arabism and pan-Islamism. The Libyan leader also prominently supported the Palestine Liberation Organization (PLO) in its struggle against Israel and aided in the revolutionaries' effort to take power in Upper Volta. Consequently, many Western leaders assumed that the CNR was a creation of the eccentric and ambitious Libyan leader.[74] However, Sankara and the CNR did not fit a priori Cold War categories or the Manichaean worldview it generated. There was, therefore, some confusion in Western foreign ministries when Sankara denounced Libya's new offensive in northern Chad that began on 24 January 1984. In the summer of 1983, Libyan-backed forces as well as regulars made significant gains in their effort to overthrow the French-backed Chadian government. Afterward, an informal truce effectively divided the country with each side pledging not to cross their lines of control. Libya violated that deal, which led to escalating French involvement in Chad. Libya's allies were mauled in French air attacks, and by spring 1984, Qaddafi proposed a mutual withdrawal of forces that was agreed to that fall. The CNR's official position was that the conflict was an internal matter for Chad, and it opposed any internationalization of the conflict. Throughout the hostilities in early 1984, the revolutionary government called for a ceasefire and withdrawal of all forces from the conflict. Qaddafi may have assumed that Sankara would unconditionally support Libya's actions, but the CNR leader made it clear that Upper Volta's foreign policy was guided by unshakeable principles, not traditional patron–client diplomacy.[75]

Relations with Libya took another hit over the conflict in the former colony of Spanish Sahara. Following Spain's withdrawal in early 1976, both Morocco and Mauritania attempted to annex the territory, with Morocco eventually gaining control over most of it. However, the rebel Polisario Front declared the independence of the Sahrawi Arab Democratic Republic and began a guerrilla war against Morocco. The Polisario Front was pro-Soviet and received support from the socialist world, Libya, and Algeria. The rebels used bases in Algeria from which to launch attacks against Moroccan forces. On 4 March 1984, the CNR officially recognized the Sahrawi Republic and established bilateral relations with the Polisario Front. Then on 31 March 1984, Sankara became the first head of state to visit the Sahrawi Republic.[76] Months later, though, Libya signed the Oujda Treaty with Morocco on 13 August 1984 that called for the union of the two countries. That agreement terminated Libya's support for the Polisario Front, forcing it to rely even more significantly on Algeria for survival. Sankara denounced the accord as a betrayal of solidarity with the forces of national liberation.[77] As a consequence, the CNR drew closer to Algeria and signed a series of treaties for economic aid to Upper Volta, established cultural exchange programs, and committed the two countries to mutual defense. By the summer of 1984, Algeria was providing significant economic assistance to Upper Volta, and the two countries were building ties in their banking sectors to facilitate future development projects.[78]

During those shifting alignments, Sankara made his first major tour of African states (23 June 1984–2 July 1984) to shore up alliances with other socialist governments in Africa. He journeyed to Ethiopia (Mengistu Haile Miriam), Angola (Dos Santos), the People's Republic of Congo (Denis Sassou-Nguesso), Mozambique (Samora Michel), and Madagascar (Ratsiraka). With each country, Upper Volta signed cooperation agreements and mutual accords of solidarity. In southern Africa, Sankara emphasized the struggle against apartheid, emerging as one of the main aspects of the CNR's foreign policy. The revolutionary government declared its solidarity and alignment with the African National Congress (ANC) and South African Communist Party (SACP), leading the fight against apartheid inside South Africa.[79] When South Africa's prime minister visited France in June 1984, Sankara denounced the trip and terminated the talks underway to reconfigure Upper Volta's cooperation agreement with the former colonizer. He also called out other African states for their relationships with the apartheid government, including Morocco and Zaire. Sankara even criticized the Nkomati Accord signed between South Africa and Mozambique on 16 March 1984 at "the risk of displeasing the Mozambican authorities." Sankara then declared that Upper Volta was boycotting the Olympic Games scheduled to be held in Los Angeles in August 1984 because of U.S. support for South Africa and that country's participation in the event. Finally, the CNR created the Mouvement Burkinabè contre le Racisme et l'Apartheid (Burkinabè movement against racism and apartheid, MOBRAP) to mobilize the population in support of the anti-apartheid cause.[80] At a press conference on 10 August 1984, Sankara explained, "Although our revolution is not made for export, we don't intend to go out of our way to shut the Burkinabè Revolution up inside an impenetrable fortress. Our revolution is an ideology that blows freely and is at the disposal of all those who feel the need to take advantage of it."[81]

By the time of that press conference, the revolution initiated on 4 August 1983 had reconfigured the nature of the state and the process of governance. The CNR brought together the revolutionary groups (PAI, former OMR, former ULC, and independent Marxists) and was the institution that formulated policy and clarified the new regime's ideology. The CDR arose among the people around the country and served as the enforcers of the CNR's programs as well as a security force for the revolution, defending it against internal and external enemies. The TPR provided the revolutionary government with a new judicial structure that bypassed the existing courts, many of which were still in the hands of those loyal to former governments and protective of the privileges of the elite. The consolidation of the revolutionary government enabled it to begin implementing policies that would bring about the transformation of society and the person, a cultural revolution needed to sustain and carry forward the Democratic and Popular Revolution as outlined in the *Discours d'Orientation Politique*. In the countryside, the effects of those actions were being felt in the liberation of the peasantry and redistribution of the land under the aegis of the CDR. The government's emphasis on the importance of culture to facilitating the country's revolutionary transformation was embodied in the first National Week of Culture and other early moves to devote financial, material, and human resources to the development of creative activity in all areas. It enhanced the availability for training in cinema and other creative activities and enabled greater access to those works. Finally, the CNR reoriented Upper Volta's foreign policy to protect it against external interference in the country's internal affairs and to create lines of cooperation that assisted economic and cultural development while preserving its sovereignty. The stage was set to embark on the campaigns to revolutionize Upper Volta and forge a new person during that struggle.

4

Cultural Revolution, Economic Reform, and Global Engagement

(1984–1985)

In its *Discours d'Orientation Politique*, the CNR warned, "The Revolution is distinguished from destructive anarchy. It demands exemplary discipline and conduct. The acts of vandalism and adventurist actions of all kinds, instead of strengthening the revolution by the adhesion of the masses, weaken and repel it far from the innumerable masses."¹ As the revolutionary government consolidated, it confronted serious internal and global challenges even as it implemented the first major programs designed to transform Burkinabè society. In the spring of 1984, the government faced two serious challenges, both from elements led by Joseph Ki-Zerbo's FPV that had already been implicated in a plot to overthrow the government as early as October 1983. On 9 March 1984, the CNR arrested three leading members of the FPV and accused them of conspiring to lead an insurrection against the revolution. In response, the FPV-directed SNEAHV declared a general strike on 20 March 1984. At first the authorities permitted the strike to occur. However, its scope expanded over the following days until the CNR received a report from minister of the interior and security, Nongoma Ernest Ouédraogo, claiming that the strike was in truth part of a "counterrevolutionary plot." This posed an existential threat to the revolution. At a meeting of the CNR on 22 March 1984, the government voted to terminate the strike by immediately firing all the teachers involved. This amounted to nearly 1,400 instructors.[2]

While Sankara expressed support for the initial decision, he was troubled by the severity of the sanctions meted out to the SNEAHV. The president reconvened the CNR on 23 March 1984 and asked it to reconsider the sanctions. The CNR nonetheless voted overwhelmingly to maintain the order. In addition, it issued a statement that declared the strike was instigated at the request of "their imperialist allies" to create "conditions favorable for the destabilization [of the country] and [to prepare] an aggression [from the outside]." Specifically, the CNR accused France, Belgium, and Israel of being behind the strike.[3] While there was some evidence to link the strike to a broader conspiracy, the strongest advocates for the most severe penalties against the teachers was the PAI/LIPAD. Its affiliated labor federation, the CSV, suffered severe repression during Saye Zerbo's regime, which was backed by Ki-Zerbo's FPV. The CSV and its affiliated teachers' union, the SUVESS, was forced underground, while the rival SNEAHV thrived. Some elements within the revolutionary government, like Valère Somé, intimated in subsequent meetings that the liquidation of the SNEAHV on 22 March 1984 constituted a measure of revenge and removed another obstacle to the growing power of the pro-Soviet PAI/LIPAD in its drive to become the vanguard party of the revolution.[4]

The repression of forces connected with Saye Zerbo's CMRPN continued the following month. On 21 April 1984, Saye Zerbo and other leading members of his regime were hauled before a TPR and charged with embezzlement of public funds, crimes of repression against the people, and acting against the interests of the country. The CMRPN leaders were found guilty with Saye Zerbo sentenced to fifteen years imprisonment and ordered to make full compensation for the money stolen by the regime.[5] Then on 28 May 1984, President Sankara announced that the CNR had uncovered a plot hatched by Colonel Didier Tiendrébéogo and other senior military officers, many of them also affiliated with the CMRPN and the FPV. However, this time the PAI pulled back from an immediate and uncritical denunciation. Instead, the pro-Soviet communist party demanded that Sankara present solid evidence to back the charges. Unlike his earlier stance regarding the punishment of the teachers, the president this time took a hard line and refused. Sankara argued that the matter required urgent action to defend the revolution. He called for a snap vote on the execution of those accused, but "the PAI refused to take part" in the deliberations. Meanwhile, the pro-Chinese ULCR headed by Valère Somé backed Sankara's position and called for carrying out "capital punishment" for the potential coup plotters. This, too, was a reversal of positions from two months earlier when the ULCR took a more moderate position although in both instances it consistently aligned with Sankara against the PAI. The TPR condemned the leader of the plot and six others to death, four were given sentences of twenty years in prison, and fifteen others were acquitted of all charges. The executions were carried out on 11 June 1984.[6]

This chapter charts how the CNR navigated myriad and escalating domestic and international challenges to the revolution even as it more aggressively implemented the reforms aimed at the transformation of Burkinabè society and the person. The subtle conflicts between the Maoist ULCR directed by Valère Somé and the Soviet-oriented PAI erupted into the open and forced Sankara to routinely serve as a mediator to keep the revolutionary coalition together. In the meantime, the officers of the former OMR maneuvered to constrain the power of the civilian parties through its hold on the CDR and other formal institutions of the revolutionary state. Regardless of those internal divisions, the Burkinabè Revolution took root in the country and made a mark on the global stage. The results of the first major social programs implemented by the CNR indicated that people's lives were improving, and the country forcefully asserted its sovereignty in the international arena. That earned it the attention of the major powers expressed in a mix of admiration, respect, and suspicion. The key to maintaining the momentum in transforming Burkinabè society was the preservation of unity among the revolutionary forces as well as broadening the revolution's base of support throughout the country.

Conflict between the PAI and ULCR

The PAI's abstention from discussions about the fate of those accused of plotting to overthrow the revolution indicated a shift in political alignments within the CNR. From the revolution's earliest months, the PAI had attempted to implement the most radical aspects of the CNR's agenda and accelerate its pace. This was reflected in Soumane Touré's aggressive actions toward the mayor of Ouagadougou, the attack on the headquarters of the post office, and the LIPAD's decision to implement its own TPR shortly after the CNR decreed their existence. Moreover, the PAI had secured control of the most powerful CDR in the capital and other major cities throughout the country. The PAI/LIPAD used its strength among the urban working masses to begin transforming the relations of power on the ground before the CNR even formulated specific policies or provided guidance for the functioning of institutions like the CDR. The teachers' strike in March 1984 provided another opportunity for the PAI and its affiliates to expand their influence in the country by crushing one of the remaining labor unions that had some power and was independent of the PAI's CSV. The motion to fire the teachers derived from a commission headed by the minister of education, Emmanuel Dadjoari, who was a leading figure within the PAI.[7]

However, Valère Somé felt threatened by those developments and countered by building the ULCR as a counterweight. At every turn, PAI members within the government blocked Valère Somé from forming mass organizations that could rival LIPAD or the CSV. Valère Somé, in turn, used his personal friendship with Sankara to ingratiate himself at the highest levels of power and sent the president messages warning of the dangers posed by the PAI's continued participation in the revolutionary government. Until the dispute over the accused plotters in May 1984, the rival groups had not disagreed on any substantive matters. The accusations against Colonel Didier Tiendrébéogo and his associates enabled the ULCR to pose as the more radical party in lockstep with the CNR leadership and isolated the PAI as having potentially questionable loyalties. Slanders against the PAI even accused it of being "an accomplice of the counterrevolution."[8]

The dispute over dismissal of the teachers in March 1984 was the first indication of Sankara's divergence from the PAI that had widened into a nearly irreconcilable breach by the time of the dispute over the move to execute Saye Zerbo's supporters in May 1984. The initial disagreement over the teachers was compounded on 5 April 1984 when the CNR announced the establishment its own official journal, *Sidwaya*, and that its director was Babou Paulin Bamouni. While not affiliated with any organization, Bamouni had become the unofficial ideologue of the revolution and was a friend and confidante to Sankara. Bamouni writes, "To encourage the people in the gigantic effort it provides, it was necessary to support it morally, ideologically, by mobilizing it, by raising awareness, day and night. Therefore, the Revolution of August inaugurated on 5 April 1984 a great daily *Sidwaya* (the truth has arrived), charged with the ideological and political formation of all the people."[9] Bamouni's appointment as director of the newspaper undercut the role of the PAI's Adama Touré who was the minister of information as well as that of Philippe Ouédraogo (PAI), the minister of equipment and communication, a point not lost on the party.[10]

Following *Sidwaya*'s founding the PAI's Ibrahima Koné in his role as minister of youth and sports announced that his agency would organize mass demonstrations of students on 20 May 1984 to commemorate the 1983 popular mobilization that had occurred after Sankara was imprisoned by the CSP. On the surface, this event would be a routine commemoration of a critical moment that brought together the forces of the revolutionary communist left in a powerful coalition that in subsequent months propelled the CNR to power. However, it also signaled the PAI's centrality to that process and staked a claim to its leadership of the revolution. It was obvious that the PAI's front organization LIPAD would dominate the event since it was the only group capable of turning out masses in the streets, and it controlled the major CDR in Ouagadougou. Pierre Ouédraogo, secretary general of the CDR and part of the former OMR, along with ULCR members within the government, objected to Ibrahima Koné overseeing the event. They argued that any commemoration of the events leading to the revolution be directed by the CNR as a whole and not fall under the purview of a single government ministry. Consequently, its organization should result from internal deliberations and reflect the diverse coalition that comprised the CNR. Sankara once more was thrust into the role of mediator to avoid a blowup over a celebration that ostensibly marked the moment when revolutionary unity was achieved. He wrote a letter to the leaders of the PAI and the ULCR to ask for their ideas about how to unite the revolutionary groups into a single vanguard party, the result of which would overcome the differences over the commemoration of 20 May. Sankara believed that the petty squabbling among the contending parties was a waste of energy that could lead to their mutual destruction.[11]

Before the parties responded to Sankara's request, on 1 May 1984, Soumane Touré issued a statement declaring that all labor federations other than the CSV were counterrevolutionaries, positioning his union as the only legitimate workers' organization in the country. According to Valère Somé, the CNR dismissed the statement as inconsequential and took no action, which he later argued was a mistake that emboldened the PAI and its affiliated groups to become even more assertive in relation to the other factions within the revolutionary government.[12] On 15 May 1984, the PAI/LIPAD produced its official response to Sankara's letter. In its reply, the pro-Soviet party criticized the CNR's failure to publish the statutes governing the CDR and claimed the delay had led to the absence of democracy within them, the dominance of military officers over the organization, and the improvisational nature of decision-making in the government.[13] The government did announce the *Statutes of the CDR* two days later, on 17 May 1984, although they were not published in *Sidwaya* until 28 May 1984, the day Sankara announced the discovery of the plot against the revolution by agents of Saye Zerbo's former regime.[14]

Rather than dismiss the PAI's complaints, Sankara convened several meetings of the CNR to resolve the two outstanding issues—the direction of the 20 May 1984 demonstrations and the organization and disciplining of the CDR to bring them firmly under the control of the government. The CNR issued a decree on 16 May 1984 that specified the organization and nature of the commemoration of "20 May." The date was named the "Anti-imperialist Day of the Youth" and Ibrahima Koné, who had initially called for the celebration, retained overall authority to organize the demonstrations, but the government "demanded that he coordinate [all his decisions] with the national secretary general of the CDR," Pierre Ouédraogo. However, the minister of youth and sports worked directly with Soumane Touré to maximize LIPAD's presence in the 20 May 1984 actions and bypassed consultations with the CDR's national general secretary. Pierre Ouédraogo learned of Ibrahima Koné's plans and planned a separate demonstration for 21 May 1984. The march of 20 May 1984 was a triumph with tens of thousands of youth flooding Ouagadougou's streets carrying LIPAD banners. Pierre Ouédraogo's subsequent rally on 21 May 1984 was a disappointment being poorly attended and hastily organized.[15] Instead of uniting, the contending forces within the government operated independently of one another and of the CNR.

Sankara was angered by Ibrahima Koné's defiance of the compromise decree worked out within the CNR. Consequently, in the evening of 21 May 1984, the PAI minister for youth and sports was dismissed from the government, the first public split since the revolution of 4 August 1983.[16] Bamouni published an editorial in *Carrefour Africain* in which he openly declared war on the PAI. "The knell was struck on 21 May 1984. The weaknesses characterized by a Lamizana, a Saye Zerbo, or a Jean-Baptiste Ouédraogo, formerly hostages of political calculators, will not be appropriate with the Revolution." He added, "Certain [groups] put the accent on their parties above the Revolution." Bamouni demanded that the groups put aside their differences and submit to revolutionary unity and discipline.[17]

The rift within the revolutionary government worsened in the following weeks. On 23 May 1983, the CDR in Ouagadougou "sounded the clarion for the purification of the CDR" and issued a declaration in which it described the PAI as a "deviationist organization, putschist, opportunist, and [a] dangerous counterrevolutionary [group]."[18] Within days, dozens of PAI/LIPAD activists were purged from the CDR.[19] Meanwhile, minister of information, Adama Touré (PAI), toured Europe throughout May and June 1984 during which he spoke openly to the foreign press about the widening rift in Upper volta's government. According to Brittain, Adama Touré told the journalists, "That unless a party based on LIPAD was immediately formed and given the leadership, the regime would degenerate into chaos." He pronounced, "It's them (the military) or us."[20] As the historian Englebert notes, Adama Touré's statements, specifically his declaration while in Albania of the "imminent creation of a single communist party" and his insistence that Upper Volta's radio repeat his speeches "up to five times a day," caused "discontent within the CNR." For his part, Arba Diallo (PAI), foreign minister, pushed for a closer and more explicit alignment with the Soviet Union and Albania, a deviation from Sankara's articulation of revolutionary neutrality in the Cold War.[21]

The rift between the civilian revolutionary parties in the government opened a space for the military officers of the former OMR to assert their power to provide more discipline and coherence to the functioning of the government. First, the CNR sought to guarantee the unity of the military and its loyalty to the revolution. This was important considering the numerous counterrevolutionary plots that it had uncovered since the previous fall. To that end, on 15 June 1984, the CNR decreed the formation of Revolutionary Discipline Councils (Conseils Révolutionnaires de Discipline, CRD) charged with "purifying the army of dubious and dangerous elements for the implementation of the August Revolution." In addition, the decree created an ideological litmus test for anyone employed in public service, giving the new CRD power even over the CDR, many of which were still led by the PAI and its affiliates. Then on 27 June 1984, the CNR met to air the grievances of the various parties within the government. At the meeting, the military members of the ruling body conceded that some of LIPAD's critiques from April and May 1984 were correct while they also criticized the

PAI for the debacle of 20–21 May 1984. Despite those overtures at reconciliation, PAI/LIPAD would not concede any mistakes on its part and sustained Adama Touré's assertion that the PAI should be the nucleus around which the vanguard party was formed.[22]

The Clarification

Most people in the country, however, did not become embroiled in the partisan fights within the government. The reforms initiated between August 1983 and August 1984 created a new judicial system (the TPR) that redressed historic injustices and showed the CNR's commitment to the eradication of corruption. The transformation of power relations in the countryside gave peasants more freedom and authority while the traditional leaders lost their authority and special privileges. People across the country mobilized in local CDR and directly engaged in formulating policies in their communities and places of work, providing them the ability to make decisions that intimately impacted their lives. Finally, the CNR had forcefully asserted its independence in international relations, even defying France in negotiations over the cooperation agreement between the two countries and challenging the United States over its actions in Central America and southern Africa. Those developments touched people's lives where they lived them and were generally applauded in most sectors.[23]

To symbolize the permanent break with the past and recognize the changes already wrought throughout society, on 18 July 1984, the CNR declared that 4 August would be commemorated as the national holiday. In addition, on 4 August 1984, the country's name was changed to Burkina Faso (The Land of Dignified People). The CNR issued a new flag and adopted a national anthem that extolled the revolution's values and celebrated the contributions of the masses to making a new society.[24] In his speech on 4 August 1984 to commemorate the revolution's first anniversary and mark its new identity, Sankara reviewed the CNR's accomplishments of the previous year. He highlighted the expansion of education, the improvement in roads and bridges, improvement in health care, and the revolutionary transformation in the nature of the Burkinabè state. The CNR leader pointed specifically to the ideological clarity of the *Discours d'Orientation Politique* and the essential role of the CDR in carrying out the revolution's objectives. Those developments had prepared the ground for even more aggressive reforms that would accelerate the transformation of Burkinabè society as well as the mentality of the people. However, Sankara warned, there were unnamed elements who had an "erroneous" interpretation of the Democratic and Popular Revolution then underway, and those mistaken perspectives contributed to counterproductive acts that threatened to undermine the unity of revolutionary forces and played into the hands of foreign foes of the CNR. He asked the people to remain vigilant and carry on the work of implementing the revolution's policies in a disciplined and united manner. To symbolize the shift to a new phase of the revolutionary process, the country would henceforward be known as "Burkina Faso," a reminder to the Burkinabè people and the rest of the world that the revolution was making a new type of person; one that had transcended the alienation produced by imperialism and was now building a new future that did not rely on instruction from the outside world.[25]

Sankara telegraphed his intentions to make changes to the government at a press conference after his speech on 4 August 1984. He stated, "The CNR would ensure the consolidation of the popular power by clarifying the political line of the Democratic and Popular Revolution.... The Revolution will be clarified and its line consolidated. The CNR will be better structured." Sankara pointedly addressed the problem of LIPAD and the tumult that had spilled into the streets since the spring of 1984. He said the PAI/LIPAD had an erroneous interpretation of the revolution, naming the group he did not single out in his speech, and criticized the organization's "sterile theorization while the people advance." A "clarification" was necessary so that the ideological line of the *Discours d'Orientation Politique* could be effectively implemented.[26]

In a dramatic move Sankara announced on 19 August 1984 that the cabinet was dissolved. In its place, a committee called the Coordonnateurs du Faso (Coordinators of Faso) assumed complete authority. The group was composed of Sankara, Compaoré, Boukary Lingani, and Zongo, the four leaders of the former OMR. In essence, the military asserted its dominance of the state. Even Valère Somé was caught off guard and said the formation of this interim group was "a structure which was not previewed anywhere, in any text and which places itself above the CNR, supposedly the supreme governing body."[27] When the Coordinators announced the new cabinet on 31 August 1984, all the ministers from PAI/LIPAD were dropped, with Adama Touré and Arba Diallo sent to the countryside to take positions assisting agricultural development.[28] The winner of the clarification, as the CNR described the change in personnel, was Valère

Somé's ULCR which augmented its presence in the reconstituted administration adding the portfolio of Foreign Affairs (Basile Guissou) to its previous positions.²⁹ However, the balance within the larger CNR, which once more directed the government when the Coordinators completed their work, shifted overwhelmingly to the military. Martens counts sixty-five military officers and four ULCR members in the General Assembly of the CNR. Moreover, he notes that the General Assembly of the CNR was "convened by and presided over by Sankara; it continued to function without statutes nor internal regulations and practically without an internal organization."³⁰

With the pro-Soviet PAI sidelined from the government, Valère Somé's ULCR sought to enhance its position as the only nonmilitary element within the CNR. In mid-September 1984, the CDR held elections for leadership of the different sectors in the major cities, and the ULCR swept some of the most critical districts. The most bitter contest was in sector five of Ouagadougou where the ULCR challenged Mahamadi Kouanda and defeated him. Kouanda was the leader of an informal group known as the Inter-CDR that formed on 3 October 1983 and pledged to "fight against all people and all movements that attack the Revolution."³¹ Kouanda refused to accept his defeat and the Inter-CDR declared in the days following the elections, "[This] is the birth of a new era that foreshadows a new era of merciless struggle with the ULCR opportunists."³²

The Inter-CDR reflected the position of Pierre Ouédraogo, the general secretary of the CDR, who officially launched the Union of Burkinabè Communists (UCB) on 10 August 1984, and Boukary Lingani, who was viewed as sympathetic to the PAI/LIPAD.³³ To counterbalance Valère Somé's ULCR within the CNR, on 22 May 1985, the CNR admitted both the UCB and the GCB into the government. The UCB was the civilian wing of the military officers, with Pierre Ouédraogo serving as its general secretary and Sankara, after August 1985, as the president. The GCB was directed by Jean-Marc Palm, who led a split from the PCRV after it refused to support the Revolution of 4 August 1983. By early 1984, Jean-Marc Palm and his comrades had formed a separate organization that supported the CNR. So, by May 1985, the revolutionary government had been rebalanced through the participation of the former members of the OMR, ULCR, GCB, and UCB.³⁴

Economic Dimensions of the PPD

While the dust settled in the "clarification process" outside observers recorded that Burkina Faso was experiencing "an unprecedented explosion of popular confidence and creativity." As the political economist Brittain concludes, "In the second year, with the problem of political unity apparently solved at the center, the regime's focus was to make as definitive a breakthrough on the economic front towards agricultural self-sufficiency as had been made on the domestic political front."[35] In addition to the agrarian reforms discussed in the previous chapter, the CNR initiated programs in four other areas of the society during 1984 and 1985. Those included anti-corruption drives tied to the issue of foreign debt, reform of the education system, a campaign against gender discrimination and patriarchy, and sweeping changes in health care. Taken together, these five areas of social change aimed not only to promote socioeconomic development but also to produce a new kind of people that matched the country's new name. In doing so, new behaviors, forms of social organization, and values were expected to emerge, enabling the Burkinabè Revolution to become self-perpetuating, propelled by the heroic action and will of its people. Sankara reflected on the collective impact of those areas of activity in an interview he gave to *L'Autre Journal* in April 1986. The Burkinabè president said, "The project . . . is above all to create a . . . lifestyle. A new mental framework. It is asking the Burkinabè to admit that happiness must be defined on our terms, not according to how others define it. It belongs to each of us, all of us." Sankara added, "We suffer too much here from a lifestyle that has been inculcated in us, imposed on us without our will, without our participation."[36] The aim was to fulfill Fanon's maxim that "everything needs to be reformed and everything thought out anew." As Fanon writes, "The extraordinary importance of this change is that it is willed, called for, demanded." This effort "brings a natural rhythm into existence, introduced by new men, and with it a new language and a new humanity."[37]

The organizing framework for the implementation of the CNR's revolutionary projects in 1984 and 1985 was the Popular Program for Development (Programme Populaire de Développement, PPD), begun on 1 October 1984 and scheduled to last fifteen months. Rather than impose a detailed plan of action on the population, the government encouraged local CDR to express their own needs and put forward proposals for how to meet them. The historian Englebert notes that the emphasis on local initiative hoped to avoid the pitfalls of earlier development efforts in Africa that aimed for spectacular and gigantic building programs beyond the capacity of the resources and capabilities of those societies. The peasants were to reveal their desires through the local CDR, which would "define in common the project deemed the highest priority." The ensemble of the microprojects would constitute the PPD. "The CNR would furnish the material or the experts when it was necessary."[38] The truly innovative aspect of the PPD and the CNR's approach to economic development in general was its emphasis on the transformation of the person through the mobilization of the masses to realize their own objectives. This derived from a Marxist analysis of the role of ideology in modern societies. Malitsky writes, "Instead of serving as an unconscious mechanism contributing to individual alienation, as it did in Western capitalist societies, ideology was seen as something that could be learned and felt by thinking and experiencing in an informed way."[39] According to Kyélem de Tambèla, "The PPD played a role of innovation and making [the people] responsible. The population ... was encouraged, not only to participate, but also and above all to create and define their own projects." The government pledged to provide the capital (19 percent obtained domestically the remainder from abroad), but the people had to come forward with their needs and organize themselves (with assistance from CDR) to carry out the projects.[40] At the conclusion of the PPD in December 1985, Burkina Faso was to have achieved a level of economic growth, popular mobilization, and rational organization of resources (human and material) so that the Democratic and Popular Revolution could leap to the next stage of a mature period of modernization and development.

Over the next fifteen months, Burkina Faso's PPD resulted in the construction of "334 schools, 284 dispensaries and maternity wards, 78 pharmacies, 25 grocery stores, 553 apartment buildings and lodgings, 258 water reservoirs, and 962 wells and boreholes." As Martens reports, citing World Bank figures, "The volume of stockpiled water went from 8.7 million tons in 1983 to 302.4 million tons in 1986."[41] The augmentation in the supply of potable water indicated the priority given to the transformation of the agrarian sector of Burkina Faso's economy. As Sankara explained, "The CNR chose to make agriculture the motor, the principal lever of our economic and social development."[42] To defend farmers from the vicissitudes of the world market and encourage them to increase output, the CNR fixed the prices paid to rural producers for foodstuffs at figures above international values and guaranteed them a market, partly by restricting the importation of competing products from neighboring countries. The state also provided funds for irrigation programs, dam construction, and engaged in a vast construction program to renovate and expand the transportation sector. The latter involved road and railroad construction on a massive scale throughout 1985, the centerpiece of which was the "Battle of the Railroad" inaugurated on 1 February 1985. It sought to extend the existing track that ran from Abidjan in Côte d'Ivoire to Ouagadougou all the way to the north of Burkina Faso.[43] The extension of the rail system to the north would also make the region's mining industry more lucrative, especially the extraction of manganese, that could augment Burkina Faso's capital earnings and provide materials to stimulate the domestic manufacturing sector.[44]

However, the CNR was clear that economic development had to be done in a way that also combatted the effects of climate change. When the CNR issued the decree nationalizing the land and resources of the country in August 1984 (prior to the announcement of the PPD), it included the provision that "all projects of social and economic development at the national or local level must of necessity include a program of reforestation in the form of planting groves of trees, plantations, green spaces, or public gardens."[45] Sankara presented his government's thinking on the link between climate change and economic development as a question of "the organization of our society." He said that the drought and desertification that ravaged the north largely went unnoticed in urban centers like Ouagadougou because of food imported from France and elsewhere. As Sankara put it, "In the city of Ouagadougou we never really knew that there was drought. . . . For the needs of the few in the city, the drought raises an issue of justice and equity."[46]

The crisis was urgent. Kyélem de Tambèla writes that, "At the time of the Revolution the desert was advancing by 10 kilometers a year." This accelerated the migration of people from the north to the west and south of Burkina Faso and added pressure on those populations and the strained resources at their disposal. To further demonstrate its commitment to battling global warming, the CNR announced on 1 January 1985, the beginning of a massive reforestation program centered primarily in the north, but eventually designed to encompass all of Burkina Faso. By the end of the PPD in December 1985, well over ten million trees had been planted by local CDR.[47] In addition, the CNR announced on 22 May 1985 the "Three Struggles," which were the fight against brush fires, indiscriminate animal herding, and excessive logging. CDR were mobilized throughout the country to combat those practices by convincing the people that they were not only harmful to the environment, but counterproductive for social and economic development. Many rural Burkinabè depended on burning wood for heat and cooking, and traditional agricultural practices encouraged clearing forests to bring more land under cultivation, a tendency also encouraged during the colonial period when France advocated to produce cotton for the world market. Consequently, success in the Three Struggles entailed a complete rethinking of established habits, a different awareness of the connections between development and the environment, and a reorientation of value systems toward sustainability and social reform.[48] The role of the CDR as institutions wherein new mentalities were forged among the people organized within them was put to the test in the Three Struggles as well as the PPD overall. Bamouni argues that people's experience within the CDR would lead to the reordering of Burkinabè society that "would permit [the country] to pass, by stages, from its current bourgeois nature to a socialist nature then a communist [one], as is the wish of all the true revolutionaries of this country, that is to say the Burkinabè communists."[49]

Dr. Hyppolyte Fofack of the African Academy of Sciences, citing figures from the World Bank as well as those produced by the Burkinabè government, reported in *African Business*, "The results and development outcomes [of the PPD by December 1985] were spectacular: increased road density and rail infrastructure networks, a booming textile industry through processing of domestically produced cotton and [a] growing market share of cotton fabric for local producers; food self-sufficiency through sensible agricultural policy." He points to the increase in wheat production from 1,700 kilograms per hectare to 3,800 kilograms per hectare in a country ravaged by drought and famine as well as "the deficit of technology for productivity enhancement" as particularly significant.[50] The journalist Harsch notes that between 1983 and 1986 "cereal production rose by a spectacular 75 percent," and the economist Paul Harrison confirms that the outcomes were "encouraging" as the government carried out its determination "to spread development out into the neglected villages."[51] According to World Bank data, the PPD had an observable impact on the environment almost immediately. While never a major contributor to carbon dioxide emissions, the setting of brush fires and other aspects of deforestation added to the general erosion of climate stability as well as long-term economic sustainability for Burkina Faso. In 1983, the World Bank measured the country's carbon dioxide emissions at 0.081 metric tons per capita, a figure that had grown virtually every year since independence in 1960 when it was 0.009 metric tons per capita. In 1984, the figure declined to 0.062 metric tons per capita, holding steady in 1985, falling to 0.061 metric tons per capita in 1986, before rising slightly in 1987 to 0.064 metric tons per capita.[52] The revolutionary government managed to lower carbon dioxide emissions while vastly expanding agricultural productivity and manufacturing as the population also increased from 7.3 million in 1983 to 8.1 million in 1987, an 11 percent increase.

Despite the positive results of the PPD, some problems emerged over the course of 1985. The CDR were highly effective at mobilizing large numbers of people for concentrated tasks and providing a sense of local empowerment in the decision-making process. However, because many of the leaders were inexperienced, prone to dogmatic interpretations of directives from the CNR, or both, abuses took place in some areas. For example, in the campaign to curtail free herding of livestock, some CDR hunted the livestock, which generated tensions with those groups like the Peul whose livelihood depended on herding. That struggle was suspended in 1986 after much public discussion.[53] Accusations also mounted against some CDR that they acted dictatorially and abused their power.[54] In other areas, the country was limited in its ability to fully realize the goals of the PPD. For one, the CNR urged peasants to switch to the use of natural gas instead of wood as a source of energy. However, as Kyélem de Tambèla points out, the price of gas was too high for most Burkinabè communities. Moreover, the burning of wood was important in many local cultural rituals, and it was difficult to persuade people to abandon their traditions in the name of conservation.[55]

Cultural Politics, Education Reform, and the PPD

Those issues pointed to the essential project of the transformation of society and the formation of new people to ensure the durability of the Democratic and Popular Revolution. To that end, the CNR embarked on a reform of Burkina Faso's education system, engaged in the cultural field with an emphasis on regeneration and creativity, and waged a battle to overcome gender discrimination and empower Burkinabè women. In December 1983, the revolutionary government initiated a campaign to increase the number of literate Burkinabè to 5.5 million within ten years, out of an estimated population of over 7 million at the time. The government selected more than a dozen languages in which to conduct the operation, not just the colonial language of French. Within that program, in February 1986, the CNR launched Operation Alpha Commando, a campaign for accelerated literacy training among select groups of the peasantry who had already been touched by the initial sweep. The goal was to raise over 30,000 farmers to official literacy within forty-eight days.[56]

However, functional literacy was not the program's only goal. As Sankara stated in a 1985 interview, "Our task today is to inject new values into our schools, so that they can produce a new man who understands ideas, who absorbs them, and who functions in total harmony with the dynamic evolution of his people." Burkina Faso's schools had to be democratized by which Sankara meant building classrooms everywhere. However, he noted that the enthusiasm of the people to expand the country's educational infrastructure had "outstripped the government's capacity to back them up technically. They're going a little too fast for us," Sankara added, "but we're certainly not going to stop something that's going well."[57] During the PPD, over 1,200 new primary school classrooms were built, more than a 25 percent increase over existing stock. This included over 350 new schools opened in time for the start of the 1986 school year alone. The CNR also attacked the problem of access to instruction by slashing school fees by about one-third. The combined results of more schools and lower cost produced immediate results. Between 1983 and 1985, according to UNICEF, attendance jumped from 16.5 percent of eligible children to nearly 21 percent and increased to 24 percent by 1986. That rate of growth in school attendance was well beyond previous years where the average advance was a meager 1 percent per year between 1975 and 1983.[58]

A factor that limited even further improvement in the country's education system was the CNR's decision to fire the 1,400 teachers of the SNEAHV in March 1984. That left a gaping hole that could not be immediately filled, especially with the addition of so many new schools being built across the country. The CNR called for all those with even a minimal educational background to volunteer to replace those fired. The state wanted revolutionary teachers that would not only educate students in the basics of reading, writing, and arithmetic, but also inculcate the younger generation with the values of the August Revolution as enunciated in the *Discours d'Orientation Politique*. Gnindé Bonzi, at the time a young student from rural Burkina Faso, was puzzled by the sudden departure of his teachers and even more dismayed at the poor quality of their replacements.

He was excited about Sankara and the revolution. Bonzi expressed with marvel the humility and strength of the country's new president. However, he also respected his teachers, whom everyone in the village knew to be decent people. Bonzi writes, referring to President Sankara, "How dare he do that? To show the door to 2,000 heads of families! And to replace them with people who lacked training!" He adds that as the years passed, Bonzi became convinced "that the PF (President of Faso) was poorly informed."[59]

Some within the CNR also objected to the direction in which education reform was moving. On 12 September 1984, the CNR appointed a special commission to "propose a new system of teaching taking into account the realities of the country." The Commission only reported back in March 1986. According to Kyélem de Tambèla, "The proposed reform . . . was radical, oriented toward the production and integration of the rural world." The proposals included stronger emphasis on agronomy and agricultural practices, veterinary sciences, and technical education that would enhance local manufacturing and production. Resources were to be directed toward "practical" education with many projects connected to the PPD's development programs, effectively integrating the students into the economic changes being undertaken by the CNR. Within the CNR, the proposal came under fierce attack primarily from those who had benefited from the school system inherited from French colonial rule. That structure favored urban populations and especially those from the middle and upper classes. Those opposed to the commission's proposals feared that foreign institutions of higher learning would question the value of the diplomas earned by Burkinabè students and that some schools could lose their accreditation. The CNR rejected the commission's proposal. The field of education reform, therefore, became another site where differences within the revolutionary government took root.[60]

Cultural Politics, FESPACO 1985, and the PPD

Reform of Burkina Faso's education system was imbricated with the promotion of a cultural revolution in the form of increased creative productivity as well as public celebrations of Burkina Faso's and Africa's artistic contributions to the world. This was on display at the Second National Week of Culture opened by the CNR on 13 December 1984. People from all walks of life and in all regions gathered to display their creative works, perform dances, hold singing competitions, and engage with the expressive arts of the country's many ethnic and religious communities. Thousands participated in or attended events during the week and leaders of the CNR as well as local CDR were prominent at the festivities. Representatives from around the world also were involved as a gesture both of international solidarity as well as expressing the goal of constructing what Fanon described as a new humanism.[61]

Beyond the weeks of culture, the CNR carried out a robust program of cultural infrastructure development. It provided funds to build sports complexes throughout the country and encouraged physical fitness as integral to both a child's education as well as their mental development. Bonzi remembers with fondness the exuberance he and his classmates experienced when it was announced that President Sankara was coming to Houndé to inaugurate a new stadium in 1985. "What a mobilization," he writes. People wore traditional masks from the local community, others played musical instruments, and then there was the impressive cortège of military vehicles escorting the CNR leader to the venue. Even "a military plane flew over the village at low altitude, something never seen [there] before." Revolutionary slogans adorned the stadium, were posted along the roadside, and carried on banners by the masses marching in formation. Bonzi witnessed Sankara shooting a basketball as well as batting a handball as part of the event. For the young student, this confirmed the government's unity with the people as well as their inexorable "glorious advancement toward a better future."[62] The adornment of the areas surrounding the stadium was part of what the film scholar Malitsky identifies as part of a project by revolutionary governments to create "transformed public spaces" where the people were immersed in the process and saw themselves as bringing the world into being as displayed in the posters and through the slogans.[63]

However, the central arena of the revolution's cultural politics was its engagement in the cinematic field. As part of the PPD, the CNR sponsored the expansion of the country's motion picture infrastructure, building movie theaters, providing increased funding for filmmakers, and forging collaborative relationships with other countries to enhance the production and distribution of films. As Sankara put it, "All political independence needs . . . a real cultural identity."[64] To realize that aim, the CNR called on the people to "go into the streets to watch films" screened in the open air.[65] The PPD also included substantial funds for mobile film units to bring motion pictures to the most remote parts of Burkina Faso and to reach the population with the revolution's message. The program to bring the cinema to the people was decentralized in structure so that local initiative could be expressed, and the people directly involved in choosing the films screened in their communities and organizing the events. That extended to FESPACO, where new venues were opened to show movies and the people were encouraged to participate actively in the festivities through workshops, discussions, and conferences as well as informal conversation.[66]

The CNR contributed substantial resources to FESPACO 1985, paying out a record XOF 25 million (at 1985 values) and doubled that to XOF 50 million for FESPACO 1987. As the Burkinabè filmmaker Gaston Kaboré told the film historian Dupré, FESPACO "was an integral part of the identity of the country and its population" because it allowed them "to represent themselves and permit[ed] the people to demonstrate a certain unity." However, to that point, Burkina Faso had not made a significant mark in African cinema through its own productivity. Kaboré's first film, *Wend Kuuni*, had appeared in 1983, and that was only the country's second full-length feature.[67] Consequently, the CNR vastly increased funding for the film training institute INAFEC as part of the PPD. While UNESCO provided some money, during the Sankara administration, the government covered upward of 80 percent of the training institute's operational costs. As part of the proceedings of FESPACO 1985, African filmmakers also petitioned UNESCO to create a feasibility study for the creation of an archive of African film history to be housed in Ouagadougou to preserve its growing legacy.[68]

The Ninth FESPACO (23 February–2 March 1985) came at a critical moment in the history of African cinema. FEPACI was in crisis and barely functioning. While the threat of a split in the organization was forestalled by the Senegalese filmmaker Sembène and the issuance of the "Niamey Manifesto" in 1982, the divisions over the nature and purpose of African cinema remained. Moreover, film productivity continued to suffer with few motion pictures being released in the previous five years when compared with the remarkable productivity of African filmmakers from the late 1960s to the end of the 1970s. It was the Democratic and Popular Revolution's commitment to cinema as an essential tool to affect a transformation of the person leading to true liberation that created the context wherein African filmmakers recovered a sense of purpose and mission while also enabling a revival in the production of motion pictures.[69] At the 1985 FESPACO, the CNR invited FEPACI to relocate to Ouagadougou and establish its permanent headquarters there. The government provided funding for physical space and guaranteed access to media and other materials needed to conduct its business. During the festival, FEPACI convened its Third Congress and revisited the radical "Algiers Charter" from 1975 to which it recommitted itself and even expanded the program for realizing the liberation of the person and society through the cinema industrial complex.[70] During that meeting, Kaboré became FEPACI's general secretary. Prior to assuming his new post, Kaboré explained, "My political choice forces me to take an active part in the struggle to restore the personality and dignity of [the] African and Burkinabè people. In my opinion," Kaboré continued, "cinema has a great role to play as a medium to promote our development policies and also as a means to rehabilitate our culture."[71] In an interview with Frank Ukadike, the Burkinabè filmmaker said, "And in an Africa that is trying to grapple with the problems of development, African cinemas are indispensable, as foreign films which are shown in our theaters contribute to keeping African peoples in a state of subjugation."[72] Kaboré and his associates in FEPACI put their rhetoric to action on 28 February 1985 when the organization decided to join the Battle of the Railroad launched a few weeks earlier by actually participating in the construction of rail track. FEPACI declared, "We, African cineastes, reunited for the III Congress of FEPACI and the 9th FESPACO, decided unanimously to participate in the Battle of the Rail. ... By this act, we wish to express our solidarity with the Burkinabè people in its struggle for development."[73]

As the film scholar Manthia Diawara writes, "The most obvious difference between [the 1985 FESPACO] and the preceding ones was in theme," which was "Cinema and Peoples' Liberation." This was the first time the festival had a theme, and it reflected the CNR's revolutionary agenda domestically and internationally. Diawara describes FESPACO 1985's effervescent atmosphere writing, "The theme of freedom was denoted by signs like 'libérez les écrans africains,' 'FESPACO '85, Arme de la Libération des Peuples,' 'FESPACO '85, Hommage aux Peuples en Lutte,' which were everywhere, on posters in front of movie theaters and hotels, on banners, flyers, newspaper headlines, radio and television." He adds, "The theme of freedom was also seen in the selection of films that were shown on a noncompetitive basis. There was a special retrospective on Algerian war epics and on Latin and Central American Third Cinema films. There were also anti-apartheid films."[74] The gathering of filmmakers, critics, and enthusiastic audiences was a whirlwind of activity aimed at advancing the festival's theme. Workshops and demonstrations against racism, imperialism, and apartheid occurred every day during FESPACO.⁷⁵ Unquestionably, the Burkinabè Revolution had become enmeshed in the entire project of African cinema. Their messages were united, and their energies combined to assist in realizing the domestic reform programs of the CNR while also facilitating the spread of the revolutionary message globally. Sankara was conspicuous at film screenings, workshops, press conferences, and awards ceremonies. He also personally presented the grand prize at the 1985 FESPACO, which went to Rahim Tsaki (Algeria) for *Histoire d'une rencontre* (1983) about two children who overcome their disabilities to bridge the cultural divide between them.⁷⁶

Dupré reports that FESPACO 1985 witnessed "record participation" and adds, from that gathering, "FESPACO officially took a revolutionary orientation."⁷⁷ To serve that goal the cinema industrial complex had to be cleansed of its imperialist contamination and instead serve the cause of peoples' liberation. As Sankara told reporters on 4 March 1985, "The purification of the cinema is a requirement of our struggle ... we must conquer our screens, reconquer our culture ... to spread the messages that are going to serve [the peoples'] interests. Cultural achievement is part of the overall strategy of the Revolution."⁷⁸ During the festivities, the CNR staged a "march of the militants" on 24 February 1985 to demonstrate the link between Africa's premier film festival and the Democratic and Popular Revolution underway in Burkina Faso. It signified the unity of the people and their participation in the global struggle for liberation, the kind of humanism Fanon insisted was an essential condition of true decolonization. The demonstration was also an extension of the gesture of solidarity indicated by the inclusion of films from throughout the world at FESPACO 1985.⁷⁹

Dupré points to the prominent presence of the Cubans at the festival that year and writes that it was no "accident" that they played such a large role in the events that week as they provided a model for using cinema to serve the revolution as well as taking action to promote international solidarity to advance the cause of global liberation.⁸⁰ Castro's government provided notable assistance to facilitate the PPD in 1984–1985 through the deployment of technicians, teachers, material aid, and committing to trade in Burkinabè-produced materials and goods.⁸¹ Cuban-Burkinabè relations did not go unnoticed by the United States. On 9 June 1985, Joseph Treaster reported in the *New York Times* that the United States was watching ongoing negotiations between Cuba and Burkina Faso over a cooperation agreement that would have Cuban "specialists in agriculture and public health" go to the African country. Kenneth N. Skoug Jr., director of the

U.S. State Department's Office of Cuban Affairs, told Treaster, "They (Cubans) engage in all sorts of activity that we don't welcome. Sometimes they go into a country and teach people to read. Yet at the same time, the things people are learning to read contain political indoctrination. Their engineers build roads, but at the same time, the roads are militarily significant."[82] One of the areas of closest cooperation between the two countries was in the cinematic field. Cuba played a prominent role as both inspiration and facilitator in the birth of FEPACI. Those bonds strengthened during the 1970s into the 1980s through Cuba's Institute of Cinematographic Art and Industry (ICAIC) and the journal *Tricontinental*, published by the OSPAAL (Organization of Solidarity with the People of Asia, Africa, and Latin America) founded in 1967. Consequently, FEPACI maintained offices in Havana; the CNR sent students to Cuba, and Cubans participated in every major cultural festival and event in Burkina Faso during the Sankara administration. There was an instant convergence in the revolutionary analytical framework of the two countries centered on the "fight against the cultural alienation that resulted from colonial image making" and how film "could contribute to national liberation."[83]

FESPACO 1985 brought to life FEPACI's aspirations as expressed in the 1975 "Algiers Charter." Ten years prior, Africa's filmmakers pointed to the "pervading ideological alienation that stems from a massive injection of cultural by-products thrust on the African markets for passive consumption" as a focus of struggle for the continent's cineastes. They must, the "Algiers Charter" proclaimed, "see themselves as creative artisans at the service of their people." Moreover, "African filmmakers must be in solidarity with progressive filmmakers, who are waging anti-imperialist struggles throughout the world."[84] In Burkina Faso's revolutionary government, the African filmmakers found a kindred force and an ally to promote the development of the continent's cinema industrial complex and fight for Africa's place in the global cinematic field. For the CNR, FEPACI and FESPACO became vehicles for aiding the revolutionary projects underway in the country and a vector of influence internationally.

Cultural Politics, Freeing Women, and the PPD

The cinematic field, however, revealed a fundamental limitation to the complete transformation of Burkinabè society. Few African women had been able to break into motion pictures by 1985. One of the changes the CNR made to address that problem was the provision of more money targeted to women who wanted to attend INAFEC. The first Burkinabè woman to make a feature-length film (*La Nuit de la Vérité*, 2004), Fanta Régina Nacro, graduated from the institute in 1986, its last year. There she studied under Idrissa Ouédraogo, one of the country's foremost filmmakers. The *Discours d'Orientation Politique* highlighted the double exploitation of women as a specific form of oppression. They suffered from the general exploitation that much of humanity experiences but also faced a distinct form of repression at the hands of men because of their being women. The goal of the Democratic and Popular Revolution was "to create the conditions for [women's] real emancipation." The *Discours d'Orientation Politique* cited the mobilization of women as full participants in every aspect of the society and the revolutionary process as the goal of full liberation. The CNR's statement of principles also linked women's emancipation to "the respect and consideration of men." As the *Discours d'Orientation Politique* states, "Will it be possible to liquidate the system of exploitation while continuing the exploitation of these women who constitute more than half of our society?"[85] The CNR issued decrees that abolished forced marriage, female circumcision, established a minimum age for marriage, and recognized the right of women to inherit property. Special emphasis was placed on encouraging girls' attendance in school as part of the revolution's education reforms and the health campaigns discussed below had female-specific dimensions to improve the health of mothers and children.[86]

Ultimately, though, women's emancipation resulted from direct female participation in the management of society and its decision-making process at all levels and in full equality with men. Within the CDR, a special Direction for Women's Mobilization and Participation (Direction de la mobilization et de participation féminine, DMOF) formed in the early months of the revolution. The DMOF played a critical role in promoting programs around family planning and sex education especially in rural Burkina Faso. Throughout the administrative structure of the revolutionary state, women gained access to positions of authority for the first time. Upon the reorganization of the country into provinces in 1984, the CNR appointed women to top positions in several of them. One of the goals of naming women as high commissioners of provincial governments was to sensitize men in those areas to the idea of women being in charge. Kyélem de Tambèla identifies nineteen female ambassadors appointed by the Burkinabè government to countries around the world. "Roughly 20% of [government] ministers were women" as well. The CNR mandated that government institutions have minimal requirements for the number of women in leadership positions, and this extended to the CDR, economic development programs, education campaigns, and healthcare.[87]

The CNR also made women the center of national celebrations, such as by recognizing International Women's Day (8 March) as a holiday. In July 1984, Sankara held a public meeting with thousands of women to learn from them their needs and the conditions in which they lived. On 22 September 1984, the CNR decreed men had to do all the shopping and tasks usually consigned to women in what it called the day of "husbands to the market." The objective was to teach men about market conditions, what it cost to feed the family, and what women had to experience in their role as sustainers of the family. During the week of 1–8 March 1985, the CNR sponsored a national conference of women at which over 3,000 delegates from throughout Burkina Faso took part. That was followed on 19 September 1985 by the founding of the Union of Burkinabè Women (Union des Femmes du Burkina, UFB).[88] Summing up the unique role of the Democratic and Popular Revolution and its leader, President Sankara, regarding women's emancipation, Fofack writes, "Sankara was the first gender-equality-sensitive president in the world. He was not only one of the first to offer cabinet positions to women, but he also launched a crusade against social norms which either perpetuated gender inequality or undermined the self-esteem of women."[89]

That extended to the government's healthcare reforms and campaigns. This was an arena wherein women gained greater control over their bodies and elevated the physical and mental well-being of the female population. Often the revolutionary government appointed women to lead its health care campaigns, and they were conspicuous in carrying out vaccination programs as well as dispensing knowledge about hygienic practices. One such program where women figured prominently was Operation Vaccine Commando that ran from 25 November to 10 December 1984. At a meeting of the CNR on 19 September 1984, the government identified infant mortality and the lack of childhood vaccinations as two areas where the revolution had not lived up to its responsibilities. To correct that deficiency, the government engaged CDR throughout the country to fully immunize all children and newborns in the country in fifteen days. The CNR partnered with UNICEF and received the support of hundreds of Cuban doctors, a result of the previous year's cultural and cooperation agreement, to realize the program. Doctors and nurses fanned out across the country, organized through the local CDR, and within fifteen days over 2.5 million children from newborns to age fourteen received vaccinations for measles, cerebral spinal meningitis, and yellow fever. UNICEF representatives on the ground marveled at the efficiency and success of the operation. The official report stated, "I was profoundly impressed by the engagement that the government displayed on the occasion of this campaign . . . as well as . . . the mobilization of the community."[90]

In addition to vaccines, the CNR constructed primary care clinics throughout the country with the goal of having one in every village. CDR built basic pharmacies in every province as part of the PPD. The state also subsidized the cost of medication so the price paid by the people was well below the global market.[91] While the impact of health care campaigns took time to be reflected statistically, some measure of the CNR's success can be gleaned from infant mortality and life expectancy data. At the time of the August Revolution in 1983, life expectancy in Burkina Faso was 48.5, according to the World Bank. By 1986, the figure rose to 49.5, where it remained for the next ten years.[92] In terms of infant mortality, Burkina Faso had a rate of over 119 deaths per 1,000 live births in 1983, among the highest levels in the world. That number dropped to around 111 per 1,000 live births by 1987, after which, again, the rate of improvement nearly stagnated for a decade.[93]

The Contribution of the Burkinabè Revolution to a New International Order

The success of the PPD and sustainability of the revolution was inextricably linked to the project of transforming the international order. The CNR identified imperialism as the root cause of many problems that afflicted the Burkinabè people, and that system had to be broken to permit true independence and the kind of development that would transform alienated subjects into a new humanity. The opportunity to present that vision to the world came with President Sankara's scheduled visit to the United Nations in October 1984 as part of that body's annual ritual of speeches by heads of state. In preparation for that trip, Sankara visited Cuba (25–30 September 1984) to strengthen the bonds of solidarity between the two revolutionary states. When the CNR leader arrived in Havana, the Cuban government gave Sankara the Order of José Martí, the highest honor bestowed by the state. In explaining its decision, a Cuban government official said it was reserved to acknowledge "those who have rendered outstanding service to the cause of their people . . . [in] the struggle against imperialism . . . and for genuine national liberation." The Cuban representative extolled Sankara's leadership of the transformation of Burkinabè society while fighting off threats to the revolution from inside and outside. Conferring the honor reaffirmed the close bond between Burkina Faso and Cuba especially in their foreign policy. Sankara replied, "Cuba and Burkina Faso are so far and yet so near, so different and yet so familiar, that only revolutionaries can understand the sincere love that pushes us irresistibly toward one another." He concluded by pointing out that the slogan he adopted for his country, "Homeland or Death, we will win!" is identical to that of Cuba's revolutionary government.[94]

Upon learning of Sankara's impending visit to the United States, Mayor Andrew Young invited him to visit Atlanta after the stopover in Cuba. However, before he arrived, the Reagan Administration demanded to see the Burkinabè leader's UN speech so that it could prepare a response. Sankara complied, and the United States requested a few alterations, which the CNR leader ignored, according to Harsch. Consequently, Sankara was denied a reception at the White House and Reagan's government blocked the visit to Atlanta as well.[95] Instead, Sankara left Cuba and travelled directly to New York City. Imitating Fidel Castro's trip in September 1960 to address the UN, Sankara stayed in Harlem. There, the Burkinabè leader was greeted as a hero, much as Fidel had been twenty-four years earlier. Sankara was invited to inaugurate an exhibit of Burkinabè art, and on 3 October 1984, he spoke before a packed crowd of over five hundred people at the Harriet Tubman School. In a rebuke to Reagan, Sankara proclaimed that "Our White House is in Black Harlem." He railed against imperialism, spoke of his efforts to build solidarity across Africa, described his friendship with Ghana's Rawlings, reminded the audience of the continuing struggle against apartheid in South Africa and the need to free the ANC's leader Nelson Mandela, and previewed the themes of his address to the world on the following day. The audience was ecstatic and frequently interrupted him with applause and shouts of approval.[96]

On Thursday 4 October 1984, thirty-four-year-old President Sankara stood in the front of the General Assembly of the UN to deliver an address on behalf of Burkina Faso. Dressed in military fatigues and wearing his trademark red beret with gold star, Sankara spoke to the world directly for the first time. Sankara said, "I bring the fraternal greetings of a country covering 274,000 square kilometers, where seven million men, women, and children refuse henceforth to die of ignorance, hunger, and thirst, even though they are not yet able to have a real life, after a quarter of a century as a sovereign State represented here at the United Nations." He came to speak "on behalf of a people which . . . has chosen from now on to assert itself and to take responsibility for its own history." Sankara provided an analysis of the state of the world, which he described as one of chaos and said he was going to speak on behalf of "the mass of people who are disinherited . . . maliciously dubbed 'the third world.'" He argued that the shared oppression of peoples had produced the alignment of countries from Latin America, Asia, and Africa to fight for their rights on the world stage. Sankara explained the urgent need for a break with the established global order in order to realize true development for the impoverished parts of the world. After lambasting Western experts, who he accused of devising numerous phony strategies for economic improvement in the Third World, and those in developing countries who were complicit with those schemes, Sankara explained the need for a revolution against all domination. He railed against international aid, which the Burkinabè president said was designed to perpetuate exploitation, underdevelopment, and dependency. Sankara instructed the General Assembly on the nature of the revolution underway in Burkina Faso, which was an example for the entire world.[97]

Sankara continued, "I speak not only on behalf of Burkina Faso . . . but also on behalf of all those who suffer, wherever they may be." He highlighted the root causes of marginalization around the world, including racism, cultural discrimination, "a structurally unjust system," and sexism. The CNR leader aligned his country with those states that were recent targets of imperialist aggression, expressing solidarity with the Palestinians, Iran, Grenada, and Ireland. Sankara placed the Burkinabè Revolution in the context of the world's great upheavals from the American Revolution through the French and Russian Revolutions to all the liberation struggles in the Third World during the twentieth century. Sankara remarked that "the new international economic order can be achieved only if we manage to do away with the old order . . . only if we insist on the place which is ours in the political organization of the world, only if we realize our importance in the world and obtain the right to decision-making with respect to the machinery governing trade, economic and monetary affairs at the world level." That old order propped up the racist regime in South Africa, sustained Israeli occupation of Palestine, permitted Morocco's aggression, and tolerated the U.S. invasion of Grenada and its aggression in Latin America. Sankara called for revision of the structures governing the UN so that the real equality of all peoples would be actualized. He urged a reprioritization of resources to promote health care, education, and protection of the environment. Sankara declared, "Down with international reaction! Down with imperialism! Down with neocolonialism! Down with 'puppetism!' Eternal glory to the peoples who are struggling for their freedom! Eternal glory to the peoples who stand shoulder to shoulder to defend their dignity! Eternal victory to the peoples of Africa, Latin America, and Asia in their struggle!"[98] The following day the *New York Times* described Sankara's address as "a fiery speech," and took note of the Burkinabè leader's call for a "new system of international economic relations."[99]

Fiscal Crisis, International Debt, and Fighting Corruption

The need to transform the world's economic system was urgent for Burkina Faso. The costs of the PPD were substantial and required a combination of sacrifice on the part of the urban population through contributions to special funds as well as reduced wages and accelerated international lending. In the early months of the Democratic and Popular Revolution, the government slashed public sector salaries to lessen expenditures. To offset the hardship that might result among those essential state workers, the CNR lowered rents on urban dwellings beginning 1 April 1984, and Sankara announced on 31 December 1984 that all housing was free for the entire year of 1985 during the PPD. The CNR also began a program to build new low-cost housing for government employees known as "Cities of 4 August."[100] The fiscal austerity imposed on urban workers, the military, and government officials was part of a strategy to build confidence among the rural population that the entire country was participating in the process of revolutionary construction.[101]

To better coordinate financing for the government's social programs, the CNR had already formed the Revolutionary Union of Banks (Union Révolutionnaire des Banques, URB) headed by Moïse Traoré (ULCR) on 11 July 1984. The head of the Bureau of Relations with Nongovernmental Organizations in the CNR, Alfred Sawadogo, writes that Sankara even suggested that all foreign agencies in the country open accounts with the new bank to provide it with liquidity. Sawadogo thought that was a dubious scheme since it would restrict those groups' ability to work without being under tight government supervision. He declares that in the end, "This bank did not ever have any great prosperity and would not survive the Revolution."[102] The aspirations as well as the problems associated with the URB reflected the persistent capital shortfall that the CNR confronted. That deficit only worsened with the advent of the programs of the PPD and the revolutionary government's insistence that Burkina Faso find the resources within the country to bring about its own development.

At the conclusion of a meeting on 19 November 1984 to discuss the coming year's budget, Sankara realized there would be a significant shortfall that could force Burkina Faso to take out more loans and undermine the political goal of real national sovereignty. This required drastic measures, so the CNR president called a national conference to discuss the budget and mobilize the people in the process of putting the country's fiscal house in order in a dignified way. On 3 December 1984, thousands of delegates from all parts of Burkina Faso and every sector of the economy assembled to deal with the fiscal crisis. The conference lasted all night, ending in the early morning of 4 December 1984. At its conclusion, the delegates accepted payroll deductions for the coming year, on top of those imposed at the start of 1984. However, the meeting was filled with tension as organized labor opposed further cuts in pay and benefits for their members. The CSB (Confédération Syndicale Burkinabè) led by Soumane Touré refused to even participate in the conference. The unions dominated by the pro-Albanian PCRV attended but would not speak.[103]

Despite the sacrifices agreed to by the delegates at the budget conference, the capital required to sustain the PPD was not available among the people. However, Sankara refused to accept the conditionality or structural adjustment that had become part of the requirements for accepting their assistance from the IMF and World Bank. Those agencies managed Burkina Faso's structural debt. Instead, the Burkinabè government sought support from friendly countries.[104] Consequently, the debt mounted. By the end of 1984, Burkina Faso's external debt stood at the equivalent of $410 million in 2019 terms, a modest increase of around 3 percent over the previous year. However, its total GDP continued to contract, falling to $1.46 billion from $1.6 billion in 1983. Per capita income fell as well, from $240 in 1983 to $210 the following year. On the positive side, inflation continued to drop in 1984 to an annualized rate of 4.85 percent, a decline of

3.31 percent over the previous year. And the economy grew 1.6 percent in 1984 after bottoming out the previous year with negative real GDP.[105] Nevertheless, the PPD did turn things around, and real economic progress was starting to be realized by December 1985. In 1985, Burkina Faso's real GDP grew by 11.3 percent, the fastest growth rate in the country's history. The size of the economy grew to $1.552 billion from the 1984 bottom of $1.46 billion. The inflation rate remained under 7 percent, the lowest in over ten years. Burkina Faso's external debt, however, jumped nearly 25 percent to over $511 million.[106]

The external debt pointed to what the Burkinabè leaders identified as an unjust international order that was structured in a way that inhibited the development of poor countries and made them dependent on continued streams of aid. As Sankara told the journalist Harsch, "Imperialism tries to dominate us from both inside and outside our country." He added, "The imperialism we're fighting is not an isolated thing. It is a system.... You have to counter a system with a system."[107] West Africa had institutions in place to facilitate trade and mutual assistance among the countries of the region, but little resulted from it. Sankara finally assumed leadership of the regional economic bloc on 28 October 1984 when the rotating presidency passed to Burkina Faso. Almost immediately a businessman, Mohamed Diawara, was arrested on charges of illegally taking funds from ECOWAS/CEDEAO and was to be tried before a TPR. Within weeks, others, including Moussa N'Gom and Moussa Diakité, were imprisoned as part of the scandal that unmasked deep corruption in ECOWAS/CEDEAO. Diawara was an Ivoirian former finance minister. Furthermore, the wife of Mali's president was implicated in the scandal. By August 1985, another Malian, Drissa Kiëta, the secretary general of ECOWAS/CEDEAO and connected with the corruption investigation, made impolitic comments in the press about the Burkinabè Revolution and was expelled from Burkina Faso.[108]

The scandal and the CNR's refusal to back down from its investigation caused renewed friction with Burkina Faso's neighbors. In January 1985, the Burkinabè government made overtures to Côte d'Ivoire to smooth relations through a visit by Compaoré to the country. During that sojourn, Compaoré met his future wife Chantal Terrasson de Fougères, raised by Houphouët-Boigny as an adopted daughter and related to a deposed Liberian leader.[109] Sankara was scheduled to visit Côte d'Ivoire in February 1985, but just prior to his arrival, a bomb exploded at the hotel where he was to stay. The Burkinabè president went anyway and received a hero's welcome from the population. As tensions escalated with Houphouët-Boigny's government, the CNR conducted joint military exercises with Ghana in March 1985, partly in response to similar maneuvers in November 1984 by France and Côte d'Ivoire. From late March to early April 1985, the TPR of the Diawara case began and resulted in convictions that led to the imprisonment of those found guilty as well as orders to make restitution to ECOWAS/CEDEAO. In May 1985, Burkina Faso suffered a series of terrorist attacks that the CNR blamed on Côte d'Ivoire and its backers. The same period also witnessed attacks and attempted coups in Niger and Togo, allies of Côte d'Ivoire. The leaders of those countries said Libya and Ghana were behind the attacks, but Burkina Faso was implicated as well. The accusers pointed to the summit of the heads of state of Benin, Ghana, Burkina Faso, and Libya on 27 April 1985 as evidence of a coordinated plot. Those tensions were the backdrop for the meeting of the Conseil de l'Entente in Côte d'Ivoire on 10 September 1985 at which the Ivoirian leader called for the creation of a regional military force.[110] The continuous escalation of tensions throughout the course of the corruption investigation around ECOWAS/CEDEAO pointed to Burkina Faso's vulnerability in the region to countries that were nervous about the Burkinabè Revolution and its potential to inspire dissent within their own states. From the spring to the fall of 1985, there appeared to be a dangerous increase in instability within and between the nations of West Africa that rose to a new level with Houphouët-Boigny's suggestion to form a multinational defense force.

The Burkinabè Revolution at the Service of the World

The CNR read developments in Côte d'Ivoire as directed at it. Sankara responded in a speech to a meeting of CDR on 11 September 1985. The CNR president said, "There are attempts to cook up all kinds of plots against our people." He continued, "I issue a firm warning to all those who would dare disturb the tranquility of a single Burkinabè, either inside the country or abroad." If Burkina Faso were invaded, those leaders would face the wrath of their people. Sankara said, "These peoples have understood that only revolution will enable them to rid themselves of all those inside and outside their countries who stand in the way of achieving this noble goal." Then Sankara broadened his warning beyond the Conseil de l'Entente to include Mali pledging, "The revolution of the Burkinabè people is at the disposal of the people of Mali, who need it." The revolutionary leader waxed triumphant about the prospects of a "revolution on the march" across Africa and around the world, one which Burkina Faso was prepared to assist in any way possible.[111]

While not named by Sankara in his speech, France's presence loomed large in the subtext. Relations between the CNR and Mitterrand's government had been fraught from the start and deteriorated over time. On 27 November 1984, the Burkinabè government cut off French access to capital in Burkina Faso to protest the failure of France to fulfill financial commitments it had made to support construction of the dam at Kompienga, a major component of the PPD. Days later, President Sankara announced his country's support for the liberation struggle underway in the French colony of New Caledonia. By December 1984, the two countries were hardly communicating, and Sankara boycotted the Franco-African summit that month.[112] Then Mitterrand received South Africa's foreign minister in another official visit in February 1985 further irritating the CNR, which formally protested. The Burkinabè president again boycotted the Franco-African summit in December 1985. Instead, Sankara received France's archenemy Qaddafi on an official state visit.[113]

By December 1985, tensions within West Africa had reached a boiling point. Sankara judged that the global context was ripe for the expansion of the revolution. Domestically, the PPD yielded impressive results, connections with Africa's and Latin America's filmmakers provided an important vehicle for promoting the revolution's message to the world, and the government appeared stable and united despite the falling out with the PAI/LIPAD. On the other hand, France bolstered its presence in the region, local leaders like Houphouët-Boigny were becoming wary of the Burkinabè Revolution's potential impact on their countries, and the United States feared that a new Soviet-Cuban foothold was emerging in Africa.[114] Burkina Faso headed into 1986 facing potentially dire headwinds and prepared to meet that challenge, whether emanating internally or externally.

5

Recalibration of the Burkinabè Revolution

(1985–1986)

Tensions between Burkina Faso and its neighbors had reached explosive levels by September 1985 when Sankara accused some of them, like Côte d'Ivoire and Mali, of plotting to destroy the revolution by invasion from without. In fact, France made a large delivery of arms to Mali in February 1985 during the escalating dispute over the scandal that involved the imprisonment by Burkina Faso of top officials of ECOWAS/CEDEAO in 1984, many of them from Mali and Côte d'Ivoire. Then in August 1985, the CNR expelled the Malian official Idrissa Keïta from Ouagadougou after he made derogatory comments about the Burkinabè Revolution. Those developments provided the backdrop to the emergency meeting of the Conseil de l'Entênte on 10 September 1985 and Sankara's speech on the following day in reaction to the gathering.[1] In retaliation, Mali's President Traoré refused to attend the summit of the West African Community in October 1985, effectively "blocking the functioning of the institution for three months." Then the Burkinabè opposition figure Joseph Ki-Zerbo paid a visit to Bamako in November 1985, which was bound to raise suspicions within the CNR of a foreign-backed plot to overthrow the revolution.² For his part, Traoré accused Sankara's government of stoking dissent in Mali. General strikes, student protests, and other disturbances unbalanced the dictatorship in November and December 1985. Those disturbances partly resulted from a severe drought throughout 1985 that was badly mismanaged by the Malian regime. While the climate issues hit Burkina Faso as well, they were mitigated by the proactive measures associated with the PPD. Finally, external elements interjected themselves into the row between the two West African countries. Qaddafi paid a visit to Ouagadougou in December 1985 to shore up relations between the radical governments. Meanwhile, France, the United States, and its regional allies viewed the advance of the Burkinabè Revolution as a mortal threat, invoking the claims that it was merely a puppet of Libya and the Soviet Union to advance those countries' interests in the area.³

The CNR then authorized a census that began on 10 December 1985. It was the first effort at a national head count since 1975. During the survey, some Burkinabè military staff accompanied census takers into the disputed villages of the Agacher Strip, which had been the territory at the center of the war between Mali and Upper Volta in 1974. Mali claimed that act violated ongoing mediation. On 25 December 1985, Mali's army crossed Burkina Faso's border in the Agacher Strip and attacked four villages. Mali's troops quickly overran several border stations and police outposts in what was called the Christmas War. While Mali had a clear military advantage, it was unable to overwhelm Burkinabè forces. Moreover, discontent with Traoré's regime mounted with some protesters displaying banners inscribed with slogans from revolutionary Burkina Faso. The CNR rallied the Burkinabè military and local CDR to retaliate and pushed Mali's military back and even bombed cities in Mali, including Sikasso. Then, Mali's air force bombarded a market in Ouahigouya resulting in many civilian casualties. Events moved quickly as the fighting between the two former French colonies became the focus of international attention and involvement. Traoré's regional allies grew worried that continuing the conflict would further destabilize the region and gain sympathy for the Burkinabè Revolution. On 26 December 1985, Qaddafi offered to mediate the dispute with no result. As fighting intensified and spread beyond the Agacher Strip, Libya joined with Nigeria on 29 December 1985 in a renewed effort to end hostilities, which failed once more. The next day, 30 December 1985, the countries agreed to a ceasefire sponsored by a sub-regional group of member states of the OAU. Over three hundred were killed, with most casualties on the Burkinabè side, many of them civilians. The two countries agreed to pull their forces back to pre-conflict positions and submit their dispute to the International Court of Justice (ICJ).[4] In early January 1986, CDR held mass demonstrations in Burkina Faso in solidarity with the Malian people that were also aimed at deescalating tensions between the two countries.[5] Houphouët-Boigny was credited with playing a major role in bringing the sides together to reach a definitive peace. On 8 January 1986, both sides exchanged prisoners and on 17 January 1986 at an extraordinary summit in Côte d'Ivoire, the belligerents agreed to a peace treaty that led to the ICJ's final ruling on 22 December 1986 to divide the disputed territory equally between the two countries.[6]

This chapter charts a shift in the direction and tenor of the Burkinabè Revolution following the Christmas War. To the leaders of the CNR and other governments in the region, the war was a shock that caused both sides to tone down their rhetoric, engage in more systematic negotiation of outstanding issues, and recalibrate regional relations. Within Burkina Faso, the CNR took stock of what had been achieved through its social programs to that point and examined those areas where results lagged expectations. Moreover, the tensions among the groups that comprised the ruling coalition exposed deep differences on the revolution's priorities, how government should be organized, and what were the ultimate objectives of the revolutionary process. President Sankara was once more forced into the role of mediator among the competing factions while he also demonstrated an increasing reluctance to directly challenge the growing power of the military within the CNR and the other institutions of governance in Burkinabè society.

Moderation and Assessment of the Revolution

As Englebert notes, the war was a turning point in regional relations as "the language and the attitudes [of the countries] considerably changed" from that point onward.[7] The shift in tone was previewed in Sankara's speech to a rally in solidarity with the Malian people in Ouagadougou on 3 January 1986. The CNR leader said, "Our politics were . . . transformed into a generalized popular defense . . . I would like each of us to try to surmount feelings of hate, rejection, and hostility toward the Malian people." He continued, "I would like each of us to achieve the most important victory: to kill inside ourselves the seeds of hostility and enmity toward anyone." Sankara concluded by looking ahead. He declared, "For 1986, which is beginning, I would like to wish all of you happiness—a happiness in keeping with the intentions we are expressing and with the efforts we are ready to make."[8] Following that rally, the Burkinabè, Malian, and Ivoirian governments worked closely to mediate an end to the conflict and permanently settle outstanding issues between them. From that point, conversations on a range of issues between the CNR and other governments in the region continued, including on trade and cultural exchanges. The Christmas War also opened a space within Burkina Faso for the CNR to begin a rapprochement with some of those on the revolutionary left and others that were not yet reconciled to the revolution. As Harsch notes, "[There was] a broader shift during 1986 and 1987 to try and ease up on coercion and reduce social tensions."[9]

The rebalancing and assessment of the state of the revolution entailed the formation of new mass organizations to bring more sectors of the population into the CNR's activities, broadening the coalition partners within the government, and addressing of the mounting criticisms against some of the Democratic and Popular Revolution's institutions like the CDR. Already in the spring of 1985, the National Pioneers Movement was founded to cultivate revolutionary consciousness among the Burkinabè youth. In August 1985, the cabinet was once more abolished, which Sankara announced would be an annual occurrence. When the new government was announced by the Coordinators, there were only minor changes in its composition. This ritual was done, according to Jaffré, "to demystify the ministerial position. The annual dissolution should be understood as one of the pedagogical methods to contribute toward that end." Ministers had become used to habitually occupying their position in previous governments. One of the revolution's innovations was to make government office one among many positions of service to the country that individuals would undertake temporarily as part of their broader contribution to advancing the revolution.[10]

In addition, the CNR began to lift the heavy hand it had used against officials of former governments as well as some of the labor federations. Jean-Baptiste Ouédraogo was remanded to house arrest, and Saye Zerbo had his sentence reduced, among other former prominent politicians who were either released or saw their sentences commuted. Some of them were incorporated into the newly created National Union of Burkinabè Elders (Union Nationale des Anciens Burkinabè, UNAB) in early 1986 under the leadership of former President Lamizana. Even the pro-FPV SNEAHV labor union and the pro-PCRV

SYNTSHA workers' organization had prosecutions against them dropped by the CNR. Finally, some of the PAI/LIPAD officials purged from the government and CDR in 1984 and subsequently arrested were rehabilitated in early 1986. Among them, Arba Diallo became a counsellor to Sankara and Adama Touré was freed from prison in February 1986.[11] In explaining the gradual release of political opponents and leaders of previous governments, Sankara said, "We know that our ideas, generous as they are, cannot fail to generate opposition. As long as these oppositions remain in the classic fight of freedom of opinion . . . it does not matter." However, Sankara cautioned, "when this opposition is organized and can compromise the serious work we do, then we are forced to crack down on it." Speaking about members of earlier regimes or even those who fell out with the revolution after the fact, the Burkinabè leader noted, "I reached out my hand to them. They grabbed it. We will see if they are opportunists. [We will see] if they want to deceive us or serve their country. . . . I accept the plurality of ideas."[12]

A further sign of the shift in the tone of the CNR involved the chastening of the CDR, which was a target of frequent criticism for abuse, incompetence, and was an arena of political strife among the revolutionary parties. The occasion was the opening of the First National Congress of the CDR on 31 March 1986. After more than two years since their founding, over 1,300 delegates from across Burkina Faso arrived in Ouagadougou to attend the meeting. According to the *Statute of the CDR*, the National Congress is the supreme body of the organization. The Congress was to convene every two years, so one was due for the spring of 1986 since the statute had been published in May 1984. Each CDR was to provide reports on the work they had done to implement the policies of the CNR. The Congress was presided over by a bureau that included the National General Secretariat of the CDR and was run by the general secretary, Pierre Ouédraogo, appointed to the post by Sankara in 1983.[13]

While celebratory in some respects, the meeting was also filled with tension among the different factions, especially between the Inter-CDR (supported by the military-led UCB) and the Maoist ULCR. As Harsch notes, "Some of the [revolution's] greatest problems came from a layer of activists within the CDRs," so the Congress was bound to involve a measure of critique and dispute. Accusations included that some CDR embezzled funds and used their position to engage in "shakedowns and armed robberies."[14] Bonzi relates one incident where he and his friend were stopped by CDR on the pretext that they were entering a forbidden zone. Despite their pleas of ignorance, they were held for a long time. Meanwhile, they witnessed other people apparently known to the young guards simply walk by unmolested. While in custody, Bonzi describes another unfortunate extorted for money before being released. In his memoir, he asks, "Is this how the Revolution is supposed to work? I like the Revolution, but not this way of doing things by these guardians."[15] The future French ambassador to Burkina Faso Alain Deschamps writes, "The CDR, too often, enrolled and empowered irresponsible adolescents."[16] Finally, since the fall of 1984, Pierre Ouédraogo had used the CDR to wage political war against the ULCR through the shadowy Inter-CDR in order to bolster the UCB, which was becoming a vehicle for the military to assert its dominance of the revolution.[17] While Guillaume Sessouma was named the first president of the UCB, the permanent secretariat formed at the group's 10 August 1984 founding included Pierre Ouédraogo and Watamou Lamien. In August 1985, Sessouma was dropped as president of the organization when he was accused of being an infiltrator working on behalf of Valère Somé's ULCR. Sankara became the new president of the UCB.[18]

In his speech closing the First National Congress of the CDR on 4 April 1986, Sankara unambiguously assailed the CDR's shortcomings and outlined his expectations for how they were to function in carrying out their duties for the revolution. He acknowledged that "there are bad CDR members among us." Sankara denounced opportunists who viewed the CDR as pathways to secure positions of power within the revolution and serve their own selfish interests. He described them as veritable despots who should be regarded as very dangerous and labelled them "anarcho-fascists." Sankara called for a shift "to a much more conscious level of organization" and argued it was time for the improvisational phase of the revolution to give way toward the methodical construction of the new society. Specifically, he tasked the CDR to produce. He returned to the theme of self-sufficiency and called on Burkinabè to "consume only what we control." Sankara urged the CDR to resist the temptation to want to achieve development by leaps. That can only lead to a trap set by the imperialists, forcing the revolution to become dependent upon and subordinate to those who do not have the revolution's best interests at heart. He told the delegates that this did not preclude cooperation with other peoples and countries. "We need the cooperation of all the peoples of the entire world," Sankara explained, "but we do not want aid that creates a welfare mentality in us." As he ended, Sankara instructed the National Congress to prepare for the next stage of the revolutionary process, which would involve "a deepening of our revolution . . . a radicalization of our revolution."[19]

Following the meeting, the CDR moved against some recalcitrant members, purged leaders identified as blatantly corrupt or abusive, and "downgraded [their] security functions."[20] Pierre Ouédraogo survived as general secretary despite widespread rumors that he was going to be sacked and replaced by the ULCR leader Valère Somé. Partly those innuendoes stemmed from a rare rebuke published by Bamouni's *Sidwaya*.[21] Rather than smooth relations among the revolutionary groups, the CDR National Congress opened a new round in the internal struggle to lead the revolution. Hardly chastened by Sankara's speech, Pierre Ouédraogo directed the CDR to launch "total war against the ULCR" right after the Congress closed. He believed that Valère Somé was behind the president's change in tone and even the plot to remove him as leader of the National General Secretariat of the CDR.[22] Sankara still hoped the divide among the parties could be bridged and preserving Pierre Ouédraogo in his post despite pressures from his close friend was a gesture in that direction.

Political Infighting and the Push for Unity on the Left

The Burkinabè president also returned to the idea of creating a united vanguard party from among the CNR's coalition partners. As Bamouni explained the vision for how such an organization would be formed, "The party is envisaged [to be created] over the long term because it is too early to envisage it in the current circumstances." One problem was the lack of a proletariat strong enough to take direction of the party. Another issue was division among the existing revolutionary forces. Bamouni observes, "The left is divided into small revolutionary parties" that often view each other as the main enemy.[23]

On 17 May 1986, the CNR issued a declaration signed by its four constituent organizations that proclaimed their commitment to unite into one communist vanguard party. The statement announced, "The following political organizations: 1. The Revolutionary Military Organization (OMR) 2. The Union of Communist Struggle Reconstructed (ULCR) 3. The Union of Burkinabè Communists (UCB) 4. The Burkinabè Communist Group (GCB) . . . solemnly affirm our will of common action within the CNR" with the aim of "forging a unique vanguard organization." It concluded with a call directed at all revolutionary forces in Burkina Faso saying, "We launch a militant appeal to all the other revolutionaries organized or not that struggle sincerely for the success and the consolidation of the Democratic and Popular Revolution, to join with us in the process of unification [now] underway."[24]

The question of political unity was becoming a matter of urgency within the CNR. Pierre Ouédraogo's use of the CDR and UCB indicated the reassertion of the military component of the revolution as dominant, negating its popular base. This was also suggested by the ad hoc body of Coordinators who annually dissolved the cabinet and held uncontested authority to announce its replacement. Partly, Sankara embraced the project of creating a united communist party to head off those within the CNR who rhetorically pushed to accelerate the revolutionary process beyond the country's capabilities. The ULCR and its rivals the UCB were among those trying to outdo each other in ultra-leftist phraseology and pose as the "true" or "pure" revolutionaries. Harsch writes, "Some [ULCR] members were becoming impatient with what they perceived as the slow pace of change." Sankara increasingly made overtures to the PAI/LIPAD and PCRV to bring them into the revolutionary fold and possibly mitigate the deleterious impact of the feud between the ULCR and UCB. A gesture of reconciliation extended to Soumane Touré, leader of the CSB, who was freed from prison on 26 October 1986. He had been imprisoned in January 1985 after publicly accusing the CNR of illicitly taking money from the social security fund. A small pro-Sankara faction of the PAI even split from the party and pledged support to the Burkinabè government.[25]

Despite signing the declaration, the UCB thwarted any hope of unity and continued its attacks on the ULCR. According to Lalsaga, "The presence of the military elements in the UCB enabled the latter to strengthen itself in relation to the other organizations, the reinforcement of which undoubtedly contributed to the sabotage of the unification process announced by the declaration of 17 May 1986." While Sankara was technically the president of the UCB, it was Pierre Ouédraogo who exercised real power within the organization, and he viewed the group as a vehicle for hegemonic power within the CNR. Lalsaga described the UCB as "considering themselves the leading figures of communism around which the communist party was to take shape." After May 1986, the distance between Sankara and the UCB widened as the project for unification of the revolutionary parties faltered.[26] Behind the scenes, a dangerous rift was emerging among the four officers who comprised the Coordinators. Pierre Ouédraogo's attacks on the ULCR were supported by Compaoré, who had never liked the ULCR, even as Sankara continued to back the leader of the CDR despite being strongly supported by Valère Somé's group. Compaoré and his allies were becoming influential throughout the UCB, and he promoted its development as a stalking horse to increase his own and the military's power within the CNR, according to Harsch.[27]

Sankara consistently opposed the idea of creating a united communist party through bureaucratic means. He explained to a journalist from Benin on 6 December 1985 that "if the masses need a party, they will have a party." Sankara pointed to the wreckage of previous attempts in Africa and elsewhere of revolutionary governments attempting to decree into existence vanguard parties because they were following preestablished models imported from outside their national experiences. They all ended in fiascos that undermined the revolution. Sankara envisioned the formation of a communist party from the voluntary action of the masses whose consciousness had been raised and whose experience provided them with the tools to form a vanguard group. Consequently, he insisted that the existing parties cooperate with the mass organizations, with each other, and reach out to other revolutionary groups to engage in a process of creating the vanguard party.[28] Compaoré and his associates, however, sought to replicate the models Sankara found troubling. According to Martens, at roughly the time Sankara told the journalist from Benin that there was no rush to create a single party, the UCB issued a call for "the Marxist-Leninists to regroup within the [UCB]" and "appeal[ed] to the other groups to join the ranks of the UCB to create a Marxist-Leninist party."[29]

Pierre Ouédraogo used the CDR to advance the UCB's battle against its political opponents. By August 1986, the University of Ouagadougou was on the frontline of the fight between the UCB and the ULCR. As Harsch argues, the fight for control of the students' CDR in August 1986 was emblematic of the bureaucratic maneuvering and intimidation that were increasingly hallmarks of the functioning of those organizations under Pierre Ouédraogo despite Sankara's reproach of such tactics. He adds that UCB members would often silence their opponents "by slapping their holstered pistols."[30] Valère Somé's ULCR had control over the students' CDR at the university. However, Pierre Ouédraogo wanted to drive the party from power, much as he had used bureaucratic methods to prevent the ULCR from gaining control of the CDR of neighborhoods in the capital in 1984 despite the ULCR winning the elections that year. When the National General Secretariat of the CDR sent a directive to the university CDR about the theme of its annual conference to be held 26–30 August 1986, the local CDR balked. Instead, it called a meeting of the board of directors to discuss its differences with the National General Secretariat. When the bureau voted down the directive from the center, Pierre Ouédraogo struck back "by liquidating the body, excluding its members from activity within the CDR for a year [and] prohibiting their election to office for three years." The National General Secretariat appointed a new body that was comprised of UCB supporters.[31]

Sankara's push for the unity of all revolutionary forces was collapsing. While it still supported the notion of a single vanguard party, even the GCB hedged on what that looked like. On 12 August 1986, it stated, "Parallel with the CNR, which continues to exist as an anti-imperialist front, we advocate the existence of a structure bringing together the representatives of the Marxist-Leninist organizations."[32] In other words, the CNR would remain as a coalition of forces, and the vanguard was to be a separate council with members from the still-separate groups. That was not what the joint declaration of 17 May 1986 envisioned.

By the time of the annual dissolution of the government on 18 August 1986, the plan to create a unified communist party was tabled. When the Coordinators announced the new government on 29 August 1986, Valère Somé was elevated to minister of higher education during the fight between the ULCR and UCB for control of the CDR of the university of Ouagadougou. With Sankara out of the country attending the Eighth Summit of Heads of Government of the Non-Aligned Movement in Harare, Zimbabwe, Boukary Lingani chaired the cabinet meeting on 1 September 1986 to discuss the matter. Valère Somé rose during the discussions and resigned his newly acquired post to protest Pierre Ouédraogo's actions against the ULCR-controlled students' CDR and the failure of the government to step in and reverse the draconian actions of the CDR's National General Secretariat. On 3 September 1986, the government met again to discuss the dispute, this time chaired by Compaoré. Valère Somé refused to attend that assembly as he had attached his loyalty exclusively to Sankara and was aware of Compaoré's animosity toward the ULCR.[33] Upon his return to Burkina Faso on 7 September 1986, Sankara once more stepped in to mediate the dispute between the National General Secretariat of the CDR (in essence representing the military dominated UCB) and Valère Somé's pro-Chinese ULCR. Consistent with his decision in May 1984 to mollify Pierre Ouédraogo in the dispute with PAI/LIPAD over the youth demonstrations, he endorsed the National General Secretariat's decision to dissolve the CDR Bureau of the University of Ouagadougou, but "he lifted some of the other sanctions" imposed on the ULCR members involved. Indicative of his continued personal loyalty to Sankara, Valère Somé accepted the decision on behalf of the ULCR and agreed to resume his post as minister of higher education. That action, taken without consulting the party as he had done in 1981 when he dissolved the original ULC, provoked the ire of many ULCR members who accused their leader of betraying them. That was the origin of a split in the ULCR that culminated on 2 February 1987 when Moïse Traoré and Kader Cissé led a rebel faction and left to form a group subsequently known as the ULC–*La Flamme* after the new group's newspaper.[34]

However, Sankara did not embrace the UCB's action unequivocally either. He was aware of the group's being transformed into a stalking horse for the military. Consequently, Sankara formally reanimated the OMR in August 1986 and encouraged the military to leave the civilian parties and regroup in their own organization.[35] According to the journalist Harsch, Sankara was worried that the UCB was seeking to recreate a Soviet model of political leadership not grounded in the unique revolutionary experiences of Burkina Faso. The CNR leader warned in August 1986 against the "emergence of a 'nomenclature of untouchable dignitaries'" that would make "it harder for people outside the party leadership to have a voice in public policy."[36]

However, throughout 1986, Sankara became more isolated within the government. His moderation in rhetoric after the Christmas War, the CNR's rejection of the education reform plan in March 1986, and his critique of the CDR in April 1986 indicated a growing separation between the president and his partners in government. Even seemingly trivial matters were sites of bitter confrontation among the revolution's leaders. In October 1985, Sankara proposed the promotion of Vincent Sigué, head of his personal security, to the rank of lieutenant. However, Compaoré led the opposition and defeated the request. Regardless, Sankara unilaterally promoted Sigué upon the latter's return from training in Cuba in October 1986. Then in November 1986, Sankara acted on his own again by appointing new members to the CNR, enlarging its overall membership in a way that reduced Compaoré and his allies' influence.[37]

Combatting Climate Change and Advancing Women's Liberation

The divergence between Sankara and Compaoré was also reflected in their analyses of the stage of the revolutionary process as it applied to socioeconomic and cultural politics. At the conclusion of the PPD, which coincided with the Christmas War, Sankara hinted at "the necessity for a pause and enlargement of the base of the revolution," according to Jaffré.[38] The Burkinabè president argued that the results of the PPD had to be assessed and a Five-Year Plan worked out before the country could resume its march forward. The reforms already underway would continue, but new initiatives had to wait until a consensus was reached as to what was needed and possible given the state of development of the society and the formation of new revolutionary people. Boukary Lingani, meanwhile, pushed openly for a more aggressive implementation of the CNR's programs that would bring the revolution closer to the establishment of a fully socialist system. His position was more aligned with the PAI/LIPAD, which he had supported in the disputes during 1984. For his part, Compaoré did not reveal a clear ideological position. Rather than intervene in the debate over how far and how fast to push the project of social transformation, Compaoré reserved his interjections for when there was a dispute among contending groups, mostly in the direction of supporting outcomes that enhanced the military's power to the detriment of the civilian-based communist parties.[39]

One policy that had general agreement among the different groups within the CNR was the reforestation program. The government expanded it in 1986 to mandate the construction of parks and gardens in every village across the country. Sawadogo says the CNR's plan aimed "to create giant green belts to block the route of the desert."[40] However, Sankara argued that saving the planet was inextricably linked to the development prospects of all societies. He carried his message to the International Silva Conference on Trees and Forests (SYLVA) held in Paris on 5 February 1986. Sankara said, "Since 4 August 1983 water, trees, and lives—if not survival itself—have been fundamental and sacred elements in all action taken by the National Council of the Revolution, which leads Burkina Faso." He related his people's experience over the previous three years as they waged a struggle to combat the desert's advance. The CNR leader pointed to a program carried out by children to build improved cooking stoves to reduce the consumption of firewood. Sankara also asserted that the vaccination and literacy campaigns of the PPD aided the fight against climate change since they improved the health and education of the population, equipping the people to be more productive contributors to the "struggle for a green Burkina." Citing the regulations imposed by the CNR and enforced through local CDR, the Burkinabè president pointed to the accelerated pace of tree planting, reduction in the consumption of forest products, restrictions on livestock grazing, and the diminished number of brush fires across the country. All of this was accomplished through the active participation of the people, making them aware of the importance of the environment and its connection to their general welfare. Sankara announced that from 10 February to 20 March 1986 "more than 35,000 peasants . . . will take intensive, basic courses on the subjects of economic management and environmental organization and maintenance." However, Burkina Faso's efforts would fail if the rest of the world did not cooperate and do its part. Sankara proclaimed, "We are not against progress, but we do not want progress that is anarchic and criminally neglects the rights of others." He proposed that governments take one percent of the money currently being invested in projects to search for life on other planets and direct it toward financing projects to save trees and lives. The CNR leader said, "Our struggle for the trees and forests is first and foremost a democratic and popular struggle. . . . [It] is above all a struggle against imperialism." Sankara told the conference "The spread of the desert no longer knows any borders."[41] Sankara explained in a subsequent interview that for the Burkinabè people the fight against the advance of the desert "poses a question of justice and equity."[42]

The campaign for women's liberation also continued to be a central focus of the CNR in 1986. As Jaffré states, "The condition of women was not able to fundamentally evolve in four years, but the question [of women's liberation] was no longer a taboo subject." The CNR extended credit to women for social programs as well as to start small enterprises. Numerous radio programs and articles in Bamouni's *Sidwaya* advocated an end to female circumcision (genital mutilation), promoted sex education, and explained the importance of using contraception to prevent the spread of disease as well as manage reproduction. However, resistance to those measures was intense across Burkina Faso, and progress beyond the appointment of women to leadership positions at all levels of government was limited.⁴³

Cinema's Role in the Formation of Dignified People

The battle for women's equality was integral to the essential project of the Democratic and Popular Revolution to create a new revolutionary culture that transcended colonial-era alienation and restored dignity to the person. Fanon explains, "A national culture . . . is the result of internal and external tensions exerted over society as a whole and at every level of that society. . . . The condition of its existence is therefore the national liberation and the renaissance of the state."⁴⁴ The alienated subject that enabled neocolonialism to persist in its oppression of the Burkinabè people had to be dissolved in the struggle to make a new world. That process began with forging new mentalities and was realized through the creative energies as expressed in the cinematic field and other cultural practices. Sankara asserted, "The human being is total. And culture is a form of expression where the human being frees itself." Responding to a question from *L'Autre Journal* about the need to prioritize feeding, educating, and sheltering the people, the Burkinabè president explained, "There is no hierarchy to make. People do not live only on bread. . . . So, material satisfaction is not enough. . . . We do not want a people sad and without passions." Sankara said, providing the people with the means and outlets to create and consume culture enabled the Burkinabè "to express their liberty. They would be able to speak their pains, their joys. That is why we are very attached to culture. One cannot make a revolution if one does not believe in humanity, with the romanticism that this entails."⁴⁵

The cinema industrial complex was critical to the advancement of that agenda, and in 1986, the CNR continued to invest significant fiscal and human resources in that direction. One recipient of that support was the Mauritanian filmmaker Med Hondo, a pioneer of African cinema and advocate of Third Cinema's revolutionary film theory. His epic *Sarraounia* (1986) was shot entirely in Burkina Faso. It tells the story of Sarraounia, queen of the Anzas, who battled invading French colonial troops in the 1890s in what is today northern Nigeria and Cameroon. She is an accomplished warrior, skilled political leader, and fierce defender of her people's independence. Hondo's ordeal in making what Ukadike describes as "a landmark of African cinema" speaks to the difficulties that confronted African cineastes as well as the important role played by the Burkinabè Revolution in mitigating those problems and reinvigorating the entire cinematic field in Africa. Originally set to be shot in Niger with that government's assistance, the contract was mysteriously terminated just as Hondo was prepared to begin shooting. He then remarks to Ukadike that "one day, during FESPACO [1985], I had the opportunity of being invited . . . for a drink by . . . Captain Thomas Sankara." The CNR leader was aware of Hondo's struggles with Niger's government and told the Mauritanian cineaste that he could film in Burkina Faso. The revolutionary government worked to arrange Hondo with funding, even reaching out to France. However, the French government attached outrageous conditions in return for its investment that included distribution rights and a significant portion of the royalties. Hondo went back to Sankara who then brokered a loan through the Ministry of Finance "because, in his view, this film must be made." Upon its release, France censored the *Sarraounia*, and it was difficult to get it distributed in Europe and North America. It was widely screened in Burkina Faso and would win the Étalon de Yennenga at the 1987 FESPACO.[46]

The intervention of Sankara's government to make the film possible validated FEPACI's position that "the state must take a leading role in building a national cinema free of the shackles of censorship or any other form of coercion likely to diminish the filmmakers' creative scope and the democratic and responsible exercise of their profession."[47] Moreover, *Sarraounia* responded to the need to fight imperialism's "deculturalization" of Third World peoples that occurs through "depersonalizing their peoples, of discrediting their culture . . . and of disfiguring their history." The Resolutions of the Third World Filmmakers' Meeting in 1973 argued then that "action must be taken to seize from imperialism the means to influence ideologically, and forge new methods adapted in content and form to the interests of the struggle of their peoples."[48] Hondo's film advanced that project through animating a hero from Africa's recent history who pointedly fought the colonizers and moreover was a woman, which undermined the patriarchal representation and oppression of women, which the Burkinabè Revolution sought to dismantle. As Dupré notes, the film demonstrated the unity of purpose between African filmmakers and the CNR and their cooperation to promote the cause of liberation for all peoples.[49] The Burkinabè government also funded Cissé's *Yeelen* (1987) and assisted with Idrissa Ouédraogo's first feature *Yam Daabo* (1987).

Beyond promoting the work of established cineastes, the CNR created programs to permit new voices to enter the filmmaking field, especially within Burkina Faso. Jaffré highlights a decision in April 1986 "to grant from now on the approval of the state to the Burkinabè cineastes for bank loans" to assist in the expansion of the country's cinema industry. That year Burkina Faso produced six socio-educational films, three documentaries, and five full-length feature films.[50] One documentary produced and distributed in that period was Idrissa Ouédraogo's *Issa le tisserand*, a film about a weaver forced to sell Western clothes to survive. It illustrated how imports destroyed local production. The short film indicates that all the materials and skills for a vibrant textile industry are present within Burkina Faso. However, it is prevented from developing because of the imperialist capitalist system that generates dependency among people like the Burkinabè. Other motion pictures distributed by the Burkinabè government at that time were *Desebagato* (made in cooperation with Cuba) and Idrissa Ouédraogo's *Yam Daabo*, both of which deal with issues of poverty, relations between urban workers and peasants, and the impact of the climate crisis on local economies.[51]

Unfortunately, those successes were offset by the unexpected closure of INAFEC in 1986 "for economic reasons." According to Dupré, the school had trained over two hundred professionals in various aspects of filmmaking during its ten-year lifespan.[52] The CNR vastly increased funding for the institute and created an array of scholarships and grants to finance students' studies, but it was not enough to counter the growing fiscal crisis in which the revolutionary state found itself. Nacro was one of its last graduates, another indication of the importance placed by the Democratic and Popular Revolution on the education of women and their promotion into professions previously reserved to men.

In addition to film, the CNR also sought to use print media to hold government officials accountable to the people. Sankara argued that it was critical to develop a press that challenged the privileges of those in power, that reflected the values and the spirit of the revolution, and that would also "touch the international sensibility." In April 1986, the Burkinabè president hinted at the prospect of founding a different kind of paper that was critical, satirical even. Sankara wanted a space that could facilitate permanent debate to prevent the revolution from becoming stale or dogmatic. "However," the CNR president warned, "the debate does not have for a goal to reinforce our enemies, it has for its goal the better understanding of our ideas to fight better."[53] Two months later, in June 1986, the satirical and humorous newspaper *L'Intrus* was launched with much fanfare. Jean Hubert Bazié, a long-time journalist in radio and ally of Sankara, was its director general. Sankara was one of the most frequent contributors, often poking fun at himself as well as his colleagues in the CNR.[54]

The Five-Year Plan of Popular Development (PQDP)

The birth of *L'Intrus* coincided with the final stages of creating Burkina Faso's first economic plan. Sankara launched the process on 3 April 1985, and the CNR laid out a rigorous procedure for its elaboration. CDR were instructed to put forward the needs and potential resources (human and material) from each village, workspace, school, and government office so that they could be collated and reconciled into a workable blueprint for national development. That was accomplished by September 1985, and the ideas were put before national sectoral commissions to coordinate and prioritize them, which were then sent back to the base. In January 1986, the sectoral commissions revised their plans, and in March 1986, the Ministry of Planning synthesized the plans and sent the reports to the provinces for more detailed elaboration. From 24–27 June 1986, the National Council of the Plan met and adopted its final blueprint, which was taken up by the CNR for final approval and implementation. The Five-Year Plan of Popular Development (Plan quinquennal de développement populaire, PQDP) went into effect on 4 August 1986 and was to run through 1990.[55] The ULCR originally headed the process of developing the PQDP through Kader Cissé's leadership of the Revolutionary Economic and Social Council. However, by the time the plan was finalized in 1986, Henri Zongo (OMR), one of the Coordinators, oversaw bringing together the various ministries, agencies, and institutions involved in fulfilling the economic plan. This further indicated the military's increasingly dominant position in the Burkinabè government.[56]

President Sankara announced the PQDP on 4 August 1986 and recounted the successes of the revolution to that point. However, he noted, there have been errors that required the attention of the state and the people to correct if the revolution were to continue to advance. Sankara pointed out the critical role to be played by the Pioneers, the UFB, and the UNAB in the "consolidation of the popular bases of the Revolution." However, he urged the people to prevent the revolution from becoming mere words and instead become a fact in the very existence of everyone's daily lives. Sankara warned that the enemies of the revolution continued their efforts to derail the aspirations of the Burkinabè people, from inside and outside the country. To resist them, it was essential to "change the conditions of life and work of the popular masses." Returning to the theme advanced at the CDR Congress in April 1986, Sankara encouraged the people to consume what they produce, to avoid dependence on the outside world, to expand the domain of their productive activities, and to be prepared to sacrifice to preserve Burkina Faso's sovereignty. He said, "We are going to proclaim: Prefabricated development: No! Customized development: Yes!" The economic plan, Sankara explained, was the result of careful and deliberate consultation with all sectors of society. He encouraged the people to work hard and in a disciplined manner to achieve the objectives of the PQDP. The Revolutionary Economic and Social Council would oversee its implementation and make sure targets were being met on time. Sankara concluded, "Forward for the Five-Year Plan of Popular Development! For economic independence! For political and cultural independence! For the liberation of Africa! For Africa for the Africans! For real power to the dignified people, to the people who struggle! Country or Death, we will win!"[57]

The plan was oriented toward rural improvement with 42.5 percent of capital commitments directed toward agriculture and a further 20.8 percent aimed at improving the country's infrastructure, specifically roads, railroads, and communications. By 1990, the plan was to have set Burkina Faso firmly on the path to economic self-sufficiency and self-directed economic development. However, as Kyélem de Tambèla observes, there was a contradiction built into the PQDP. Burkina Faso did not have the capital to finance the programs. Therefore, it would have to increase the level of borrowing from the outside world. He writes, "It is a paradox that to want to construct an independent economy relying essentially on the exterior which, on the contrary, should only be used for extra funds." In its design and ambition, the PQDP was not "realistic" given the circumstances of the country in 1986.[58]

To secure financing for the plan, the CNR entered negotiations with the IMF and World Bank to fund specific development programs that were integral to the overall PQDP. The Burkinabè government signed an agreement with the World

Bank on 21 May 1985 to finance the construction of primary schools in rural areas at a cost of over $23 million with roughly $21 million coming from the World Bank. The project was to begin in June 1986; however, the lender refused to release the funds because Sankara would not accept the terms of structural adjustment that the World Bank (pressured by the IMF) sought to impose on Burkina Faso. That money was not disbursed until October 1987, after Sankara's assassination. The World Bank claimed in a subsequent report that "the project start-up was delayed by 16 months (from June 1986 to October 1987) due to the political changes in Burkina Faso."[59] This, obviously, was not true as there was no political change in the country's leadership until October 1987. As Jaffré notes, "Throughout the revolutionary period, Burkina Faso faced hostility, even pressure from the donors" leading to conflict between the two.[60] The Burkinabè government signed two other agreements with the World Bank in 1985. One was a "Fertilizer and Food Policy Credit Project" of nearly $14 million signed on 26 February 1985 that was delayed several times as the World Bank attempted to impose more conditions on the CNR as part of the implementation strategy. The funds were partially released late in 1985.[61] The other was a "Health Services Development" project signed on 11 June 1985 for nearly $27 million that included financing for anti-malaria programs as well as family planning services. The World Bank noted that "very little activity was carried out under the project in the first two years of its implementation." The lender blamed the government for this lack of activity since it wanted to prioritize "funds to finance activities in the social sector" and noted that "a much stronger policy dialogue" emerged in the early 1990s that led to smoother relations between Burkina Faso and the World Bank.[62] Relations with the IMF were even worse. The CNR did not take out any additional loans from the IMF during the entire period of Sankara's presidency, although it continued to make payments on the debt incurred by previous governments. It remanded nearly $8 million to the lender between 1984 and 1987. Only in 1991 did Burkina Faso accept a massive new loan from the IMF of over $6 million and agree to its structural adjustment program.[63]

The difficulties in obtaining external capital for its development plans led the CNR to rely more extensively on measures to extract wealth from its own people to finance the PQDP. In January 1986, it announced the Popular Investment Effort (l'Effort populaire d'investissements, EPI), which would require an obligatory contribution of either one month or half a month's salary from all public workers. Military officers were scheduled to contribute the most to the EPI, with lesser amounts coming from junior officers and civilian government employees. A third tier was created for the lowest-paid employees who were expected to contribute 5 percent of their annual wages. According to the CNR, "[The EPI] should translate the will and the determination of the salaried employees to life with the masses and to vanquish with the masses all the problems and all the obstacles that emerge to [prevent] the fulfillment [of the aspirations] of the people."[64] However, the EPI was unpopular, especially within the military. Resistance to its implementation grew in the armed forces, which extended into the CNR as well. Consequently, the program was terminated in early 1987.[65]

Not willing to relent on having the military and other civil servants contribute to the development plan, Sankara imposed new regulations on 24 October 1986 that delineated the proper behavior of government employees. This was a further step in the campaign by the CNR to root out corruption among public officials as both a means to inculcate new values and work habits in society as well as a cost-saving measure to streamline government expenditures. Those measures were supplemented by further fiscal monitoring and restrictions of public sector workers on 1 January 1987 that reclassified their salaries downward to reduce the budgetary commitments of the state.[66]

The continued caustic confrontations between the ULCR and UCB spilled into the direction of the PQDP. Kader Cissé was one of the sharpest critics of Valère Somé's acceptance of Sankara's compromise over the disputed control of the CDR at the University of Ouagadougou. In the face of continued criticism of both Pierre Ouédraogo and Valère Somé from Kader Cissé and other dissidents within the ULCR, Sankara decided in November 1986 to appoint Kader Cissé, Moïse Traoré, and Train Raymond Pooda as high commissioners to remote provinces of Burkina Faso, a move reminiscent of the demotion of PAI cabinet members in August 1984. They refused the reassignment upon which Sankara accused them of "refusing to serve the peasant masses."[67] Kader Cissé and Moïse Traoré were thereupon dismissed from the Revolutionary Economic and Social Council. This intensified the schism within the ULCR and resulted in the formation of the ULC–*La Flamme* on 2 February 1987, which definitively broke from Valère Somé, further isolating him and Sankara within the government. It also left Captain Henri Zongo (OMR), minister of planning, in charge of the country's economy, which included management of the PQDP. This was another sign of the military officers' growing prominence in the government and throughout Burkinabè society throughout 1986.[68]

By far the greatest challenge to the success of the PQDP, however, was Burkina Faso's deepening debt crisis. By the end of 1986, the external debt stood at $640 million, a 25 percent increase over the previous year and the second straight year of approximately 25 percent jumps.[69] This put more pressure on the government to accept the conditions associated with loans from the IMF and World Bank. This Sankara would not do under any circumstances.[70] The CNR leader expressed confidence that the success of the self-directed development strategy would produce outcomes that enabled the country to avoid being subjected to structural adjustment and its concomitant dependency on the imperialist powers. The country was growing and living standards were improving by the end of 1986. Burkina Faso's GDP grew to $2.036 billion in 1986, a 31 percent leap from 1985 and the largest in the country's history. After bottoming out at $210 in 1984 and 1985, Burkina Faso's per capita GNI grew to $240 in 1986, returning to 1983 levels, the first annual increase since 1980. While the economy grew and the people's share of it increased, the country's carbon dioxide emissions continued to fall, dropping to 0.061 metric tons per capita in 1986, a drop from 0.081 metric tons per capita in 1983. Finally, life expectancy at birth ticked up to 49.492, an improvement of one full year since 1983.[71] According to the IMF, Burkina Faso experienced negative inflation in 1986 with prices dropping 2.7 percent while the real GDP grew at a brisk 8 percent following on from the 11.3 percent achieved in 1985.[72]

Breaking the Hold of Imperialism to Meet the People's Needs

Those positive results, however, could only be sustained and built upon if the neocolonialist framework of international relations were replaced by a system based on people-to-people solidarity and mutual assistance. Symbolic of that project was the CNR's effort to reconfigure Burkina Faso's connections to France, especially the desire to undo and renegotiate the treaty of cooperation signed between the two countries on 24 April 1961. As discussed earlier, shortly after taking power the CNR announced that it would not abide by the existing cooperation treaty and opened negotiations to reframe it. Those discussions stalled for more than two years over disputes about France's relationship with apartheid South Africa and its provision of military support to countries in

West Africa that were hostile to the Burkinabè Revolution. Then at the end of 1985, France passed new immigration laws that imposed a visa requirement on all Africans entering the country, for the first time including those from the former French colonies. The CNR responded by requiring French citizens to obtain a visa to visit Burkina Faso.[73]

Finally, on 4 February 1986, France and Burkina Faso signed a new agreement. The treaty released French funds for the dam project at Kompienga as well as retained the deployment of military instructors in Burkina Faso. However, France refused to move its embassy from the security perimeter of the Burkinabè presidential palace. The embassy was only fifty meters outside the seat of power creating the impression of being an overseer to the Burkinabè government. France demanded the CNR build a new compound before it would relocate its diplomatic staff. They also did not resolve the visa issue. Therefore, citizens of each country henceforward needed a visa to enter the other. France also refused to renew the judicial cooperation aspects of the previous treaty, claiming that it could not recognize the "popular justice" of the Burkinabè Revolution, specifically the convocation of the TPR.[74]

The CNR also sought to ease tensions with Côte d'Ivoire. The opening came when Houphouët-Boigny helped to bring the Christmas War to a conclusion. The CNR hosted the Ivoirian leader on a state visit to Burkina Faso on 26–27 March 1986 during the ECOWAS/CEDEAO summit. In his speech, Sankara noted Houphouët-Boigny's critical role in the fight for independence from France through his leadership of the RDA and thanked his guest for his support of Burkina Faso's presidency of ECOWAS/CEDEAO. Following their meeting Côte d'Ivoire agreed to provide aid to renovate and expand the airport at Bobo-Dioulasso and contribute other assistance for drought relief in the Sahel. In exchange, Englebert intimates that there was an implicit understanding that Sankara would moderate the revolutionary language directed at Côte d'Ivoire and other countries in the region.[75]

However, even as Sankara and Houphouët-Boigny moved to overcome some of their differences, global events caused renewed tensions between the imperialist camp and the developing countries. Elections in France on 16 March 1986 returned a conservative majority to the National Assembly and produced a shift in that country's foreign relations in a more hostile direction toward revolutionary, progressive, or socialist states and movements. Then on 15 April 1986, U.S. President Reagan ordered air bombardments of Libya in retaliation for its suspected role in the bombing of a disco in Berlin days earlier. The attack led to the deaths of forty-five Libyans, including Qaddafi's adopted daughter and two U.S. pilots. The attack ratcheted tensions around the world leading to a UN General Assembly vote to condemn the United States, denunciations from the Non-Aligned Movement and the OAU, as well as statements of outrage from China, the Soviet Union, and other countries, including Burkina Faso.[76]

In southern Africa on 19 May 1986, South Africa escalated its aggression across the entire region with coordinated strikes against Zambia, Zimbabwe, and Botswana as well as renewed invasions of Angola in a wider effort to crush the anti-apartheid uprising unfolding within South Africa. As the *New York Times* reported on 20 May 1986, "The American raid on Libya last month may have emboldened the South Africans, since Pretoria depicts its campaign as part of an international effort against terrorism."[77] In an interview with Radio Havana Cuba, Sankara described apartheid as "a form of Nazism. Apartheid is a living element of imperialism in our times." He called for an intensification of the struggle to overthrow the racist regime in Pretoria as part of the broader fight to end the exploitation of people by other people. The Burkinabè president called on the people of the world to join forces to "exterminate this cancer that oppresses not only Africa but also all of humanity."[78] The campaign to end apartheid in South Africa was a centerpiece of the CNR's foreign policy from its inception. It symbolized the role that Burkina Faso sought as part of its global engagement to overcome imperialism and realize the liberation of humanity. MOBRAP was one of the mass organizations created by the revolutionary government to mobilize its people in solidarity with those fighting for freedom around the world. At the 1985 FESPACO, it held meetings with the ANC and other liberation movements to coordinate activities and build networks of solidarity.[79] Throughout South Africa's escalation of violence in 1986, MOBRAP staged numerous demonstrations in support of those resisting the racist regime. It was also another area in which Burkina Faso and Cuba found common cause on the world stage. Castro committed his entire country to the destruction of apartheid, which he described as "the most beautiful cause."[80]

Tensions also ratcheted up in West Africa as well through the summer and fall of 1986. Sankara cut short a visit to Nigeria in June 1986, following rumors of a coup plot in Burkina Faso against his government. The CNR accused France and its partners in West Africa of being behind the attempted overthrow of the Democratic and Popular Revolution. In August 1986, the Burkinabè government demanded that France recall its ambassador for meddling in the country's internal affairs. The French government refused. Then dissidents in Togo's military, a close ally of France and Côte d'Ivoire, attempted to topple the dictatorship of Gnassingbé Eyadéma on 23–24 September 1986. Eyadéma declared that Ghana and Burkina Faso were behind the coup. Sankara responded by denouncing Togo's strongman for his involvement in several efforts to overthrow the CNR since 1983, in collusion with France and Côte d'Ivoire.[81] France dispatched emergency military aid to Togo as did Mobutu Sese Seko of Zaire. French Prime Minister Jacques Chirac made strident pronouncements about the security of Eyadéma's regime and pledged to stand side-by-side with Togo against any effort to overthrow the rightist regime.[82] Once more, the Burkinabè government confronted the prospect of invasion from without to overthrow the revolution. Those regional tensions increased anxiety within the military and contributed to the officers' push to dominate the state. They also undermined Sankara's position within the CNR since he had spent a year reaching out to neighboring governments, France, and internal critics to precisely avoid the situation in which Burkina Faso found itself at the end of 1986. Those efforts appeared to have failed and emboldened the CNR's enemies.[83]

During those mounting threats, Sankara engaged in whirlwind diplomacy to shore up support for the revolution among Burkina Faso's allies. In August 1986, he welcomed Daniel Ortega, president of Nicaragua and leader of that country's anti-imperialist revolution in 1979, to Ouagadougou for a state visit, a clear affront to the United States, which was engaged at that time in a massive effort to overthrow the Sandinista regime. Sankara expressed support for the Nicaraguan Revolution and pledged, "We intend to join forces to safeguard and defend this ideal at a time when imperialism is arrogantly spreading its tentacles." The CNR leader reasserted Burkina Faso's commitment to non-alignment in the Cold War, but that did not mean the revolutionary government would hesitate to stand with those peoples fighting imperialism. Sankara asserted, "Though we are willing to cooperate with both (the USSR and U.S.), we demand the right to be different." The Burkinabè president said, "We denounce the aggression against Nicaragua as we protest that perpetrated against Libya and the Frontline States. We denounce the invasion of Grenada as we do the occupation of Namibia."[84]

Sankara carried that message to the Eighth Summit of the Movement of Non-Aligned Countries in Zimbabwe, 1–6 September 1986. In his address on

3 September 1986, Sankara pleaded for a more activist stance on the part of the non-aligned community in support of liberation struggles as well as in defense of progressive and revolutionary states. He said, "We believe the world is divided into two antagonistic camps: the camp of the exploiters and the camp of the exploited." He called on the Non-Aligned Movement to develop a permanent struggle against those powers that would subjugate the countries who fought dearly for their recent independence. Sankara expressed his feeling of disappointment at the failure of the Non-Aligned Movement to fulfill its self-proclaimed historic destiny. He implored the dignitaries to wake up to their duty and do something about the brutal apartheid government in South Africa, the ongoing occupation of Namibia, and the oppression of the Palestinian people. He asked, "What is the Non-Aligned Movement doing?" Sankara urged them to go beyond speeches denouncing the attacks on the Frontline States, messages of condolences to the victims of imperialist aggression, or other symbolic acts that do not change the dynamic on the ground. He said there must be unity when confronting international creditors over the debt because "we're all making repayments in whatever way the capitalists wish, because we're disunited." Sankara forcefully called for a cessation of repayment on the international debt because "we cannot continue to repay it," and because the nature of the obligation is inherently unjust. He also discussed the climate crisis pointing out the global advance of the deserts, the spread of insect infestations, and irregularities in the weather patterns making agriculture unsustainable in a growing part of the world. Sankara reminded his audience that the stances and actions they take then will be recalled by future generations and judged accordingly.[85]

Sankara's speech in Harare synthesized the myriad escalations against developing countries since the spring of 1986 and indicated his deepening frustration with those countries who the Burkinabè revolutionaries expected to be their natural allies in resisting imperialism. He also gave his address amid the rift over control of the CDR at the University of Ouagadougou that imperiled the CNR's unity. Consequently, it reflected the dangers that Burkina Faso's government faced internally and externally. The inaction by the delegates at Harare to the global crises paralleled Sankara's own incapacity to direct the revolution at home and his isolation among the forces that brought the CNR to power in 1983.

After a brief stop back in Ouagadougou where Sankara mediated the dispute between Valère Somé and Pierre Ouédraogo, the president headed a large delegation on a lengthy visit to the Soviet Union, led since March 1985 by Mikhail Gorbachev. From 6 to 12 October 1986 over fifty representatives of the Burkinabè government met with leaders of the Soviet administration, officials of the Communist Party of the Soviet Union, and representatives of its youth section, the Komsomol. During that trip, Gorbachev's government pledged increased economic and military aid to Burkina Faso. Sankara indicated his favor with the reform programs Gorbachev had launched within the Soviet Union (perestroika and glasnost) since it aligned with his own interpretation of the revolutionary process. Symbolic of their new relationship, Burkina Faso voted with the USSR at the UN when the United States pushed resolutions condemning the Soviet Union's role in Afghanistan. The CNR also released the CSB leader and member of the pro-Soviet PAI Soumane Touré from prison on 26 October 1986.[86]

Sankara followed that trip with visits to Cuba and Nicaragua, 8–9 November 1986. A new accord between Burkina Faso and Cuba that was signed in February 1987 allowed over six hundred Burkinabè pioneers to study in Cuba. Castro's government augmented the number of doctors, teachers, and advisors sent to Burkina Faso while also expanding its technical assistance for a range of activities that included further literacy operations and construction of light manufacturing facilities.[87] Other Burkinabè delegations journeyed to North Korea. In September 1985, North Korea and Burkina Faso signed a cooperation treaty that provided much-needed agricultural assistance. North Korea built or financed the construction of sixty water retention facilities, provided material and capital for a two hundred–bed hospital and many smaller clinics, and was a significant donor to the program to build new housing. In February 1986, North Korea provided another round of agricultural assistance through provision of heavy equipment. Then on 20 September 1986, the two governments agreed to a new cultural exchange program that enabled Burkina Faso to import over 4,400 books on subjects including peasant conditions, industrialization, socialist economic transformation, and how to build "organs of popular power."[88] Those agreements enabled the Democratic and Popular Revolution to maintain its momentum despite the rising international tensions and divisions within the CNR. As Sankara put it, "There is no better strategy than the reinforcement of South-South cooperation in the matter of technical assistance."[89]

The Great Debate between Sankara and Mitterrand

Shortly after Sankara's visit to Cuba and Nicaragua, the CNR hosted French President Mitterrand on his first official visit to Burkina Faso since the August 1983 Revolution. In October 1986, Guy Penne, President Mitterrand's special advisor for African affairs was replaced by Jean-Christophe Mitterrand, the French leader's son. He accompanied his father to Burkina Faso in November 1986. In the evening of 17 November 1986, Sankara hosted his visitor during a state dinner. Sankara gave a welcome speech that began with an exposition of the revolution's achievements over the previous three years. He noted the jump in the number of students attending school from 10 to 22 percent, the irrigation projects that brought water to farms and vastly increased the amount of potable water for the people, the improvements in health care that provided at least a minimum of medical attention to the most remote parts of the country, the vaccination program, and so on. Sankara expressed his hope that the French president would "get to know these realities" and take the truth back to France with him. The CNR leader turned to international affairs and cited a litany of conflicts from the Palestinian issue to imperialist aggression against Nicaragua. He highlighted the fight to end apartheid in South Africa and invoked his friend Samora Machel, leader of Mozambique, who died in a mysterious plane crash the previous month, as a hero in that struggle. Sankara demanded that France, as a country advocating peace and standing in a long tradition of human rights, take the side of justice, saying it had a special role to play to end the suffering of the victims of imperialism. Sankara continued, "It is in this context, Mr. François Mitterrand, that we did not understand how bandits like Jonas Savimbi (leader of the South-African backed UNITA in Angola) and killers like [South African Prime Minister] Pieter Botha, have been allowed to travel up and down France." The Burkinabè president added, "All those who have made it possible for them to carry out these actions will bear full responsibility here and everywhere, today and forever." Sankara explained that he would be willing to sign a military pact with France on the condition that the weapons would be transited directly to those fighting to overthrow apartheid in South Africa.[90]

Sankara then raised the issue of international debt, characterizing it as a major inhibitor to the development of countries such as Burkina Faso. He said, "We are not at all responsible for these loans, these debts of yesterday." He turned to President Mitterrand and implored him to join with Burkina Faso to resist these debts and free up the energies of people around the world to develop their societies and live lives of dignity. Sankara reminded his visitor of the plight of African immigrants in France who do honest work and contribute to France's economy yet are discriminated against and abused because of their race or place of origin. Finally, the CNR leader spoke of the behavior of some French citizens in Burkina Faso who have spread lies about the Burkinabè Revolution and worked to undermine its objectives. Sankara asked his guests to raise their glasses to "drink to friendship and to unity in struggle against those who, here, in France, and elsewhere, exploit us and oppress us."[91]

In a 2017 interview Jean-Christophe Mitterrand recalled the events of that encounter. He said that François Mitterrand "appreciated strong characters like Sankara." Jean-Christophe Mitterrand continued, "I remember his famous speech during the official visit of my father to Ouagadougou, 17 November 1986, where he spoke for an hour without a single note. In response, François Mitterrand put aside the speech he had prepared and responded point by point to Sankara. It was a captivating debate."[92] Alexandra Reza describes François Mitterrand as listening to the speech stoically staring straight ahead with hardly any movement. The video of the event shows a leader unaccustomed to being addressed so frankly and forcefully by the head of an African country.[93] The French president then rose and asked if he could speak in response to the points raised by the Burkinabè leader. Appearing almost nervous, François Mitterrand said, "This is a somewhat troublesome man, Thomas Sankara."[94] France's leader asserted the Burkinabè president had a sharp tongue and was going too far in his accusations, especially against France. François Mitterrand tried to make the comment appear as if it was part of a jocular exchange by reaching a hand toward the now-seated Sankara, but the Burkinabè leader did not respond.[95] France's president stated, "With him it is not possible to sleep in peace. He does not leave us with a tranquil conscience." President Mitterrand defended his actions and positions, none of which Sankara found exculpatory for legitimizing the leaders of apartheid South Africa and its agents.[96]

The visit generated a firestorm of controversy. In France, the political right was livid at Sankara's "impertinence" toward the leader of the former colonial power. François Mitterrand faced growing pressure from Chirac's government to act against the upstart revolutionary leader.[97] The French ambassador to Burkina Faso, Jacques Le Blanc, indicated that there was some frustration with Sankara's insistence that he was correct on all things without considering that

France might have an honest difference of opinion but did not suggest that this opened any hostility between the two countries.[98]

Regardless, relations between the two countries deteriorated notably in the ensuing months. On 2 December 1986, Burkina Faso voted in favor of UN Resolution 41/41A to add New Caledonia to the list of unfree territories and recognize its right to independence, a significant diplomatic rebuke directed at France, the colonial ruler of the territory that was then the site of a bitter armed conflict. Two weeks later, France's National Assembly voted overwhelmingly to cut all aid to Burkina Faso. That vote coincided with the visit of Jacques Foccart to Burkina Faso, 16–17 December 1986. Foccart was a notorious imperialist who had served many French presidents from the establishment of the Fifth Republic in 1958, advising them on African affairs. He was deeply involved in espionage networks spread throughout the former French colonial empire and was directly involved in many military coups after 1960. When Jacques Chirac became prime minister in March 1986, he recalled Foccart from retirement as his advisor on African affairs, the counterpart to Jean-Christophe Mitterrand for the president. As Frédéric Marchand described Foccart, "He is a real crocodile, he specializes in the troubled Franco-African waters." Foccart was very close to Houphouët-Boigny as well as Eyadéma. Consequently, while François Mitterrand's office may have brushed aside the 17 November 1986 exchange, Chirac's office appeared to stir into activity regarding Africa and especially Burkina Faso. According to Marchand, Chirac gave Foccart "one precise mission: to affirm France's lost and/or contested authority in West Africa." In that regard, he turned to his long-time partner Houphouët-Boigny, the "appointed representative of the metropolis in the West African zone."[99] With the start of 1987, the Burkinabè Revolution faced unprecedented challenges from within and without while trying to keep the momentum going toward a complete transformation of society and its people.

6

Twilight of the Revolution and Sankara's Murder

(1986–1987)

ON 5 JULY 1987, PRESIDENT THOMAS SANKARA GAVE AN INTERVIEW TO AN Ivoirian journalist in which he said, "The Burkinabè Revolution is a part of the movement toward the transformation of humanity. . . . [It has] its specificities and nuances. Now it must be said right away that the Burkinabè Revolution is not a copy of any other revolution." Sankara quoted the Bolshevik leader Lenin when he stated, "Each revolution must follow the path that is the most appropriate." The CNR leader admitted that the Democratic and Popular Revolution was in a state of crisis. Nevertheless, Sankara was optimistic that the revolution would survive its present troubles because it was founded on the mobilization of the masses, not simply the power of the military. He did not believe it would be possible to reverse the regime through a military coup because the people would not allow it. Sankara added, though, that the threat to the revolution was not only internal. He noted, "We are menaced by invasion from other armies, other powers." To mitigate against the external threats, the CNR intensified its policy of achieving economic self-sufficiency, especially in food production during 1987.[1] As the walls closed in on the revolution from the outside and the

CNR experienced a series of ever-deeper schisms that debilitated its functioning, Sankara pushed the Burkinabè people to reengage in the project of the radical transformation of the society and of the person to defend the revolutionary process from the forces undermining it.

By 1987, the Burkinabè Revolution had become a beacon of hope, an inspiration across Africa and around the world. For many inside and outside Burkina Faso, Sankara had come to embody the revolution. Much had become invested in his person, and the CNR leader's increasing unilateralism in policy matters and reliance on personal friendships to conduct government business only reinforced that perception. As one writer cited by the *New York Times* expressed it, "Sankara incarnates African youth. Elevated, poised, incisive. It is the style of the black man of the modern age. After so many cruel deceptions and wounds inflicted on Africans by so-called 'revolutionary' leaders, I cannot help but be sympathetic to the style and thought of Thomas Sankara."[2] Another journalist wrote, "Sankara [was] extremely popular within the country as well as around the continent for his honest leadership and commitment to the welfare of his impoverished people."[3]

However, Sankara's mediation of disputes among the groups that comprised the CNR was often rewarded by the hostility of all those involved, and his decisions were frequently ignored. In response, the Burkinabè president tended to go around and over the heads of those who comprised the revolutionary government, and throughout 1987, he appealed directly to the people to implement the goals of the Democratic and Popular Revolution. Simultaneously, the military asserted a stranglehold over the state even as Sankara lost influence among the officers he had brought together in alliance with the civilian revolutionary groups in the coalition that took power on 4 August 1983. This chapter charts the final tumultuous year of the Burkinabè Revolution as the CNR became dysfunctional and Sankara and his few remaining allies were increasingly isolated in the government. In that environment, enthusiasm for the revolution waned among the Burkinabè people, the pace of progress in many of its social programs slowed, and the fiscal crisis reached the breaking point. President Sankara decided that the only hope to salvage the revolution was to push more aggressively the project of transforming the people's mentality.

Paralysis of the Revolutionary State

Relations among the constituent parties of the CNR were toxic by early 1987. On 7 February 1987, Sankara announced the formation of the People's Commission Charged with the Prevention of Corruption (Commission du peuple chargée de la prevention de la corruption, CPPC). The CPPC was comprised of nine members hand-picked by the Burkinabè president. Four came from the CNR, and a minimum of five came from CDR. Its first session was on 20 February 1987 with Sankara presiding. He gave a full accounting of his assets and was followed by several other members of the government. However, some officials refused, and opposition to the CPPC was intense within the CNR.[4] Those charged with corruption included Moïse Traoré and Kader Cissé (both ULC–*La Flamme*), who were dismissed from the cabinet. That move, like the dismissal of the PAI ministers in August 1984, demonstrated Sankara's loyalty to Valère Somé (ULCR). However, their removal unintentionally undermined confidence in the PQDP since both were integral to its formulation and initial implementation, and it opened the door to the formation of a broader political coalition aimed against Valère Somé and by extension President Sankara.[5]

By April 1987, the GCB (former members of the pro-Albanian PCRV) allied with the ULC–*La Flamme* then extended that anti-Valère Somé front to include his arch-nemesis the military-dominated UCB in May 1987. According to Martens, the GCB-ULC–*La Flamme*-UCB alliance was politically aimed at "the line developed by Sankara" regarding policy-orientation and the modality of decision-making within the government. The anti-Sankarists claimed that during the first two years of the revolution, the "communists" had asserted the correct path through the *Discours d'Orientation Politique* and the establishment of the CDR "as organs of the democratic dictatorship of the working class and the petit-bourgeoisie." However, from 1986, the communists had lost influence causing "the disappearance of the hope and the confidence of the people." They pointed to Sankara's decision to rehabilitate the country's former presidents as a sign of the Burkinabè president's abandonment of the revolution's core principles. In contrast, those parties called for a more aggressive move toward socialist construction with the full nationalization of the economy and the collectivization of agriculture. At the head of that coalition stood Compaoré.[6]

Sankara was convinced that the radical rhetoric espoused by the groups coalescing around Compaoré was a mask used to settle personal scores. He argued that their approach to policy implementation would result in the development of a bureaucratized revolutionary state along models imported from abroad. Sankara insisted that the Burkinabè Revolution had to reflect the lived experience of the people and correspond to the current stage of the Democratic and Popular Revolution. He emphasized the need to mobilize the masses and have them direct the revolution to transform the person, a fundamental precondition to real development and independence.[7] As Stoneman writes, "[This] was integral to a process of remaking [Burkina Faso's] identity at a moment of revolutionary change." That transformation was embodied in the country's name, which means Land of Dignified People, or the space of the unalienated subject.[8]

FESPACO 1987 and the Cultural Revolution on the March

That objective informed the theme of the Tenth FESPACO (21–28 February 1987), which was "Cinema and Cultural Identity." Despite the unexpected closure of INAFEC at the end of 1986, the Burkinabè Revolution continued to place the cinema industrial complex at the center of its cultural politics and, as such, at the core of the revolutionary process. Vieyra highlighted the cultural combat characteristic of the atmosphere at the 1987 FESPACO. He writes in his report of the event, "At FESPACO, in the beginning was the cinema, the art of the present. And now around the film, its essential component, is the cultural struggle for the rebirth of African civilization. This is the message of Burkina Faso that will surely meet all the African and progressive countries of the world" and to which they "cannot fail to respond."[9] Dupré observes that the festival's theme was "above all characteristic of Sankarism [that sought] to raise the consciousness of the Black people in its identity and its culture." Dupré quotes Sankara as he explains, "African cinema has to reflect the revolutionary collective memory of our peoples and project their rich experiences in the fight for a more fraternal world that is more just and freer."[10]

As during the previous FESPACO, Sankara was ubiquitous at the 1987 festival. Ukadike writes, "President Sankara brought energizing candor to the Tenth FESPACO."[11] Moreover, the event transpired at a moment of heightened tension with France and its allies in the region. The winner of the grand prize, Hondo's *Sarraounia*, spoke directly to the history of imperial conquest and served to focus public attention on the connections between Africa's past and its present. In that light, the Burkinabè Revolution continued the struggle for independence and people's dignity in the face of oppressive forces from inside and outside the continent. Diawara situates *Sarraounia* as part of the genre of "colonial confrontation" films that "position the spectators to identify with the African people's resistance against European colonialism and imperialistic drives." As such, movies like Hondo's "valorize African cultures to emphasize the dehumanizing effect of colonization which is intent on destroying them."[12] Hondo sought to depict an event that transpired "at a crucial time when Africa's freedom, dignity, and pride were at stake," a moment that corresponded to the context of the mid-1980s. He explained that his motivation stemmed from a desire "to show the true 'historical value of traditional culture' by bringing to light an important period in Africa's history."[13]

The Tenth FESPACO was noted for establishing three major developments in the nature of the festival, all of which reflected the Democratic and Popular Revolution's influence on the trajectory of African cinema more broadly and the participation of filmmakers in the making of the Burkinabè Revolution. One was the inauguration of an ambitious project to create an African-controlled distribution network for the continent's films. As Sankara said at FESPACO, "Whoever controls distribution controls the cinema."[14] The CNR's determination to create a vibrant African film distribution company resulted from the limitations that followed Lamizana's nationalization of the country's movie theaters in 1970.[15] While the Voltaic government had taken control of the country's viewing spaces, it lacked access to films that could be screened in them. That forced Lamizana to accede to demands that the French-based companies continue to provide the products viewed in Upper Volta's movie theaters. The frustrations of African filmmakers with the lack of a viable African-based distribution system and market for their films was reflected in FEPACI's "Niamey Manifesto" in 1982 where the African cineastes declared, "It is not possible to have a viable cinema industry on a national level in Africa." It recommended that "every state should organize, support, safeguard and develop its movie theater market and encourage and collaborate with neighboring states to form a regional common market for the importation and exploitation of films."[16] When Sankara was prime minister during the 1983 FESPACO, the filmmakers created the International Market of African Film (Marché International du Film Africain, MIFA). The concept involved setting up stalls for the sale of African motion pictures, film equipment, and information on African cinema. The first version was small but, at the 1985 FESPACO, vastly expanded and increased further in 1987. In 1985, MIFA was joined with a separate market devoted to television, the first serious attempt to integrate African cinema with that medium. However, evidence of the fiscal pressures that beset the Burkinabè state manifested in the poor organization of the 1987 MIFA, according to Dupré. He adds that "not a single film was sold" during the 1987 FESPACO.[17]

The second major focus of the Tenth FESPACO was the attention paid to oral cultures and tradition in the liberation struggle as well as their transmission via television and radio. The festival included a Colloquium on Oral Tradition and its connection to new media, which Vieyra describes as "the axis of orientation for future African cinematographic production." The objective of such meetings was to bring together "cultural workers to make their work relevant [with regard to] reflecting the African reality [and] be at the service of development."[18] Directors were urged to listen to the people, learn their traditions, and deploy them in a manner that would enhance the people's ability to improve their lives while resisting domination and exploitation. Sankara hosted a meeting of representatives from African television, radio, and filmmakers in the presidential palace where he explained that investment in the expansion of new media across the continent was a matter of achieving economic independence. Promotion of television would, according to the CNR leader, create another outlet for the distribution of African films and function as a vehicle for drawing upon the rich oral culture that animates the continent's societies. Therefore, Sankara urged filmmakers "to adapt themselves" to the new media and to "search for the means of [greater] cooperation with those who work in television."[19] By engaging in those collaborative enterprises, they would contribute to "teaching the people how to love [and make] art." In a wide-ranging interview with Serge Daney of the French newspaper *Libération*, Sankara explained that "cinema is an elegant and pleasant way to develop among African peoples the attitudes we want for the construction of our happiness in Africa." However, the Burkinabè leader cautioned, "A people is never great when they are not aware of the culture, and the culture of a people does not exist so long as [they] themselves cannot amplify together something beautiful." Sankara called for intimate engagement between filmmakers and their audience so that there could be a productive exchange of ideas and perspectives with each enhancing the work of the other. Finally, the Burkinabè president explained, "Cinema, an alliance between sound and image, is for us a useful vector in Africa because we are a culture of orality, but cinema should not be [means] that distills indirectly or in a malicious manner messages of [counterrevolutionary] propaganda."[20]

FESPACO 1987's emphasis on cultural identity both reflected and furthered a trend in African cinematic production evident from the early 1980s. Increasingly, African filmmakers explored historical events in their films as demonstrated in Hondo's *Sarraounia* as well as Sembène's *Camp de Thiaroye* (1988) to reclaim the past and project a vision of African heroic resistance against imperialist oppression. African identity is recovered as a vehicle to overcome neocolonialism and realize a modernity rooted in Africa's needs and in accordance with its traditions. In Hondo's film an African woman leads her people in the fight to retain their sovereignty during the colonial conquest. Sembène's motion picture chronicles African soldiers who fought to liberate humanity from Nazi oppression in rebellion against the brutal conditions in their military camp. In the end, they are horribly massacred by French troops.[21] However, history was also presented from the perspective of rural traditions and the lives of peasants as they struggle against local forms of exploitation while grappling with their place in the modern world. This theme is elaborated by Idrissa Ouédraogo in *Yam Daabo* (1986), Cissé's *Yeelen* (1987), and Kaboré's *Zan Boko* (1988). All, in unique ways, delve into the intimate lives of peasant families, rural communities, and the role of tradition as either a source of power or a barrier to the self-development of the person and society. They continued and deepened a stylistic shift evident in Kaboré's *Wend Kuuni* (1983) that, according to Ukadike, "illustrates how oral narrative techniques affect cinematic structure and how cinematic convention affects oral art." It is part of what he describes as the "Africanization of the film language whereby the narrative style transcends the spoken word."[22]

The third major innovation at FESPACO 1987 was its global emphasis through the addition of new categories and prizes. "Window on the World" showcased films from outside Africa and marked the internationalization of FESPACO. In 1987, FEPACI created the category of "diaspora" the winner of which was awarded the "Paul Robeson Prize," named after the African American communist and civil rights activist. While the prize was announced at the 1987 FESPACO, it was not awarded for the first time until the 1989 version. Dupré writes that these developments had a profound impact on African cinema, "First of all in terms of participation, professionalization, and exposure, which are essential elements [of the cinema industrial complex], and then in terms of the international aura." Cubans were once more highly visible at FESPACO 1987 as were the Soviets and other representatives of progressive and socialist states. The result was increased financing of the festival from outside Africa as well as a significant jump in attendance to 400,000 visitors, double the figure for 1983.[23] One of the highest profile celebrities at FESPACO 1987 was the Nigerian singer and political activist Fela Kuti. At a press conference upon his arrival at the Ouagadougou airport, the musician explained that he came to witness, support, and participate in "the cinema of combat" promoted at the festival. He expressed his support for Sankara and the Burkinabè Revolution as a beacon for Africa.[24] FESPACO's organizers, in collaboration with the CNR, explicitly linked the cultural politics of film to social and economic development, as exemplified in workshops, press events, and seminars held throughout the event. Vieyra remarked in his summary of that year's exhibition, the construction of cultural identity through film must be "in the service of development." Even Jack Lang, France's former minister of culture, led a meeting titled, "Culture and Economy, the Same Struggle."[25]

Women's Liberation and the Fight for Self-Directed Development

The Democratic and Popular Revolution continued its campaign to combat patriarchy and draw more women into revolutionary work. On 8 March 1987, International Women's Day, Sankara in conjunction with the UFB held a mass demonstration in Ouagadougou that highlighted the critical role of women's liberation in the realization of the revolutionary project. The CNR leader admitted the shortcomings of the Democratic and Popular Revolution saying, "[Woman] has been excluded from this joyful procession." Sankara declared, "Starting now, the men and women of Burkina Faso should profoundly change their image of themselves. For they are part of a society that is not only establishing new social relations but is also provoking a cultural transformation, upsetting the relations of authority between men and women and forcing each to rethink the nature of both." The Burkinabè president stated, "Women's emancipation is at the heart of the question of humanity itself." Sankara insisted that women's oppression would not be overcome without abolishing the imperialist capitalist economic system that sustains it. However, he warned, it would be an error to subordinate the fight against women's exploitation to the class struggle. The UFB was an organization to combat sexism within the revolution and raise women's consciousness. Sankara called on the UFB members to "break with the kind of practices and behavior traditionally thought of as female." The CNR leader served notice that every ministry and administrative committee would be assessed according to their success in implementing the goal that justice be done to women. This was critical to destroying the neocolonial state apparatus that has held the people back. To realize the ambitious goals of the revolution, the UFB needed "to carry out vast political and ideological educational campaigns." Sankara asserted, "Comrades, only the revolutionary transformation of our society can create the conditions for your liberation. You are dominated by both imperialism and by men." However, "there is no true social revolution without the liberation of women," and this must be accomplished without resorting to bureaucratic means.[26]

Sankara called for the creation of a National Bureau for the UFB that was independent from the CDR. The new body was to be self-administering and charged with implementing a "Plan of Action" regarding women's emancipation that would check the patriarchal practices of the government ministries and their associated organizations.[27] That was an allusion to the persistent resistance of traditional authorities in rural areas to accepting the authority of women appointed as judges, leaders of CDR, directors of social campaigns, or as heads of economic development programs.[28]

Discontent with the CNR's policies was already spreading in the cities after years of austerity designed to promote development of the countryside. That disquiet was exacerbated with the announcement of the EPI in 1986, which reduced public sector wages by up to 12 percent. According to Arsène Yé, a leading member of the CNR, there was general consternation upon Sankara's announcement of the program. He claims the decision was solely that of Sankara since he was "surprised to hear the proclamation of that measure, as were the functionaries." EPI was terminated at the start of 1987.[29] However, by then, the PQDP was underway and required significant revenue to realize its objectives. Sankara argued the resources the people needed were already present in the country, but self-directed development was thwarted by the dominant classes who remained tethered to the imperialist world. He asked, "What can our workers do if the Burkinabè wealthy organize, encourage, and maintain the importation of competitive products?"[30] The PQDP emphasized the use of materials produced domestically such as cotton, fruits, and vegetables. Agricultural raw materials would enable domestic manufacturing, which would be protected from international competition through increased duties on imports or prohibitions on the sale of certain goods from outside. One critical sector was cotton textile production. The CNR raised tariffs on imported cotton textiles, and the government invested to expand the cultivation of cotton domestically that could feed newly established state-run textile mills supervised by Zongo's Ministry of Economic Development. In addition, on 12 November 1986, the cabinet "following a proposal of the Minister of Culture" announced that, from 1 January 1987, all top administrators of the state were required to wear domestically produced cotton textiles called Faso Dan Fani. The proclamation explained that the measure was "part of the economic struggle for the defense of our national cotton production." It argued that the purchase of foreign goods "functionally contributes" to the profit of foreign factories, to "help alleviate the unemployment of others while adding to unemployment in [Burkina Faso]. It is [also] to nourish the social tensions among us and lower them for others." Kyélem de Tambèla concludes that, "Faso Dan Fani gave birth to an autonomous economic circuit."[31] UNICEF and other international agencies recorded that "the production of cotton increased from 79,000 to 176,000 tons between 1983 and 1987, that of cereals from 1.1 to 1.64 million tons (peaking at 1.93 million in 1986)."[32]

Financing Development and the Neoliberal Capitalist Order

Despite the difficulties and the hardship imposed on certain parts of the Burkinabè population, the economy continued to improve under the CNR. GDP reached $2.37 billion in 1987, school enrollment hit nearly 30 percent that year up from 22 percent four years earlier, carbon dioxide emissions remained well below where they were in 1982, life expectancy improved by two years from 47.81 in 1982 to 49.55 in 1987, and per capita income reached $270.[33] Even with rising incomes and productivity, Burkina Faso experienced negative inflation for the second straight year in 1987. That meant purchasing power throughout the country continued to increase.[34] However, the prospects for further development were constrained by Burkina Faso's mounting external debt. In 1987, the country's total foreign obligations reached over $827 million, a 29 percent jump from the previous year and more than double what it had been in 1983.[35]

On 29 July 1987, Sankara spoke at the twenty-fifth conference of the member states of the OAU in Addis Ababa, Ethiopia, and focused his remarks on the problem of debt for developing countries. He echoed Castro's earlier call to cancel the foreign debt imposed on poor peoples by the imperialist powers. Sankara chastised those African heads of state who found excuses for not attending meetings of the OAU, but never missed a chance to dash off to Western capitals whenever the opportunity presented itself. The Burkinabè leader suggested that sanctions be imposed on those who failed to show up and the countries that did appear should be rewarded with favored treatment in the disbursement of funds from the African Development Bank. Sankara asked, "Are we going to allow heads of state to seek individual solutions to the problem of the debt, at the risk of creating, in their own countries, social conflicts that could endanger their stability and even the building of African unity?" He said, "The debt has nothing to do with us. That is why we cannot pay it." Sankara said the debt enabled the "reconquest of Africa" and turned its people "into a financial slave." The CNR leader told the gathering that "the lender won't die" if Africans refused to pay the debt; however, "if we do pay, we are the ones who will die." Sankara called for the OAU to form a "united front . . . against the debt." He pledged that the money saved from not repaying the debt would be used for productive development projects, not for vanity or to import more arms. In fact, Sankara called for disarmament and pushed for economic cooperation among African countries to make the most efficient use of the continent's abundant resources. In an extension of domestic policies within Burkina Faso, he added, "Produce what we need and consume what we produce, in place of importing it," and pointed to the Faso Dan Fani he was wearing as an example of his country's commitment to the strategy.[36]

Sankara's address to the OAU echoed his remarks the previous year to the Non-Aligned Movement summit in Harare. In Addis Ababa, the Burkinabè president argued that confronting international debt and the imperialist system that thrived because of it was a basis for building pan-Africanist solidarity and would be the foundation for closer cooperation among the countries of the global south. Sankara's alignment with Castro's campaign to make eradication of the debt owed to wealthy countries and international banks also reaffirmed their shared anti-imperialist ideology. The CNR leader confronted his own internal political crises that at least in part were connected to Burkina Faso's debt. Those obligations hampered the fulfilment of urgent development projects and forced the government to ask the Burkinabè people to tighten their financial belts even further, perhaps beyond what was tolerable for many. Consequently, south–south solidarity and cancellation of the debt would alleviate some of the domestic pressures that threatened to cause the collapse of the revolutionary government.

A Peasant-Based Revolution in Conflict with Organized Labor

Despite the frequent bouts of applause at the OAU, no agreements were reached on the debt or even cooperation among African states. It was a familiar pattern—Sankara's message was enthusiastically received and after the accolades trailed off the same order persisted. Consequently, the Democratic and Popular Revolution focused more intently on mobilizing the Burkinabè peasantry and emphasized self-reliance as the only path forward to realize and defend the revolution. To that end, the government promoted a cooperative movement to socialize production and transform rural mentalities. The CNR convened a National Seminar on the Cooperative Movement, 23–28 March 1987, to spur the drive toward socialism in the countryside. The gathering extolled the benefits of cooperative agriculture and outlined the state's role to support farmers in their enterprises. The seminar linked cooperative farming to combatting desertification since it would "put an end to [the soil's] anarchic utilization."[37]

The seminar was timed to coincide with Second National Congress of the CDR (30 March–3 April 1987). The agenda of the Second Congress was limited to a discussion of the CDR's role in realizing the objectives of the PQDP with an enhanced position for the peasantry. For some, the meeting was a breaking point in their relationship with the revolution. According to Mamadou Traoré, who was a CDR leader, commissar of youth, head of the CDR of services, and an organizer of the Congress, the opening of the Congress set an ominous tone. The proceedings were to open at 3:00 p.m. on 30 March 1987 in the city of Dédougou. However, Sankara's Libyan pilots got lost flying the president from Ouagadougou. Mamadou Traoré did his best to stall by parading officials before the 1,700 delegates until Sankara arrived three hours late. Mamadou Traoré describes a scene where one delegate after another rose to make wild motions aimed at realizing the self-sufficiency at the core of the plan. Some bordered on the absurd and included relabeling hotels from "five stars" to "five cowries." Mamadou Traoré claims that he and Achille Tapsoba, another high-ranking leader of the CDR, warned Sankara about the "populist drift" of the revolution, which they saw as an abandonment of the principles expressed in the *Discours d'Orientation Politique*. Despite those warnings, Mamadou Traoré claims what he heard in Sankara's closing remarks was "a very strong populist speech" that caused the CDR leader to break with the revolution.[38] Martens describes other "confused propositions" delegates made in a bid to outdo one another in their revolutionary rhetorical flourishes. Pierre Ouédraogo, the CDR general secretary, even suggested that each Burkinabè contribute three weeks of voluntary labor every year to achieve the plan's goals. The pro-Albanian and anti-CNR PCRV denounced the idea as the "return of forced labor" from the colonial period.[39]

The Congress ended on 3 April 1987 with Sankara's speech called, "We Produce and Consume Burkinabè." In it, he announced a ban on the importation of alcohol, fruits, and vegetables. This violated Article 5 of the Treaty of the Economic Community of West African States (ECOWAS/CEDEAO) and hit Côte d'Ivoire's economy the hardest as it was a major supplier of fruits and vegetables to Burkina Faso.[40] For those like Mamadou Traoré, however, Sankara's interdiction of imports was read as another blow to urban public sector workers. He said the drive for self-sufficiency was becoming absurd and appeared to be aimed at punishing those who lived in the cities. Mamadou Traoré even pointed to instances where rural people would refuse to use toilet paper because "city-dwellers use them." He characterized Sankara's ideas as "anti-intellectual and anti-civil servant. We, senior executives of the Revolution were still small officials. We had the same things as everyone else, we had no compensation as part of the Revolution." Moreover, he resented Sankara's targeting of those who Mamadou Traoré said had made the revolution in the first place while the peasants stayed on the sidelines. He said, "[The August Revolution] was [carried out by] the small officials, the agents of the Administration, the journalists, the teachers."[41] Diallo argues, "This austerity, a sort of ascetic policy, as well as the scale of the efforts required of the Burkinabè, but also a certain authoritarianism, had the consequence of displeasing or fatiguing even certain sections of the population who were rather favorable to the revolution."[42]

Nevertheless, Sankara pressed forward with his campaign to base the revolution among the peasants. In August 1986, the CNR created a ministry for the peasant question, and then shortly after the Second National Congress of the CDR, Sankara announced on 11 April 1987 the formation of the National Peasants Union of Burkina (Union nationale des paysans du Burkina, UNPB). The UNPB was loosely associated with the CDR but independent. That was followed up with a national symposium on the cooperative movement at which over 2,500 peasants participated (28 April–2 May 1987).[43] Sankara's understanding of the Democratic and Popular Revolution was consistent with Fanon's ideas of national liberation in a colonial (or neocolonial) context. Fanon highlighted the sharp division colonialism fostered between rural and urban communities. He argued that the nationalist parties of the decolonization period were constrained to action in the cities and failed to mobilize the peasantry. That contributed to peasant resistance to the development schemes pushed by those groups and the civil service that comprised the politically active sector of society. Fanon emphasized the need for revolutionary movements to base themselves among the people, in this case the peasant masses. By structural necessity, they were the force that would rupture the bonds of the imperialist system of exploitation. Finally, he argued, "If you really wish your country to avoid regression, or at best halts and uncertainties, a rapid step must be taken from national consciousness to political and social consciousness. The nation does not exist in a program which has been worked out by revolutionary leaders and taken up with full understanding and enthusiasm by the masses." Fanon wrote, "The nation's effort must be constantly adjusted into the general background of underdeveloped countries."[44]

However, resistance in the cities only intensified. On 17 April 1987, the labor federations issued a joint declaration that openly criticized the CNR's policies and demanded a lessening of austerity imposed on civil servants. They protested Sankara's announcement at the CDR National Congress banning the importation of fruits, vegetables, and alcohol. Then on 21 April 1987, Soumane Touré's CSB filed a formal protest with the International Labor Organization (ILO) claiming that the government was violating union rights. The unions followed up with a more detailed elaboration of demands forwarded to the CNR on 27 April 1984, just prior to the opening of the National Peasants' Symposium. The petitions put organized labor at odds with the official position of the CDR as validated by the delegates at its Second National Congress. Specifically, the unions refused to cooperate further in austerity measures and rejected the ban on imports at the heart of the CNR's directive to consume Burkinabè.⁴⁵

On 1 May 1987, crowds gathered to commemorate May Day in rival groups, holding distinct demonstrations alongside the official procession. When organizers of the dissident marches arrived, their designated assembly space was filled with soldiers sent by the CNR. Consequently, the unions cancelled their festivities, and the CSB denounced the revolutionary government. Elements allied with Compaoré used the cover of the turn toward a peasant-based revolution exhibited by the conferences throughout the spring 1987 and the Second National Congress of the CDR to use the instruments of popular power to repress organized labor. Ernest Nongoma Ouédraogo, the CNR's minister of territorial administration and security, announced via radio on 4 May 1987 that the unions must "convene their congresses and renew their directorship before 15 June 1987." Failure to comply would result in the unions being dissolved. On 26 May 1987, Soumane Touré issued a statement on behalf of the CSB that protested the "crass and unacceptable interference of the government in the life of the unions." The statement continued, "With the repressive arsenal in place, the repression aimed at the labor organizations and their leaders." On 30 May 1987, the CDR of Ouagadougou arrested Soumane Touré and accused him of joining the forces of the counterrevolution. Meeting in extraordinary session 31 May 1987–1 June 1987, the CDR pronounced the CSB leader guilty and sentenced him to death, and Compaoré convened a meeting of the CNR's politburo at which he demanded the arrest of other leaders of the pro-Soviet PAI, like Philippe Ouédraogo and Adama Touré. The next day, 1 June 1987, Adama Touré was arrested by the CDR. Throughout June 1987, the CDR raided union offices across Burkina Faso imprisoning dozens of labor leaders. By the end of June 1987, the CDR had purged the leadership of the labor federations and replaced them with loyalists of the military-dominated UCB.⁴⁶

Contrary to all available evidence and even his public actions demanding the arrest of the PAI leadership, Compaoré would claim Sankara was behind the repression of organized labor, and he "distanced himself from the policy" and worked to protect the unions.⁴⁷ In fact, when the CDR and CNR took extraordinary steps to eliminate the PAI as a political force, Sankara and his allies intervened to mitigate those moves. On 3 June 1987, Valère Somé delivered a letter on behalf of the ULCR to the CNR that strongly protested the arrest of Soumane Touré as well as the other leaders of the PAI/LIPAD and demanded their immediate release. President Sankara called a meeting of the CNR Central Committee that day to address the events of the previous weeks. The meeting devolved into a vitriolic shouting match with elements of the OMR, UCB, and GCB aligned behind the verdict and sentence against Soumane Touré. Sankara sided with the ULCR and argued persuasively against the CSB leader's execution. He could not reverse the verdict, but at least Soumane Touré's execution was stayed.[48] For Valère Somé this was a significant shift in political alignment from the early days of the revolution when he worked to eliminate the PAI/LIPAD from government and often advocated the execution of the regime's opponents. His change of heart reflected Sankara's work at rapprochement with the PAI/LIPAD since early 1986 that reached the point by spring 1987 of negotiations about the return of the PAI to the government. The moves by the CDR against organized labor, the PAI/LIPAD, and the PCRV undermined those efforts and led the PAI on 12 June 1987 to formally end all conversations with the CNR concerning its reintegration within the government.[49]

Revisiting the Project of a Unified Vanguard Party

Even as the CDR attacked the labor groups, divisions within the CNR reached new depths in May and June 1987 and once more the University of Ouagadougou was at the center of the conflict. As Burkina Faso prepared to commemorate the annual "Anti-Imperialist Days," the university organized a series of events, 11–17 May 1987. In the run up to those festivities, Valère Somé issued a series of public denunciations and warned that the revolution was in danger of being overthrown by a restoration of the bourgeoisie that was being facilitated by elements within the CNR. In his party's paper and *Sidwaya*, the ULCR leader lambasted his former comrades Kader Cissé and Moïse Traoré (both ULC–*La Flamme*) as "traitors" who sought to use their government posts to undermine the revolution. He attacked the leaders of the UCB, Etienne Traoré and Gabriël Tamini, and accused them of being "careerists" who contravened the anti-corruption policies of the revolution. Valère Somé then labeled the CDR general secretary, Pierre Ouédraogo, a "bureaucrat" and his cohort as "opportunists," who charged the ULCR with being "anarcho-fascists" "to mask their own opportunism." Following that series of broadsides, Compaoré met with the leaders of the ULC–*La Flamme* for the first time and urged them to respond to the ULCR leader in kind. This marked a new stage of the consolidation of Compaoré's leadership of a constellation of forces arrayed against Sankara and his allies in the CNR.[50]

Valère Somé writes that he fully mobilized his comrades to attend the meetings of the students at the University of Ouagadougou during the Anti-Imperialist Days. However, the armed forces anticipated the ULCR's actions and filled the campus with troops loyal to the UCB and other rivals to Valère Somé's group. The ULCR leader claims the soldiers escorted Etienne Traoré (UCB) to the gatherings. The ULCR members were barred from entering the meeting halls. Not content to accept their exclusion, the ULCR militants forced their way into the room and were confronted by soldiers and elements of the CDR. Several ULCR activists were imprisoned following the melee. The minister of information, Basile Guissou (ULCR), denounced the violence directed against his comrades and published an article in *Sidwaya* where he warned against the "upsurge in the militarism of the Revolution," by which he meant the growing power of the soldiers.[51] Confrontations continued throughout the week despite Sankara's appeal for calm. Basile Guissou and minister of transports, Alain Coefe (ULCR), went to the campus along with other contingents from the ULCR to reclaim control of the situation. This led to more arrests of ULCR activists. Then in retaliation, Basile Guissou used his ministerial post to cut short the address by Etienne Traoré (UCB) that was being broadcast over the radio.[52]

As he had done publicly twice before—in the dispute over the marches in May 1984 and in the conflict at the University of Ouagadougou in August/September 1986—Sankara sided with his military friend Pierre Ouédraogo, whom he had appointed as general secretary of the CDR in 1983. This dismayed Sankara's most uncritically loyal ally in the CNR, Valère Somé. He writes that the Burkinabè president knew the CDR and UCB were behind the violence but, nonetheless, accused the ULCR of provoking the incidents.[53]

In the wake of this conflict, the UCB called for a general mobilization to prepare for "a final assault against the opportunist holdouts who in the final analysis are reactionaries and counterrevolutionaries," a clear call to arms against the ULCR. Even Sankara was targeted by scurrilous attacks in anonymous tracts. The first appeared on 17 May 1987 in a missive titled "Open Letter to Emperor Sankara" that denounced the arbitrariness of his leadership. Martens attributes its source as the National Bureau of Students controlled by the UCB. That was followed by "Open Letter Number 2 to the Emperor of Faso" in early June 1987 that denounced Sankara's government as dictatorial and called for people to come out for the final fight to overthrow "the dictatorship, repression, [and] the cult of personality" centered on the CNR leader.

Regardless, Sankara still tried to hold the revolutionary coalition together. On 27 May 1987, he called a meeting of representatives of the parties within the CNR to air their differences, but nothing was resolved. Consequently, the Burkinabè president reached for the nuclear option and ordered all the political parties to dissolve by 13 June 1987. He was ignored.[54]

On 27 June 1987, Sankara called another meeting of representatives from the CNR's constituent groups. This time, he revisited the project of unifying the parties into a vanguard organization, something attempted in 1984 and 1986 to no avail. The only item on the agenda was "the dissolution of the said organizations within the Conseil National de la Révolution." The OMR was represented by Zongo, the ULCR by Valère Somé, the UCB by Watamou Lamien, and the GCB by Jean-Marc Palm. Following the meeting, Sankara classified the positions of the parties as follows: the GCB "is opposed to the self-dissolution of the Marxist-Leninist organizations in favor of an anti-imperialist front constituting the CNR"; the OMR "agreed to the self-dissolution within the CNR"; the UCB "demands the restart of the process of unification of the previous year on the basis of the platform already clarified"; and the ULCR agreed to renew the process of unification that "resulted in the development of the platform" in 1986 and agreed to "put into place a Provisional Committee for the Party" to guide the unification of the parties. Sankara used his authority to revive the minimal platform for unity developed in 1986 (UCB's position, partially agreed to by the ULCR) and called for putting into place a Provisional Committee for the Party as recommended by the ULCR. Then, Sankara wrote, "After the organizations have dissolved themselves, the CNR [will] elaborate a program (economic, political, and social)" that will be the policy basis of the emerging united organization. The Burkinabè president instructed the parties to come back with their final recommendations within one week after consulting with their members.[55]

Valère Somé writes that the main differences at the meeting were between the GCB and ULCR with the UCB remaining silent through most of the deliberations. The ULCR leader says that Jean-Marc Palm (GCB) wanted the Provisional Committee to be composed of two members from each group whereas Valère Somé countered by arguing Sankara should, in his capacity as president, decide on its composition. Compaoré opposed the entire process and called out Valère

Somé, calling him a loose cannon. Moreover, he advocated the inclusion of the ULC–*La Flamme* within the discussions and its addition to the CNR. Valère Somé was incensed and adamantly refused. He threatened to resign and have the ULCR leave the CNR if that happened. He claims that Zongo followed "the views of President Thomas Sankara" and the OMR was on board with the project.[56]

The showdown between Sankara and the military officers behind the UCB came at its meeting on 4 July 1987 to review the results of the previous week's meeting. One pro-Compaoré delegate at the conference, Béatrice Damiba, told Martens that Sankara brought the motion to the UCB to dissolve the organizations within the CNR, "but he found himself very isolated." Damiba viewed the proposal as another sign of improvisation, which was excusable at the beginning of the revolution. She said Sankara was to blame for the failure to construct a vanguard party to that point since "the party means democracy and discipline and Sankara does not support either the one or the other." Another attendee at the conference, Kilimité Hien, highlighted the militant opposition of the students to the proposal and told Martens that Sankara accused Compaoré of inciting the students. This, according to Kilimité Hien, put into the open for the first time that "Blaise was not in agreement with him."[57]

Sankara pushed the UCB to accept the unity plan and urged a pause in the reform programs to allow time for the base of the revolution to expand, referencing his outreach to the peasants throughout 1987. Despite some contradiction among eyewitnesses to the conference, it appears that the UCB supported the idea of a pause, although one delegate, Etienne Traoré, says Sankara wanted to accelerate the revolution. The main point of contention was over the unification of parties. Sankara could not persuade the representatives to support his proposition. Jaffré argues the UCB wanted to delay the process to consolidate its position within the CNR to the exclusion of the ULCR. The meeting adjourned, acrimoniously. While the UCB agreed to continue engagement in the unification process by conducting discussions with the ULCR outside the CNR, that was an obvious ploy to avoid reaching a deal to dissolve the parties and merge into a vanguard party within the CNR, the main objective of the entire process. Sankara realized this and threatened to resign his post. He no longer participated in UCB meetings.[58]

On 6 July 1987, the CNR assessed the responses of the four groups. The GCB advocated "the enrichment of the platform, the putting in place of an organizing committee by parity and the elaboration of a program (economic, political, and social)" before it would go forward with dissolving. The OMR unequivocally agreed with the call to dissolve the groups without elaborating. The UCB "agreed with the self-dissolving" of the groups and demanded that "after putting in place an organizing committee, discussions should be engaged [in that body] where there have been difficulties between the different organizations in view of creating a climate of confidence among the militants of the organizations." Only then would the UCB entertain the idea of self-dissolution. Finally, the ULCR agreed with "the procedure expressed by the UCB, that is to say on the basis of the platform elaborated and adopted by all, putting in place an organizing committee for the party, after which it will entertain the dissolution of the organization." The ULCR also "insists on the necessity to instantiate a climate of confidence among the militants of these organizations." Sankara then gave "details about the organizing committee," which will be "outside the CNR," "on the elaboration of a Marxist-Leninist platform and on a program." He urged all the militants to work together for unity. Then Sankara charged Compaoré, Boukary Lingani, and Zongo "to organize meetings on points where there have been tensions among organizations" to create a climate of confidence in which they can pursue unity. Sankara declared that once "unification was realized, the CNR will work with organizations that are not members of the CNR with a view toward their integration."[59] Effectively, the Coordinators (minus Sankara) were to direct the process of creating a united vanguard party, and, with the PAI/LIPAD and PRCV suppressed, the only functioning party outside the CNR was the ULC–*La Flamme*, allied to Compaoré and enemy to Valère Somé and the ULCR.

On 23 July 1987, the CNR reconvened to assess the progress toward unification. At the meeting, the GCB and ULCR offered amendments, which became the basis of discussion. All the parties agreed that there would be a resumption of the discussion on further elaboration of the platform, which involved the collection of different amendments for their enrichment and adoption and that there will be established a "Provisional Organizing Committee for the Party." That group would be constituted on "a parity basis of which the practical modalities remain to be determined." They also committed to elaborating a political program that Sankara wrote and would include a maximum and a minimum program. According to the CNR leader, "Only the minimum program will be discussed and adopted at the level of the CNR." A timeline for the dissolution of the groups would be developed after the Provisional Committee had achieved specific tasks regarding organizational structure, the platform, and so on. That put the potential date for unification after 4 August 1987.[60]

A Revolution off the Rails

On 4 August 1987, Sankara took the stage in Bobo-Dioulasso at the festivities marking the fourth anniversary of the Democratic and Popular Revolution. The other leaders of the CNR sat to the side with the foreign dignitaries. Compaoré sat stone-faced as his erstwhile friend delivered the keynote address. The Libyan ambassador whispered periodically to those seated beside him. Dressed in a ceremonial blue tunic with gold collar and epaulettes and wearing his trademark red beret, Sankara spoke in a calm and measured tone saying, "The fourth anniversary of our Revolution takes place under the banner of our dynamic peasantry," and he noted the founding of the National Union of Peasants of Burkina (UNPB). The transformation of the countryside was leading to "the birth of the new peasant.," echoing Fanon's notion of creating new people. That process was guaranteed through the self-reliant development strategies of the PQDP and enforced by the work of the CDR "as laid out by [its] Second National Congress." The Burkinabè president said the revolution aimed "to reduce the gap between town and country through selflessness and sacrifice." This "has required that the mentality of the Burkinabè people cease being a reproduction of the culturally alienated and politically servile individual created to perpetuate imperialist domination in the newly independent countries." Sankara asserted "we need a new people" to carry out the revolution's ambitions. However, the CNR president noted that the previous "political year . . . has certainly been stormy."[61]

At that point in the speech, Sankara's tone changed. He stiffened up, projected his torso forward, and declared, "The Democratic and Popular Revolution needs a convinced people, not a conquered people; a convinced people, not a submissive people passively enduring their fate." He warned that the revolution's internal and external enemies had not ceased their efforts to destroy it. Sankara pointed to "erroneous ideas and practices" that have emerged among the masses and "among the revolutionaries." He described the "fragility of our own ranks" and the rifts tearing at the revolution's unity. This resulted from opportunism and "a frenetic search for selfish personal gain." Sankara acknowledged the "slanderous attacks . . . springing from the ranks of the Revolution itself; from impatient people infected with the dubious zeal of the novice, when it's not from a frenzy of schemers with undisguised personal ambitions." The Burkinabè president pointed to the ultra-left mask behind which the opportunists hide. Those extremists took premature initiatives and went "after the wrong target pure and simple." That was an unmistakable reference to the assault on the PAI/LIPAD and PCRV in May–June 1987. Sankara said the coming year must be one of "assessment, a year of scientifically organized ideological and political work." The CNR leader asserted, "The Revolution cannot go forward and achieve its goals without a vanguard organization, able to guide the people in all its battles and on all fronts."[62]

"Year Five," Sankara said, "calls on us to throw all our energies into the organizational fight, into political and ideological consolidation, into the overriding importance of political leadership." Now it was time for the different revolutionary groups to cast aside their petty theoretical nuances that are "destined for contemplation [only] by a few dreamers and self-gratifying fanatics." He proclaimed, "It's the quality of life that's changing in Burkina, and that's the result of a qualitative evolution of minds." The failures of the revolution, Sankara argued, were the result of inadequacies at the top, not of the people. He said, "We should prefer one step forward together with the people to ten steps forward without the people." The Burkinabè leader affirmed, "The Revolution is neither sadness nor bitterness. On the contrary, it is the embodiment of the enthusiasm and pride of an entire people taking responsibility for itself, and thereby discovering its own dignity." He added, "I invite you to stand firm together in order to pursue the march we have begun at an even more accelerated pace, but which at the same time is experiencing a pause; a pause in the pursuit of a number of projects, a pause we need in order to devote our energies to the task of political and ideological organization."[63]

On 8 August 1987, the National Conference of Students in Ouagadougou was the scene of bitter denunciations of the president's remarks orchestrated by elements of the UCB. Then the CNR called another conference of its constituent parties on 18 August 1987 to discuss the progress toward unification. However, Valère Somé had the ULCR boycott the meeting. According to the ULCR leader, Compaoré used that meeting to strike against his party and called for the immediate "unification of the consenting organizations and since the ULCR refused to attend, too bad for it." Sankara rejected the proposal and convened a roundtable to discuss what had taken place in the days before the meeting.[64] Sankara issued a circular to government ministers on 19 August 1987, reminding them of the message of his anniversary address. He called on them to explore the reinstatement of those fired during the crackdown on schoolteachers in 1984 as well as the labor unrest of May–June 1987. Sankara told them, "You must bravely engage in the debate of ideas. . . . Comrades have proved that political differences do not exclude, within certain limits, a good performance of the worker." He concluded, "The fact remains that you must remain firm vis-à-vis all those who, fanatical or subtle provocateur saboteurs, confuse dialogue and weakness." In that note and a subsequent one distributed on 21 August 1987, Sankara also called for the liberation of Soumane Touré from prison.[65]

The increasingly venomous anonymous tracts aimed against Sankara that had circulated since May 1987 returned in the fall and routinely portrayed the revolutionary leader as an autocrat and mentally unstable, "a paranoiac like Hitler, N'guéma, Bokassa."[66] To counter those perceptions, Sankara formed a special cabinet of advisors on 22 August 1987 that included Paulin Bamouni, Christophe Saba, Bonaventure Compaoré, Frédéric Kiemde, Patrice Zagré, and Alouna Traoré. Its purpose was to help Sankara improve his decision-making, develop a less spontaneous and improvisational style of leadership, and signaled a willingness to withdraw somewhat from government tasks to refine his political thinking.[67] The parties were each asked to nominate a representative to sit in this new presidential secretariat. The ULCR proposed Train Raymond Pooda, but Compaoré objected and the ULCR decided not to offer a replacement. The GCB objected when Salif Diallo nominated himself and the UCB selected Patrice Zagré. Consequently, only the party closest to Compaoré had official representation on Sankara's new inner circle of advisors.[68]

On 26 August 1986, the CNR met to prepare for the annual dissolution of the government. One official rose to denounce Pierre Ouédraogo and demand his removal as general secretary of the CDR. The motion was rejected. Normally the Coordinators—Sankara, Compaoré, Boukary Lingani, and Zongo—exercised authority between governments and collectively agreed to the new list of cabinet officials. However, at that meeting, Sankara and Compaoré openly feuded when the Burkinabè president again called for the reinstallation of those fired or imprisoned for counterrevolutionary acts. Compaoré objected and posed as the arch-defender of the revolution, aligning with the most rhetorically extremist factions within the CNR—the UCB, GCB, and OMR. Sankara gave an interview following the meeting in which he said, "There is no risk in taking back the wrongdoers of the past, if each revolutionary does their work. The greater risk would be to find oneself on a beautiful morning, sitting on illusions and having convinced no one."[69] That same day he told journalists at *Sidwaya* that his proposal of 21 August 1987 had provoked "suspicions, discomfort among the militants." He warned against a mechanical merger of the groups into a unified party since it would squelch discussion and create an organization that was paralyzed and sterile. He urged the formation of a vanguard that would include a diversity of opinions that could be debated with respect through criticism and self-criticism. The revolutionaries, Sankara reiterated, should always be conscious of their task of improving the lives of the people and developing policies "in the interest of the masses."[70] Since the four Coordinators could not agree on a new government, they left the decision in the hands of the CNR's Political Bureau, dominated by Compaoré's allies. That body was comprised mostly of military officers almost universally members of the UCB and OMR. Sankara had publicly ruptured with the UCB in July 1987, and the OMR routinely sided with Compaoré in disputes within the CNR, like those around control over the students' CDR at the University of Ouagadougou and the repression of the PAI along with organized labor in May and June 1987.

Compaoré's Emerging Network Inside and Outside Burkina Faso

Even as the CNR's unity frayed, there were worrying shifts internationally that also threatened the Democratic and Popular Revolution. Foremost among those concerns was the widening gulf between Qaddafi and Sankara. Every year since the August 1983 Revolution, the Burkinabè president had attended the celebrations of the Libyan Revolution on 1 September. However, since early 1984, the two had feuded over the Libyan leader's renewed aggression in Chad. In 1987, heavy fighting erupted again in Chad with Libyan territory vulnerable to French-backed incursions for the first time that August 1987.

Another source of tensions between Sankara and Qaddafi was the latter's plan to train a rebel force commanded by Charles Taylor that could be inserted into Liberia to overthrow that government. Sankara wanted no part of the adventure.[71] The project was backed by Houphouët-Boigny as well as Compaoré who had befriended Taylor and was close to the Ivoirian leader through his 1985 marriage to Chantal de Fougères. Compaoré's wife was also related to the deposed Liberian leader, William Tolbert, who was overthrown by Samuel Doe in 1980. Recent evidence suggests that the rift with Libya over Taylor's adventure played a role in the political drama unfolding in Burkina Faso during the autumn of 1987. The dispute between Sankara and Compaoré included a sharp divergence over Qaddafi's plans to insert the Liberian rebel into his home country to overthrow Doe's government. In addition, Taylor not only worked for Libya, but he was also suspected of being an agent of the U.S. CIA. It was because of the latter that he had been arrested twice in Ghana (February to May 1986 and again in January 1987). Taylor made his way to Africa after a daring escape from a U.S. prison on 15 September 1985, which is now believed to have been orchestrated by the CIA to make him an asset that could infiltrate Libya and other radical governments in Africa.[72] The speculation around Taylor's true benefactors as well as Sankara's own aversion to having Burkina Faso be used as an instrument in other countries' objectives combined to form the basis of his animosity to Qaddafi's and Compaoré's schemes regarding Liberia.

By 1987, a small group of Liberian exiles were being trained in Burkina Faso after transferring from bases in Libya. Taylor had headquarters in Ouagadougou and travelled between that city and Tripoli throughout the year. As minister of state, Compaoré had direct liaisons with those training camps, supervision over them, and provided them with weapons.[73] The split between Sankara and Qaddafi led to the Burkinabè leader's decision to not attend Libya's Revolution Day celebrations on 1 September 1987. Instead, Compaoré headed the country's delegation. Also attending the celebrations was Ghana's President Rawlings and Uganda's leader, Yoweri Museveni, with whom Compaoré confirmed he had extensive consultations, the substance of which was not revealed.

Compaoré returned to Burkina Faso on 3 September 1987, just prior to an emergency meeting of the OMR called by Sankara. The Burkinabè leader called the gathering to address the odious tracts aimed at him and his family. According to Compaoré, Sankara absented himself from the meeting for an hour during which many of his allies charged other members of the OMR with being the source of the tracts. Compaoré believed he was being accused of being the architect of the slander campaign. Other Compaoré allies claimed Sankara's absence indicated he was preparing a coup to remove his rivals. According to Compaoré ally Arsène Yé, Sankara returned to the meeting and charged that the authors of the scurrilous attacks against him and his wife were seated at the table and demanded that they "have the courage to reveal themselves." Boukary Lingani asserted that false rumors were conveyed to Sankara saying that he was planning a coup against the Burkinabè leader. Zongo said it was not true that he "wanted to be [Sankara's] successor." Finally, Compaoré rose and exclaimed that the sole purpose of the meeting was to "attack and insult" him. Compaoré claimed later that he said, "[This room] is full of people who understand nothing of politics. In fact, it is an affair between Thomas and me. If Thomas has things to reproach me for since '83, let him say [them]."[74] The meeting adjourned amid great tension.

On 8 September 1987, Sankara called another meeting of the OMR and proposed that all military withdraw from the UCB, and the OMR should define its statutes.[75] The following day, the CNR announced the new government for Year V of the revolution. All members of the ULCR were dropped, and the UCB picked up substantial representation within the cabinet, not surprising since they dominated the CNR's Political Bureau and had the exclusive authority to form the new administration. Valère Somé lost his post as minister of education and Basile Guissou as minister of information.[76] On 10 September 1987, Sankara again convened the OMR to approve a draft of the group's new statutes. The OMR declared that its "immediate task [was] to realize the union of the Burkinabè left with the aim of the creation of a Marxist-Leninist party."[77]

At this point, another front opened in the conflict between Sankara and Compaoré that centered on control of the state's security apparatus. Vincent Sigué served as the head of Sankara's personal security detail, and in January 1987, he was given command of a newly constituted elite paramilitary unit known as the Force d'Intervention du Ministère de l'Administration Territoriale et de la Sécurité (intervention force of the ministry of territorial administration and security, FIMATS). That ministry was headed by Ernest Nongma Ouédraogo, a close associate of Sankara. By the spring of 1987, he had recruited dozens of cadres from local police units for the new organization.[78] One of the main purposes behind creating FIMATS was to circumvent if not undercut Compaoré's exclusive command over the military. Englebert writes, "Unlike those CNR officers, Sankara had no direct military command, so he proposed the creation of [FIMATS]." That move ultimately backfired as it "alienat[ed] his military friends."[79]

While Sankara was in Ethiopia on a state visit, on 16 September 1987, Compaoré convened a meeting of the cabinet during which he tabled the proposal to reorganize the ministry of territorial administration and security and give it direct command of FIMATS. On 21 September 1987, with Sankara back in the country, the Political Bureau of the CNR convened to discuss the political program that was to be the basis for creating a vanguard party. However,

Compaoré brought up the controversy over FIMATS. Sankara, though, would not be diverted from the project of forming a unified communist party to lead the revolution. After the meeting, he issued directives to the leaders of the parties "to prepare an outline of a program" of the CNR. Valère Somé notes that, around this time, there was unusual movement within the command structure of the Burkinabè armed forces as Compaoré loyalists were appointed to leadership of strategic units, such as those at Pô and the rapid intervention force at the airport (BIA). To avoid a final rupture with his friend, Sankara invited Compaoré to a meeting of his political secretariat on 24 September 1987 to demonstrate that there was no plot against him and that the CNR president was operating transparently.[80] The Coordinators then met on 1 October 1987, the first time in nearly a month, to discuss a pathway toward repairing their differences. While not resolving the rift among them, Sankara proposed that the four leave together in a sign of unity. None of his three comrades followed when the Burkinabè president departed. Regardless, that evening Sankara convened his secretariat to outline more details of their responsibilities. Those included instructions to Bamouni to start a new journal for the CNR. In addition, Christophe Saba was charged with drafting a "revolutionary code of conduct" that would be discussed at their next meeting.[81]

Final Days

On 2 October 1987, Sankara and the other leaders of the August Revolution gathered to commemorate the anniversary of the *Discours d'Orientation Politique* in Tenkodogo. The Burkinabè president delivered the keynote address in which he praised the heroic work of the masses of Boulgou province for their accomplishments over the previous four years. Sankara said the people's work "allows us to believe in miraculous transformations, in leaps forward with the people, always with the people, without surging prematurely." Sankara denounced those who twist and turn revolutionary phrases and said the revolution must distance itself from all erroneous ideas. He highlighted the Democratic and Popular Revolution's role in changing the world as part of "the collective struggle of all humanity." Sankara said the revolution had to be grounded in the reality of the country to avoid the "spouting [of] slogans that are no more than signals used by manipulators trying to use them as catchwords." The CNR leader explained that the goal of the revolution was the happiness of the people, achieved through having "clean water to drink . . . abundant, sufficient food, because they're in excellent health, because they have education, because they have decent housing." If the revolution did not meet those needs, then it will have been nothing more than "a bunch of mummies who represent nothing but a lifeless collection of decaying values." He implored the urban population to embrace the policies of self-sufficiency at the heart of the ongoing PQDP and insisted that the revolutionary institutions should adhere to their statutes and to the moral standards of the revolution to lead by example. "The goal of the Revolution," Sankara opined, "is not to scatter revolutionaries. The goal of the revolution is to consolidate our ranks. We are eight million Burkinabè; our goal is to create eight million revolutionaries." He announced that all militants in the CDR would be evaluated according to their revolutionary conduct. Sankara also informed the gathering that he was going to free all the detainees "whose social behavior harmed the people" because "victory lies in the disappearance of prisons." That amounted to eighty-eight individuals released. Finally, the Burkinabè president said the CNR had abolished the tax on stockbreeders to end punitive measures against the herding populations that were part of the "Three Struggles" launched in 1984 and that had caused conflict between the CDR and rural communities. As Sankara put it, "Joy for some should not mean sadness for others."[82]

Sankara's remarks came toward the end of the festivities after leaders of the other mass organizations had spoken, including the president of the National Bureau of Students, Jonas Somé. Jonas Somé told Martens that the speech had been cleared by Kilimité Hien (UCB), second to Pierre Ouédraogo in the National General Secretariat of the CDR. The student praised the work of the CDR for having created the revolution in reality. He warned against opportunists who sabotaged the work of unity among the revolutionaries. Jonas Somé stated, "Where there is revolution, there is counterrevolution." He "reproached Sankara for not respecting [organizational] structures and for cutting off debates [within them]." The student leader labeled the ULCR as opportunists, who were intent on "liquidating the revolutionaries." For the Sankarists, the speech was "the work of Blaise Compaoré."[83] Attention turned to Kilimité Hien's role in permitting the speech to go forward with its critiques of the Burkinabè president. Captain Kilimité Hien was one of the officers "most loyal to Blaise Compaoré" and remained so throughout the latter's regime.[84]

On 6 October 1987, the Provincial Revolutionary Authority of Houet, the government of the province, convened in Bobo-Dioulasso and produced a statement in which it recalled "the strong points" made by Sankara but highlighted the declaration made by the National Bureau of Students as a "clear-sighted" analysis of the *Discours d'Orientation Politique* that "was positively appreciated by the Council."[85] Both Sankara and Pierre Ouédraogo were alarmed by the regional committee's statement, and the Burkinabè president instructed them to clarify their position vis-à-vis the two speeches of 2 October 1987 since it appeared to support both speeches, but clearly embraced Jonas Somé's remarks that were highly critical of Sankara. On 8 October 1987, the CNR leader called a meeting of the Coordinators to present a united front against the criticisms leveled by Jonas Somé. Boukary Lingani was not in Ouagadougou and did not participate. Sankara demanded that the three in attendance issue a statement denouncing Jonas Somé's speech and the declaration of the Revolutionary Council of Houet. Compaoré and Zongo refused. Sankara rose, headed out the door, and slammed it behind him. The rupture was irreparable.[86]

After the acrimonious meeting that evening Sankara placed critical units of the military and some paramilitary groups on high alert. Youssouf Diawara, a Burkinabè citizen working for the ACCT, received an urgent call from a friend in Sankara's security detail that night asking that he return immediately from Bordeaux, France. The unnamed officer said Sankara and Compaoré were on the verge of "an armed confrontation." The next day, 9 October 1987, Youssouf Diawara was in Ouagadougou. That evening he went to the presidential offices and met with Sankara, conducting the last known interview with the Burkinabè president. Sankara explained that it was "true, we are informed that Blaise has the intention to attack me." According to Youssouf Diawara, the CNR leader said, "Contacts have even been established with Liberians, Togolese and perhaps Ivoirians to precipitate a coup." Sankara waxed historic and asserted that Compaoré had wanted to be "number one" from the first day of the revolution. Youssouf Diawara expressed his dismay and confusion. He suggested that a new office of vice president or prime minister be created to assuage Compaoré's ego. Sankara shook his head, and the conversation turned to more personal matters.[87] Sankara's allusion to the role played by Liberians in the emerging plot to overthrow the CNR was later confirmed by the Liberian Truth and Reconciliation Commission (TRC). According to the final report of the TRC, "Accounts suggest that Compaoré ordered former Burkinabè President

Thomas Sankara's assassination and that Taylor, who arrived in Burkina Faso at approximately the time of President Sankara's assassination in October 1987, was involved in the murder." The report also notes the "strong relationship between Compaoré and Houphouët-Boigny and their shared hostility toward Doe." Finally, it asserts that "perhaps one of Compaoré's most significant acts was his introduction of Taylor to the Libyan leader Colonel Muammar Qaddafi."[88]

Meanwhile, Pierre Ouédraogo mobilized CDR across the country and called on them to stage demonstrations in support of Sankara's speech of 2 October 1987. That move in some way repaid Sankara's loyalty to the CDR's general secretary in several previous rifts within the CNR, like that between it and the PAI in May 1984 and the fight with the ULCR in September 1986. Many CDR obeyed the mobilization orders, but others refused. Pierre Ouédraogo then sent a letter on 10 October 1987 to Jonas Somé in which the CDR head labeled the student leader "a plotter and putschist." Jonas Somé was suspended as leader of the National Bureau of Students and ordered to produce a self-criticism by the next day. According to Kilimité Hien, the student leader wanted to be defiant, but Kilimité Hien and others edited it to make a more humble and self-critical final statement. Pierre Ouédraogo accepted the student leader's mea culpa on 12 October 1987, the same day he ordered a purge of the Revolutionary Council of Houet for its equivocation over the speeches of 2 October 1987.[89]

Then on 13 October 1987, the OMR met and affirmed the decision to withdraw all soldiers from the UCB. Finally, Sankara convened a meeting of the cabinet on 14 October 1987 at which Compaoré was absent. He also failed to attend the gathering of the OMR on 13 October 1987, feigning illness, although he was well enough to consult with Zongo and Boukary Lingani on 11 October 1987. The government took up the matter of FIMATs and approved it. The cabinet also took up other reforms, including a project to create an additional 2,000 civil service jobs, an increase in urban salaries of up to 20 percent in the coming year, and the "elaboration of a revolutionary code of conduct." Sankara proclaimed that the crisis was over and the differences among the revolution's leaders were resolved. That evening he informed the UCB that all military members had withdrawn from the group, and Sankara convened a meeting of the heads of the security services to coordinate the defense of the revolution.[90] Compaoré interpreted those developments differently. Kyélem de Tambèla writes, "Compaoré's military power which remained [his] last rampart was on the path of being neutralized.

For Compaoré, who wanted to achieve his ambitions [of leading Burkina Faso], there was no time to lose. It was now or never to take action."[91]

On 15 October 1987, Sankara consulted with Valère Somé and called Compaoré's wife to express his desire to mend their relationship. Throughout the day, he worked on a statement that outlined the path toward reestablishing revolutionary discipline and unity of action. Sankara was to present his ideas before a CNR meeting scheduled for that evening. In the statement Sankara admitted, "The prestige of the Revolution and the confidence the masses had placed in him had suffered a great shock." A source of the problems that undermined the Democratic and Popular Revolution was the organizational and ideological immaturity of the new state institutions. Another font of discord resided in the realm of human relations. They reflected the entry within the CNR of certain elements engaged in intrigue and who viewed their membership there as a guarantee against any attack on their label as a revolutionary. They masquerade as people of the left, using the most extreme rhetoric to hide their opportunism. Sankara invoked the tragedies of South Yemen, Grenada, Lebanon, and Chad where governments splintered and civil war followed. He asserted, "We are responsible before our people, but also responsible before the international progressive movement for the future of this hope that has been aroused by the Revolution of 4 August 1983." The Burkinabè president said, "It is urgent that we go out, that we speak, that we reassure our people." Sankara called for the "elimination within our ranks" of those causing trouble. "Our Revolution will advance through purifying itself." Lastly, Sankara moved that the government implement, without delay, the "economic, political, social, and military program" of the CNR through which they will gather all revolutionaries "based on their ability to contribute to the real well-being of our people." It should also approve the Revolutionary Code of Ethics as the basis for participation in leadership of the Democratic and Popular Revolution.[92]

The Burkinabè leader never had the chance to present those proposals. Compaoré had already given orders to the units under his control in Pô to march on the capital. In the afternoon of 15 October 1987, the heads of the branches of state security (including Ernest Nongma Ouédraogo, Vincent Sigué, and Boukary Lingani) met in response to the unusual troop movements detected from Pô, and the forces loyal to Sankara accused those units from Pô of intending to carry out a coup against the CNR. The meeting broke apart amid extreme acrimony with the officers racing to get into contact with their various associates around the country. At around 4:00 p.m., Sankara left his home for the Conseil de l'Entênte building to confer with his secretariat and prepare for that evening's CNR gathering. At the same time, the commandos from Pô, assisted by elements associated with Taylor's Libyan-trained forces, arrived outside. At 4:20 p.m. shots were fired. Sankara and his associates heard shouts demanding that all come outside with their hands in the air. Alouna Touré, the sole survivor of the attack, said Sankara rose and told the others to stay behind because "it is me they want." With hands raised, the captain exited the building. As he stepped into the sunshine at 4:30 p.m., Sankara was hit with a barrage of automatic weapons fire; two shots to the head and ten to the body. The soldiers then burst into the room and massacred the remaining members of the presidential secretariat. Among the killed were Paulin Bamouni, Christophe Saba, Bonaventure Compaoré, Frédéric Kiémende, and Patrice Zagré, the last a member of the UCB and double agent. Only Alouna Touré escaped. Two guards outside were also murdered. The bodies were hastily buried in an unmarked grave on the outskirts of Ouagadougou. Several Sankara allies were killed throughout the country that day, with many others thrown into prison. By 6:00 p.m., national radio was playing the ominous martial music to signal a change in regime. Then a voice read a proclamation announcing the formation of the Popular Front government, signed by Compaoré, the new president of Burkina Faso.[93]

Conclusion

AFTER SANKARA'S ASSASSINATION AND THE OVERTHROW OF THE CNR, small groups of people gathered somberly throughout Ouagadougou and other cities and villages across Burkina Faso. According to Harsch, "Thousands began pilgrimages to the tiny, weed-infested cemetery where Sankara and 12 others had been hastily buried during the night. Flowers were deposited on Sankara's grave, also pieces of paper with messages on them: 'We will all be Sankaras' and 'Mama Sankara, your son will be avenged.'"[1]

There was confusion throughout the country. Information was scarce; a curfew imposed; and Compaoré, the nation's new ruler, remained missing and reportedly confined to his bed with an illness. The national radio was filled with venomous attacks against Sankara labeling him a "'traitor' to the revolution," a "messianist," and a "fascist." Popular Front communiqués said Sankara was leading "Burkina into economic, political, and social chaos." He was vilified as an autocrat bent on arresting and executing his associates in the revolutionary government. Compaoré claimed in subsequent interviews, "It was either him or me."[2] There was even confusion over whether Sankara was dead. An article in the French paper *Libération* on 16 October 1987 claimed that the CNR president had been arrested and charged with treason against the revolution.[3]

The inaugural proclamation of the Popular Front on 15 October 1987 claimed the new government moved to save the revolution from Sankara. The revolution was to continue "although 'corrections' were needed to check 'a demobilization of the masses and a degeneration of the revolution.'" Compaoré's new regime labeled this process a "rectification."[4] However, as the *New York Times* reported, "So far, no African leader has sent a public message of congratulations to President Compaoré. Neighboring Ghana declared one week of mourning. The Congolese radio lamented the loss of 'a worthy son of Africa' and assailed 'Compaoré's treason.'" The article also documented the relentless pilgrimage to Sankara's burial site in the days after the massacre. The paper pointed out that efforts by the new government to engineer mass rallies in its support had failed so miserably that they had to be cancelled and the Popular Front issued orders banning all ceremonies for Sankara and his associates.[5]

It was not until 19 October 1987 that Compaoré addressed the country. By then, he had moderated the scurrilous attacks directed at his predecessor and simply posited that his former friend had gone astray and insisted that he did not order the assassination. In fact, he claimed that his troops had moved without his knowledge or authorization to arrest Sankara, and that when the CNR leader resisted, they had mistakenly killed him. As Harsch writes, "The accusations did not match their image of Sankara or of the revolution he had been leading for over four years. Some observed that the charges of bureaucratic and repressive conduct applied much more to the perpetrators of the coup than to Sankara."[6]

Resistance emerged within the Burkinabè military as units under the command of Captain Boukary Kaboré in Koudougou raised the banner of revolt in the name of saving the Burkinabè Revolution. Compaoré and his associates attempted for several days to break the resistance of the "Lion of Bulkiemdé," as he was popularly known. Support for the rebellion grew to the extent that Compaoré had to send teams to the countryside to persuade the people that Sankara's "death was an accident of the revolution."[7] Students staged impromptu demonstrations in their classrooms in support of Sankara, and the Popular Front increasingly turned to the very repression the ex-president warned against. The Popular Front shut down schools, imprisoned thousands of Sankara supporters, dissolved the CNR, and made plans to eliminate the CDR.

Finally, on 27 October 1987, Compaoré ordered his troops from Pô to attack the garrison at Koudougou. Many rebels were killed, and Captain Kaboré fled across the border to Ghana. The Popular Front had finally clamped down on the organized, outward signs of resistance to its counterrevolution.[8] In early 1988, the CDR were shut down, directly contradicting the Popular Front's claim that it sought to reenergize the masses in support of the revolution. Within two years, Compaoré had successfully consolidated all power in his hands when he had his other two close associates, Boukary Lingani and Zongo, executed on 19 September 1989 for attempting a coup against him.

Compaoré stood alone atop Burkinabè politics until his own overthrow in a popular uprising on 31 October 2014. The people in the streets that day carried pictures of Sankara, chanted his name, and held aloft posters with quotations from the long-deposed leader. As one reporter described the scene, "Streets and squares flooded by demonstrators, many of whom were women brandishing wooden spatulas," and the tenor of the protests gave evidence of "a resurgence of interest in the man many protesters credit as their inspiration—Thomas Sankara."[9] As Harsch writes, "Clearly, for many in Burkina Faso today, the Sankara revolution is not just a chapter in the country's past. Its echoes continue to reverberate, as the Burkinabè people consider ways to reshape their society."[10]

African Cinema and the Burkinabè Revolution

The echoes and durability of that revolutionary project stemmed from its essential objective to make new people in society that would generate a new global humanism. The CNR's policies and transformation of the country's institutional structures between 1983 and 1987 were designed to furnish the space wherein the Burkinabè could take proprietorship of the revolution, improve their lives, and realize their full creative potential. This would result in the transcendence of the mentalities that arose from and served the interests of imperialism, which would resolve in the formation of unalienated subjects, a people with dignity who stood as equal and sovereign participants in the world, forging humanity's destiny in harmony with others and with the environment in which they lived.

The Burkinabè Revolution sought to accomplish the process of national liberation from colonialism that, according to Fanon, entailed "a complete calling in question of the colonial situation.... [It] sets out to change the order of the world [and consequently involves] a program of complete disorder." He summarizes, "Decolonization is the veritable creation of new [people]."[11] Sankara repeatedly articulated that theme throughout his tenure as president. In his speech on the revolution's fourth anniversary (4 August 1987), the CNR leader stated that the Democratic and Popular Revolution "has required that the mentality of the Burkinabè people cease being a reproduction of the culturally alienated and politically servile individual created to perpetuate imperialist domination in the newly independent countries.... [W]e need a new people."[12] The formation of those new, unalienated subjects would further "the collective struggle of humanity," as he reminded the audience at the celebration of the fourth anniversary of the *Discours d'Orientation Politique* on 2 October 1987.[13]

Within the revolution's cultural politics conceived to form unalienated people in the context of a new universal humanity, the cinema occupied a prominent place. The revolutionaries viewed film as a vehicle to project the Democratic and Popular Revolution's message domestically and internationally as well as an endeavor within which people could create their own culture and identity, as Sankara affirmed during the 1985 FESPACO. The CNR's consistent and deep engagement with the cinema industrial complex fundamentally impacted the nature and trajectory of African cinema while also reviving the productivity and activity of the continent's filmmakers. It also stimulated the making of motion pictures by Burkinabè directors who became some of the most important figures in the global film field.[14] The revolutionary government's commitment to the cinema was materially manifested in its construction of movie theaters in every major city and village across the country, as well as mobile cinemas for more remote areas, to provide the physical space wherein the people had access to films and could engage with the movies in a manner that recalled Sembène's conception of them as reports that would "participate in their awareness."[15]

With the CNR in power, FESPACO became a different kind of event than it had been to that point. The 1985 and 1987 iterations became enmeshed in the revolutionary process underway in Burkina Faso. Dupré describes the 1985 FESPACO as "a veritable anti-imperialist summit and event of African Marxism."[16] At that gathering, the festival for the first time had a theme, "Cinema and People's Liberation." In addition to the traditional screening of films and conferences of filmmakers, the Ninth FESPACO included marches of militants organized by the CDR, vastly expanded public viewing spaces to allow for more popular participation in the festival, meetings of anti-apartheid and anti-racist movements, and workshops on the anti-imperialist struggle. Representatives from throughout the world became integral parts of the event, signaling its internationalization in ways that linked the work of African cinema with the transformation of the global environment and participated in the creation of a new humanism. The festival became a space of cultural exchange that generated tangible agreements to share their products, ideas, and even people on a continual basis. The theme of the Tenth FESPACO in 1987, "Cinema and Cultural Identity," deepened the imbrication of African film practices with the project of personal and social transformation at the core of the Democratic and Popular Revolution. It also built upon the changes instantiated in 1985 with the creation of new competitive categories such as "Window on the World" and "Films of the Diaspora," the winner of the latter receiving the Paul Robeson Prize that was awarded for the first time at the 1989 FESPACO. The introduction of themes, and the specific ones chosen for the 1985 and 1987 FESPACOs marked the revolution's commitment to fulfilling one of the main aspirations of African filmmakers that dated to the decolonization era, which was "the necessity for Africans to appropriate for themselves the means of self-expression to raise consciousness" and create their own culture freed from imperialism.[17] That year's winner of the Étalon de Yennenga, Hondo's *Sarraounia* (1986), fit with the framework of the Tenth FESPACO and embodied the project of seizing the tools of filmmaking to forge an anti-imperialist and liberated sense of self in the course of remaking the world.

Africa's filmmakers testified to the importance of the Democratic and Popular Revolution in the cinematic field through their actions after the CNR was removed from power in Compaoré's coup. In anticipation of the 1989 FESPACO, many directors, led by Hondo and Hailé Gerima, tried to organize a boycott to express their unwillingness to cooperate with the Popular Front regime on any level. Others argued it was important to attend to pay homage to Sankara and the ideals of the CNR government. Most went to Ouagadougou, and there were conspicuous acknowledgments of Sankara's impact on African cinema and FEPACI's continued adherence to the revolution's mission of transforming the person and the world.[18]

Despite the CNR's violent overthrow in 1987, the changes to African cinema persisted in subsequent decades as evidenced in the transformed nature of FESPACO and the films produced by the continent's directors. In terms of style and content, there was a palpable shift inaugurated under the influence of the Burkinabè Revolution. Increasingly, African films tackled historical subjects, often linked to local, largely rural traditions. Such was the case with Hondo's *Sarraounia* (1986) as well as Sembène's *Camp de Thiaroye* (1988), and Cissé's *Yeelen* (1987). The move toward a deeper analysis of peasant and precolonial life was most evident in the increased production of Burkinabè films, already presaged with Kaboré's *Wend Kuuni* (1982) and built upon by Idrissa Ouédraogo's *Yam Daabo* (1986), Kaboré's *Zan Boko* (1988), as well as Idrissa Ouédraogo's *Yaaba* (1989) and *Tilaï* (1990). Those films shared an aesthetic that valorized rural life, indigenous customs, and explored themes like the pursuit of justice, self-discovery, and adaptation to a changing world. Consequently, the effect was to position the peasantry as part of the larger world, shaped by and transforming it.

They participated in a process described by Fanon as opening the space for a new humanism. He writes, "the two cultures can affront each other, enrich each other. . . . [U]niversality resides in this decision to recognize and accept the reciprocal relativism of different cultures, once the colonial status is irreversibly excluded."[19] Ukadike notes how collectively the films from Burkina Faso during the 1980s and early 1990s effectively deployed the techniques of oral storytelling transposed into the cinematographic framework. Prominently exhibited in Idrissa Ouédraogo's work, he explains that a new wave of African cinema emerged "in which the humanistic and the universalist interweave with the ancient and the present" as part of a conscious effort "to internationalize black African cinema to gain larger audiences."[20]

That trend carried into the 1990s and beyond as African filmmakers explored the ways in which the continent's societies fit into and were impacted by neoliberal capitalist globalization, another reflection of the ways that the Burkinabè Revolution established the discursive and ideological framework for understanding global dynamics. The Sankara government repeatedly challenged the strictures of the IMF, World Bank, and Western governments that used debt as an instrument of control and manipulation of people around the world. Those concerns found expression through films by Abderrahmane Sissako (*La Vie sur Terre*, 1998; *Bamako*, 2006; and *Timbuktu*, 2014) as well as Mambèty's *Hyènes* (1992) among others. Sissako says that *Bamako* resulted from a felt sense "of urgency to bring up the hypocrisy of the North toward the Southern countries." His work as well as others of the generation of African cineastes that came to prominence well after Sankara's assassination revived explicit political filmmaking while incorporating and foregrounding African cultures, languages, and the experiences of people from all parts of society, most notably from rural communities. That synthesis, emerging from the context of the impact of the Burkinabè Revolution on African cinema, spoke to an aspirational new global humanism in which African voices had their equal place.[21]

More formal recognition of the enduring influence of the Burkinabè Revolution on African cinema had to await Compaoré's removal from power in October 2014. The next month, in November 2014, the Guilde Africaine de Réalisateurs et Producteurs (GARP) created the Prix Thomas Sankara. It was awarded for the first time at the next FESPACO on 6 March 2015. The award assisted in the production of a short film that demonstrated "dramatic creativity, narrative talent, technical excellence, and a positive representation of the pan-African imagination."[22] Four years later, at the 2019 FESPACO, the African filmmakers marked the festival's fiftieth anniversary by declaring that year's theme to be a reprise of the 1985 FESPACO's focus on "Cinema and People's Liberation." In addition, the event included the unveiling of a statue of Sankara.[23]

Transformation of Burkinabè Society

The revolution's cultural politics were expressed through three areas of structural change that were implemented to create the space for the creation of new people and a new global humanism. That entailed a thorough remaking of the institutions of governance, altering social conditions in rural communities, and changing the international order. The CNR's policies produced tangible and almost immediate positive results in people's daily lives. Burkina Faso's GDP expanded from $1.6 billion to almost $2.4 billion between 1983 and 1987. School enrollment improved from 21.8 percent to 29.8 percent during those years. Life expectancy rose by a full year from 48.5 to 49.5 years at birth. And per capita GNI recovered from the period of sharp declines in the early 1980s, rising from $240 to $270 during the CNR's period in power. Carbon dioxide emissions dropped from 0.081 metric tons per capita to 0.064 over the period 1983–1987. Real GDP growth soared during the years of Sankara's presidency from –1.2 percent when he came to office to 1.6 percent in 1984, 11.3 percent in 1985 (the pear of the PPD), and 8.0 in 1986 percent (as the PQDP got underway), falling to –0.2 percent in the turbulent year of 1987.²⁴ The one area where conditions did not improve was in Burkina Faso's external debt, which rose from nearly $398 million in 1983 to $827.5 million in 1987.²⁵

From its inception, the Burkinabè Revolution sought to break down the structures of patriarchy that undermined the contribution of half of the country's population to its development, which was intricately linked to a transformation of practices in rural Burkina Faso. The *Discours d'Orientation Politique* pronounced, "The Revolution and women's liberation go together. . . . It is a fundamental necessity for the triumph of the Revolution." That emancipation involved a basic transformation of men's and women's mentalities, to think and act differently than before.²⁶ This was part of the project of having the people rely on themselves and their resources at hand (human and material) to lift the country out of poverty and underdevelopment. Women were appointed to leadership positions across Burkina Faso, notably in rural communities. Peasants organized collectives to initiate development programs that would make their lives better. People dug wells, participated in reforestation programs, rationalized agricultural techniques, and improved the transportation and communication infrastructure. Economic policies were tied to the objective of building self-confidence among the people and solidarity between communities. Bonzi, recalled with excitement the "Day of the Peasant" in 1987 when Sankara arrived to give a speech in Houndé. He declared, "Yes, the Revolution was conscious that the peasantry was the motor of our economy and that it would not be neglected." Bonzi describes with amazement his use of the "X9" bus system established by the revolution as he made his way to Ouagadougou for the first time. He remarks, "In our days it was a luxury to travel, that is why the Revolution launched this program," which included "Faso Tours" to organize vacation trips for people throughout the country.²⁷ Those impacts, subtle as they were in some instances, remained imprinted on the Burkinabè people's memory of the revolution as was displayed during the upheaval decades later when Compaoré was removed from power.

Global Impact

The CNR positioned the unfolding domestic changes in the global context. The revolution was in danger so long as the world order was dominated by imperialism. The Burkinabè government pursued an aggressive foreign policy based on an unshakable core set of principles that included justice, transparency, equality, solidarity, resistance to oppression in all forms, and the liberation of all peoples. As Sankara said in a 1985 interview, "But we face a dilemma: We either remain silent on positions we believe to be correct, consciously lying to enjoy the good graces of those who can help us, to please our delicate and powerful partners. Or we tell the truth in the firm conviction that we are helping our own people and others."[28] Burkina Faso forged close relationships with Cuba, Nicaragua, Ghana, North Korea, China, and anti-imperialist movements, especially with the Sahrawi, Kanaks, and those resisting apartheid on all fronts (ANC, Angola, Mozambique, SWAPO). From Sankara's disquisition before the General Assembly of the UN in October 1984 to his remarks before the meeting of the Non-Aligned Movement in September 1986 and his speech to the OAU in July 1987, the Burkinabè leader highlighted the injustices of the current world system, demanding that those in positions of responsibility take the actions needed to remedy the plight of the poor and the oppressed.[29] The CNR refused to accept the imposition of structural adjustment programs from the IMF or World Bank and called on the people to contribute what they could to support its programs while also building networks of solidarity with friendly countries on the basis of mutual exchange of people and resources. The Burkinabè Revolution worked to break the neocolonial bonds with France that dated to Upper Volta's independence in 1960.

The Burkinabè Revolution brought to the fore critical issues that impacted the country and the world, again highlighting how they were interconnected. Those included international debt, food dependency, and climate change. The CNR enacted a reforestation program at the start of 1984, followed by the institutionalization of tree planting as part of every region's development projects. As Harsch points out, it would be nearly a decade before the rest of the world began to catch up to where Burkina Faso was on the link between environmental preservation and development.[30] Fofack adds, "Although global warming has become a major concern in the international community in recent years, the tree-planting initiative was criticized at the time as a misplaced priority for a poor country which had no control over carbon pollution.... Sankara had the courage to identify and confront the major constraints to the implementation of his development strategy."[31]

Empowerment at the Grassroots, Instability at the Top

While the CNR represented the pinnacle of the state, the CDR were intended as the base of popular mobilization. People from all walks of life organized in those committees to defend the revolution, and to articulate and carry out the objectives of the Democratic and Popular Revolution. Those institutions were dismantled in March 1988 by the Compaoré regime.[32] The revolutionary government instituted TPR as a new system of jurisprudence that freed justice from corrupt officials and politicians and enabled the people to call to account those who had exploited them and robbed the country. Kyélem de Tambèla writes, "By the clear exposition of the fact, by the debates that they carried out, and by the grace of the often-admirable competence of the judges, the TPR permitted the citizens to be informed, to be instructed, and to be familiarized with the problems related to the management of the records and resources of the state. . . . The success of the TPR led the CNR to extend the system to all parts of the country."[33]

Unfortunately, the CNR failed to achieve unity, and over the years, it was division among the revolution's leaders that led to its undoing. The Burkinabè Revolution was born of a coalition of revolutionary and progressive forces forged over decades in the fires of political struggle against colonialism, corruption, poverty, environmental catastrophe, and most importantly through the articulation of a vision of the future where the people shaped their destiny in ways that met their basic needs and aspirations. Shortly after their triumph on 4 August 1983, the partners within the CNR began to turn on one another. Initially, differences arose over the pace and depth of the revolution, but soon personal conflicts and political jealousies arose that were masked by increasingly radical rhetoric enforced through reactionary practices. Sankara often played the role of mediator, but he frequently did not enjoy the support of most of the country's ruling committee. He hoped that, by merging the groups into a vanguard party, it would compel them to work together. That goal was never realized, and the base of the CNR and Sankara's position within it narrowed over time. That was reflected in the gradual reassertion of the military's role in leadership from governing institutions like the CDR to control over implementation of the PQDP. In the end, Harsch writes, "A small group of army officers, acting in secret, chose to resolve their differences with Sankara through the method they knew best—military force."[34]

In one of his last public acts, Sankara dedicated a street in Che Guevara's name to his memory and cited the oft-repeated line that you can kill the individual, but "you cannot kill ideas."[35] The CNR leader asserted that "we must dare to invent the future. . . . 'Everything man is capable of imagining, he can create.' I'm convinced that's true."[36] The *Discours d'Orientation Politique* defined the revolution as having the "primordial task of the liquidation of imperialist domination and exploitation . . . [and] the purging of . . . all the social, economic, and cultural obstacles that keep [the people] in a state of backwardness" to "create a new society, free, independent, and prosperous."[37] As the *Guardian* described the scene over twenty-seven years after Sankara's murder, "When residents of Ouagadougou took to the streets last week to protest against a military coup, there was one name on their lips. Wearing T-shirts bearing the image of the legendary former Burkina Faso leader, Thomas Sankara, they chanted the slogan of his government: 'Homeland or death, we will win!'"[38] Sankara became the personification of the Burkinabè Revolution and through the invocation of his name, the people of Burkina Faso resurrected the ideals of the Democratic and Popular Revolution. The work of African filmmakers, in important ways, was a bridge connecting the revolutionary years to the twenty-first century and has kept alive what the CNR leader described as "the glorious march of our people toward happiness."[39]

Notes

PREFACE

1. "A Sad Day for Africa," *Update Africa Report* 32, no. 6 (1 November 1987): p. 5.
2. Kingsley Kobo, "Burkina Faso: Ghost of 'Africa's Che Guevara,'" *Al Jazeera America*, 30 October 2014.
3. Eduardo Molano, "Jazz, Rivalry and Revolution: Burkina Faso Recalls the Spirit of Sankara," *Guardian*, 27 September 2015, https://theguardian.com/world/2015/sep/27/jazz-and-revolution-burkina-faso-recalls-the-spirit-of-sankara.
4. International Monetary Fund (IMF), "Burkina Faso: Transactions with the Fund from May 01, 1984 to December 31, 2019," https://www.imf.org/external/np/fin/tad/extrans1.aspx?memberKey1=95&endDate=2099%2D12%2D31&finposition_flag=YES.
5. Stephen Ellis, *The Mask of Anarchy: The Destruction of Liberia and the Religious Dimension of an African Civil War* (London: Hurst & Company, 2007), pp. 2, 15, 66–67, 68.
6. Ernest Harsch, *Thomas Sankara: An African Revolutionary* (Athens: Ohio University Press, 2014), pp. 88–91.
7. Clément Tapsoba, "Préface," in Colin Dupré, *Le FESPACO, une affaire d'état(s): 1969–2009* (Paris: L'Harmattan, 2012), p. 9.
8. James E. Genova, *Cinema and Development in West Africa* (Bloomington: Indiana University Press, 2013), pp. 153–55; Colin Dupré, *Le FESPACO, une affaire d'état(s):*

1969–2009 (Paris: L'Harmattan, 2012), pp. 162, 167, 169.

9. Dupré, *Le FESPACO*, pp. 171–72; Nwachukwu Frank Ukadike, *Black African Cinema* (Berkeley: University of California Press, 1994), pp. 199–200; Manthia Diawara, *African Cinema: Politics & Culture* (Bloomington: Indiana University Press, 1992), p. 137.

10. Apollinaire J. Kyélem de Tambèla, *Thomas Sankara et la Révolution au Burkina Faso: Une experience de développement autocentré*, 2nd ed. (Ouagadougou: Harmattan Burkina, 2012), pp. 238–39.

11. Dupré, *Le FESPACO*, p. 188.

12. Dupré, *Le FESPACO*, pp. 177–78.

13. Speech by Thomas Sankara before the UN General Assembly, Thirty-Ninth Session, Twentieth Plenary Meeting, Agenda Item 9, A/39/PV.20 (4 October 1984), https://undocs.org/fr/A/39/PV.20. Throughout the speech Sankara talked about the "cultural alienation" and search for the essence of the person in Africa that has shaped the continent's political history since colonialism and even beyond. All translations are mine unless otherwise noted.

14. I am using the concept of the limits of the possible as articulated first by Karl Marx and elaborated upon later by Pierre Bourdieu. See Karl Marx, *The Eighteenth Brumaire of Louis Bonaparte* (New York: International Publishers, 1990), p. 15; Pierre Bourdieu and Loïc J. D. Wacquant, *An Invitation to Reflexive Sociology* (Chicago: University of Chicago Press, 1992), pp. 98–99. Fanon also warns against the recourse to "biological justifications" for communal identity. See Frantz Fanon, *Toward the African Revolution* (New York: Grove, 1967), p. 43.

15. Pierre Englebert, *La Révolution Burkinabè* (Paris: L'Harmattan, 1986), p. 41.

16. Frantz Fanon, *The Wretched of the Earth* (New York: Grove, 1963), pp. 35, 36.

17. Fanon, *Toward the African Revolution*, pp. 38, 41, 42, 43.

18. I explore the emergence of this social group and Fanon's contemporaneous critique of it in: James E. Genova, *Colonial Ambivalence, Cultural Authenticity, and the Limitations of Mimicry in French-Ruled West Africa, 1914–1956* (New York: Peter Lang, 2004), pp. 281–82.

19. Fanon, *The Wretched of the Earth*, pp. 246, 241, 203.

20. Karl Marx, *The Economic & Philosophic Manuscripts of 1844* (New York: International Publishers, 1993), pp. 149, 150, 187.

21. Marx, *The Economic & Philosophic Manuscripts of 1844*, p. 140.

22. Fanon, *The Wretched of the Earth*, p. 150. The revolutionaries' emphasis on the will of the people to carry out the revolution's aims also indicates the influence of Mao

Zedong's philosophy on the leaders of the CNR. See Bruno Jaffré, *Biographie de Thomas Sankara: La patrie ou la mort* (Paris: L'Harmattan, 1997), p. 106.
23. Englebert, *La Révolution Burkinabè*, pp. 18–19, 82–83.
24. Englebert, *La Révolution Burkinabè*, p. 208.
25. Ludo Martens, *Sankara, Compaoré et la révolution Burkinabè* (Anvers, Belgium: EPO Dossier International, 1989), pp. 46, 68, 298–99, 301.
26. Bruno Jaffré, *Burkina Faso: Les années Sankara de la révolution à la rectification* (Paris: L'Harmattan, 1989), pp. 282, 261, 263, 265–66.
27. Jaffré, *Biographie de Thomas Sankara*, pp. 77, 100, 103, 106, 108, 175–79.
28. Harsch, *Thomas Sankara*, pp. 9–10.
29. Brian J. Peterson, *Thomas Sankara: A Revolutionary in Cold War Africa* (Bloomington: Indiana University Press, 2021), pp. 12, 13, 284–87, 304–5.
30. Victoria Brittain, "Introduction to Sankara & Burkina Faso," *Review of African Political Economy* 32 (April 1985): pp. 39–47; Guy Martin, "Ideology and Praxis in Thomas Sankara's Populist Revolution of 4 August 1983 in Burkina Faso," *Issue* 15 (1987): pp. 77–90; Charles Kabeya, "Évolution et rôle des syndicats au Burkina Faso," *Présence Africaine* 142 (1987): pp. 130–47; Guy Martin, "Démocratie révolutionnaire, conflits socio-politiques et pouvoir militaire au Burkina Faso, 1983–1988," *Labor, Capital and Society/Travail, capital, et société* 23, no. 1 (April 1990): pp. 38–68; Elliott P. Skinner, "Sankara and the Burkinabè Revolution: Charisma and Power, Local and External Dimensions," *Journal of Modern African Studies* 26, no. 3 (September 1988): pp. 437–55.
31. Kyélem de Tambèla, *Thomas Sankara et la Révolution au Burkina Faso*, pp. 298–322.
32. René Otayek, Filiga Michel Sawadogo, and Jean-Pierre Guinganè, eds., *Le Burkina entre révolution et démocratie (1983–1993)* (Paris: Éditions Karthala, 1996); Ndongo Samba Sylla, ed., *Redécouvrir Sankara: Martyr de la liberté* (Douala, Cameroon: Africavenir, 2012); Jean-Emmanuel Pondi, *Thomas Sankara et l'émergence de l'Afrique au XXIe siècle* (Yaoundé, Cameroon: Éditions Afric'Eveil, 2016).
33. Pierre Englebert, *Burkina Faso: Unsteady Statehood in West Africa* (New York: Routledge, 2018); this is a reissue and update of a book first published in 1996. Ernest Harsch, *Burkina Faso: A History of Power, Protest, and Revolution* (London: Zed Books, 2017).
34. Dupré, *Le FESPACO*, pp. 23–24, 317.
35. See my earlier work on the "cinema industrial complex" for a full discussion of its origins and development in West Africa: Genova, *Cinema and Development in West Africa*, pp. 7–10.

36. Fanon, *Toward the African Revolution*, pp. 43–44, 102.

CHAPTER 1. POLITICS AND CULTURE IN UPPER VOLTA (1960S–1982)

1. Bruno Jaffré, *Biographie de Thomas Sankara: La patrie ou la mort* (Paris: L'Harmattan, 1997), p. 16.
2. For work that explores how France attempted to manage the decolonization process in West Africa, see James E. Genova, *Colonial Ambivalence, Cultural Authenticity, and the Limitations of Mimicry in French-Ruled West Africa, 1914–1956* (New York: Peter Lang, 2004); Tony Chafer, *The End of Empire in French West Africa: France's Successful Decolonization?* (New York: Berg, 2002); Elizabeth Schmidt, *Cold War and Decolonization in Guinea, 1946–1958* (Athens: Ohio University Press, 2007); Phillip C. Naylor, *France and Algeria: A History of Decolonization and Transformation* (Gainesville: University Press of Florida, 2000).
3. B. P. Bamouni, "L'Évolution politique de la Haute-Volta," *Peuples noirs, Peuples africains* 34 (July–August 1983): pp. 54–55; Babou Paulin Bamouni, *Burkina Faso: Processus de la Révolution* (Paris: L'Harmattan, 1986), p. 31.
4. Genova, *Colonial Ambivalence*, pp. 281, 282; Frantz Fanon, *The Wretched of the Earth* (New York: Grove, 1963), p. 36; Achille Mbembe, *On the Postcolony* (Berkeley: University of California Press, 2001), pp. 142–43.
5. James E. Genova, *Cinema and Development in West Africa* (Bloomington: Indiana University Press, 2013), pp. 93–96.
6. Genova, *Colonial Ambivalence*, pp. 239–41, 253; Elizabeth Schmidt, *Cold War and Decolonization in Guinea, 1946–1958* (Athens: Ohio University Press, 2007), pp. 60, 110; and Jaffré, *Biographie de Thomas Sankara*, p. 42.
7. Pierre Englebert, *La Révolution Burkinabè* (Paris: L'Harmattan, 1986), pp. 26, 27–28.
8. Englebert, *La Révolution Burkinabè*, pp. 30–31; Jaffré, *Biographie de Thomas Sankara*, 44–45; and Bamouni, "L'Évolution politique de la Haute-Volta," pp. 62–63.
9. Elliott P. Skinner, "The Changing Status of the 'Emperor of the Mossi' under Colonial Rule and since Independence," in *West African Chiefs: Their Changing Status under Colonial Rule and Independence*, ed. Micheal Crowder and Obaro Ikime (New York: Africana, 1970), pp. 108–11; Joseph-Roger Benoist, *L'Afrique occidentale française de 1944 à 1960* (Dakar, Senegal: Les Nouvelles Éditions Africaines, 1982), pp. 114–15.
10. Philippe Lippens, *La République de Haute-Volta* (Paris: Berger-Levrault, 1972), p. 21;

"Resolution of the RDA Congress in February 1962," cited in Englebert, *La Révolution Burkinabè*, p. 35.

11. Bamouni, "L'Évolution politique de la Haute-Volta," p. 63. Bamouni cites figures for the mounting debt incurred by the Yaméogo regime, much of which went to him and his family.
12. Englebert, *La Révolution Burkinabè*, pp. 37–38. See also Jaffré, *Biographie de Thomas Sankara*, p. 45.
13. Bamouni, "L'Évolution politique de la Haute-Volta," p. 63. See also Englebert, *La Révolution Burkinabè*, p. 38; Bamouni, *Burkina Faso*, pp. 46–47; Jaffré, *Biographie de Thomas Sankara*, p. 46.
14. Bamouni, "L'Évolution politique de la Haute-Volta," p. 64; Bamouni, *Burkina Faso*, pp. 48–49; Englebert, *La Révolution Burkinabè*, p. 44.
15. Jaffré, *Biographie de Thomas Sankara*, pp. 49–50.
16. Brian J. Peterson, *Thomas Sankara: A Revolutionary in Cold War Africa* (Bloomington: Indiana University Press, 2021), p. 48.
17. Peterson, *Thomas Sankara*, pp. 50–51; Jaffré, *Biographie de Thomas Sankara*, pp. 49–51; and Mamadou Diallo, "Thomas Sankara and the Revolutionary Birth of Burkina Faso," *Viewpoint Magazine* 6, no. 1 (February 2018), https://www.viewpointmag.com/2018/02/01/thomas-sankara-revolutionary-birth-burkina-faso/; and Ernest Harsch, *Burkina Faso: A History of Power, Protest, and Revolution* (London: Zed Books, 2017), pp. 26–27.
18. Peterson, *Thomas Sankara*, p. 52.
19. Jaffré, *Biographie de Thomas Sankara*, p. 51.
20. Colin Dupré, *Le FESPACO, une affaire d'état(s): 1969–2009* (Paris: L'Harmattan, 2012), p. 85. Dupré cites Stanislas Bemile Méla, *Le film africain face à la competition, analyse des étalons du Fespaco de 1972 à 2005* (doctoral thesis, IUT Michel de Montaigne–Université de Bordeaux 3, 2006).
21. Fanon, *The Wretched of the Earth*, pp. 209, 245–47.
22. Genova, *Cinema and Development in West Africa*, pp. 117–23, p. 144.
23. James E. Genova, "Re-Thinking African Cinema in the Context of Third Cinema: From *Mandabi* to *Bamako* and the Mediascape of Postcolonial Identity," in *Rethinking Third Cinema: The Role of Anti-colonial Media and Aesthetics in Postmodernity*, ed. Frieda Ekotto and Adeline Koh (Berlin: Lit Verlag, 2009), p. 126. See also Kenneth W. Harrow, *Postcolonial African Cinema: From Political Engagement to Postmodernism* (Bloomington: Indiana University Press, 2007), p. 23.
24. Frantz Fanon, *Toward the African Revolution* (New York: Grove, 1967), p. 44.

25. Genova, *Cinema and Development in West Africa*, pp. 146–47; Paulin Soumanou Vieyra, "African Cinema: Solidarity and Difference," in *Questions of Third Cinema*, ed. Jim Pines and Paul Willemen (London: British Film Institute, 1991), pp. 196–97; Dupré, *Le FESPACO*, pp. 56–59.
26. Genova, *Cinema and Development in West Africa*, p. 147.
27. Dupré, *Le FESPACO*, pp. 88–91; Genova, *Cinema and Development in West Africa*, pp. 149–50.
28. *Le Manifeste Culturel Panafricain*, adopted at the First Pan-African Cultural Festival, Algiers, Algeria, 1 August 1969, https://ocpa.irmo.hr/resources/docs/Pan_African_Cultural_Manifesto-fr.pdf.
29. Genova, *Cinema and Development in West Africa*, p. 147; Rod Stoneman, "South/South Axis: For a Cinema Built by, with and for Africans," in *African Experiences of Cinema*, ed. Imruh Bakari and Mbye Cham (London: British Film Institute, 1996), p. 176.
30. Genova, *Cinema and Development in West Africa*, pp. 38–44, 133–41.
31. Dupré, *Le FESPACO*, pp. 115–16; Genova, *Cinema and Development in West Africa*, pp. 153–54.
32. Genova, *Cinema and Development in West Africa*, pp. 154–55; Dupré, *Le FESPACO*, pp. 115–16, 123.
33. Englebert, *La Révolution Burkinabè*, p. 47; Dupré, *Le FESPACO*, p. 98; Genova, *Cinema and Development in West Africa*, pp. 154–55.
34. Dupré, *Le FESPACO*, pp. 127, 133.
35. "Burkina Faso External Debt 1971–2019," published by *Macrotrends*, citing World Bank data, https://www.macrotrends.net/countries/BFA/burkina-faso/external-debt-stock.
36. Englebert, *L Révolution Burkinabè*, p. 49.
37. Englebert, *L Révolution Burkinabè*, p. 50.
38. Ludo Martens, *Sankara, Compaoré et la révolution Burkinabè* (Anvers, Belgium: EPO Dossier International, 1989), p. 108; Jaffré, *Biographie de Thomas Sankara*, pp. 97–98.
39. Jaffré, *Biographie de Thomas Sankara*, pp. 63–66; Harsch, *Thomas Sankara*, pp. 27–29; and Peterson, *Thomas Sankara*, pp. 53–60.
40. Said Bouamama, *Figures de la révolution africaine de Kenyatta à Sankara* (Paris: Éditions la Découverte, 2014), p. 277. Bouamama cites an interview Sankara gave in 1986 in which he also listed V. I. Lenin's *State and Revolution*, the Bible, and the Quran as the three most influential books in his life.
41. Antonio Gramsci, *Selections from the Prison Notebooks*, edited and translated by

Quintin Hoare and Geoffrey Nowell Smith (New York: International, 1992), pp. 418–19. Here Gramsci describes the process whereby thought is translated into action in the material world, calling it "praxis."

42. Harsch, *Thomas Sankara*, pp. 27–28; Jaffré, *Biographie de Thomas Sankara*, pp. 66, 70; and Peterson, *Thomas Sankara*, p. 60.
43. Jaffré, *Biographie de Thomas Sankara*, pp. 72–73.
44. Harsch, *Thomas Sankara*, p. 30; Jaffré, *Biographie de Thomas Sankara*, pp. 87–88; Diallo, "Thomas Sankara and the Revolutionary Birth of Burkina Faso."
45. Bamouni, *Burkina Faso*, p. 50.
46. Bamouni, "L'Évolution politique de la Haute-Volta," pp. 65–66; Englebert, *La Révolution Burkinabè*, pp. 51–52; Jaffré, *Biographie de Thomas Sankara*, p. 88; Bamouni, *Burkina Faso*, p. 53.
47. Emmanuel Salliot, "A Review of Past Security Events in the Sahel 1967–2007," published by the Sahel and West Africa Club Secretariat of the OECD (2010), pp. 22–23.
48. Jaffré, *Biographie de Thomas Sankara*, pp. 91–95; Harsch, *Thomas Sankara*, p. 31–32; and Peterson, *Thomas Sankara*, pp. 68–69.
49. Martens, *Sankara, Compaoré et la révolution Burkinabè*, 71. The interview was given on 28 February 1989, a little over a year after Sankara was murdered and only months before Boukary Lingani was executed by Compaoré. The information is also reproduced in Jaffré, *Biographie de Thomas Sankara*, pp. 94–95. See also Bridgette Kasuka, *Prominent African Leaders since Independence* (New York: New Africa, 2013), p. 296.
50. Jaffré, *Biographie de Thomas Sankara*, pp. 99–100; Englebert, *La Révolution Burkinabè*, pp. 54–55; Martens, *Sankara, Compaoré et la révolution Burkinabè*, p. 72; Bamouni, *Burkina Faso*, pp. 54–55; Bamouni, "L'Évolution politique de la Haute-Volta," p. 66.
51. Englebert, *La Révolution Burkinabè*, pp. 56–57; Bamouni, *Burkina Faso*, pp. 56–58; Jaffré, *Biographie de Thomas Sankara*, p. 110; Bamouni, "L'Évolution politique de la Haute-Volta," pp. 66–68.
52. "Burkina Faso External Debt 1971–2019."
53. "Burkina Faso Data Bank," published by the World Bank, https://data.worldbank.org/country/burkina-faso.
54. Bamouni, *Burkina Faso*, pp. 58–60.
55. "Burkina Faso Data Bank," World Bank.
56. Diallo, "Thomas Sankara and the Revolutionary Birth of Burkina Faso."

57. Jaffré, *Biographie de Thomas Sankara*, pp. 100–108.
58. Jaffré, *Biographie de Thomas Sankara*, pp. 103, 106; Harsch, *Thomas Sankara*, pp. 26–27.
59. Jaffré, *Biographie de Thomas Sankara*, p. 103.
60. Martens, *Sankara, Compaoré et la révolution Burkinabè*, pp. 117–21; Peterson, *Thomas Sankara*, pp. 58–59.
61. *Le Manifeste Culturel Panafricain*, First Pan-African Cultural Festival.
62. "Resolutions of the Third World Film-Makers' Meeting, Algiers, 1973," in *African Experiences of Cinema*, ed. Imruh Bakari and Mbye Cham (London: British Film Institute, 1996), p. 20.
63. "Resolutions of the Third World Film-Makers' Meeting, Algiers, 1973," in *Cinemas of the Black Diaspora: Diversity, Dependence and Oppositionality*, ed. Michael T. Marti (Detroit: Wayne State University, 1995), p. 472. For further discussion of the 1973 Third World Filmmakers' Conference, see Maria Roof, "African and Latin American Cinemas: Contexts and Contacts," in *Focus on African Films*, ed. Françoise Pfaff (Bloomington: Indiana University Press, 2004), p. 243; Genova, *Cinema and Development in West Africa*, 148–49; and Dupré, *Le FESPACO*, pp. 74–77.
64. "The Algiers Charter on African Cinema, 1975," in *African Experiences of Cinema*, ed. Imruh Bakari and Mbye Cham (London: British Film Institute, 1996), pp. 25–26.
65. Genova, *Cinema and Development in West Africa*, p. 154.
66. Vieyra, "African Cinema," in *Questions of Third Cinema*, ed. Jim Pines and Paul Willemen (London: British Film Institute, 1991), p. 197; and Dupré, *Le FESPACO*, pp. 78, 131–32.
67. Manthia Diawara, *African Cinema: Politics & Culture* (Bloomington: Indiana University Press, 1992), p. 61; and Harrow, *Postcolonial African Cinema*, p. 44.
68. Genova, "Re-Thinking African Cinema in the Context of Third Cinema," pp. 145–46.
69. Dupré, *Le FESPACO*, pp. 78–79.
70. "Niamey Manifesto of African Filmmakers, 1982," in *African Experiences of Cinema*, ed. Imruh Bakari and Mbye Cham (London: British Film Institute, 1996), pp. 27–30.
71. Bamouni, "L'Évolution politique de la Haute-Volta," p. 67.
72. Jaffré, *Biographie de Thomas Sankara*, pp. 117–18.
73. Englebert, *La Révolution Burkinabè*, p. 61. See also Jaffré, *Biographie de Thomas Sankara*, pp. 117–18; Bamouni, *Burkina Faso*, pp. 60–61.
74. Englebert, *La Révolution Burkinabè*, p. 61; Bamouni, *Burkina Faso*, pp. 61–62; Bamouni, "L'Évolution politique de la Haute-Volta," p. 69; Jaffré, *Biographie de Thomas Sankara*, p. 118.

75. René Odou, "Haute-Volta—Une rêve se brise," *Afrique Nouvelle* 1642 (December 1980): p. 15. Also cited in Kyélem de Tambèla, *Thomas Sankara et la Révolution au Burkina Faso*, p. 46.
76. Englebert, *La Révolution Burkinabè*, p. 62. He quotes an article on the coup from *Le Monde*, 12 December 1980, p. 7.
77. Bamouni, *Burkina Faso*, pp. 63–65; Englebert, *La Révolution Burkinabè*, p. 63; Jaffré, *Biographie de Thomas Sankara*, p. 118; Bamouni, "L'Évolution politique de la Haute-Volta," pp. 70–71.
78. Jaffré, *Biographie de Thomas Sankara*, p. 121.
79. Martens, *Sankara, Compaoré et la révolution Burkinabè*, pp. 125–26.
80. Martens, *Sankara, Compaoré et la révolution Burkinabè*, p. 132.
81. Peterson, *Thomas Sankara*, p. 78.
82. "Burkina Faso Inflation Rate 1961–2019," Macrotrends; "Burkina Faso Databank," World Bank; "Country Data of Burkina Faso," published by the International Monetary Fund, https://www.imf.org/en/Countries/BFA.
83. Englebert, *La Révolution Burkinabè*, pp. 64–65; Jaffré, *Biographie de Thomas Sankara*, p. 122; Bamouni, *Burkina Faso*, pp. 65–66; Bamouni, "L'Évolution politique de la Haute-Volta," p. 71.
84. Harsch, *Thomas Sankara*, p. 39.
85. Jaffré, *Biographie de Thomas Sankara*, p. 123; Harsch, *Thomas Sankara*, p. 39; Englebert, *La Révolution Burkinabè*, p. 66; Diallo, "Thomas Sankara and the Revolutionary Birth of Burkina Faso," pp. 82–85.
86. Jaffré, *Biographie de Thomas Sankara*, p. 123.
87. Jaffré, *Biographie de Thomas Sankara*, pp. 123–24; Harsch, *Thomas Sankara*, p. 40.
88. "Letter from Thomas Sankara to Colonel Félix Tiemtaraboum," 23 December 1981, reprinted in Bamouni, *Burkina Faso*, pp. 171–72. Bamouni also produces the letter from 9 September 1981 in which he initially refused the appointment, p. 170.
89. Diallo, "Thomas Sankara and the Revolutionary Birth of Burkina Faso."
90. Colette Drabo, "Fidèle Toé Ancien Compagnon de Thomas Sankara: 'Si Blaise Compaoré s'entête, le peuple peut l'amener à regagner les rangs,'" in *Le Pays*, 15 October 2014, http://lepays.bf/fidele-toe-ancien-compagnon-thomas-sankara-blaise-compaore-sentete-peuple-lamener-regagner-les-rangs/. For a discussion of the circumstances under which Fidèle Toé and Sankara became friends as well as Toé's appointment as chief of staff at the Ministry of Information, see Peterson, *Thomas Sankara*, pp. 39–40, 82.
91. Jaffré, *Biographie de Thomas Sankara*, pp. 124–25; Harsch, *Thomas Sankara*, pp.

40–41; Martens, *Sankara, Compaoré et la révolution Burkinabè*, p. 148.
92. "Letter from Thomas Sankara to Saye Zerbo," (L'interpellation du Directeur de l'A.V.P. à la Sûreté Nationale), dated 4 March 1982, reprinted in Bamouni, *Burkina Faso*, pp. 172–73. Also quoted in Jaffré, *Biographie de Thomas Sankara*, p. 127.
93. "Country Data of Burkina Faso," published by the International Monetary Fund, https://www.imf.org/en/Countries/BFA; "Burkina Faso Databank," published by the World Bank, https://data.worldbank.org/country/burkina-faso.
94. Jaffré, *Biographie de Thomas Sankara*, pp. 127–28; Harsch, *Thomas Sankara*, p. 42; "Letter from Thomas Sankara to Saye Zerbo," 12 April 1982, reprinted in Bamouni, *Burkina Faso*, pp. 173–74; Englebert, *La Révolution Burkinabè*, p. 66; Dupré, *Le FESPACO*, pp. 170–71; and Peterson, *Thomas Sankara*, p. 85.
95. Roland Fayel, "Haute-Volta: L'Inlisement," *Aujourd'hui Afrique* 26 (1982): pp. 28–29; also cited in Jaffré, *Biographie de Thomas Sankara*, p. 129.
96. Cited in Jaffré, *Biographie de Thomas Sankara*, p. 130. The work of the commission is also related in Martens, *Sankara, Compaoré et la révolution Burkinabè*, p. 75.
97. Jaffré, *Biographie de Thomas Sankara*, pp. 133–36; Bamouni, *Burkina Faso*, p. 69; Harsch, *Thomas Sankara*, pp. 43–44; Englebert, *La Révolution Burkinabè*, pp. 68–71; Bamouni, "L'Évolution politique de la Haute-Volta," pp. 71–72; Diallo, "Thomas Sankara and the Revolutionary Birth of Burkina Faso."

CHAPTER 2. DUAL POWER AND THE TRIUMPH OF THE BURKINABÈ REVOLUTION (1982–1983)

1. "Proclamation of the Council for the Salvation of the People," published in *Carrefour Africain* 752 (12 November 1982):, p. 6. Cited in Bruno Jaffré, *Biographie de Thomas Sankara: La patrie ou la mort* (Paris: L'Harmattan, 1997), pp. 134–35.
2. Jaffré, *Biographie de Thomas Sankara*, p. 130.
3. Babou Paulin Bamouni, *Burkina Faso: Processus de la Révolution* (Paris: L'Harmattan, 1986), pp. 70–71; B. P. Bamouni, "L'Évolution politique de la Haute-Volta," *Peuples noirs, Peuples africains* 34 (July–August 1983): p. 72.
4. Apollinaire J. Kyélem de Tambèla, *Thomas Sankara et la Révolution au Burkina Faso: Une experience de développement autocentré*, 2nd ed. (Ouagadougou: Harmattan Burkina, 2012), pp. 56–57.
5. Jaffré, *Biographie de Thomas Sankara*, pp. 136–37. See also Pierre Englebert, *La Révolution Burkinabè* (Paris: L'Harmattan, 1986), p. 71.

6. Jaffré, *Biographie de Thomas Sankara*, p. 137; Ernest Harsch, *Thomas Sankara: An African Revolutionary* (Athens: Ohio University Press, 2014), p. 44; Kyélem de Tambèla, *Thomas Sankara et la Révolution au Burkina Faso*, pp. 57–59.
7. Bamouni, "L'Évolution Politique de la Haute-Volta," p. 72.
8. Jaffré, *Biographie de Thomas Sankara*, p. 137; Bamouni, "L'Évolution politique de la Haute-Volta," pp. 72–73; Englebert, *La Révolution Burkinabè*, p. 71.
9. Thomas Sankara, "Discours prononcé devant le congrès de SUVESS le 10 décembre 1982," published in *L'Observateur*, 4 January 1983, and in *Politique africaine* 9 (March 1983), Thomas Sankara Archives, http://www.thomassankara.net/discours-prononce-devant-le-congres-du-suvess-le-10-decembre-1982/.
10. Ludo Martens, *Sankara, Compaoré et la révolution Burkinabè* (Anvers, Belgium: EPO Dossier International, 1989), p. 76. Martens conducted the interview with Compaoré on 23 July 1988, several months after he had taken power upon Sankara's murder. Also cited in Jaffré, *Biographie de Thomas Sankara*, p. 137. Fidèle Toé and Bamouni do not mention this meeting in their accounts. Moreover, Valère Somé does not discuss such a meeting in his retelling of the events. See Colette Drabo, "Fidèle Toé, Ancien Compagnon de Thomas Sankara: 'Si Blaise Compaoré s'entête, le peuple peut l'amener à regagner les rangs,'" in *Le Pays*, 15 October 2014, http://lepays.bf/fidele-toe-ancien-compagnon-thomas-sankara-blaise-compaore-sentete-peuple-lamener-regagner-les-rangs/; Bamouni, "L'Évolution politique de la Haute-Volta," pp. 73–74; Valère D. Somé, *Thomas Sankara: L'Espoir Assassiné* (Paris: L'Harmattan, 1990).
11. Kyélem de Tambèla, *Thomas Sankara et la Révolution au Burkina Faso*, pp. 59–60.
12. Jaffré, *Biographie de Thomas Sankara*, p. 137. See also: Bamouni, *Thomas Sankara*, p. 71; Martens, *Sankara, Compaoré et la révolution Burkinabè*, p. 76; Harsch, *Thomas Sankara*, p. 76; Englebert, *La Révolution Burkinabè*, p. 71; Mamadou Diallo, "Thomas Sankara and the Revolutionary Birth of Burkina Faso," *Viewpoint Magazine* 6, no. 1 (February 2018), https://www.viewpointmag.com/2018/02/01/thomas-sankara-revolutionary-birth-burkina-faso/.
13. Bamouni, *Burkina Faso*, pp. 72–73.
14. Thomas Sankara, "Discours d'investiture de Thomas Sankara comme premier minister du CSP 11 January 1983," published in *Carrefour Africain* 764 (4 February 1983), Thomas Sankara Archives, http://www.thomassankara.net/dicours-dinvestiture-de-thomas-sankara-comme-premier-ministre-du-csp-2-en-janvier-1983/.
15. Anne Chia, "Ghana Must Go: Nigeria's Expulsion of Immigrants," published as part of Anne Chia's blog, *Immigration, Life, Politics, and International Affairs*, 20

April 2015, https://annechia.com/2015/04/20/ghana-must-go-nigerias-expulsion-of-immigrants/; Johnson Olaosebikan Aremu, "Responses to the 1983 Expulsion of Aliens from Nigeria: A Critique," in *African Research Review* 7(3), no. 30 (July 2013):pp. 340–41; Associated Press, "Expelled Foreigners Pouring Out of Nigeria," *New York Times*, 5 May 1985, p. 100. The article discussed the 1985 second mass expulsion from Nigeria but references the events of 1983.

16. Daouda Gary-Tounkara, "A Reappraisal of the Expulsion of Illegal Immigrants from Nigeria in 1983," *International Journal of Conflict and Violence* 9, no. 1 (2015):p. 29.
17. Chia, "Ghana Must Go"; Gary-Tounkara, "A Reappraisal of the Expulsion of Illegal Immigrants from Nigeria in 1983," p. 26.
18. Jaffré, *Biographie de Thomas Sankara*, p. 138.
19. Chia, "Ghana Must Go."
20. "Conseil de l'Entênte: De la création à la réforme," http://www.conseildelentente.org/index.php/institution/historique.
21. Report on the Conseil de l'Entênte, in *Carrefour Africain* 765 (11 February 1983): p. 12. Also cited in Jaffré, *Biographie de Thomas Sankara*, pp. 139–40. For the history of the Conseil de l'Entênte, see its official site at http://conseildelentente.org/index.php/institution/historique.html.
22. Aremu, "Responses to the 1983 Expulsion of Aliens from Nigeria," pp. 346–47. Aremu cites reports from the *African Economic Digest* (1983): 6726.
23. Manthia Diawara, *African Cinema: Politics & Culture* (Bloomington: Indiana University Press, 1992), pp. 43–44.
24. "Niamey Manifesto of African Filmmakers, 1982," in *African Experiences of Cinema*, ed. Imruh Bakari and Mbye Cham (London: British Film Institute, 1996), pp. 27–30.
25. Colin Dupré, *Le FESPACO, une affaire d'état(s): 1969–2009* (Paris: L'Harmattan, 2012), p. 170.
26. Dupré, *Le FESPACO*, pp. 170–71. Sankara's speech is quoted in *Africultures* and cited by Dupré.
27. James E. Genova, *Cinema and Development in West Africa* (Bloomington: Indiana University Press, 2013), pp. 136, 146–47.
28. Lindiwe Dovey, *Curating Africa in the Age of Film Festivals* (New York: Palgrave Macmillan, 2015), p. 102; Dupré, *Le FESPACO*, p. 167, citing a press conference, the transcript of which was published in *Sidwaya*, 4 March 1985.
29. Dovey, *Curating Africa in the Age of Film Festivals*, p. 102.
30. Dupré, *Le FESPACO*, p. 181.
31. Nwachukwu Frank Ukadike, *Black African Cinema* (Berkeley: University of

California Press, 1994), p. 199.
32. Jaffré, *Biographie de Thomas Sankara*, pp. 140–41; Harsch, *Thomas Sankara*, p. 46; Brian J. Peterson, *Thomas Sankara: A Revolutionary in Cold War Africa* (Bloomington: Indiana University Press, 2021), p. 96.
33. "Recent Unsuccessful Coup Attempt Explained," published in *West Africa*, 28 March 1983, pp. 770–71; "Coup Plot Discovered," published in *Africa Research Bulletin*, 1983, p. 6781.
34. Peterson, *Thomas Sankara*, p. 96.
35. "Report on the Non-Aligned Movement," *Jeune Afrique* 1161 (6 April 1983):p. 35. Cited in Jaffré, *Biographie de Thomas Sankara*, p. 142.
36. Dupré, *Le FESPACO*, pp. 165–66.
37. Sankara, "Discours prononcé au Sommet des Non alignés de New Delhi en mars 1983."
38. Simon Malley, "Interview with Thomas Sankara," *Afrique Asie* 297 (6 June 1983), cited in Jaffré, *Biographie de Thomas Sankara*, p. 142, note 16.
39. Jaffré, *Biographie de Thomas Sankara*, pp. 143–44.
40. Harsch, *Thomas Sankara*, p. 47.
41. Thomas Sankara, "Qui sont les ennemis du people?" speech delivered in Ouagadougou, Upper Volta, 26 March 1983, published in *Carrefour Africain*, 1 April 1983, Thomas Sankara Archives, http://www.thomassankara.net/qui-sont-les-ennemis-du-peuple-26-mars-1983/.
42. Kyélem de Tambèla, *Thomas Sankara et la Révolution au Burkina Faso*, pp. 62–63. For other accounts of the mood during Jean-Baptiste Ouédraogo's presentation, see Harsch, *Thomas Sankara*, pp. 47–48; Englebert, *La Révolution Burkinabè*, pp. 72–73; Jaffré, *Biographie de Thomas Sankara*, pp. 144–48.
43. President Jean-Baptiste Ouédraogo's speech was published in *Carrefour Africain* 772 (1 April 1997):pp. 22–25, cited by Jaffré, *Biographie de Thomas Sankara*, p. 148.
44. Jaffré, *Biographie de Thomas Sankara*, pp. 148–49.
45. Siradiou Diallo, "La Chute de l'aigle," *Jeune Afrique* 1169 (1 June 1983): p. 24. Cited in Skinner, "Sankara and the Burkinabé Revolution," *Journal of Modern African Studies* 26, no. 3 (September 1988): p. 441.
46. Englebert, *La Révolution Burkinabè*, p. 73.
47. Martens, *Sankara, Compaoré et la révolution Burkinabè*, p. 77.
48. "1983–1987 The Revolution: The 1983 Putsch: Compaoré Installs Sankara," https://www.blaisecompaore.com/en/political-and-military-career/1983-1987-the-revolution/.

49. Kyélem de Tambèla, *Thomas Sankara et la Révolution au Burkina Faso*, p. 67.
50. Thomas Sankara, "Un chat est un chat," speech at Bobo-Dioulasso, Upper Volta, 14 May 1983, http://www.thomassankara.net/discours-de-thomas-sankara-en-direction-de-le-jeunesse-14-mai-1983-a-bobo-dioulasso/.
51. Saglba Yaméogo, "17 Mai 1983: Prémices de la Révolution d'août," in *lefaso.net*, 12 August 2012, https://lefaso.net/spip.php?article49628.
52. Bamouni, *Burkina Faso*, pp. 74–75.
53. Guy Martin, "Ideology and Praxis in Thomas Sankara's Populist Revolution of 4 August 1983 in Burkina Faso," *Issue* 15 (1987): p. 78. Martin cites Victoria Brittain, "Introduction to Sankara & Burkina Faso," *Review of African Political Economy* 32 (April 1985): p. 44.
54. Bamouni, *Burkina Faso*, pp. 75–76; Jaffré, *Biographie de Thomas Sankara*, pp. 150, 152; Kyélem de Tambèla, *Thomas Sankara et la Révolution au Burkina Faso*, pp. 68–69; Martens, *Sankara, Compaoré et la révolution Burkinabè*, pp. 77–78; Harsch, *Thomas Sankara*, p. 48.
55. Jean-Baptiste Ouédraogo, "Déclaration du Président du CSP," 17 May 1983, reprinted in Bamouni, *Burkina Faso*, p. 174.
56. Kyélem de Tambèla, *Thomas Sankara et la Révolution au Burkina Faso*, pp. 69–70.
57. Englebert, *La Révolution Burkinabè*, pp. 74–76. Englebert discusses at some length the speculation of French direction of the coup of 17 May 1983, including the significance of forestalling Libyan influence in Upper Volta considering the ongoing conflict between France and Libya over Chad.
58. Elliott P. Skinner, "Sankara and the Burkinabè Revolution: Charisma and Power, Local and External Dimensions," *Journal of Modern African Studies* 26, no. 3 (September 1988), pp. 442–43.
59. Jaffré, *Biographie de Thomas Sankara*, p. 452.
60. Mohamed Maïga, "Douze heures avec Thomas Sankara," in *Afrique Asie* 305 (26 September 1983), Thomas Sankara Archives, http://www.thomassankara.net/douze-heures-avec-thomas-sankara-exclusif-mensuel-afrique-asie-1983/.
61. "1983–1987 The Revolution: The 1983 Putsch: Compaoré Installs Sankara," https://www.blaisecompaore.com/en/political-and-military-career/1983-1987-the-revolution/.
62. Yaméogo, "17 Mai 1983: Prémices de la Révolution d'août."
63. Jaffré, *Biographie de Thomas Sankara*, p. 153.
64. Diallo, "Thomas Sankara and the Revolutionary Birth of Burkina Faso."
65. Yaméogo, "17 Mai 1983: Prémices de la Révolution d'août"; Jaffré, *Biographie de*

Thomas Sankara, pp. 153–55; Martens, *Sankara, Compaoré et la révolution Burkinabè*, p. 78; Bamouni, *Burkina Faso*, pp. 78–80; Kyélem de Tambèla, *Thomas Sankara et la Révolution au Burkina Faso*, p. 71; Harsch, *Thomas Sankara*, p. 49. As an eyewitness to the events described herein, Bamouni provides a detailed and graphic portrayal of the tumultuous events of those days.

66. Ouédraogo, "La marche des élèves," reprinted in Bamouni, *Burkina Faso*, p. 175; Kyélem de Tambèla, *Thomas Sankara et la Révolution au Burkina Faso*, p. 71; Englebert, *La Révolution Burkinabè*, p. 77; Jaffré, *Biographie de Thomas Sankara*, p. 155; Michael Wilkins, "The Death of Thomas Sankara and the Rectification of the People's Revolution in Burkina Faso," *African Affairs* 88, no. 352 (July 1989): p. 381.

67. "Press Conference of President Jean-Baptiste Ouédraogo," in *Carrefour Africain* 758 (1 July 1983): p. 10, cited by Jaffré, *Biographie de Thomas Sankara*, p. 153; and Englebert, *La Révolution Burkinabè*, p. 75.

68. Jaffré, *Biographie de Thomas Sankara*, pp. 155–56; Martens, *Sankara, Compaoré et la révolution Burkinabè*, p. 78.

69. Kyélem de Tambèla, *Thomas Sankara et la Révolution au Burkina Faso*, pp. 71–72; Englebert, *La Révolution Burkinabè*, pp. 77–78; Martens, *Sankara, Compaoré et la révolution Burkinabè*, p. 78; Bamouni, *Burkina Faso*, pp. 80–81; Jaffré, *Biographie de Thomas Sankara*, pp. 155–56; Skinner, "Sankara and the Burkinabè Revolution," p. 443; Wilkins, "The Death of Thomas Sankara and the Rectification of the People's Revolution in Burkina Faso," p. 381.

70. "Lettre du capitaine Blaise Compaoré aux autres officiers," summer 1983, reprinted in Bamouni, *Burkina Faso*, pp. 176–78. Also cited in Martens, *Sankara, Compaoré et la révolution Burkinabè*, p. 79.

71. Martens, *Sankara, Compaoré et la révolution Burkinabè*, p. 79.

72. "1983–1987 The Revolution: The 1983 Putsch: Compaoré Installs Sankara."

73. Jaffré, *Biographie de Thomas Sankara*, pp. 156–58; Bamouni, *Burkina Faso*, pp. 81–82; Martens, *Sankara, Compaoré et la révolution Burkinabè*, pp. 78–79; Kyélem de Tambèla, *Thomas Sankara et la Révolution au Burkina Faso*, pp. 72–74.

74. Kyélem de Tambèla, *Thomas Sankara et la Révolution au Burkina Faso*, p. 74; Yaméogo, "17 May 1983: Prémices de la Révolution d'août"; "1983–1987 The Revolution: The 1983 Putsch: Compaoré Installs Sankara"; Jaffré, *Biographie de Thomas Sankara*, p. 158.

75. World Bank data on Burkina Faso, https://data.worldbank.org/country/burkina-faso; "Burkina Faso External Debt 1971–2019," reported by Macrotrends using World Bank Data, https://www.macrotrends.net/countries/BFA/burkina-faso/external-debt-stock;

"Burkina Faso Inflation Rate 1961–2019," reported by Macrotrends using World Bank Data, https://www.macrotrends.net/countries/BFA/burkina-faso/inflation-rate-cpi; Burkina Faso Country Report, produced by the IMF, https://www.imf.org/en/Countries/BFA.

76. Yaméogo, "17 May 1983: Prémices de la Révolution d'août"; Martens, *Sankara, Compaoré et la révolution Burkinabè*, pp. 147–49, 155–56; Bamouni, *Burkina Faso*, pp. 80, 176.
77. Jaffré, *Biographie de Thomas Sankara*, p. 161.
78. Jaffré, *Biographie de Thomas Sankara*, p. 162. In an interview with *Jeune Afrique* conducted by Benjamin Roger and published on 13 October 2019, Jean Christophe Mitterrand makes no mention of this interaction, and there is no evidence that the message ever reached the desk of the French president. Benjamin Roger, "Jean-Christophe Mitterrand: 'L'assassinat de Sankara? Selon moi, un accident," *Jeune Afrique*, 13 October 2017, https://www.jeuneafrique.com/mag/481423/politique/jean-christophe-mitterrand-lassassinat-de-sankara%e2%80%89-selon-moi-un-accident/.
79. Mohamed Maïga, "Douze heures avec Thomas Sankara," *Afrique Asie* 305 (26 September 1983), Thomas Sankara Archives, http://www.thomassankara.net/douze-heures-avec-thomas-sankara-exclusif-mensuel-afrique-asie-1983/.
80. Bamouni, *Burkina Faso*, pp. 85–87.
81. Bamouni, *Burkina Faso*, pp. 87–88; "1983–1987 The Revolution: The 1983 Putsch: Compaoré Installs Sankara"; Jaffré, *Biographie de Thomas Sankara*, p. 165.
82. Skinner, "Sankara and the Burkinabé Revolution," p. 443.
83. Bamouni, *Burkina Faso*, pp. 88–91; also reproduced in Jaffré, *Biographie de Thomas Sankara*, pp. 166–70; Diallo, "Thomas Sankara and the Revolutionary Birth of Burkina Faso"; "1983–1987 The Revolution: The 1983 Putsch: Compaoré Installs Sankara"; Skinner, "Sankara and the Burkinabé Revolution," p. 443.
84. Bamouni, *Burkina Faso*, p. 91.
85. Thomas Sankara, "La Déclaration du 4 août 1983," Thomas Sankara Archives, http://www.thomassankara.net/la-declaration-du-4-aout-1983/; also reprinted in Bamouni, *Burkina Faso*, pp. 91–93.
86. Associated Press, "13 Killed in Coup in Upper Volta," published in *New York Times*, 6 August 1983, https://www.nytimes.com/.

CHAPTER 3. BUILDING REVOLUTIONARY STRUCTURES AND MAKING NEW PEOPLE (1983–1984)

1. Babou Paulin Bamouni, *Burkina Faso: Processus de la Révolution* (Paris: L'Harmattan, 1986), p. 93.
2. Ludo Martens, *Sankara, Compaoré et la révolution Burkinabè* (Anvers, Belgium: EPO Dossier International, 1989), pp. 82–83, 157–58.
3. Interview of Ernest Nongma Ouédraogo on Radio Burkina on 15 October 2017, transcribed by Ousmane Hébié and published on 16 October 2017 by *Les Echos du Faso*, "La Grande Révélation de Nongma Ernest sur Blaise Compaoré," http://lesechosdufaso.net/grande-revelation-de-nongma-ernest-blaise-compaore/.
4. Bruno Jaffré, *Biographie de Thomas Sankara: La patrie ou la mort* (Paris: L'Harmattan, 1997), p. 171.
5. Victoria Brittain, "Introduction to Sankara & Burkina Faso," *Review of African Political Economy* 32 (April 1985): p. 45.
6. Apollinaire J. Kyélem de Tambèla, *Thomas Sankara et la Révolution au Burkina Faso: Une experience de développement autocentré*, 2nd ed. (Ouagadougou: Harmattan Burkina, 2012), pp. 76–88.
7. Sennen Andriamirado, *Sankara le rebelle* (Paris: Jeune Afrique Livres, 1987), p. 17. Also cited in Kyélem de Tambèla, *Thomas Sankara et la Révolution au Burkina Faso*, p. 89.
8. Med Hondo, "What Is Cinema for Us?" *African Experiences of Cinema*, ed. Imruh Bakari and Mbye Cham (London: British Film Institute, 1996), pp. 40–41. The essay was reprinted from 1979.
9. Roy Armes, *Third World Film Making and the West* (Berkeley: University of California Press, 1987), p. 99.
10. Colin Dupré, *Le FESPACO, une affaire d'état(s): 1969–2009* (Paris: L'Harmattan, 2012), p. 169.
11. Pierre Englebert, *La Révolution Burkinabè* (Paris: L'Harmattan, 1986), p. 73; Brian J. Peterson, *Thomas Sankara: A Revolutionary in Cold War Africa* (Bloomington: Indiana University Press, 2021), p. 96; Elliott P. Skinner, "Sankara and the Burkinabè Revolution: Charisma and Power, Local and External Dimensions," *Journal of Modern African Studies* 26, no. 3 (September 1988), p. 441.
12. Peterson, *Thomas Sankara*, pp. 8, 9, 10; Michael Wilkins, "The Death of Thomas Sankara and the Rectification of the People's Revolution in Burkina Faso," *African Affairs* 88, no. 352 (July 1989): pp. 381, 383, 385.

13. Englebert, *La Révolution Burkinabè*, p. 123; Bamouni, *Burkina Faso*, pp. 107, 182–83; Jaffré, *Biographie de Thomas Sankara*, pp. 177–81.
14. Jaffré, *Biographie de Thomas Sankara*, p. 184.
15. Mohamed Maïga, "Douze heures avec Thomas Sankara," *Afrique Asie* 306 (10 October 1983), Thomas Sankara Archives, http://www.thomassankara.net/douze-heures-avec-thomas-sankara-exclusif-mensuel-afrique-asie-1983/.
16. Bamouni, *Burkina Faso*, pp. 93, 106–7.
17. Kyélem de Tambèla, *Thomas Sankara et la Révolution au Burkina Faso*, p. 101.
18. *Statut General des Comités de Défense de la Révolution*, 17 May 1984, pp. 7, 21, Thomas Sankara Archives, http://www.thomassankara.net/statut-general-des-cdr-comites-de-defense-de-la-revolution/.
19. Martens, *Sankara, Compaoré et la révolution Burkinabè*, p. 85; Jaffré, *Biographie de Thomas Sankara*, pp. 176–77; Englebert, *La Révolution Burkinabè*, pp. 124–25; Bamouni, *Burkina Faso*, p. 144.
20. *Statut General des Comités de Défense de la Révolution*, pp. 4–5; also found in Englebert, *La Révolution Burkinabè*, pp. 238–54.
21. *Statut Général des Comités de Défense de la Révolution*, pp. 7, 11–13.
22. Jaffré, *Biographie de Thomas Sankara*, pp. 181–82; Martens, *Sankara, Compaoré et la révolution Burkinabè*, p. 134–35.
23. Ernest Harsch, "A Revolution Derailed," *Africa Report* 33, no. 1 (January–February 1988): p. 34; X, "L'Ascension du Capitaine Sankara," *Esprit* 85, no. 1 (January 1984): p. 164; Guy Martin, "Ideology and Praxis in Thomas Sankara's Populist Revolution of 4 August 1983 in Burkina Faso," *Issue* 15 (1987): pp. 78–79; Charles Kabeya, "Évolution et role des syndicats au Burkina Faso," *Présence Africaine* 142 (1987): p. 146.
24. Martens, *Sankara, Compaoré et la révolution Burkinabè*, p. 87. Martens cites the "Declaration of the Central Committee of the PAI," 24 October 1987, p. 4. It should be noted that this document was produced after Sankara's assassination and long after the PAI broke with the CNR. Curiously, the head of the party, Philippe Ouédraogo, was intimately involved in drafting the *Discours d'Orientation Politique* and apparently had no objection at the time to the content or process of its adoption.
25. Ernest Harsch, "A Revolution Derailed," *Africa Report* 33, no. 1 (January–February 1988): pp. 34–35.
26. Guy Martin, "Démocratie révolutionnaire, conflits socio-politiques et pouvoir militaire au Burkina Faso, 1983–1988," *Labor, Capital and Society/Travail, capital, et société* 23, no. 1 (April 1990), p. 47.
27. *Discours d'Orientation Politique*, 2 October 1983, released by the Ministry of

Information on behalf of the CNR, pp. 1, 3, Thomas Sankara Archives, http://www.thomassankara.net/discours-d-orientation-politique-2/.
28. *Discours d'Orientation Politique*, pp. 3, 6, 7–9.
29. *Discours d'Orientation Politique*, pp. 9, 10, 11, 12–15. Frantz Fanon, *The Wretched of the Earth* (New York: Grove, 1963), pp. 35–37.
30. *Discours d'Orientation Politique*, pp. 16–20. James E. Genova, *Cinema and Development in West Africa* (Bloomington: Indiana University Press, 2013), pp. 70–96.
31. *Discours d'Orientation Politique*, pp. 21–22.
32. *Discours d'Orientation Politique*, pp. 4, 12–13, 14, 20.
33. Frantz Fanon, *Toward the African Revolution* (New York: Grove, 1967), p. 33; Fanon, *The Wretched of the Earth*, pp. 210, 223, 233, 246.
34. Englebert, *La Révolution Burkinabè*, pp. 100–101. Abdoulaye Barro, "Pensée et système politiques chez Thomas Sankara," LeFaso.net, 21 October 2016, https://lefaso.net/spip.php?article73792; Jaffré, *Biographie de Thomas Sankara*, pp. 100–106; and Bruno Jaffré, *Burkina Faso: Les années Sankara de la révolution à la rectification* (Paris: L'Harmattan, 1989), pp. 280–83.
35. Babou Paulin Bamouni, *Burkina Faso: Processus de la Révolution* (Paris: L'Harmattan, 1986), p. 145.
36. Martens, *Sankara, Compaoré et la révolution Burkinabè*, p. 28.
37. Bamouni, *Burkina Faso*, pp. 145–46.
38. Howard Schissel, "Six Months into Sankara's Revolution," *Africa Report* 29, no. 2 (March–April 1984): p. 16.
39. Bamouni, *Burkina Faso*, pp. 145–46.
40. Englebert, *La Révolution Burkinabè*, p. 192; Bamouni, *Burkina Faso*, p. 146; Jaffré, *Burkina Faso*, pp. 163–64.
41. Bamouni, *Burkina Faso*, p. 145.
42. Jaffré, *Burkina Faso*, p. 122.
43. Thomas Sankara, "Les Tribunaux populaires de la révolution," 3 January 1984, pp. 1, 2, Thomas Sankara Archives, http://www.thomassankara.net/les-tribunaux-populaires-de-la-revolution-3-janvier-1984/.
44. Jaffré, *Burkina Faso*, pp. 126, 118–19.
45. Interview with Blaise Compaoré published in *Carrefour Africain* 896 (16 August 1985): p. 13. Also cited in Martens, *Sankara, Compaoré et la révolution Burkinabè*, p. 227.
46. Jaffré, *Burkina Faso*, pp. 123, 124; Martin, "Ideology and Praxis in Thomas Sankara's

Populist Revolution of 4 August 1983 in Burkina Faso," pp. 79–81; Martin, "Démocratie révolutionnaire, conflits socio-politiques et pouvoir militaire au Burkina Faso, 1983-1988," pp. 49–51; Kyélem de Tambèla, *Thomas Sankara et la Révolution au Burkina Faso*, p. 133.

47. Martens, *Sankara, Compaoré et la révolution Burkinabè*, p. 112.
48. Martens, *Sankara, Compaoré et la révolution Burkinabè*, pp. 138–40. The letter is taken from the personal archives of Valère Somé. It is also partly cited in Jaffré, *Biographie de Thomas Sankara*, p. 178.
49. Martens, *Sankara, Compaoré et la révolution Burkinabè*, pp. 112–13.
50. Interview with Soumane Touré in *Afrique Asie* 312 (2–15 January 1984). Also cited in Martens, *Sankara, Compaoré et la révolution Burkinabè*, p. 113.
51. Valère D. Somé, *Thomas Sankara: L'espoir assassiné* (Paris: L'Harmattan, 1990), p. 208; Martens, *Sankara, Compaoré et la révolution Burkinabè*, p. 28; Bamouni, *Burkina Faso*, pp. 146–47; Kyélem de Tambèla, *Thomas Sankara et la Révolution au Burkina Faso*, pp. 191–92; Martin, "Démocratie révolutionnaire, conflits socio-politiques et pouvoir militaire au Burkina Faso, p. 58.
52. *Discours d'Orientation Politique*, pp. 9, 19.
53. Kyélem de Tambèla, *Thomas Sankara et la Révolution au Burkina Faso*, pp. 101–2; Jaffré, *Burkina Faso*, p. 141; Englebert, *La Révolution Burkinabè*, pp. 166–67.
54. James E. Genova, *Colonial Ambivalence, Cultural Authenticity, and the Limitations of Mimicry in French-Ruled West Africa, 1914–1956* (New York: Peter Lang, 2004), pp. 101–11.
55. Kyélem de Tambèla, *Thomas Sankara et la Révolution au Burkina Faso*, pp. 113–14; Martin, "Ideology and Praxis in Thomas Sankara's Populist Revolution of 4 August 1983 in Burkina Faso," p. 85.
56. *Discours d'Orientation Politique*, p. 19.
57. Kyélem de Tambèla, *Thomas Sankara et la Révolution au Burkina Faso*, p. 114.
58. Ordinance 84-50, *Journal Officiel*, 16 August 1984, pp. 806–9. Cited also in Englebert, *La Révolution Burkinabè*, p. 167; Bamouni, *Burkina Faso*, p. 156.
59. Bamouni, *Burkina Faso*, p. 156.
60. Kyélem de Tambèla, *Thomas Sankara et la Révolution au Burkina Faso*, p. 114.
61. *Discours d'Orientation Politique*, p. 9.
62. Genova, *Cinema and Development in West Africa*, pp. 128–41; James E. Genova, "Re-Thinking African Cinema in the Context of Third Cinema: From *Mandabi* to *Bamako* and the Mediascape of Postcolonial Identity," in *Rethinking Third Cinema:*

The Role of Anti-colonial Media and Aesthetics in Postmodernity, ed. Frieda Ekotto and Adeline Koh (Berlin: Lit Verlag, 2009), pp. 132–39; Armes, *Third World Film Making and the West*, pp. 286–88.

63. Englebert, *La Révolution Burkinabè*, p. 204. Englebert has the wrong date, stating that Sankara arrived in France on 20 October 1983 when in fact it was on 2 October 1983.
64. "Conférence de presse de Thomas Sankara à l'issue du sommet France-Afrique de Vittel en octobre 1983," Thomas Sankara Archives, https://www.thomassankara.net/conference-de-presse-de-thomas-sankara-a-lissue-du-sommet-france-afrique-de-vittel-en-octobre-1983-retranscription-integrale/; Peterson also covers this moment in: Peterson, *Thomas Sankara*, pp. 147.
65. Englebert, *La Révolution Burkinabè*, p. 193; Jaffré, *Burkina Faso*, pp. 164–65.
66. Béatrice Damiba, "Rassurer nos voisins," *Carrefour Africain* 797 (23 September 1983): p. 21. Also cited in Englebert, *La Révolution Burkinabè*, p. 188.
67. Kyélem de Tambèla, *Thomas Sankara et la Révolution au Burkina Faso*, p. 269.
68. Kyélem de Tambèla, *Thomas Sankara et la Révolution au Burkina Faso*, p. 265.
69. Jaffré, *Burkina Faso*, p. 164.
70. Kyélem de Tambèla, *Thomas Sankara et la Révolution au Burkina Faso*, p. 268; Jaffré, *Burkina Faso*, p. 160.
71. Kyélem de Tambèla, *Thomas Sankara et la Révolution au Burkina Faso*, p. 227.
72. Kyélem de Tambèla, *Thomas Sankara et la Révolution au Burkina Faso*, pp. 228–29, 234, 238–39, 296–97; Peterson, *Burkina Faso*, p. 192.
73. Kyélem de Tambèla, *Thomas Sankara et la Révolution au Burkina Faso*, pp. 293–94.
74. Peterson, *Thomas Sankara*, pp. 135–37.
75. Englebert, *La Révolution Burkinabè*, p. 200. See also the article in *Carrefour Africain* 844 (17 August 1984): p. 26.
76. Kyélem de Tambèla, *Thomas Sankara et la Révolution au Burkina Faso*, p. 287.
77. Englebert, *La Révolution Burkinabè*, p. 202.
78. Kyélem de Tambèla, *Thomas Sankara et la Révolution au Burkina Faso*, pp. 282–84.
79. Kyélem de Tambèla, *Thomas Sankara et la Révolution au Burkina Faso*, p. 284.
80. Englebert, *La Révolution Burkinabè*, pp. 200–201. See also the message sent by Sankara to the Organization of African Unity on 13 July 1984 announcing that Upper Volta would not participate in the Olympic Games published in *Africa Research Bulletin*, July 1984, p. 7327.
81. Press Conference with President Thomas Sankara, transcript published in *Carrefour Africain*, August 1984, reprinted in: Thomas Sankara, *Thomas Sankara Speaks: The*

Burkina Faso Revolution 1983–1987 (New York: Pathfinder Press, 2007), p. 135.

CHAPTER 4. CULTURAL REVOLUTION, ECONOMIC REFORM, AND GLOBAL ENGAGEMENT (1984–1985)

1. *Discours d'Orientation Politique*, issued 2 October 1983, p. 15, Thomas Sankara Archives, http://www.thomassankara.net/discours-d-orientation-politique-2/.
2. Ludo Martens, *Sankara, Compaoré et la révolution Burkinabè* (Anvers, Belgium: EPO Dossier International, 1989), p. 28; Pierre Englebert, *La Révolution Burkinabè* (Paris: L'Harmattan, 1986), pp. 151–52.
3. Order published in the *Journal officiel de la République de Haute-Volta* 26, no. 18 (3 May 1984): pp. 338–55. Also cited in Apollinaire J. Kyélem de Tambèla, *Thomas Sankara et la Révolution au Burkina Faso: Une experience de développement autocentré*, 2nd ed. (Ouagadougou: Harmattan Burkina, 2012), p. 119.
4. Englebert, *La Révolution Burkinabè*, pp. 152–53.
5. Kyélem de Tambèla, *Thomas Sankara et la Révolution au Burkina Faso*, pp.179–80; Valère D. Somé, *Thomas Sankara: L'espoir assassiné* (Paris: L'Harmattan, 1990), p. 209.
6. Martens, *Sankara, Compaoré et la révolution Burkinabè*, pp. 113, 84; Babou Paulin Bamouni, *Burkina Faso: Processus de la Révolution* (Paris: L'Harmattan, 1986), pp. 153, 154; Somé, *Thomas Sankara*, p. 209.
7. Brian J. Peterson, *Thomas Sankara: A Revolutionary in Cold War Africa* (Bloomington: Indiana University Press, 2021), p. 164.
8. Martens, *Sankara, Compaoré et la Révolution au Burkina Faso*, p. 113.
9. Bamouni, *Burkina Faso*, p. 111.
10. Martens, *Sankara, Compaoré et la Révolution au Burkina Faso*, p. 160.
11. Bruno Jaffré, *Biographie de Thomas Sankara: La patrie ou la mort* (Paris: L'Harmattan, 1997), p. 184.
12. Somé, *Thomas Sankara*, p. 116.
13. Martens, *Sankara, Compaoré et la Révolution au Burkina Faso*, p. 88.
14. *Statut General des Comités de Défense de la Révolution*, 17 May 1984, pp. 2, 4–5, Thomas Sankara Archives, http://www.thomassankara.net/statut-general-des-cdr-comites-de-defense-de-la-revolution/.
15. Martens, *Sankara, Compaoré et la Révolution au Burkina Faso*, p. 113.
16. Bamouni, *Burkina Faso*, p. 153.
17. B. P. Bamouni, "Le Glas de la clarification," *Carrefour Africain* 832 (25 May 1984): p.

7. Also cited in Martens, *Sankara, Compaoré et la Révolution au Burkina Faso*, p. 113; and Kakiswendépoulmdé Marcel Marie Anselme Lalsaga, "Les Comités de Défense de la Révolution (CDR) dans la politique du Conseil National de la Révolution (CNR) de 1983 à 1987: Une approche historique à partir de la ville de Ouagadougou," Memoire Online, 2007, https://www.memoireonline.com/05/12/5889/m_Les-Comites-de-Defense-de-la-RevolutionCDR-dans-la-politique-du-Conseil-National-de-la-Revolut57.html.
18. Bamouni, "Le Glas de la clarification," p. 11. Also cited in Lalsaga, "Les Comités de Défense de la Révolution (CDR) dans la politique du Conseil National de la Révolution (CNR) de 1983 à 1987."
19. Lalsaga, "Les Comités de Défense de la Révolution (CDR) dans la politique du Conseil National de la Révolution (CNR) de 1983 à 1987"; Martens, *Sankara, Compaoré et la Révolution au Burkina Faso*, p. 114.
20. Victoria Brittain, "Introduction to Sankara & Burkina Faso," *Review of African Political Economy* 32 (April 1985): p. 46.
21. Englebert, *La Révolution Burkinabè*, pp. 125–26.
22. Bamouni, *Burkina Faso*, pp. 154–55.
23. Gnindé Bonzi, *Souvenirs de la Révolution: Des moments de la révolution sankariste vue par un adolescent. Récit* (Paris: L'Harmattan, 2015), p. 41; Alfred Yambangba Sawadogo, *Le Président Thomas Sankara: Chef de la Révolution Burkinabè; 1983–1987, portrait* (Paris: L'Harmattan, 2001), p. 29.
24. Bamouni, *Burkina Faso*, pp. 154–55.
25. "Le people concevra ses besoins économiques: discours de Thomas Sankara du 4 Août 1984," Thomas Sankara Archives, https://www.thomassankara.net/le-peuple-concevra-ses-besoins-economiques-discours-de-thomas-sankara-du-4-aout-1984/.
26. Thomas Sankara, "Press Conference and Address to the Nation," *Carrefour Africain* 843 (10 August 1984): pp. 10, 12, 14. Also cited in Englebert, *La Révolution Burkinabè*, p. 126.
27. Somé, *Thomas Sankara*, p. 210.
28. Martens, *Sankara, Compaoré et la Révolution au Burkina Faso*, pp. 114.
29. Brittain, "Introduction to Sankara & Burkina Faso"; Ernest Harsch, "A Revolution Derailed," *Africa Report* 33, no. 1 (January–February 1988): p. 36.
30. Martens, *Sankara, Compaoré et la Révolution au Burkina Faso*, p. 88.
31. Lalsaga, "Les Comités de Défense de la Révolution (CDR) dans la politique du Conseil National de la Révolution (CNR) de 1983 à 1987."
32. Dramane Pare, "Ouagadougou à l'ère des CDR sectoriels: La discipline a prévalu,"

Carrefour Africain 849 (21 September 1984): p. 12, cited by Lalsaga, "Les Comités de Défense de la Révolution (CDR) dans la politique du Conseil National de la Révolution (CNR) de 1983 à 1987."
33. Englebert, *La Révolution Burkinabè*, p. 127.
34. Martens, *Sankara, Compaoré et la Révolution au Burkina Faso*, p. 136; and Lalsaga, "Les Comités de Défense de la Révolution (CDR) dans la politique du Conseil National de la Révolution (CNR) de 1983 à 1987."
35. Brittain, "Introduction to Sankara & Burkina Faso," pp. 46–47.
36. Guy Delbrel and Marie-Laure de Decker, "Entretien avec Thomas Sankara," *L'Autre Journal*, 3–8 April 1986, Thomas Sankara Archives, http://www.thomassankara.net/lautre-journal-entretien-avec-thomassankara-avril-1986-premiere-partie/.
37. Frantz Fanon, *The Wretched of the Earth* (New York: Grove, 1963), pp. 100, 35, 36–37. See also Kyélem de Tambèla, *Thomas Sankara et la Révolution au Burkina Faso*, p. 205; Joshua Malitsky, *Post-Revolution Nonfiction Film: Building the Soviet and Cuban Nations* (Bloomington: Indiana University Press, 2013), p. 61.
38. Englebert, *La Révolution Burkinabè*, p. 167. See also Ordinance 84–069, published in *Carrefour Africain* 851 (5 October 1984): p. 17.
39. Malitsky, *Post-Revolution Nonfiction Film*, p. 16.
40. Kyélem de Tambèla, *Thomas Sankara et la Révolution au Burkina Faso*, p. 186.
41. Martens, *Sankara, Compaoré et la Révolution Burkinabè*, p. 168. See also: First Conference of the CDR, Final Documents, SN-CDR, p. 66, published in *Carrefour Africain* 947 (8 August 1986): p. 8.
42. Guy Delbrel and Marie-Laure de Decker, "Entretien avec Thomas Sankara," *L'Autre Journal*, 3–8 April 1986, Thomas Sankara Archives, http://www.thomassankara.net/lautre-journal-entretien-avec-thomassankara-avril-1986-premiere-partie/.
43. Martens, *Sankara, Compaoré et la Révolution Burkinabè*, pp. 166–68.
44. Kyélem de Tambèla, *Thomas Sankara et la Révolution au Burkina Faso*, pp. 206–7, 224–25.
45. Ordinance No. 84–050/CNR/PRES, Article 22, issued 8 August 1984, cited also by Kyélem de Tambèla, *Thomas Sankara et la Révolution au Burkina Faso*, p. 204.
46. Delbrel and de Decker, "Entretien avec Thomas Sankara."
47. Kyélem de Tambèla, *Thomas Sankara et la Révolution au Burkina Faso*, pp. 203–4.
48. Martens, *Sankara, Compaoré et la Révolution Burkinabè*, pp. 166–70; Kyélem de Tambèla, *Thomas Sankara et la Révolution au Burkina Faso*, pp. 204–5; Englebert, *La Révolution Burkinabè*, p. 166; Paul Harrison, *The Greening of Africa: Breaking through in the Battle for Land and Food* (London: Paladin Grafton, 1987), pp. 218–19;

and Bruno Jaffré, *Burkina Faso: Les années Sankara de la révolution à la rectification* (Paris: L'Harmattan, 1989), pp. 131–34.
49. Bamouni, *Burkina Faso*, p. 119.
50. Hyppolyte Fofack, "Thomas Sankara: A Leader before His Time?," *African Business*, December 2012, p. 73.
51. Harsch, *Thomas Sankara*, p. 96; and Harrison, *The Greening of Africa*, pp. 219, 218, 269–70.
52. World Bank, Country data for Burkina Faso, https://data.worldbank.org/country/burkina-faso.
53. Jaffré, *Burkina Faso*, p. 132; Harsch, *Thomas Sankara*, p. 102.
54. Gnindé Bonzi, *Souvenirs de la Révolution: Des moments de la révolution sankariste vue par un adolescent. Récit* (Paris: L'Harmattan, 2015), pp. 81–88.
55. Kyélem de Tambèla, *Thomas Sankara et la Révolution au Burkina Faso*, p. 205.
56. Jaffré, *Burkina Faso*, pp. 89–90; and Kyélem de Tambèla, *Thomas Sankara et la Révolution au Burkina Faso*, pp. 240–41.
57. "Dare to Invent the Future," interviews of Thomas Sankara by Jean-Philippe Rapp, 1985 series of interviews, published in *Thomas Sankara Speaks: The Burkina Faso Revolution 1983–1987* (New York: Pathfinder Press, 2007), p. 223.
58. Jean-Emmanuel Pondi, *Thomas Sankara et l'émergence de l'Afrique au XXIe siècle* (Yaoundé, Cameroon: Éditions Afric'Eveil, 2016), p. 110; Jaffré, *Burkina Faso*, p. 93. Jaffré cites the *Annuaire statistique du Burkina Faso*, published by UNICEF, see page 64 for the first range of figures and page 38 in *ONU Flash*, published by the Centre d'information des Nations uniés pour Burkina, le Mali, le Niger et le Tchad, for the second numbers from 1986.
59. Bonzi, *Souvenirs de la Révolution*, p. 54.
60. Kyélem de Tambèla, *Thomas Sankara et la Révolution au Burkina Faso*, pp. 244–46.
61. Bamouni, *Burkina Faso*, p. 161; Jaffré, *Biographie de Thomas Sankara*, p. 100; Peterson, *Thomas Sankara*, pp. 183–84; and Kyélem de Tambèla, *Thomas Sankara et la Révolution au Burkina Faso*, pp. 244–46.
62. Bonzi, *Souvenirs de la Révolution*, pp. 59–65.
63. Malitsky, *Post-Revolution Nonfiction Film*, p. 28.
64. Emmanuelle Spiesse, "L'Artiste et le pouvoir sous Sankara (1983–1987)," in *Burkina Faso: Cent ans d'histoire, 1895–1995*, 2 vols., ed. Yénouyaba Georges Madiéga and Oumarou Nao (Ouagadougou: Éditions Karthala, 2003), p. 2143.
65. Michel Lachkar, "Féstival de cinéma de Ouagadougou: Fespaco 1985, une année particulière," *Franceinfo: Afrique*, 24 February 2019, https://www.francetvinfo.fr/

monde/afrique/societe-africaine/festival-de-cinema-de-ouagadougou-fespaco-1985-une-annee-particuliere_3191779.html.

66. Colin Dupré, *Le FESPACO, une affaire d'état(s): 1969–2009* (Paris: L'Harmattan, 2012), p. 194, 177; Ousmane Sembène, "Continuons à travailler sans relâche," in *Afriques 50: Singularités d'un cinéma pluriel*, ed. Catherine Ruelle, Clément Tapsoba, and Alessandra Speciale (Paris: L'Harmattan, 2005), pp. 13–15.
67. Dupré, *Le FESPACO*, pp. 177, 145–46.
68. Filippe Sawadogo, "Ouagadougou, future mémoire du cinéma africain," in *L'Afrique et le Centenaire du cinema / Africa and the Centenary of Cinema*, ed. Gaston Kaboré (Dakar: Présence Africaine, 1995), p. 320.
69. Kyélem de Tambèla, *Thomas Sankara et la Révolution au Burkina Faso*, pp. 238–39.
70. Paulin Soumanou Vieyra, "African Cinema: Solidarity and Difference," in *Questions of Third Cinema*, ed. Jim Pines and Paul Willemen (London: British Film Institute, 1991), p. 197.
71. Françoise Pfaff, "Africa from Within: The Films of Gaston Kaboré and Idrissa Ouédraogo as Anthropological Sources," in *African Experiences of Cinema*, ed. Imruh Bakari and Mbye Cham (London: British Film Institute, 1996), p. 227. Pfaff quotes Kaboré as published by Cherifa Benabdessadok, "Wend Kuuni, le don de Dieu," *Afrique-Asie* 319 (9 April 1984): p. 57.
72. Nwachukwu Frank Ukadike, *Questioning African Cinema: Conversations with Filmmakers* (Minneapolis: University of Minnesota Press, 2002), p. 117.
73. "Les temps forts du Fespaco," *Carrefour Africain* 873 (8 March 1985). Also cited in Dupré, *Le FESPACO*, p. 190.
74. Manthia Diawara, *African Cinema: Politics & Culture* (Bloomington: Indiana University Press, 1992), pp. 132, 137.
75. Dupré, *Le FESPACO*, p. 196.
76. Lachkar, "Festival de cinema de Ouagadougou: Fespaco 1985, une année particulière."
77. Dupré, *Le FESPACO*, p. 172.
78. Thomas Sankara, "Conférence de presse du Camarade président—la conquête Culturelle de nos écrans fait partie de la stratégie globale de la Révolution," *Sidwaya*, 4 March 1985, cited also in Dupré, *Le FESPACO*, p. 167.
79. Dupré, *Le FESPACO*, p. 191.
80. Dupré, *Le FESPACO*, pp. 172–74; Piero Gleijeses, *Visions of Freedom: Havana, Washington, Pretoria, and the Struggle for Southern Africa, 1976–1991* (Raleigh: University of North Carolina Press, 2016), p. 274.
81. Harsch, *Thomas Sankara*, p. 116.

82. Joseph B. Treaster, "Cuba Expanding Activity in African Nations," *New York Times*, 9 June 1985, p. 9.
83. Victoria Pasley, "*Kuxa Kanema*: Third Cinema and Its Transatlantic Crossings," in *Rethinking Third Cinema: The Role of Anti-colonial Media and Aesthetics in Postmodernity*, ed. Frieda Ekotto and Adeline Koh (Berlin: Lit Verlag, 2009), pp. 111–12. See also Jaffré, *Burkina Faso*, p. 167; Jaffré, *Biographie de Thomas Sankara*, p. 191; Harsch, *Thomas Sankara*, p. 116.
84. FEPACI, "The Algiers Charter on African Cinema, 1975," in *African Experiences of Cinema*, ed. Imruh Bakari and Mbye Cham (London: British Film Institute, 1996), pp. 25–26.
85. *Discours d'Orientation Politique*, 2 October 1983, pp. 17–18.
86. Jaffré, *Burkina Faso*, pp. 107–8.
87. Kyélem de Tambèla, *Thomas Sankara et la Révolution au Burkina Faso*, pp. 257–58.
88. Jaffré, *Burkina Faso*, pp. 108, 110; Harsch, "A Revolution Derailed," p. 35.
89. Fofack, "Thomas Sankara: A Leader before His Time?," p. 74.
90. "Message of the President of UNICEF," published by the UNICEF Bureau in Ouagadougou, March 1985.
91. Kyélem de Tambèla, *Thomas Sankara et la Révolution au Burkina Faso*, pp. 252–53; Jaffré, *Burkina Faso*, pp. 80–81, 82.
92. World Bank, Country data for Burkina Faso, https://data.worldbank.org/country/burkina-faso.
93. United Nations—World Population Prospects, "Burkina Faso Infant Mortality Rate 1950–2019," published by Macrotrends, https://www.macrotrends.net/countries/BFA/burkina-faso/infant-mortality-rate.
94. Thomas Sankara, "Our Struggle Draws Strength from Cuba's Example and Support," speech in Cuba 25 September 1984. Reprinted in *Thomas Sankara Speaks*, pp. 137–42.
95. Harsch, *Thomas Sankara*, p. 114.
96. Thomas Sankara, "Our White House is in Black Harlem," in *Thomas Sankara Speaks*, pp. 147–53.
97. Speech by Thomas Sankara before the UN General Assembly, Thirty-Ninth Session, Twentieth Plenary Meeting, Agenda Item 9, A/39/PV.20 (4 October 1984), https://undocs.org/fr/A/39/PV.20. The address was delivered in French and the UN translated it into English for the official record, which is available here at https://undocs.org/en/A/39/PV.20.
98. Speech by Thomas Sankara before the UN General Assembly, Thirty-Ninth Session, Twentieth Plenary Meeting, Agenda Item 9, A/39/PV.20 (4 October 1984), https://

undocs.org/en/A/39/PV.20.
99. James Feron, "African, in U.N., Demands Rights for Third World," *New York Times*, 5 October 1984, p. 13.
100. Speech of Thomas Sankara, 31 December 1984, reported in *Carrefour Africain* 864–65 (11 January 1985): p. 12. Also cited in Martens, *Sankara, Compaoré et la Révolution Burkinabè*, p. 169.
101. Michael Wilkins, "The Death of Thomas Sankara and the Rectification of the People's Revolution in Burkina Faso," *African Affairs* 88, no. 352 (July 1989): p. 383.
102. Alfred Yambangba Sawadogo, *Le Président Thomas Sankara: Chef de la Révolution Burkinabè: 1983–1987, portrait* (Paris: L'Harmattan, 2001), pp. 151–52, 71–72.
103. "Thomas Sankara Speech at the Gold Mine of Poura," published in *Carrefour Africain* 854, (26 October 1984). Also cited in Martens, *Sankara, Compaoré et la Révolution Burkinabè*, pp. 30–31.
104. Abdoulaye Barro, "Pensée et système politiques chez Thomas Sankara," LeFaso.net, 21 October 2016, https://lefaso.net/spip.php?article73792; Mamadou Diallo, "Thomas Sankara and the Revolutionary Birth of Burkina Faso," *Viewpoint Magazine* 6, no. 1 (February 2018), https://www.viewpointmag.com/2018/02/01/thomas-sankara-revolutionary-birth-burkina-faso/.
105. World Bank, "Burkina Faso External Debt 1970–2019," published by Macrotrends, https://www.macrotrends.net/countries/BFA/burkina-faso/external-debt-stock; World Bank, Country data for Burkina Faso, https://data.worldbank.org/country/burkina-faso; World Bank, "Burkina Faso Inflation Rate 1960–2019," published by Macrotrends, https://www.macrotrends.net/countries/BFA/burkina-faso/inflation-rate-cpi; IMF, Country Data Burkina Faso, https://www.imf.org/en/Countries/BFA.
106. International Monetary Fund Country Report, "Burkina Faso," https://www.imf.org/en/Countries/BFA; World Bank, Country data for Burkina Faso; "Burkina Faso Inflation Rate 1960–2019"; "Burkina Faso External Debt 1970–2019."
107. "We Must Fight Imperialism Together," interview of Thomas Sankara with Ernest Harsch, first published in *Intercontinental Press*, 29 April 1985, reprinted in *Thomas Sankara Speaks*, pp. 178, 186.
108. Kyélem de Tambèla, *Thomas Sankara et la Révolution au Burkina Faso*, p. 277.
109. Harsch, *Thomas Sankara*, p. 126.
110. Martens, *Sankara, Compaoré et la Révolution Burkinabè*, p. 235.
111. Thomas Sankara, "There Are Attempts to Unleash an Unjust War Against Us," speech given in Ouagadougou on 11 September 1985, published in *Sidwaya*, 13 September 1985, and reprinted in *Thomas Sankara Speaks*, pp. 233–38. See also Martens,

Sankara, Compaoré et la Révolution Burkinabè, pp. 235–36; *Carrefour Africain* 901 (20 September 1985): pp. 11–14.
112. Kyélem de Tambèla, *Thomas Sankara et la Révolution au Burkina Faso*, p. 289.
113. Englebert, *La Révolution Burkinabè*, p. 204.
114. Peterson, *Thomas Sankara*, p. 220.

CHAPTER 5. RECALIBRATION OF THE BURKINABÈ REVOLUTION (1985–1986)

1. Pierre Englebert, *La Révolution Burkinabè* (Paris: L'Harmattan, 1986), p. 194; Emmanuel Salliot, "A Review of Past Security Events in the Sahel 1967–2007," published by the Sahel and West Africa Club Secretariat of the OECD (2010), pp. 23–24.
2. Yacouba Zerbo, "Les relations politiques entre le Mali et le Burkina-Faso de 1983 à 1985: Les causes du conflit frontalier de décembre 1985," in *Guerres mondiales et conflits contemporains* 196 (December 1999): p. 94. Zerbo cites an article published in *Libération*, 26 December 1985, p. 9.
3. Zerbo, "Les relations politiques entre le Mali et le Burkina-Faso de 1983 à 1985: Les causes du conflit frontalier de décembre 1985," p. 95; Salliot, "A Review of Past Security Events in the Sahel 1967–2007," p. 23.
4. Sidy Gaye, "Truce, New Fighting Reported in Mali-Burkina Faso War," *United Press International* (*UPI*), 28 December 1985, https://www.upi.com/Archives/1985/12/28/Truce-new-fighting-reported-in-Mali-Burkina-Faso-war/6521504594000/; "A New Cease-Fire Is Announced in Mali-Burkina Faso Border War," *New York Times*, 28 December 1985, https://www.nytimes.com/; Salliot, "A Review of Past Security Events in the Sahel 1967–2007," p. 22.
5. Zerbo, "Les relations politiques entre le Mali et le Burkina-Faso de 1983 à 1985," p. 100.
6. Ludo Martens, *Sankara, Compaoré et la révolution Burkinabè* (Anvers, Belgium: EPO Dossier International, 1989), pp. 237–38.
7. Englebert, *La Révolution Burkinabè*, pp. 197–98.
8. Thomas Sankara, "The Malian Troops are No Longer Prisoners, They are Our Brothers," in *Thomas Sankara Speaks: The Burkina Faso Revolution 1983–1987* (New York: Pathfinder Press, 2007), pp. 250–53.
9. Ernest Harsch, *Thomas Sankara: An African Revolutionary* (Athens: Ohio University

Press, 2014), pp. 135–36.
10. Bruno Jaffré, *Biographie de Thomas Sankara: La patrie ou la mort* (Paris: L'Harmattan, 1997), p. 188.
11. Englebert, *La Révolution Burkinabè*, pp. 128–30.
12. Guy Delbrel and Marie-Laure de Decker, "Entretien avec Thomas Sankara," *L'Autre Journal*, 3–8 April 1986, Thomas Sankara Archives, http://www.thomassankara.net/lautre-journal-entretien-avec-thomassankara-avril-1986-premiere-partie/.
13. *Statut General des Comités de Défense de la Révolution*, 17 May 1984, pp. 11–12, 20–21, Thomas Sankara Archives, http://www.thomassankara.net/statut-general-des-cdr-comites-de-defense-de-la-revolution/.
14. Harsch, *Thomas Sankara*, pp. 132–33.
15. Gnindé Bonzi, *Souvenirs de la Révolution: Des moments de la révolution sankariste vue par un adolescent. Récit* (Paris: L'Harmattan, 2015), pp. 85–87.
16. Alain Deschamps, *Burkina Faso (1987–1992): "Le pays des hommes intègres"* (Paris: L'Harmattan, 2001), p. 22.
17. Kakiswendépoulmdé Marcel Marie Anselme Lalsaga, "Les Comités de Défense de la Révolution (CDR) dans la politique du Conseil National de la Révolution (CNR) de 1983 à 1987: Une approche historique à partir de la ville de Ouagadougou," Memoire Online, 2007, https://www.memoireonline.com/05/12/5889/m_Les-Comites-de-Defense-de-la-RevolutionCDR-dans-la-politique-du-Conseil-National-de-la-Revolut57.html.
18. Ludo Martens, *Sankara, Compaoré et la révolution Burkinabè* (Anvers, Belgium: EPO Dossier International, 1989), pp. 148, 85.
19. Thomas Sankara, "The CDRs' Job is to Raise Consciousness, Act, Produce," in *Thomas Sankara Speaks*, pp. 279, 281, 283, 284, 288, 290, 291, 292, 293, 296.
20. Harsch, *Thomas Sankara*, p. 134.
21. Jaffré, *Burkina Faso*, p. 190; Apollinaire J. Kyélem de Tambèla, *Thomas Sankara et la Révolution au Burkina Faso: Une experience de développement autocentré*, 2nd ed. (Ouagadougou: Harmattan Burkina, 2012), p. 245.
22. Lalsaga, "Les Comités de Défense de la Révolution (CDR) dans la politique du Conseil National de la Révolution (CNR) de 1983 à 1987."
23. "Interview with B. P. Bamouni," *Carrefour Africain* 839 (13 July 1984): p. 7. Also cited in Englebert, *La Révolution Burkinabè*, pp. 133–34.
24. Englebert, *La Révolution Burkinabè*, pp. 130–32, cited in its entirety. See also, Lalsaga, "Les Comités de Défense de la Révolution (CDR) dans la politique du Conseil National de la Révolution (CNR) de 1983 à 1987."

25. Ernest Harsch, "A Revolution Derailed," *Africa Report* 33, no. 1 (January–February 1988): pp. 36–37.
26. Lalsaga, "Les Comités de Défense de la Révolution (CDR) dans la politique du Conseil National de la Révolution (CNR) de 1983 à 1987."
27. Harsch, "A Revolution Derailed," p. 37.
28. Apollinaire J. Kyélem de Tambèla, *Thomas Sankara et la Révolution au Burkina Faso: Une experience de développement autocentré*, 2nd ed. (Ouagadougou: Harmattan Burkina, 2012), pp. 172–73. He cites an interview given to a Beninois journalist on 6 December 1985, unattributed source.
29. Martens, *Sankara, Compaoré et la révolution Burkinabè*, p. 162. He cites the appeal published in *Voie prolétarienne* 2 (December 1985): p. 10.
30. Harsch, "A Revolution Derailed," p. 37.
31. Lalsaga, "Les Comités de Défense de la Révolution (CDR) dans la politique du Conseil National de la Révolution (CNR) de 1983 à 1987."
32. Martens, *Sankara, Compaoré et la révolution Burkinabè*, p. 162. He cites a statement, "Letter of 12 August 1986," published as an appendix (*annexe*) of *En Avant* 3.
33. Valère D. Somé, *Thomas Sankara: L'espoir assassiné* (Paris: L'Harmattan, 1990), p. 213.
34. Martens, *Sankara, Compaoré et la révolution Burkinabè*, p. 39; Lalsaga, "Les Comités de Défense de la Révolution (CDR) dans la politique du Conseil National de la Révolution (CNR) de 1983 à 1987"; Somé, *Thomas Sankara*, p. 213.
35. Martens, *Sankara, Compaoré et la révolution Burkinabè*, p. 85.
36. Harsch, "A Revolution Derailed," p. 37.
37. Martens, *Sankara, Compaoré et la révolution Burkinabè*, pp. 89–90, 91.
38. Jaffré, *Biographie de Thomas Sankara*, p. 200.
39. Guy Martin, "Ideology and Praxis in Thomas Sankara's Populist Revolution of 4 August 1983 in Burkina Faso," *Issue* 15 (1987): pp. 85–86.
40. Alfred Yambangba Sawadogo, *Le Président Thomas Sankara: Chef de la Révolution Burkinabè; 1983-1987, portrait* (Paris: L'Harmattan, 2001), p. 150.
41. Thomas Sankara, "Imperialism Is the Arsonist of Our Forests and Savannas," in *Thomas Sankara Speaks*, pp. 254–57, 258–60.
42. Delbrel and de Decker, "Interview with Thomas Sankara."
43. Jaffré, *Burkina Faso*, pp. 107–8, 109, 110; Harsch, *Thomas Sankara*, pp. 80–81; Iris Berger, *Women in Twentieth-Century Africa* (Cambridge: Cambridge University Press, 2016), p. 104; Hyppolyte Fofack, "Thomas Sankara: A Leader before His Time?," *African Business*, December 2012, p. 74; Delbrel and de Decker, "Interview with Thomas Sankara."

44. Fanon, *The Wretched of the Earth*, pp. 233, 244.
45. Delbrel and de Decker, "Interview with Thomas Sankara."
46. Nwachukwu Frank Ukadike, *Black African Cinema* (Berkeley: University of California Press, 1994), pp. 290–94; Nwachukwu Frank Ukadike, *Questioning African Cinema: Conversations with Filmmakers* (Minneapolis: University of Minnesota Press, 2002), pp. 62–64.
47. FEPACI, "The Algiers Charter on African Cinema, 1975," in *African Experiences of Cinema*, ed. Imruh Bakari and Mbye Cham (London: British Film Institute, 1996), p. 26.
48. "Resolutions of Third World Filmmakers' Meeting, Algiers, Algeria, 1973," in *African Experiences of Cinema*, ed. Imruh Bakari and Mbye Cham (London: British Film Institute, 1996), pp. 18, 20.
49. Colin Dupré, *Le FESPACO, une affaire d'état(s): 1969–2009* (Paris: L'Harmattan, 2012), p. 192.
50. Jaffré, *Burkina Faso*, p. 103.
51. Paulin Soumanou Vieyra, "Fespaco 87," *Présence Africaine* 143, no. 3 (1987): pp. 190–94.
52. Dupré, *Le FESPACO*, pp. 215–16.
53. Delbrel and de Decker, "Interview with Thomas Sankara."
54. Somé, *Thomas Sankara*, p. 212; See also Jean Hubert Bazié, *Chronique du Burkina (1985–1986)* (Ouagadougou: Imprimerie de la Presse écrite, 1986), Thomas Sankara Archives, http://www.thomassankara.net/chronique-du-burkina-1985-1986-de-jean-hubert-bazie/.
55. Martens, *Sankara, Compaoré et la Révolution Burkinabè*, p. 169. See also, Kyélem de Tambèla, *Thomas Sankara et la Révolution au Burkina Faso*, p.186.
56. Englebert, *La Révolution Burkinabè*, p. 161, 170; Martens, *Sankara, Compaoré et la Révolution Burkinabè*, p. 169; Jaffré, *Burkina Faso*, p. 145.
57. Thomas Sankara, "Développement prêt-à-porter: Non! Développement sur mesure: Oui!," speech of 4 August 1986, Thomas Sankara Archives, http://www.thomassankara.net/developpement-pret-a-porter-non-developpement-sur-mesure-oui-discours-du-president-thomas-sankara-du-4-aout-1986/.
58. Kyélem de Tambèla, *Thomas Sankara et la Révolution au Burkina Faso*, pp. 188–89.
59. World Bank, "Implementation Completion Report, Burkina Faso, Primary Education Development Project," 4 May 1995, p. iii.
60. Jaffré, *Biographie de Thomas Sankara*, pp. 218–19.
61. World Bank, "Project Completion Report, Burkina Faso, Fertilizer Project," 29

December 1994, pp. 6–8.
62. World Bank, "Implementation Completion Report, Burkina Faso, Health Services Development Project," 27 December 1995, pp. 12, iv.
63. International Monetary Fund, "Burkina Faso: Transactions with the Fund from 1 May 1984 to 31 October 2019," https://www.imf.org/external/np/fin/tad/extransl.aspx?memberKey1=95&endDate=2099%2D12%2D31&finposition_flag=YES.
64. Kyélem de Tambèla, *Thomas Sankara et la Révolution au Burkina Faso*, p. 192.
65. Skinner, "Sankara and the Burkinabè Revolution," *Journal of Modern African Studies* 26, no. 3 (September 1988): p. 444.
66. Skinner, "Sankara and the Burkinabè Revolution," p. 444.
67. Martens, *Sankara, Compaoré et la révolution Burkinabè*, p. 39.
68. Martin, "Ideology and Praxis in Thomas Sankara's Populist Revolution of 4 August 1983 in Burkina Faso," p. 83.
69. "Burkina Faso External Debt 1970–2019," data from the World Bank, published by Macrotrends, https://www.macrotrends.net/countries/BFA/burkina-faso/external-debt-stock.
70. Michael Wilkins, "The Death of Thomas Sankara and the Rectification of the People's Revolution in Burkina Faso," *African Affairs* 88, no. 352 (July 1989): Wilkins, "The Death of Thomas Sankara and the Rectification of the People's Revolution in Burkina Faso," in *African Affairs*, Vol, 88 No. 352 (July 1989), p. 385.
71. "Burkina Faso Country Data," published by the World Bank, https://data.worldbank.org/country/burkina-faso.
72. "Burkina Faso Country Report," published by the International Monetary Fund, https://www.imf.org/en/Countries/BFA.
73. Kyélem de Tambèla, *Thomas Sankara et la Révolution au Burkina Faso*, p. 288; Englebert, *La Révolution Burkinabè*, pp. 204–5.
74. Englebert, *La Révolution Burkinabè*, p. 205; Jaffré, *Burkina Faso*, p. 169.
75. Englebert, *La Révolution Burkinabè*, p. 191.
76. Jaffré, *Burkina Faso*, p. 154.
77. Alan Cowell, "Pretoria's Forces Raid 3 Neighbors in Move on Rebels," *New York Times*, 20 May 1986, p. 1.
78. "La Revolucion de Burkina Faso se esta consolidando," interview with President Thomas Sankara conducted by Radio Havana Cuba, 19 July 1986, and reprinted in *Granma*, Thomas Sankara Archives, https://www.thomassankara.net/entrevista-con-thomas-sankara-la-revolucion-de-burkina-faso-se-esta-consolidando-granma-19-7-1986/?lang=es.

79. Dupré, *Le FESPACO*, pp. 196–97.
80. Piero Gleijeses, *Visions of Freedom: Havana, Washington, Pretoria, and the Struggle for Southern Africa, 1976–1991* (Raleigh: University of North Carolina Press, 2016), p. 524.
81. Englebert, *La Révolution Burkinabè*, p. 188; Jaffré, *Burkina Faso*, p. 159.
82. Kyélem de Tambèla, *Thomas Sankara et la Révolution au Burkina Faso*, p. 273.
83. Richard Bernstein, "France Sending Forces to Togo in Wake of Attack," *New York Times*, 26 September 1986, p. 6; Associated Press, "Togo Officials Report Crushing Well-Armed Coup Attempt; 13 Die," *Los Angeles Times*, 25 September 1986.
84. Thomas Sankara, "At Nicaragua's Side: Remarks Greeting Daniel Ortega, 27 August 1986," in *Thomas Sankara Speaks*, pp. 298, 299. Originally published in *Sidwaya*, 29 August 1986.
85. Thomas Sankara, "What Is the Non-Aligned Movement Doing?," in *Thomas Sankara Speaks*, pp. 304, 305, 309, 312. Published originally in *Carrefour Africain*, 12 September 1986.
86. Jaffré, *Burkina Faso*, p. 167; Kyélem de Tambèla, *Thomas Sankara et la Révolution au Burkina Faso*, p. 292.
87. Jaffré, *Burkina Faso*, p. 167.
88. Kyélem de Tambèla, *Thomas Sankara et la Révolution au Burkina Faso*, pp. 295–96.
89. APASH/CADTM Brazza, "La révolution Burkinabè: Les grandes orientations," published by the Association Pour une Alternative au Service de l'Humanité (APASH), based in Brazzaville, Congo, Thomas Sankara Archives, http://www.thomassankara.net/la-revolution-burkinabe-les-grandes-orientations/.
90. Thomas Sankara, "Against Those Who Exploit and Oppress Us—Here and In France," speech given at the official reception for French President François Mitterrand, 17 November 1986, in *Thomas Sankara Speaks*, pp. 326–27, 328–29.
91. Sankara, "Against Those Who Exploit and Oppress Us—Here and In France," pp. 331, 333–34.
92. Benjamin Roger, "Jean-Christophe Mitterrand: 'L'Assassinat de Sankara? Selon moi, un accident,'" *Jeune Afrique*, 13 October 2017, https://www.jeuneafrique.com/mag/481423/politique/jean-christophe-mitterrand-lassassinat-de-sankara%e2%80%89-selon-moi-un-accident/.
93. Alexandra Reza, "Short Cuts," *London Review of Books* 36, no. 23 (4 December 2014): 39. For the video of the speech, see "17 novembre 1986 : Thomas Sankara et François Mitterrand," YouTube video, 5:45, 13 October 2017, https://www.youtube.com/watch?v=tbJqVBO_XNY.

94. Harsch, *Thomas Sankara*, p. 17.
95. Reza, "Short Cuts," p. 39.
96. Kyélem de Tambèla, *Thomas Sankara et la Révolution au Burkina Faso*, p. 290.
97. Tirthankar Chanda, "Mitterrand-Sankara: Le vieux president et le capitaine impertinent," *RFI Afrique*, 10 January 2016, http://www.rfi.fr/afrique/20160109-mitterrand-sankara-le-vieux-sage-le-capitaine-impertinent.
98. Martens, *Sankara, Compaoré et la révolution Burkinabè*, p. 239; Chanda, "Mitterrand-Sankara."
99. Frédéric Marchand, "15 octobre 87: La part de Jacques Chirac et de la droite française," *Le Libérateur*, no. 43, 5–19 November 2007. See also the Thomas Sankara Archives, http://www.thomassankara.net/15-octobre-87-la-part-de-jacques-chirac-et-de-la-droite-francaise/.

CHAPTER 6. TWILIGHT OF THE REVOLUTION AND SANKARA'S MURDER (1986–1987)

1. D. Bailly interview of Thomas Sankara, "La Révolution Burkinabè et les courants révolutionnaires?" *Ivoire Dimanche* 856 (5 July 1987), Thomas Sankara Archives, http://www.thomassankara.net/interview-du-5-juillet-1987/.
2. James Brooke, "Young Voice in Africa: Sports and Clean Living," *New York Times*, 23 August 1987, p. 10. The author cites an essay published in a recent issue of *Jeune Afrique*.
3. "A Sad Day for Africa," *Update: Africa Report* 32, no. 6 (1 November 1987): p. 5.
4. Apollinaire J. Kyélem de Tambèla, *Thomas Sankara et la Révolution au Burkina Faso: Une experience de développement autocentré*, 2nd ed. (Ouagadougou: Harmattan Burkina, 2012), pp. 196–97.
5. Bruno Jaffré, *Burkina Faso: Les années Sankara de la révolution à la rectification* (Paris: L'Harmattan, 1989), p. 145.
6. Ludo Martens, *Sankara, Compaoré et la révolution Burkinabè* (Anvers, Belgium: EPO Dossier International, 1989), pp. 144–45; Bruno Jaffré, *Biographie de Thomas Sankara: La patrie ou la mort* (Paris: L'Harmattan, 1997), pp. 204–5.
7. Jean Philippe Rapp interview with Thomas Sankara, "Sankara: Un nouveau pouvoir africain," conducted in 1985, published in 1986 as "Oser inventer l'avenir," pp. 4, 9–10, 22, Thomas Sankara Archives, http://www.thomassankara.net/interview-de-jean-philippe-rapp-realise-en-1985-oser-inventer-lavenir/; P. Labazée, "Une nouvelle

phase de la révolution au Burkina Faso," *Politique Africaine* 24 (December 1986): pp. 114, 118, 119.

8. Rod Stoneman, "African Cinema: Perspective Correction," in *African Cinema and Human Rights*, ed. Mette Hjort and Eva Jorholt (Bloomington: Indiana University Press, 2019), p. 45.
9. Paulin Soumanou Vieyra, "Fespaco 87," *Présence Africaine* 143, no. 3 (1987): pp. 190, 194.
10. Colin Dupré, *Le FESPACO, une affaire d'état(s): 1969-2009* (Paris: L'Harmattan, 2012), pp. 180, 193.
11. Nwachukwu Frank Ukadike, *Black African Cinema* (Berkeley: University of California Press, 1994), pp. 199, 200.
12. Manthia Diawara, *African Cinema: Politics & Culture* (Bloomington: Indiana University Press, 1992), pp. 152, 153.
13. Ukadike, *Black African Cinema*, pp. 295, 290.
14. "Inauguration du marché de films Africains," *Sidwaya*, 24 February 1987, p. 9.
15. James E. Genova, *Cinema and Development in West Africa* (Bloomington: Indiana University Press, 2013), pp. 153-54.
16. "Niamey Manifesto of African Filmmakers, 1982," in *African Experiences of Cinema*, ed. Imruh Bakari and Mbye Cham (London: British Film Institute, 1996), pp. 27, 28.
17. Dupré, *Le FESPACO*, pp. 181-82; Kyélem de Tambèla, *Thomas Sankara et la Révolution au Burkina Faso*, pp. 238-39; Jaffré, *Burkina Faso*, p. 103.
18. "Colloque sur 'Tradition Orale et Nouveaux Medias' des communications importantes," *Sidwaya*, 25 February 1987, p. 7; Vieyra, "FESPACO 87," p. 194.
19. D. B., "Les responsables de media africains chez le president du Faso," *Sidwaya*, 25 February 1987, p. 5; Dupré, *Le FESPACO*, pp. 182-83.
20. Serge Daney, interview with Thomas Sankara, "Sankara: le cinema, un bon prétexte," *Libération*, 5 March 1987.
21. Mbye Cham, "Film and History in Africa: A Critical Survey of Current Trends and Tendencies," in *Focus on African Films*, ed. Françoise Pfaff (Bloomington: Indiana University Press, 2004), pp. 64-66.
22. Ukadike, *Black African Cinema*, pp. 210-12.
23. Dupré, *Le FESPACO*, pp. 172-73, 174, 199, 176, 178.
24. Video of Fela Kuti at FESPACO 1987, Thomas Sankara Archives, http://www.capitainethomassankara.net/pages_fr/archives_video/archives_videoFela.html.
25. Vieyra, "FESPACO 87," pp. 194, 192; Press Conference of Jack Lang, "Culture et Economie, même combat," *Sidwaya*, 25 February 1987, p. 10.

26. Thomas Sankara, "The Revolution Cannot Triumph without the Emancipation of Women," *Women's Liberation and the African Freedom Struggle* (New York: Pathfinder Press, 1990), pp. 3, 4, 6, 8, 12, 23, 26, 27, 29, 34, 31.
27. Jaffré, *Burkina Faso*, pp. 108, 110.
28. Ernest Harsch, *Thomas Sankara: An African Revolutionary* (Athens: Ohio University Press, 2014), p. 81.
29. Martens, *Sankara, Compaoré et la révolution Burkinabè*, pp. 91–92.
30. Thomas Sankara, "Développement prêt-à-porter: Non! Développement sur mesure: Oui," speech delivered on 4 August 1986, Thomas Sankara Archives, http://www.thomassankara.net/developpement-pret-a-porter-non-developpement-sur-mesure-oui-discours-du-president-thomas-sankara-du-4-aout-1986/.
31. Kyélem de Tambèla, *Thomas Sankara et la Révolution au Burkina Faso*, pp. 219–20, 221.
32. Jaffré, *Biographie de Thomas Sankara*, p. 220, citing figures from UNICEF/ICDI, "The Impact of Self-Imposed Adjustment: The Case of Burkina 1983–1989," published in 1993.
33. World Bank, "Burkina Faso," https://data.worldbank.org/country/burkina-faso.
34. Macrotrends, "Burkina Faso Inflation Rate 1960–2019," using World Bank data, https://www.macrotrends.net/countries/BFA/burkina-faso/inflation-rate-cpi.
35. Macrotrends, "Burkina Faso External Debt 1970–2019," using World Bank data, https://www.macrotrends.net/countries/BFA/burkina-faso/external-debt-stock.
36. Thomas Sankara, "A United Front Against the Debt," speech before the 25th Conference of the Organization of African Unity (OAU), Addis Ababa, Ethiopia, 29 July 1987, in *Thomas Sankara Speaks: The Burkina Faso Revolution 1983–1987* (New York: Pathfinder Press, 2007), pp. 374, 375, 376, 376–77, 378, 380, 380–81.
37. Jaffré, *Burkina Faso*, p. 130.
38. Interview with Mamadou Traoré by Mouor Aimé Kambire, "Dédougou était la fin de la Révolution," published first in *Sidwaya* (date not specified), Thomas Sankara Archives, http://www.thomassankara.net/mamadou-traore-avocat-ancien-cadre-de-la-revolution-dedougou-etait-la-fin-de-la-revolution/?fbclid=IwAR2-x3El2NEvw6_1hTnQihDQ-rmGKc4AMhP2uJ7yEihgGKuONwooJlhiiR8.
39. Martens, *Sankara, Compaoré et la révolution Burkinabè*, pp. 105–6.
40. Statement of Adèle Ouédraogo in *Jeune Afrique* 1387 (5 August 1987): p. 76, cited in Kyélem de Tambèla, *Thomas Sankara et la Révolution au Burkina Faso*, pp. 218–19.
41. Interview with Mamadou Traoré by Mouor Aimé Kambire, "Dédougou était la fin de la Révolution."

42. Mamadou Diallo, "Thomas Sankara and the Revolutionary Birth of Burkina Faso," *Viewpoint Magazine* 6, no. 1 (February 2018), https://www.viewpointmag.com/2018/02/01/thomas-sankara-revolutionary-birth-burkina-faso/.
43. Jaffré, *Burkina Faso*, p. 131.
44. Frantz Fanon, *The Wretched of the Earth* (New York: Grove, 1963), pp. 116, 117, 202, 203.
45. Jaffré, *Biographie de Thomas Sankara*, p. 232.
46. Martens, *Sankara, Compaoré et la révolution Burkinabè*, pp. 36, 37. Martens cites Soumane Touré, "Lettre de 26 Mai 1987," in *L'Unité, organe de liaison et de la lute de la CSB*, BP 1469, no. 72.
47. Martens, *Sankara, Compaoré et la révolution Burkinabè*, pp. 37–38.
48. Valère D. Somé, *Thomas Sankara: L'espoir assassiné* (Paris: L'Harmattan, 1990), p. 214.
49. Jaffré, *Biographie de Thomas Sankara*, pp. 204–6.
50. Martens, *Sankara, Compaoré et la révolution Burkinabè*, pp. 40–41.
51. Somé, *Thomas Sankara*, pp. 21–22.
52. Kakiswendépoulmdé Marcel Marie Anselme Lalsaga, "Les Comités de Défense de la Révolution (CDR) dans la politique du Conseil National de la Révolution (CNR) de 1983 à 1987: Une approche historique à partir de la ville de Ouagadougou," Memoire Online, 2007, https://www.memoirconline.com/05/12/5889/m_Les-Comites-de-Defense-de-la-RevolutionCDR-dans-la-politique-du-Conseil-National-de-la-Revolut57.html.
53. Somé, *Thomas Sankara*, p. 22.
54. Martens, *Sankara, Compaoré et la révolution Burkinabè*, pp. 43, 42.
55. Thomas Sankara, "Procès-Verbal" of the CNR, 27 June 1987, reprinted in Somé, *Thomas Sankara*, p. 221.
56. Somé, *Thomas Sankara*, pp. 20–21.
57. Martens, *Sankara, Compaoré et la révolution Burkinabè*, p. 42.
58. Jaffré, *Biographie de Thomas Sankara*, pp. 200–201.
59. Sankara, "Procès-Verbal," reprinted in Somé, *Thomas Sankara*, pp. 222–23.
60. Sankara, "Procès-Verbal," reprinted in Somé, *Thomas Sankara*, pp. 224–25.
61. Thomas Sankara, "4ème anniversaire de la RDP, AN IV," 4 August 1987, Thomas Sankara Archives, http://www.capitainethomassankara.net/pages_fr/archives_video/archives_video_4aout1987.html. This is a video of the entire address (minus the last minute or so). See also Thomas Sankara, "Our Revolution Needs a People Who Are Convinced, Not Conquered," in *Thomas Sankara Speaks*, 389, 390, 391, 392.

62. Sankara, "4ème anniversaire de la RDP, AN IV." This is a video of the entire address (minus the last minute or so). See also Sankara, "Our Revolution Needs a People Who Are Convinced, Not Conquered," pp. 393, 394, 395, 396.
63. Sankara, "4ème anniversaire de la RDP, AN IV." See also Sankara, "Our Revolution Needs a People Who Are Convinced, Not Conquered," pp. 397, 398, 399, 400, 401.
64. Valère D. Somé, "Letter to President Thomas Sankara, 18 August 1987," reprinted in Somé, *Thomas Sankara*, p. 226; Somé, *Thomas Sankara*, pp. 22–23.
65. K. Marcel Marie Anselme Lalsaga, "Avènement du 15 octobre 1987: La crise au sein du Conseil National de la Révolution (CNR) et l'échec des tentatives de conciliation," *LeFaso.net*, 15 October 2017, https://lefaso.net/spip.php?article79904. The circular was also reprinted in *Jeune Afrique* 1401 (21 November 1987): p. 41. See also Jaffré, *Biographie de Thomas Sankara*, p. 202. The circular cited was published in *Sidwaya*, 31 August 1987, giving it the force of an official edict of state.
66. Ansel Marcel Kammanl, "La guerre des tracts sous la révolution entre 1986 et 1987: un des prémices du octobre 1987 au Burkina Faso," *LeFaso.net*, 12 October 2017.
67. Jaffré, *Biographie de Thomas Sankara*, p. 203.
68. Somé, *Thomas Sankara*, p. 214.
69. Martens, *Sankara, Compaoré et la révolution Burkinabè*, p. 46. Martens cites an interview published in *Carrefour Africain* 1002 (4 September 1987): p. 8.
70. Jaffré, *Biographie de Thomas Sankara*, p. 203. He cites *Sidwaya*, 31 August 1987.
71. Howard W. French, "How Qaddafi Reshaped Africa," *The Atlantic*, 1 March 2011, https://www.theatlantic.com/international/archive/2011/03/how-qaddafi-reshaped-africa/71861/.
72. "Charles Taylor and His Six Prison Journeys," *The New Dawn*, 23 January 2013. See also Nick Allen, "Liberian Despot Charles Taylor Worked with U.S. Intelligence," *Telegraph* (UK), 17 January 2012, https://www.telegraph.co.uk/news/worldnews/africaandindianocean/liberia/9021153/Liberian-despot-Charles-Taylor-worked-with-US-intelligence.html.
73. Stephen Ellis, *The Mask of Anarchy: The Destruction of Liberia and the Religious Dimension of an African Civil War* (London: Hurst & Company, 2007), pp. 2, 15, 66–67, 68.
74. Martens, *Sankara, Compaoré et la révolution Burkinabè*, p. 47.
75. Kyélem de Tambèla, *Thomas Sankara et la Révolution au Burkina Faso*, pp. 364–65.
76. Somé, *Thomas Sankara*, p. 214; Jaffré, *Biographie de Thomas Sankara*, p. 205; Lalsaga, "Avènement du 15 octobre 1987."

77. Martens, *Sankara, Compaoré et la révolution Burkinabè*, p. 48.
78. Martens, *Sankara, Compaoré et la révolution Burkinabè*, pp. 89–90, 58.
79. Pierre Englebert, *Burkina Faso: Unsteady Statehood in West Africa* (New York: Routledge, 2018), p. 60.
80. Somé, *Thomas Sankara*, pp. 227, 32, 215. On the first page cited, Somé reproduces the letter he received from President Sankara following the 21 September 1987 CNR Political Bureau meeting, dated 22 September 1987.
81. Somé, *Thomas Sankara*, p. 215.
82. Thomas Sankara, "Eight Million Burkinabè, Eight Million Revolutionaries," in *Thomas Sankara Speaks*, pp. 404, 405, 406, 407–8, 409, 410, 411, 412, 414, 415, 416, 417.
83. Martens, *Sankara, Compaoré et la révolution Burkinabè*, pp. 49–53.
84. Obituaries, "Kilimité Théodore Hien n'est plus," *LeFaso.net*, 22 December 2014, https://lefaso.net/spip.php?article62422.
85. "Statement of the Provincial Revolutionary Council of Houet," published in *Sidwaya*, 13 October 1987, p. 2, cited also in Martens, *Sankara, Compaoré et la révolution Burkinabè*, p. 53.
86. Martens, *Sankara, Compaoré et la révolution Burkinabè*, pp. 53–54; Lalsaga, "Avènement du 15 octobre 1987"; Martens, *Sankara, Compaoré et la révolution Burkinabè*, p. 55; Somé, *Thomas Sankara*, pp. 34, 215.
87. Youssouf Diawara, *Dernière entrevue avec Thomas Sankara Président du Faso (9–10 octobre 1987): À la veille d'un meurtre programmé* (Ouagadougou: Harmattan Burkina, 2015), pp. 59–63.
88. *Republic of Liberia Truth and Reconciliation Commission*, vol. 2, *Consolidated Final Report, 30 June 2009* (Monrovia: Twidan Grafix, 2009), p. 310.
89. Martens, *Sankara, Compaoré et la révolution Burkinabè*, pp. 56–57.
90. Jaffré, *Biographie de Thomas Sankara*, p. 208; Kyélem de Tambèla, *Thomas Sankara et la Révolution au Burkina Faso*, p. 365; Somé, *Thomas Sankara*, pp. 215–16; Harsch, *Thomas Sankara*, p. 140.
91. Kyélem de Tambèla, *Thomas Sankara et la Révolution au Burkina Faso*, p. 365.
92. Thomas Sankara, "Le dernier texte de Thomas Sankara," in *Redécouvrir Sankara: Martyr de la liberté*, ed. Ndongo Samba Sylla (Douala, Cameroon: Africavenir, 2012), pp. 158–62.
93. Martens, *Sankara, Compaoré et la révolution Burkinabè*, p. 61–68; Somé, *Thomas Sankara*, p. 37, 216; Kyélem de Tambèla, *Thomas Sankara et la Révolution au Burkina Faso*, pp. 365–66; Jaffré, *Biographie de Thomas Sankara*, p. 209; Harsch, *Thomas*

Sankara, pp. 144–45; "US Freed Taylor to Overthrow Doe, Liberia's TRC Hears," *Mail & Guardian* (Johannesburg), 27 August 2008; Alpha Sesay, "Taylor's Former Vice-President Describes Training, Arms Deliveries and Atrocities, Claims Cannibalism Was Required to Join Taylor's Presidential Guard," *International Justice Monitor*, 15 May 2008, https://www.ijmonitor.org/2008/05/taylors-former-vice-president-describes-training-arms-deliveries-and-atrocities-claims-cannibalism-was-required-to-join-taylors-presidential-guard/.

CONCLUSION

1. Ernest Harsch, "A Revolution Derailed," *Africa Report* 33, no. 1 (January–February 1988): p. 33.
2. Harsch, "A Revolution Derailed," p. 34; "A Sad Day for Africa," *Africa Report*, November–December 1987, p. 5.
3. "Coup d'état à Ouagadougou," *Libération*, 16 October 1987, p. 1 of World Section. See also Abiyan Agencias, "El 'número dos' de Burkina Faso protagoniza un golpe de Estado que produce numerosas víctimas," *El País*, 16 October 1987.
4. "Burkina Faso Ruler Overthrown in Coup Staged by Deputy," *Times* (London), 16 October 1987, p. 1.
5. James Brooke, "A Friendship Dies in a Bloody Coup," *New York Times*, 26 October 1987, p. A8.
6. Harsch, "A Revolution Derailed," p. 34.
7. Richard Everett, "Coup Chief Battles to Gain Support: Tension in Burkina Faso," *Times* (London), 24 October 1987, p. 1.
8. Harsch, "A Revolution Derailed," p. 34; Ernest Harsch, *Thomas Sankara: An African Revolutionary* (Athens: Ohio University Press, 2014), p. 147; Valère D. Somé, *Thomas Sankara: L'espoir assassiné* (Paris: L'Harmattan, 1990), p. 58; Ludo Martens, *Sankara, Compaoré et la révolution Burkinabè* (Anvers, Belgium: EPO Dossier International, 1989), p. 242.
9. Aaron Leaf, "How Burkina Faso Rediscovered a Revolutionary Hero—and Overthrew a Dictator," *Quartz*, 5 December 2014, https://qz.com/305056/how-burkina-faso-rediscovered-a-revolutionary-hero-and-overthrew-a-dictator/.
10. Ernest Harsch, "Burkina Faso: Echoes of a Revolution Past," South African History Online, 22 December 2014, https://www.sahistory.org.za/archive/

burkina-faso-echoes-revolution-past-ernest-harsch-december-22nd-2014. See also Lassane Ouedraogo, "Mediated Sankarism: Reinventing a Historical Figure to Reimagine the Future," *African Studies Quarterly* 18, no. 1 (September 2018): p. 19; Mamadou Diallo, "Thomas Sankara and the Revolutionary Birth of Burkina Faso," *Viewpoint Magazine* 6, no. 1 (February 2018), https://www.viewpointmag.com/2018/02/01/thomas-sankara-revolutionary-birth-burkina-faso/; Peter Dôrrie, "25 Years On: The Mixed legacy of Burkina Faso's Thomas Sankara, Socialist Soldier," *Think Africa Press*, 15 October 2012, http://thyinkafricapress.com/burkina-faso/mixed-legacy-thomas-sankara-socialist-soldier-25-year-anniversary; Kingsley Kobo, "Burkina Faso: Ghost of 'Africa's Che Guevara,'" *Al Jazeera America*, 30 October 2014.

11. Frantz Fanon, *The Wretched of the Earth* (New York: Grove, 1963), pp. 37, 36.
12. Thomas Sankara, "4ème anniversaire de la RDP, AN IV," 4 August 1987, Thomas Sankara Archives, http://www.capitainethomassankara.net/pages_fr/archives_video/archives_video_4aout1987.html. This is a video of the entire address (minus the last minute or so). See also, Thomas Sankara, "Our Revolution Needs a People Who Are Convinced, Not Conquered," in *Thomas Sankara Speaks: The Burkina Faso Revolution 1983–1987* (New York: Pathfinder Press, 2007), p. 392.
13. Thomas Sankara, "Eight Million Burkinabè, Eight Million Revolutionaries," in *Thomas Sankara Speaks*, p. 405.
14. Colin Dupré, *Le FESPACO, une affaire d'état(s): 1969–2009* (Paris: L'Harmattan, 2012), pp. 167, 169.
15. James E. Genova, "Re-Thinking African Cinema in the Context of Third Cinema: From *Mandabi* to *Bamako* and the Mediascape of Postcolonial Identity," in *Rethinking Third Cinema: The Role of Anti-colonial Media and Aesthetics in Postmodernity*, ed. Frieda Ekotto and Adeline Koh (Berlin: Lit Verlag, 2009), p. 126.
16. Dupré, *Le FESPACO*, p. 189.
17. Clément Tapsoba, "Cinéastes d'Afrique noire: parcours d'un combat révolu," in *Afriques 50: Singularités d'un cinéma pluriel*, ed. Catherine Ruelle, Clément Tapsoba, and Alessandra Speciale (Paris: L'Harmattan, 2005), p. 148.
18. Dupré, *Le FESPACO*, pp. 218–19.
19. Frantz Fanon, *Toward the African Revolution* (New York: Grove, 1967), p. 44.
20. Nwachukwu Frank Ukadike, *Black African Cinema* (Berkeley: University of California Press, 1994), pp. 212, 267, 277, 283.
21. Genova, "Re-Thinking African Cinema in the Context of Third Cinema," p. 139.
22. "Fespaco—création du Prix Thomas Sankara," press communication, *Africultures: Les Mondes en Relation*, February 2015, http://africultures.com/

murmures/?no=17197&utm_source=newsletter&utm_medium=email&utm_campaign=451; Moses Opobo, "Dusadejambo on Scooping Thomas Sankara Prize at FESPACO," *New Times* (Kigali, Rwanda), 12 March 2017, https://www.newtimes.co.rw/section/read/208808.

23. Michel Lachkar, "Féstival de cinéma de Ouagadougou: Fespaco 1985, une année particulière," *Franceinfo: Afrique*, 24 February 2019, https://www.francetvinfo.fr/monde/afrique/societe-africaine/festival-de-cinema-de-ouagadougou-fespaco-1985-une-annee-particuliere_3191779.html; Hawa Suleiman Issah, "Burkina Faso: Thomas Sankara's Statue Inaugurated in Ouagadougou," *africanews*, 2 March 2019, https://www.africanews.com/2019/03/02/burkina-faso-thomas-sankara-s-statue-inauguration-in-ouagadougou//.

24. The World Bank, "Burkina Faso: Country Data," https://data.worldbank.org/country/burkina-faso; IMF, "Burkina Faso: Country Data," https://www.imf.org/en/Countries/BFA.

25. "Burkina Faso External Debt 1970–2019," published by Macrotrends using World Bank Data, https://www.macrotrends.net/countries/BFA/burkina-faso/external-debt-stock.

26. *Discours d'Orientation Politique*, 2 October 1983, released by the Ministry of Information on behalf of the CNR, p. 18.

27. Gnindé Bonzi, *Souvenirs de la Révolution: Des moments de la révolution sankariste vue par un adolescent. Récit* (Paris: L'Harmattan, 2015), pp. 81, 109.

28. Thomas Sankara interview with Jean-Philippe Rapp, "Dare to Invent the Future," in *Thomas Sankara Speaks*, p. 213.

29. "Angry Man's Tall Words," *New York Times*, 23 August 1987, p. 10.

30. Harsch, *Thomas Sankara*, p. 99.

31. Hyppolyte Fofack, "Thomas Sankara: A Leader before His Time?," *African Business*, December 2012, pp. 73, 74.

32. Bruno Jaffré, *Burkina Faso: Les années Sankara de la révolution à la rectification* (Paris: L'Harmattan, 1989), pp. 189, 192–93.

33. Apollinaire J. Kyélem de Tambèla, *Thomas Sankara et la Révolution au Burkina Faso: Une experience de développement autocentré*, 2nd ed. (Ouagadougou: Harmattan Burkina, 2012), p. 181.

34. Harsch, "A Revolution Derailed," p. 39.

35. Thomas Sankara, "You Cannot Kill Ideas," speech in Ouagadougou 8 October 1987, in *Thomas Sankara Speaks*, p. 421.

36. Thomas Sankara interview with Jean-Philippe Rapp, "Dare to Invent the Future," in *Thomas Sankara Speaks*, p. 232.

37. *Discours d'Orientation Politique*, 2 October 1983, pp. 1, 10.
38. Eduardo Molano, "Jazz, Rivalry and Revolution: Burkina Faso Recalls the Spirit of Sankara," *Guardian*, 27 September 2015, https://theguardian.com/world/2015/sep/27/jazz-and-revolution-burkina-faso-recalls-the-spirit-of-sankara.
39. Thomas Sankara, "Eight Million Burkinabè, Eight Million Revolutionaries," in *Thomas Sankara Speaks*, p. 404.

Bibliography

Andriamirado, Sennen. *Sankara le rebelle*. Paris: Jeune Afrique Livres, 1987.

Aremu, Johnson Olaosebikan. "Responses to the 1983 Expulsion of Aliens from Nigeria: A Critique." *African Research Review* 7(3), no. 30 (July 2013): pp. 340–52.

Armes, Roy. *Third World Film Making and the West*. Berkeley: University of California Press, 1987.

Bakari, Imruh, and Mbye Cham, eds. *African Experiences of Cinema*. London: British Film Institute, 1996.

Bamouni, Babou Paulin. "L'Évolution politique de la Haute-Volta." *Peuples noirs, Peuples africains*, no. 34 (July–August 1983): pp. 53–74.

———. *Burkina Faso: Processus de la Révolution*. Paris: L'Harmattan, 1986.

Barro, Abdoulaye. "Pensée et système politiques chez Thomas Sankara." LeFaso.net, 21 October 2016, http://lefaso.net/spip.php?article73792.

Benoist, Joseph-Roger. *L'Afrique occidentale française de 1944 à 1960*. Dakar, Senegal: Les Nouvelles Éditions Africaines, 1982.

Berger, Iris. *Women in Twentieth-Century Africa*. Cambridge: Cambridge University Press, 2016.

Bonzi, Gnindé. *Souvenirs de la Révolution: Des moments de la révolution sankariste vue par *un adolescent, Récit*. Paris: L'Harmattan, 2015.

Bouamama, Said. *Figures de la révolution africaine de Kenyatta à Sankara*. Paris: Éditions la Découverte, 2014.

Bourdieu, Pierre, and Loïc J. D. Wacquant. *An Invitation to Reflexive Sociology*. Chicago: University of Chicago Press, 1992.

Brittain, Victoria. "Introduction to Sankara & Burkina Faso." *Review of African Political Economy*, no. 32 (April 1985): pp. 39–47.

Chafer, Tony. *The End of Empire in French West Africa: France's Successful Decolonization?* New York: Berg, 2002.

Cham, Mbye. "Film and History in Africa: A Critical Survey of Current Trends and Tendencies." In *Focus on African Films*, ed. Françoise Pfaff, pp. 48–68. Bloomington: Indiana University Press, 2004.

Chanda, Tirthankar. "Mitterrand-Sankara: Le vieux et le capitaine impertinent." *RFI Afrique*, 10 January 2016, https://www.rfi.fr/fr/afrique/20160109-mitterrand-sankara-le-vieux-sage-le-capitaine-impertinent.

Chia, Anne. "Ghana Must Go: Nigeria's Expulsion of Immigrants." *Immigration, Life, Politics, and International Affairs*, annechia.com, 20 April 2015.

Crowder, Micheal, and Obaro Ikime, eds. *West African Chiefs: Their Changing Status under Colonial Rule and Independence*. New York: Africana, 1970.

Deschamps, Alain. *Burkina Faso (1987–1992): "Le pays des hommes intègres."* Paris: L'Harmattan, 2001.

Diallo, Mamadou. "Thomas Sankara and the Revolutionary Birth of Burkina Faso." *Viewpoint Magazine* 6, 1 February 2018, https://viewpointmag.com/2018/02/01/thomas-sankara-revolutionary-birth-burkina-faso/.

Diawara, Manthia. *African Cinema: Politics & Culture*. Bloomington: Indiana University Press, 1992.

Diawara, Youssouf. *Dernière entrevue avec Thomas Sankara Président du Faso (9–10 octobre 1987): À la veille d'un meurtre programmé*. Ouagadougou: Harmattan Burkina, 2015.

Dôrrie, Peter. "25 Years On: The Mixed legacy of Burkina Faso's Thomas Sankara, Socialist Soldier." *Think Africa Press*, 15 October 2012, https://allafrica.com/stories/201210160444.html.

Dovey, Lindiwe. *Curating Africa in the Age of Film Festivals*. New York: Palgrave Macmillan, 2015.

Drabo, Colette. "Fidèle Toé Ancien Compagnon de Thomas Sankara: 'Si Blaise Compaoré s'entête, le peuple peut l'amener à regagner les rangs." *Le Pays*, 15 October 2014, https://lepays.bf/fidele-toe-ancien-compagnon-thomas-sankara-blaise-compaore-sentete-peuple-lamener-regagner-les-rangs/.

Dupré, Colin. *Le FESPACO: Une affaire d'état(s): 1969–2009*. Paris: L'Harmattan, 2012.

Ellis, Stephen. *The Mask of Anarchy: The Destruction of Liberia and the Religious Dimension of an African Civil War*. London: Hurst, 2007.

Ekotto, Frieda, and Adeline Koh, eds. *Rethinking Third Cinema: The Role of Anti-colonial Media and Aesthetics in Postmodernity*. Berlin: Lit Verlag, 2009.

Englebert, Pierre. *La Révolution Burkinabè*. Paris: L'Harmattan, 1986.

———. *Burkina Faso: Unsteady Statehood in West Africa*. New York: Routledge, 2018.

Fanon, Frantz. *The Wretched of the Earth*. New York: Grove Press, 1963.

———. *Toward the African Revolution*. New York: Grove Press, 1967.

Fofack, Hypolyte. "Thomas Sankara: A Leader before His Time?" *African Business*, December 2012, pp. 72–74.

French, Howard W. "How Qaddafi Reshaped Africa." *Atlantic*, 1 March 2011, https://www.theatlantic.com/international/archive/2011/03/how-qaddafi-reshaped-africa/71861/.

Gary-Tounkara, Daouda. "A Reappraisal of the Expulsion of Illegal Immigrants from Nigeria in 1983," *International Journal of Conflict and Violence* 9, no. 1 (2015): pp. 25–38.

Genova, James E. *Cinema and Development in West Africa*. Bloomington: Indiana University Press, 2013.

———. "Re-Thinking African Cinema in the Context of Third Cinema: From *Mandabi* to *Bamako* and the Mediascape of Post-Colonial Identity." In *Rethinking Third Cinema: The Role of Anti-colonial Media and Aesthetics in Postmodernity*, ed. Frieda Ekotto and Adeline Koh, pp. 125–46. Berlin: Lit Verlag, 2009.

———. *Colonial Ambivalence, Cultural Authenticity, and the Limitations of Mimicry in French Ruled West Africa, 1914–1956*. New York: Peter Lang, 2004.

Gleijeses, Piero. *Visions of Freedom: Havana, Washington, Pretoria, and the Struggle for Southern Africa, 1976–1991*. Raleigh: University of North Carolina Press, 2016.

Gramsci, Antonio. *Selections from the Prison Notebooks*. Ed. and trans. Quintin Hoare and Geoffrey Nowell Smith. New York: International Publishers, 1992.

Harrison, Paul. *The Greening of Africa: Breaking through the Battle for Land and Food*. London: Paladin Grafton, 1987.

Harrow, Kenneth W. *Postcolonial African Cinema: From Political Engagement to Postmodernism*. Bloomington: Indiana University Press, 2007.

Harsch, Ernest. *Thomas Sankara: An African Revolutionary*. Athens: Ohio University Press, 2014.

———. *Burkina Faso: A History of Power, Protest, and Revolution*. London: Zed Books, 2017.

———. "Burkina Faso: Echoes of a Revolution Past." *South African History Online*, 22 December 2014, https://www.sahistory.org.za/archive/burkina-faso-echoes-revolution-past-ernest-harsch-december-22nd-2014.

Hjort, Mette, and Eva Jorholt, eds. *African Cinema and Human Rights*. Bloomington: Indiana University Press, 2019.

Hondo, Med. "What Is Cinema for Us?" In *African Experiences of Cinema*, ed. Imruh Bakari and Mbye Cham, pp. 39–41. London: British Film Institute, 1996.

Jaffré, Bruno. *Biographie de Thomas Sankara: La patrie ou la mort*. Paris: L'Harmattan, 1997.

———. *Burkina Faso: Les années Sankara de la révolution à la rectification*. Paris: L'Harmattan, 1989.

Kabeya, Charles. "Évolution et rôle des syndicats au Burkina Faso." *Présence Africaine*, no. 142 (1987): pp. 130–47.

Kaboré, Gaston, ed. *L'Afrique et le Centenaire du cinema / Africa and the Centenary of Cinema*. Dakar: Présence Africaine, 1995.

Kammanl, Ansel Marcel. "La guerre des tracts sous la révolution entre 1986 et 1987: Un des prémices du octobre 1987 au Burkina Faso." LeFaso.net, 12 October 2017, https://lefaso.net/spip.php?article79842.

Kasuka, Bridgette. *Prominent African Leaders since Independence*. New York: New Africa Press, 2013.

Kobo, Kingsley. "Burkina Faso: Ghost of 'Africa's Che Guevara.'" Al Jazeera America, 30 October 2014, https://www.aljazeera.com/features/2014/10/31/burkina-faso-ghost-of-africas-che-guevara.

Kyélem de Tambèla, Apollinaire J. *Thomas Sankara et la Révolution au Burkina Faso: Une expérience de développement autocentré*, 2nd ed. Ouagadougou: Harmattan Burkina, 2012.

Lachkar, Michel. "Féstival de cinéma de Ouagadougou: Fespaco 1985, une année particulière." Franceinfo:Afrique, 24 February 2019, https://www.francetvinfo.fr/monde/afrique/societe-africaine/festival-de-cinema-de-ouagadougou-fespaco-1985-une-annee-particuliere_3191779.html.

Lalsaga, Kakiswendépoulmdé Marcel Marie Anselme, "Les Comités des Défense de la Révolution (CDR) dans la politique du Conseil National de la Révolution (CNR) de 1983 à 1987: Une approche historique à partir de la ville de Ouagadougou." Memoire Online, 2007, https://www.memoireonline.

com/05/12/5889/m_Les-Comites-de-Defense-de-la-RevolutionCDR-dans-la-politique-du-Conseil-National-de-la-Revolut57.html.

———. "Avènement du 15 octobre 1987: La crise au sein du Conseil National de la Révolution (CNR) et l'échec des tentatives de conciliation." LeFaso.net, 15 October 2017, https://lefaso.net/spip.php?article79904.

Lippens, Philippe. *La République de Haute-Volta*. Paris: Berger-Levrault, 1972.

Madiéga, Yénouyaba Georges, and Oumarou Nao, eds. *Burkina Faso: Cent ans d'histoire, 1895–1995*. 2 vols. Ouagadougou: Éditions Karthala, 2003.

Malitsky, Joshua. *Post-Revolution Nonfiction Film: Building the Soviet and Cuban Nations*. Bloomington: Indiana University Press, 2013.

Marchand, Frédéric. "15 octobre 1987: La part de Jacques Chirac et de la droite française." *Le Libérateur*, no. 43, 5–19 November 2007, https://www.thomassankara.net/15-octobre-87-la-part-de-jacques-chirac-et-de-la-droite-francaise/.

Martens, Ludo. *Sankara, Compaoré et la révolution Burkinabè*. Anvers, Belgium: EPO Dossier International, 1989.

Martin, Guy. "Ideology and Praxis in Thomas Sankara's Populist Revolution of 4 August 1983 in Burkina Faso." *Issue* 15 (1987): pp. 77–90.

———. "Démocratie révolutionnaire, conflits socio-politique et pouvoir militaire au Burkina Faso, 1983–1988." *Labor, Capital and Society/Travail, capital, et société* 23, no. 1 (April 1990): pp. 38–68.

Martin, Michael T., ed. *Cinemas of the Black Diaspora: Diversity, Dependence and Oppositionality*. Detroit: Wayne State University, 1995.

Marx, Karl. *The 18th Brumaire of Louis Bonaparte*. New York: International, 1990.

———. *The Economic & Philosophic Manuscripts of 1844*. New York: International, 1993.

Mbembe, Achille. *On the Postcolony*. Berkeley: University of California Press, 2001.

Molano, Eduardo. "Jazz, Rivalry and Revolution: Burkina Faso Recalls the Spirit of Sankara." *Guardian*, 27 September 2015, https://www.theguardian.com/world/2015/sep/27/jazz-and-revolution-burkina-faso-recalls-the-spirit-of-sankara.

Naylor, Phillip C. *France and Algeria: A History of Decolonization and Transformation*. Gainesville: University Press of Florida, 2000.

Otayek, René, Filiga Michel Sawadogo, and Jean-Pierre Guingané, eds. *Le Burkina entre révolution et démocratie (1983–1993)*. Paris: Éditions Karthala, 1996.

Ouedraogo, Lassane. "Mediated Sankarism: Reinventing a Historical Figure to Reimagine the Future." *African Studies Quarterly* 18, no. 1 (September 2018): pp. 19–30.

Pasley, Victoria. "*Kuxa Kanema*: Third Cinema and Its Transatlantic Crossings." In *Rethinking Third Cinema: The Role of Anti-colonial Media and Aesthetics in*

Postmodernity, ed. Frieda Ekotto and Adeline Koh, pp. 107–24. Berlin: Lit Verlag, 2009.

Peterson, Brian J. *Thomas Sankara: A Revolutionary in Cold War Africa*. Bloomington: Indiana University Press, 2021.

Pfaff, Françoise. "Africa from Within: The Films of Gaston Kaboré and Idrissa Ouédraogo as Anthropological Sources." In *African Experiences of Cinema*, ed. Imruh Bakari and Mbye Cham, pp. 223–38. London: British Film Institute, 1996.

———, ed. *Focus on African Films*. Bloomington: Indiana University Press, 2004.

Pines, Jim, and Paul Willemen, eds. *Questions of Third Cinema*. London: British Film Institute, 1991.

Pondi, Jean-Emmanuel. *Thomas Sankara et l'émergence de l'Afrique au XXIe siècle*. Yaoundé, Cameroon: Éditions Afric'Eveil, 2016.

Reza, Alexandra. "Short Cuts: Sankara and Mitterrand." *London Review of Books* 36, no. 23 (4 December 2014), https://www.lrb.co.uk/the-paper/v36/n23/alexandra-reza/short-cuts.

Roger, Benjamin. "Jean-Christophe Mitterrand: L'Assassinat de Sankara? Selon moi, un accident." *Jeune Afrique*, 13 October 2017, https://www.jeuneafrique.com/mag/481423/politique/jean-christophe-mitterrand-lassassinat-de-sankara-selon-moi-un-accident/.

Roof, Maria. "African and Latin American Cinemas: Contexts and Contacts." In *Focus on African Films*, ed. Françoise Pfaff, pp. 241–70. Bloomington: Indiana University Press, 2004.

Ruelle, Catherine, Clément Tapsoba, and Alessandra Speciale, eds. *Afriques 50: Singularités d'un cinéma pluriel*. Paris: L'Harmattan, 2005.

Salliot, Emmanuel. "A Review of Past Security Events in the Sahel 1967–2007." Sahel and West Africa Club Secretariat of the OECD, 2010.

Sankara, Thomas. *Thomas Sankara Speaks: The Burkina Faso Revolution 1983–1987*. New York: Pathfinder, 2007.

———. *Women's Liberation and the African Freedom Struggle*. New York: Pathfinder, 1990.

Sawadogo, Alfred Yambangba. *Le Président Thomas Sankara: Chef de la Révolution Burkinabè; 1983–1987, portrait*. Paris: L'Harmattan, 2001.

Sawadogo, Filippe. "Ouagadougou, future mémoire du cinema africain." In *L'Afrique et le Centenaire du cinema / Africa and the Centenary of Cinema*, ed. Gaston Kaboré, pp. 276–81. Dakar: Présence Africaine, 1995.

Schmidt, Elizabeth. *Cold War and Decolonization in Guinea, 1946–1958*. Athens: Ohio University Press, 2007.

Sembène, Ousmane. "Continuons à travailler sans relâche." In *Afriques 50: Singularités d'un cinéma pluriel*, ed. Catherine Ruelle, Clément Tapsoba, and Alessandra Speciale, pp. 13–16. Paris: L'Harmattan, 2005.

Skinner, Elliott P. "Sankara and the Burkinabè Revolution: Charisma and Power, Local and External Dimensions." *Journal of Modern African Studies* 26, no. 3 (September 1988): pp. 437–55.

———. "The Changing Status of the 'Emperor of the Mossi' under Colonial Rule and since Independence." In *West African Chiefs: their Changing Status under Colonial Rule and Independence*, ed. Michael Crowder and Obaro Ikime, pp. 98–124. New York: Africana, 1970.

Somé, Valère D. *Thomas Sankara: L'Espoir Assassiné*. Paris: L'Harmattan, 1990.

Spiesse, Emmanuelle. "L'Artiste et le pouvoir sous Sankara (1983–1987)." In *Burkina Faso: Cent ans d'histoire, 1895–1995*, 2 vols, ed. Yénouyaba Georges Madiéga and Oumarou Nao, pp. 2141–68. Ouagadougou: Éditions Karthala, 2003.

Stoneman, Rod. "South/South Axis: For a Cinema Built by, with and for Africans." In *African Experiences of Cinema*, ed. Imruh Bakari and Mbye Cham, pp. 175–80. London: British Film Institute, 1996.

———. "African Cinema: Perspective Correction." In *African Cinema and Human Rights*, ed. Mette Hjort and Eva Jorholt, pp. 38–59. Bloomington: Indiana University Press, 2019.

Sylla, Ndongo Samba, ed. *Redécouvrir Sankara: Martyr de la liberté*. Douala, Cameroon: Africavenir, 2012.

Tapsoba, Clément. "Cinéastes d'Afrique noire: parcours d'un combat révolu." In *Afriques 50: Singularités d'un cinéma pluriel*, ed. Catherine Ruelle, Clément Tapsoba, and Alessandra Speciale, pp. 147–52. Paris: L'Harmattan, 2005.

———. "Préface." In *Le FESPACO: Une affaire d'état(s): 1969–2009*, ed. Colin Dupré, pp. 9–11. Paris: L'Harmattan, 2012.

Ukadike, Nwachukwu Frank. *Black African Cinema*. Berkeley: University of California Press, 1994.

———. *Questioning African Cinema: Conversation with Filmmakers*. Minneapolis: University of Minnesota Press, 2002.

Vieyra, Paulin Soumanou. "African Cinema: Solidarity and Difference." In *Questions of Third Cinema*, ed. Jim Pines and Paul Willemen, pp. 195–98. London: British Film Institute, 1991.

Wilkins, Micheal. "The Death of Thomas Sankara and the Rectification of the People's Revolution in Burkina Faso." *African Affairs* 88, no. 352 (July 1989): pp. 375–88.

Yaméogo, Saglba. "17 Mai 1983: Prémices de la Révolution d'août." Lefaso.net, 12 August 2012, https://lefaso.net/spip.php?article49628.

Zerbo, Yacouba. "Les rélations politiques entre le Mali et le Burkina-Faso de 1983 à 1985: Les causes du conflit frontalier de décembre 1985." *Guerres mondiales et conflits contemporains*, no. 196 (December 1999): pp. 89–104.

Index

African cinema: and the Burkinabè Revolution, xiii, 185–89; censorship, 22, 23, 135; center of, xiii, xxii, 2–3, 10–14; cinema industrial complex, 3, 12–13, 23; film as mechanism for social change, x; funding by France cut, 24, 41; Hondo, 134–35; nationalization of cinematic infrastructure, 3, 14; Niamey Manifesto of African Filmmakers, 41; open air screenings, 106–7; radicalization within, 21–24; relationship with France, 81–82; Sankara on, 154; women in film, 110–11, 136. *See also* FEPACI; FESPACO; FESPACO 1983; FESPACO 1985; FESPACO 1987; training in filmmaking

African filmmakers: "The Algiers Charter on African Cinema," 22, 41, 110; Burkinabè Revolution embraced, xiii, 136; call for a "cultural revolution," 21; censorship and prohibition of films, 23; collaboration with government, 3; cooperation with Cuba, 21; film used to counter cultural alienation, 10–13, 21, 157, 187–88; France's funding of, 41, 81; Niamey Manifesto of African Filmmakers, 24; relationship with France for control, 12–13, 155; support to Lamizana, 14; UNESCO petition, 107. *See also* FEPACI

Agacher Strip, 17, 82, 122

Agacher Strip War. *See* Christmas War

Algeria: FEPACI Second Congress, 22; at FESPACO 1985, 108, 109; liberation war, 4; Meeting of Third World Filmmakers, 21; support for Polisario Front, 86–87

"Algiers Charter on African Cinema, The," 22, 41, 110

Algiers Cultural Festival (1969), 12, 13

alienation, xiv, xv; enabled neocolonialism, 134; film as a tool to counter, 11; Hondo on, 64; in the manifesto from Algiers Cultural Festival, 13; role in Burkinabè Revolution, 97; as significant inhibitor to social development, 21.
Angola, 37, 74, 85, 87, 143
anti-apartheid, 87, 108–9, 143, 187–89
Anti-Imperialist Days, 94, 166–67
anti-racism, 11, 186–87
apartheid: anti-apartheid uprising in South Africa, 143; Burkina Faso, 191; CNR's foreign policy to end, xxiv, 85, 87; Cuba, 143; Sankara and, 45, 82, 87, 114, 143, 145, 147, 148
Autre Journal, L', 99

Bamouni, Babou Paulin, xi; on 5 August 1983, 57–58, 61; on the CMRPN, 25; CNR leader, 66; declared war on PAI, 94–95; dual power of CSP, 37–38; Fanon's true decolonization, 69–70; financial crisis, 19; four groups opposed to Saye Zerbo regime, 34; on 17 May 1983, 49–50; on move to communist country, 102; murder of, 182; on neocolonialism, 2; Sankara letter of December 1981, 28; *Sidwaya*, 92–93, 127; in special cabinet of advisors, 173; to start new journal for CNR, 17; on vision for vanguard party, 127; women's emancipation, 133. See also *Sidwaya*
Benin, 5, 39, 40, 47–48, 119, 129. See also Kérékou, Mathieu
Boukary Lingani, Jean-Baptiste, xi; arrest of, 50; control of student's CDR, 130; creation of underground military group, 3; defence of false rumors against Sankara, 175; execution of, 185; Inter CDR, 98; member of Coordinators of Faso, 63, 97, 173; minister of defense, 66, 83; OMR, 46, 50–51, 97; PAI and, 52–53, 98; push for socialism, 132; ROC, 18, 34, 35, 36–37; role in vanguard party plans, 170; Sankara and, xi, 17, 19; visit to Ghana, 83
Boyer, Gaston, 49, 53
Burkina Faso, xiv; agreements with Cuba and North Korea, 146; Conseil de l'Entente, 40; and Cuba, 143, 191; drought, 101; external debt, 160–61; GDP, 118, 141, 160; implicated in attempted coups in West Africa, 119; Inflation, 117–18, 160; life expectancy in, 113, 141, 160; name change, 96, 97; New Caledonia, 149; relations with France, 141–42. See also Upper Volta

Cabral, Amilcar, xiv, xx
Castro, Fidel: call to eradicate debt, 161; commitment to eradicate apartheid, 143, 161; and Sankara, xiv, xiv–xv, 44–45, 114
CATC (Confédération Africaine des Travailleurs Croyants), 6–7, 15
CDR (Comités de défense de la révolution), 92; authority in newly created districts, 80; Christmas War, 125; enforcer of CNR programs, 87–88; formation, role, and membership, 66, 67; on PAI as dangerous, 95; People's Commission

Charged with the Prevention of Corruption (CPPC), 153; Sankara on rift over control of the student's CDR, 145; Second National Congress of the CDR, 162–64. *See also* Ouédraogo, Pierre

CFAV (Council of the Voltaic Armed Forces), 8

Chad, 43, 50, 54, 59, 82, 86, 174, 181

chieftaincies: CMRPN support from, 25; control of TPR, 77, 79; "enemy of the people," 71; obstacle to revolutionary government, 64, 79–81

China, 7; in *Discours d'Orientation Politique*, 74; influence on Sankara, xiv–xv, 20; at National Week of Culture, 84; relationship with Burkina Faso, 191; ULCR pro-China, 69; on U.S. bombing of Libya, 143. *See also* ULC

Chirac, Jacques, 144, 148, 149

Christmas War, 17–18, 121–23, 124, 132, 142; after the war, 123–27, 131

CIDC (Consortium Interafricain de Distribution Cinématographique), 22, 24, 30

CIPROFILM (Centre Interafricain de Production de Films), 23, 24, 30

Cissé, Kader: criticism of Somé, 140; *Discours d'Orientation Politique*, 70; dismissal of, 140, 153; formed ULC–*La Flamme*, 131; Revolutionary Economic and Social Council, 137; Somé on, 166

Cissé, Souleymane: Algiers Cultural Festival (1969), 13; *cinq jours d'une vie* (1972), 23; *Den Muso* (1975), 22; *Finyé*, 42; influence of Third Cinema, 21; persecuted, 23, 42; political didacticism of, 41; *Yeelen* (1987), 136, 157, 188

climate change, xii, xxiv; carbon dioxide emissions, 102–3, 141; PPD programs to fight, 101–2, 122, 132–33, 191; relationship to economics, 14–15, 101, 136, 145, 191

CMRPN (Comité Militaire de Redressement pour le Progrès National), 25–29, 30–31, 33, 35, 41, 56–57, 90

CNR (National Council of the Revolution/ Conseil national de la révolution): admitted UCB and GCB into government, 98; Algeria, 86–87; and Bamouni, 17, 66; challenge to imperialism, 85; the clarification process, 96–98; creation of new political networks, 67; and Cuba, 84, 112–13; donations to CSR, 78–79; election of National General Secretariat, 68–69; formation of CDRs, 95; founding of SOCI-B, 84; identified inhibitors to early independence movement, xii; international relations, 65; and Kérékou, 83; nationalism, xv; PAI/LIPD and Anti-Imperialist Day of the Youth, 94, 95–96; relationship with Ghana, 76; relationship with Houphouët-Boigny, 83, 118–19; relations with Qaddafi, 85–86; renegotiated treaties with France, 81–82; reorganized chieftaincy, 80; restructuring of the state and governance, 63; root out corruption among officials, 140; seized power, ix;

SNEAHV strike, 89–90, 104; solidarity with ANC and SACP, 87; *Statutes of the CDR*, 94; *Statut Général des Comités de Défense de la Révolution*, 68; support for, 62; use of cinema to transform people, xii; vanguard party, 127–31, 166–70, 177. *See also* FESPACO 1985; PPD

CNR foreign policy: aligned with anti-imperialism, 85; core principles, 86, 191; and Cuba, 114; to end apartheid, xxiv, 87, 143; insulation from counterrevolutionary pressures, 65, 88; tied to creating new people, 84. *See also* PPD

colonialism: alienation and, xv; in *Discours d'Orientation Politique*, 74; division between rural and urban communities, 164; substituted with neocolonialism, 73. *See also* Fanon, Frantz; neocolonialism

COMACICO, 14

communism, xi, 62, 66, 102

Communist Party of the Soviet Union, 146

Compaoré, Blaise: age, xi, 20; animosity towards ULCR, 130, 172; arrest, 30; cabinet meeting, 176–77; Coordinators of Faso, 63, 97, 170, 173; creation of underground military group, 3; and CSP, 35; demanded arrest of PAI leaders, 165; exiled, 30, 33; greeting the masses, 74; influential throughout UCB, 129; Jonas Somé's speech, 178–79; minister of state, 66; National Liberation Army, 54, 57; offered himself as president, 62; OMR, 36–37, 55, 62, 97, 174, 180; opposition to vanguard party, 168–69; ordered Sankara's assassination, 179–80, 181–82; overthrown, ix–x, 185; at PMK, 9; in Pô, 50, 51, 53–54, 57–58; relationship with Libya, 43, 48, 51, 54, 171, 174–76, 179–80; relationship with Sankara, xi, 3, 17, 19, 28, 132, 153–54, 165, 167, 169, 171, 173–77, 179; to replace Sankara at Pô, 28; restored to position, 31; ROC, 18, 34, 36–37; seized power in coup (15 October 1987), ix, xix, 181, 184; and Sigué, 131; and Chantal Terrasson de Fougères (wife), 118, 174, 181; on TPR, 77; ULC–*La Flamme*, 166–67, 170

Conseil de l'Entente, 40, 119, 121, 182

Coordinators of Faso (Coordonnateurs du Faso), 97–98, 124, 128–29, 130, 170, 173–74, 177

Côte d'Ivoire, 35, 45, 82; Christmas War, 142; Compaoré's visit to, 118; Conseil de l'Entente, 40; dual citizenship for Voltaïc workers, 6–7; joint military exercises with France, 119; Nigerian migrant crisis, 39; opposition to new regime, 75; railroad extension, 101; summit to exchange Christmas War prisoner, 123. *See also* Houphouët-Boigny, Félix

Coulibaly, Ouezzin, 4–5, 6

CSB (Confédération Syndicale Burkinabè), 117, 128, 146, 164, 165, 166. *See also* CSV; Touré, Soumane

CSP (Council for the Salvation of the People/Conseil de Salut du Peuple): attempted coup by Saye Zerbo, 44;

consolidation of revolutionary forces within, 36–38; coup (May 1983), 49–50; coup to remove CMRPN, 31; crisis of dual power within, 46–49; explanation of coup, 33–34; *Finyé* (Cissé), 42; and Guébré, 34; hosted Penne, 50; influence of progressive officers, 35; internal split, 51–55; Nigerian migrant crisis, 38–40; panic at Qaddafi visit, 48; Sankara imprisoned, 93; Sankara's policies, 38

CSP II, 53–58, 61

CSV (Confédération Syndicale Voltaïque): donation program, 79; general strikes, 18, 27; legalized by CSP, 35; only legal labor federation, 93; and Sankara, 19; Soumane Touré, 15, 63, 78–79, 93; suppression of, 25, 27, 28, 90. *See also* CSB

Cuba: and Burkina Faso, 143; at FESPACO 1985, 109; at FESPACO 1987, 157; influence on Sankara, xiv–xv; at "National Week of Culture," 84–85; new accord with Burkina Faso, 146; at Non-Aligned Movement meeting, 44–45; Operation Vaccine Commando, 112–13; relationship with Burkina Faso, 143, 191; relationship with Upper Volta, 37, 67, 74, 84; role in birth of FEPACI, 110; Sankara visit to, 146; Sigué training in, 131; support for African filmmakers, 21, 84–85; use of cinema to promote revolution, 45. *See also* Castro, Fidel

Damiba, Béatrice, 169
de Gaulle, Charles, 4–5
Deschamps, Alain, 126

Diallo, Arba: on ban on consumables, 163; counselor to Sankara, 125; on CSP upheavals, 52; foreign minister, 66, 95; LIPAD leader, 15; sent to countryside, 97

Discours d'Orientation Politique: anniversary commemoration, 177, 186; areas for restructuring, 72–73; clarification needed to implement, 97; CSV donation program, 79; double exploitation of women as a specific form of oppression, 111; educational reform, 104–5; government consolidation, 88; imperialism, 70–72, 193; National Bureau of Students analysis of, 179; reorganization of the peasants, 80–81; revolution is not anarchy, 89; warning of populist drift, 163; women's emancipation, 72, 190

DMOF (Direction for Women's Mobilization and Participation), 111
dos Santos, Eduardo, 85

ECOWAS/CEDEAO, 118, 142, 163; corruption scandal, 118, 119, 121
EPI (Popular Investment Effort), 139–40, 159
Ethiopia, 87, 161, 176
Eyadéma, Gnassingbé, 144, 149

Fanon, Frantz: analysis of the liberation process, xv–xvi; destruction of the colonial system needed for sovereignty, 2; effects of imperial domination, 74; humanism, 106, 109; on importance of reform, 99; inspiration for movements, xiv; on national culture, 11; national liberation in a colonial context, 164; true decolonization, 69–70

Faso Dan Fani, 160, 161

FEPACI (Fédération Panafricaine des Cinéastes): The Algiers Charter on African Cinema, 22, 108; Cissé identified with, 42; in crisis, 41, 107; Cuba role in, 110; on cultural domination, 22; establish a permanent secretariat in Cuba, 21; First International Conference on Cinema Production in Africa, 41; formation of, 13; invited to relocate, 107–8; involvement in film festival, 14; means for government to connect with cineastes, xiii; Niamey Manifesto of African Filmmakers, 24, 41, 42, 107, 155; role of cinema in construction of people, 64; and Sankara, 30, 43; Third Congress, 108

FESPACO (Festival Panafricain de Cinéma et de Télévision de Ouagadougou): changes to, xii–xiv; connected to government, xxi; Cuba integrated into, 21; funding for African film, xiv; grand prize to *Finyé* (Cissé), 42; new venues opened, 107. *See also* Dupré, Colin

FESPACO 1983, 30, 41–43, 64, 155

FESPACO 1985: CNR contributions to, xiii–xiv, 107–10; context for, 107–8; international impact of, xxiii; MIFA, 156; MOBRAP, 143

FESPACO 1987, 135, 154–55, 156–57, 158

Festival Mondial des Arts Nègres de Dakar (1966), 12

First National Congress of the CDR, 125–27

Foccart, Jacques, 149

FPV, 25, 75, 89, 90

France, xii, 35, 45; aid cut to Burkina Faso, 149; arms delivery to Mali, 121; assistance for Jean-Baptiste Ouédraogo's government, 50; Burkinabè Revolution as puppet of Libya and USSR, 122; Chad, 82, 86; Côte d'Ivoire, 82; defied by CNR, 96; encouraged clearing forests, 102; Fifth French Republic, 4–5; food exported from, 101; funding for African filmmaking, 7, 23–24, 41, 81, 135; implicated in coup (17 May 1983), 65; intervention to arrest Sankara, 49; investment in Upper Volta cinema, 13–14; joint military exercises with Côte d'Ivoire, 119; Libya, 50; Ministry of Cooperation, 11, 23, 81; new agreement with Burkina Faso for dam project, 142; relationship to Upper Volta, 1–2; rumored to be behind coup plot, 143–44; SNEAHV strike, 90; treaty renegotiation, 81–82; use of Upper Volta for labor in other colonies, 5; visa requirements, 142. *See also* Chirac, Jacques; Mitterrand, François

GCB (Groupe Communiste Burkinabè), 128–29, 130, 153, 168–69

Ghana: attempted coup in Togo, 144; Boukary Lingani's visit to, 83; Compaoré, 51, 54; implications in attempted coups, 119; influence on Sankara, xiv–xv; Jean-Baptiste Ouédraogo, 47, 54; joint military exercises with Upper Volta/Burkina Faso, 76, 119; Joseph Ouédraogo, 7; Kaboré fled to, 185; and Libya, 35, 119; migrants expelled from Nigeria, 39; mourning for Sankara, 184; Taylor arrested in, 175. *See also* Rawlings, Jerry

Grenada, 85, 115, 116, 144, 181

Guébré, Fidèle, 31, 34, 53

Guissou, Basile, 51–52, 66, 98, 167

Havana Cultural Congress in Cuba (1968), 12

Hien, Kilimité, 35, 46, 169, 178, 180

Hondo, Med: Algiers Cultural Festival (1969), 13; on alienation, 64; influence of Third Cinema, 21; Ministry of Cooperation, 81; political didacticism, 41; role in early African filmmaker networks, 12; *Sarraounia* (1986), 134–36, 154–55, 157, 187; *Soleil Ô* (1969), 11

Houphouët-Boigny, Félix: backing Taylor project, 174; Christmas War, 142; Compaoré, 180; CSP, 37; displeasure with Sankara's actions while prime minister, 65; Mali, 75, 123; Nigerian migrant crisis, 40; raised Chantal Terrasson de Fougères, 118; refusal to meet with Jean-Baptiste Ouédraogo, 47; relationship with CNR, 83, 118–19; relationship with France, 4, 120, 149; suggestion to form a multinational force, 119; Yaméogo, 6, 7

humanism, xvi, 11, 74, 106, 109, 185, 187, 188–89. *See also* making new people

ICJ (International Court of Justice), 123

ILO (International Labor Organization), 164

IMF (International Monetary Fund): on Burkina Faso inflation, 141; influence of, xii, xxii; loan conditions for Upper Volta, 19; PPD and requirements for assistance, 117–18; PQDP Five-Year Plan negotiations, 138–39, 141; Structural Adjustment Programs (SAPS) of, x, 188, 191; Upper Volta's GDP, 55

imperialism: CNR, 65, 71, 85; combat with film, 11–12, 21–22; CSP, 35, 37; cultural domination, 16, 22; *Discours d'Orientation Politique*, 70–72; Fanon on, xv–xvi, 74; France, 5, 9, 23, 37, 40, 57, 65; international, 71; reforestation program and, 133; role in Burkinabè Revolution, 97; and Sankara, 10, 118; Sankara's denunciation of, ix, 45, 46, 47; in Sankara's speech to United Nations, 115–16; *Sarraounia* (Hondo), 135; Valère Somé, 20; workshops against, 108. *See also* racism

INAFEC, 22–23, 111, 136, 154

Inter-CDR, 98, 125–26

Intrus, L', 137

Israel, 90, 116

JCC (Journées Cinématographiques de Carthage), 12, 13

Kaboré, Gaston: Algiers Cultural Festival

(1969), 13; on cinema, 108; on
FESPACO, 107; head of CNC, 22–23;
Wend Kuuni (1983), 107, 157; *Zan Boko*
(1988), 157
Kamboulé, Jean-Claude, 33, 34, 36, 49, 53, 75
Keïta, Modibo, 4, 17
Kérékou, Mathieu, 44, 47, 83–84
Ki-Zerbo, Joseph: in exile, 75; MLN, 6, 8; power behind Saye Zerbo's administration, 25; renamed the MLN as UPV, 18; visit to Mali, 121–22
Koné, Ibrahima, 50–52, 93, 94
Kountché, Seyni, 43

Lamien, Watamou, 29, 126, 168
Lamizana, Sangoulé, 31; acquittal, 77; allowing one party and multiparty elections, 18; blames strikes on conspiracy, 24; coup (3 January 1966), 7–8; creation of MNR, 18; dealing with debt crisis, 14–15; declaration of GNR, 17; election 1978, 18–19; founded the PMK, 9; nationalization of country's movie theaters, 155; released, 53
Lang, Jack, 158
Le Collectif l'Oeil Vert, 41
Lenin, Vladimir, 151
Libya, 35, 37, 46, 48, 74, 119; conflict with France, 50; implications in attempted coups, 119; influence on Sankara, xiv–xv; Oujda Treaty with Morocco, 86; solidarity with revolution of the Voltaïc people, 48; support for Polisario Front, 86; U.S. bombing of, 42–43. *See also* Qaddafi, Muammar

LIPAD (Ligue patriotique pour le développement), 15, 18, 25; demonstrations by, 93, 94; invasion of OPT headquarters, 77–78; Sankara, 19. *See also* PAI/LIPAD; Touré, Soumane

Machel, Samora, 147
Madagascar, xx, 15–16, 87
making new people: areas of structural change, 189; birth of the new peasant, 171; CDR, 72; Fanon, xvi, 72–73; FEPACI's core mission, 64–65; manifesto from Algiers Cultural Festival, 13; name change to reflect, 97; objective of Burkinabè Revolution, 185–86; reforms needed, 103; relationship to alienation in Burkina Faso, xiv–xvii; Sankara on, 186. *See also* alienation; humanism
Mali, 4; CEAO, 83; Christmas War, 121–23; Cissé, 42; laborers from Upper Volta, 5; Sankara support of, 119–20; Summit of West African States, 75; tensions with Upper Volta, 17, 82; UMOA, 83
Mali Federation, 5, 40
Mambèty, Djibril-Diop, 22, 23
Maoism, 69, 91
Mao Zedong, xiv, 20
Marx, Karl, xiv, xvi–xvii
Marxism: in CNR, 69; *Discours d'Orientation Politique*, 71; ideology in modern societies, 100; introduced to Sankara at PMK, 10; RDA in Guinea aligned with Soviet Union, 4; U.S. invasion of Grenada, 85; within the military, xi. *See also* UCB

MDV (Mouvement Démocratique Voltaïque), 4
Meeting of Third World Filmmakers, 21
Mitterrand, François, 4, 82, 120, 147–49
Mitterrand, Jean-Christophe, 147, 148
MLN (Mouvement de Libération National), 6, 8, 15
MNR, 18
MOBRAP, 87, 143
Mobutu Sese Seko, 144
Morocco, 20, 73, 86, 116
Mossi, the, 2, 5
Mozambique, 37, 87, 147

Nacro, Fanta Régina, 111, 136
Namibia, 73, 145
National Bureau of the UFB, 159
National Pioneers Movement, 124, 137–38
National Seminar on the Cooperative Movement, 162
National Week of Culture, 84, 88
neocolonialism: *Camp de Thiaroye* (Sembène), 157; *Discours d'Orientation Politique*, 71; enabled by alienation, 134; as more dangerous than colonialism, 2; Sankara's denunciation of, 46; *Sarraounia* (Hondo), 157; South Africa's military support, 141–42; substitute for colonialism, 73; Touré's analysis of, 10. *See also* colonialism
New Caledonia, 120
Niamey Manifesto of African Filmmakers. *See* FEPACI
Nicaragua, 144, 146. *See also* Ortega, Daniel
Niger: attempted coup, 119; Conseil de l'Entente, 40; FEPACI Third Congress, 24; laborers from Upper Volta, 5; Sankara at Summit of West African States, 75; Sankara travel to, 43, 47, 83. *See also* Kountché, Seyni
Nigeria, 38–40, 143
Non-Aligned Movement: denunciation of U.S. bombing in Libya, 143; Eight Summit of the Movement of Non-Aligned Countries, 144–45, 161; meeting 7–12 March 1983, 44–45; Summit of Heads of Government of the Non-Aligned Movement, 130
North Korea, 37, 44, 46, 48, 84, 146

OAU, 17, 122, 143
OCV (Organization Communiste Voltaïque), 20–21
OMR (Organisation Militaire Révolutionnaire): cabinet of, 37; constraining civilian powers, 91; planning for possible coup, 50–51; to replace ROC, 37; vanguard party, 128–29, 168–70
Ortega, Daniel, 44, 144
Ouédraogo, Ernest Nongoma, 62, 89–90, 165
Ouédraogo, Gérard Kango, 4, 15
Ouédraogo, Idrissa, 111, 136, 157
Ouédraogo, Jean-Baptiste: acceptance of OMR proposals, 37; agreements with France in coup, 65; appointed head of commission by Saye Zerbo, 30–31, 33–34; conspired with Somé Yorian, 49; coup, 50; dismissed protests, 52; on eviction of Sankara, 52–53; house-arrest, 124; at "Meeting of Truth,"

46–47; named leader of the CSP, 31; Nigerian migrant crisis, 40; pledge to establish order and security, 44; as president, 35; speech by, 47; tour, 47–48

Ouédraogo, Joseph, 6, 7, 15, 18

Ouédraogo, Philippe, 51–52; Bamouni's appointment to *Sidwaya*, 92–93; *Discours d'Orientation Politique*, 70; minister of equipment and communication, 66; PAI and, xi

Ouédraogo, Pierre, 33–34; animosity to ULCR, 129; appointed general secretary, 125; CDR, 128; directed CDR against UCLR, 127; dispute with PAI/LIPD, 131; fight for control of CDR, 129–31; Inter-CDR, 98; launched UCB, 98; Marxist, xi; national secretary of the CDR, 94; in OMR, 36; secretary general of the CDR, 66; Somé on, 166; three weeks of voluntary labor to achieve PQDP, 163; UCB, 128; use of Inter-CDR, 126

PAI (African Independence Party), xi, 15, 51, 52–53; actions through LIPAD, 67–68; Adama Touré, xi, 27; autonomy, 69; conflict with ULCR, 91–96; distancing from LIPAD hostage taking, 77; ended conversations with CNR, 166; formed LIPAD, 15; founded, 9; and OMR, 36, 37; opposed to Compaoré's candidacy for president, 62; Ouédraogo, Philippe, xi; elect secretary general, 63; role in Upper Volta politics, 9–10; Sankara, 19; Soumane Touré, 27; Tiendrébéogo's plot, 91. *See also* Bamouni, Babou Paulin; PAI/LIPAD; PAI/LIPAD/CSV

PAI/LIPAD, 35, 63, 128; in cabinet seats, 66; demonstrations by, 93; dropped from cabinet, 97; interpretation of the revolution, 97; officials rehabilitated, 125; purged from government, 95–96; SNEAHV strike, 90; Somé, 78; strength among urban working class, 92. *See also* LIPAD; PAI

PAI/LIPAD/CSV, 25, 51

Palestine, 73, 115, 116

Palm, Jean-Marc, 62, 98, 168

Pan-African Cultural Festival 1969, 21

patriarchy, xxiv, 99, 135, 158, 159, 190. *See also* women's emancipation

PCRV (Parti Communiste Révolutionnaire Voltaïque), 21, 25, 52, 128; cabinet seats, 66; Lamien, 29; opposition to CNR, 62; Palm, 98; and Saye Zerbo regime, 26

Penne, Guy, 49, 50, 82, 147

People's Commission Charged with the Prevention of Corruption (CPPC), 153

PLO (Palestine Liberation Organization), 85–86

PMK (Prytanée Militaire de Kadiogo), 9–10, 15

Pooda, Train Raymond, 66, 140

Popular Tribunals of the Revolution. *See* TPR

PPD (Plan populaire de développement): Battle of the Railroad, 101, 108; climate change programs, 101–2, 122, 132–33, 191; cultural infrastructure development, 106; dam at Kompienga, 120; economics of, 99–103; education reform, 99, 104, 111; excessive logging,

101–2; expanded motion picture infrastructure, 106–10; fiscal crisis, 116–17; foreign debt, 99; healthcare reforms, 99, 112–13; indiscriminate animal herding, 101–2; international debt, 117–18; literacy programs, xii, 104, 133; reform of local administrative structures, xii; requirements for assistance from IMF and World Bank, 117–18; start of, 99–100; vaccination campaigns, xii, 112–13, 133, 147; women's emancipation, 110–13, 133–34, 158–59. *See also* CNR foreign policy

PQDP Five-Year Plan of Popular Development (Plan quinquennal de développement populaire), 137–41; agriculture, 138, 159–60; CDR's role in realization of, 162; country's infrastructure, 138; debt crisis, 141; Faso Dan Fani, 160; healthcare, 139; negotiations with IMF and World Bank, 138–39, 141; Popular Investment Effort, 139–40, 159; revenue needed, 159; voluntary labor to achieve, 163

PRA (Parti du régroupement Africain), 5, 8

Présence Africaine (journal), 13

Prieux, Claude, 12–13

Qaddafi, Muammar, 46; *Green Book*, 20, 43, 48; influence on Sankara, xiv–xv, 43, 44; relations with CNR, 85–86; Sankara and, 65; visit to Burkina Faso, 122; visit with Sankara, 47–48

racism: alienation and, xv; apartheid, 14, 116; cause of marginalization, 115–16; defining nonalignment, 45; MOBRAP, 87, 143; workshops against, 108–9. *See also* apartheid; imperialism

Rawlings, Jerry: and CNR, 76, 83; expulsion of African migrants, 39; friendship with Sankara, 114; influence on Sankara, xiv–xv; Non-Aligned Movement meeting, 44

RDA (Rassemblement Démocratique Africain): allied with the PCF, 1–2, 4; in Côte d'Ivoire, 4; early decades of Upper Volta, 3–5; formation, 1; in Guinea, 4; merge with PRA, 5; presidential elections 1978, 18; teachers' strike (1973), 15

Reagan, Ronald, 29, 85, 142–43

Reagan administration, 65, 114

Resolutions of the Third World Filmmakers Meeting (1973), 135

Revolutionary Union of Banks. *See* URB (Union Révolutionnaire des Banques)

RIA (Régiment Inter-Armes d'Appui), 24

ROC (Rassemblement des Officiers Communistes), 19–20, 25; forced into hiatus by Saye Zerbo, 26; founders, 18; replaced by OMR, 37

Sahrawi Arab Democratic Republic, 86

Sankara, Thomas (general biography): Agacher Strip War, 17; age, xi; on agreement with Moscow, 85; apartheid and, 45, 82, 87, 114, 143, 145, 147, 148; arrest, 30; associated cinema with social transformation, 41–42; Catholic faith, xx; on civic responsibilities of the military, 16;

commander of CNC, 19–20; creation of underground military group, 3; death of, ix; denouncement of Saye Zerbo's administration, 30; early life, 9; Fanon's true decolonization, 69–70; on his arrest, 51; influence of Fanon on, xv; liberation theology, xx; Madagascar and, xx, 15–16; minister of information for the CMRPN, 27–29; minister of information resignation speech, 30, 35, 41; mythologization of, ix–x, xx; "patriotic progressives," 34; Qaddafi, 43, 44, 46, 47–48; refused offer of presidency by CSP, 31; relationship with Compaoré, xi, 3, 17, 19, 28, 132, 153–54, 165, 167, 169, 171, 173–77, 179; relationship with Touré, 10; ROC founder, 18; speech at "Meeting of Truth," 46–47; speech to XI Congress of SUVESS, 36. *See also* imperialism

Sankara, Thomas (president): account PQDP, 137–38; address to Eight Summit of the Movement of Non-Aligned Countries, 144; address to OAU on debt for developing countries, 161; alignment with Castro on eradication of debt, 161–62; on apartheid, 45, 143, 145; ban on imported consumables, 163, 164–65; call for calm during Anti-Imperialist Days 1987, 167; call for engagement between filmmakers, 156–57; climate change, 101, 133, 145; closing speech to First National Congress of the CDR, 127; creating a united communist party via bureaucracy, 129; on creating new people, 99; on cultural identity, 106; debate with Mitterrand, 147–49; denounced Libya's offensive in Chad, 86; on developments in Côte d'Ivoire, 119; discovery of plot against revolution, 94; on education reform, 104; first major tour of African states, 87; on gradual release of political opponents, 125; intervening in Hondo's filmmaking, 135; Koné's dismissal, 94; on Lenin, 151; letter to PAI and ULCR, 93–94; loyalty to Somé, 153; named president, 62–63, 66; opening address to TPR, 76; press to hold government officials accountable, 136–37; on prioritization of culture, 134; Qaddafi, 120; on reforestation, 132; on repayment of international debt, 145; speeches, 96–97, 113–16, 123–24; Tenth Franco-African Summit of Heads of State, 82; Tiendrébéogo's plot, 90–91; on using agriculture for reform, 100; visit to USSR, 146

Sankara, Thomas (prime minister): arrest of, 49–50; Castro and, 44–45; first official foreign trip, 43–45; initial speech outlining policies, 38; invested as, 37; at Non-Aligned Movement meeting, 44–45; speech in Bobo-Dioulasso, 48–49; trip to Libya, 43–44

Savimbi, Jonas, 147

Sawadogo, Alfred, 116–17, 132

SECMA, 14

Sédogo, Laurent, 33

Sembène, Ousmane, 41; Algiers Cultural Festival (1969), 13; *Camp de Thiaroye*

(1988), 157; *Ceddo* (1976), 23; censorship, 23; FEPACI, 107; influence of Third Cinema, 21; *La noire de* . . . (1966), 11; *Mandabi* (1968), 11–12; Ministry of Cooperation, 81; role in early African filmmaker networks, 12; trained in Soviet Union, 11; *Xala* (1974), 23

Sessouma, Guillaume, 126

Shagari, Shehu, 39

Sidwaya, 16, 94, 127, 166. *See also* Bamouni, Babou Paulin

Sigué, Vincent, 131

SNEAHV teachers' union: denounced new government, 75; general strike, 89–90; general strikes launched, 15, 24; Ki-Zerbo's PFV, 27; prosecution dropped, 124–25; support pledged for Saye Zerbo regime, 27; teachers fired by CNR, 104

Somé, Valère, xi, 21, 36, 51–52, 63, 93; advice to Sankara to erode Saye Zerbo's administration, 28; attack on PAI/LIPAD, 78; called loose cannon by Compaoré, Blaise, 168–69; on Coordonnateurs du Faso, 97; counsel to Sankara, 27; *Discours d'Orientation Politique*, 70; effect of removal of Traore and Cissé, 153; in fight for control of student's CDR, 130; letter protesting arrest of Soumane Touré, 165–66; minister of higher education, 131; no part of government, 66; in OMR, 36, 37; in Pô, 50; Sankara, 20; in *Sidwaya*, 166; on SNEAHV, 90; UDR, 78; ULC, 21, 26, 69; ULCR, 78, 92, 168; on Zongo, 169

Somé Yorian, Gabriel, 31, 34, 47, 49, 53

SONAVOCI, 14

South Africa: backing of Angolan rebels, 85; efforts to crush anti-apartheid uprising, 143; Nkomati Accord, 87; as part of the old order, 116; visit to Mitterrand, 120. *See also* apartheid; CNR

Soviet Union. *See* USSR

Summit of West African States, 75

SUVESS, 36

SWAPO, 45, 73

SYLVA (International Silva Conference on Trees and Forests), 132

SYNTSHA, 124–25

Terrasson de Fougères, Chantal, 118, 174, 181

Third Cinema: at FESPACO 1985, 108; Hondo, 134; movement, 45; theory, 11, 21, 64

Tiendrébéogo, Didier, 90, 92

Toé, Fidèle, 10, 28, 66

Togo, 40, 45, 47, 119, 144

Touré, Adama, 18, 51–52; arrest, 165; Bamouni's appointment to *Sidwaya*, 92–93; broadcast of *Discours d'Orientation Politique*, 70; counsel to Sankara, 27; freed from prison, 125; influence on students, 10; member of SNEAHV, 15; minister of information, 66; PAI and, xi; at PMK, 9–10, 15; on rift in government, 95–96; Sankara, 19; sent to countryside, 97

Touré, Sékou, 4

Touré, Soumane, xi, 15, 18, 63, 91; arrest of, 165; counsel to Sankara,

27; CSB to participate in national budget, 117; fighting over arrest of, 166; imprisonment, 30, 128; labor federations declared counterrevolutionaries, 93; LIPAD's presence in Anti-Imperialist Day of the Youth, 94; popularity of, 27; public employee salaries, 79; release from prison, 35, 146; Sankara, 19; warrant for arrest issued, 27

TPR (Tribunaux Populaires de la Révolution): chieftaincies, 77, 79; CMRPN found guilty and sentenced at, 90; creation and structure of, 63–64, 76–77, 88, 96; France's refusal to recognize, 142; LIPAD's TPR, 91–92; of Mohamed Diawara, 118, 119; Office of Posts and Telecommunications, 77–78; Saye Zerbo charged, 90; success of, 192; Tiendrébéogo's plot, 90–91

training in filmmaking: CIPROFILM, 23; Cuba, 84–85, 110, 131; France's role, 7, 23–24, 41, 81; funding, xiv, 22, 24, 41, 81, 84, 106–7, 135, 136; INAFEC, 22–23, 84, 107, 136; needed to make new people, xiii, 11, 84, 88; recommendations in Algiers Charter, 41; Sembène trained in Soviet Union, 11

Traoré, Etienne, 166, 167, 169

Traoré, Mamadou, 162–63, 166

Traoré, Moïse, 116, 131, 140, 153

Traoré, Moussa, 17, 82–83, 121

UCB (Union des Communistes Burkinabè): confrontations with ULCR, 140; considered themselves as leading figure of communism, 128; founding, 126; intimidation tactics, 129; Pierre Ouédraogo, 126; role in vanguard party, 168; Sessouma, Guillaume, 126; Somé on, 166; vanguard party, 128–29

UFB (Union des Femmes du Burkina), 12, 137–38, 158, 159

ULC (Union de Lutte Communiste), xi, 21, 25, 26, 35, 51, 66

ULC–*La Flamme*, 131, 140, 153, 170

ULCR (Union de Lutte Communiste-Reconstruite): accused Somé of betrayal, 131; call for capital punishment, 91; conflict with PAI, 91–96; confrontations with UCB, 140; control of student's CDR, 125–31; formation, 69, 78; impatience of, 128; Maoism, 91; in new administration, 97–98; role in vanguard party, 168; swept elections, 98; tension with Inter-CDR, 125–26; vanguard party, 128–29. *See also* Ouédraogo, Pierre

UNAB (National Union of Burkinabè Elders), 124, 137–38

UNDD (Union Nationale pour la Défense de la Démocratie), 18–19

UNESCO, 22, 107

UNICEF, 112–13, 160

Union of Burkinabè Women (UFB). *See* UFB (Union des Femmes du Burkina)

Union Syndicale des Travailleurs Voltaïques (USTV), 6

United Nations: Burkina Faso, 146; condemnation of United States for attack on Libya, 143; New Caledonia added as unfree territory, 149; Sankara's visit to, 113–16; Upper Volta elected to Security Council, 75; USSR, 146

United States: backing of Angolan rebels, 85; challenged by CNR, 96; Chile, 67; CIA, 75; claim Burkinabè Revolution puppet of Libya and USSR, 120, 122; Cold War ideology, xi; condemning USSR in Afghanistan, 146; deflationary policies, 29; invasion of Grenada, 85, 116, 144; watching Cuba Burkina Faso relations, 109–10. *See also* Reagan, Ronald; Reagan administration; United Nations

UNPB (National Peasants Union of Burkina), 164

UNSTHV (l'Union Nationale des Syndicates des Travailleurs de Haute-Volta), 6

Upper Volta, 1; boycotting the 1984 Olympic Games, 87; debt, 14; economic crisis, 29–30; elected to United Nations' Security Council, 75; foreign debt crisis, 19; GDP, 27; GNI per capital income, 27; inflation, 27; joining Mali Federation, 5; military of, 20; name changed to Burkina Faso, 96; national debt, 27; nationalization of the theater system, 22; people used as reserve of labor for other French colonies, 5, 7; renamed to Burkina Faso, xiv, xxi–xxii; tensions with Mali, 17; USTV, 6, 7; working-class organizations became the site for resistance, 6. *See also* Burkina Faso

UPV (Union Progressiste Voltaïque), 31

URB (Union Révolutionnaire des Banques), 116–17

USSR, 42, 74, 143; Cold War ideology, xi; Communist Party of the Soviet Union, 146; Diallo's push for alignment with, 95; at FESPACO 1987, 157; at National Week of Culture, 84; Sembène trained in, 11; visit by Sankara, 146. *See also* Marxism

USTV (l'Union Syndicale des Travailleurs Voltaïques), 6, 7

Vieyra, Paulin Soumanou, 11, 12, 154, 156

Week of African Cinema (1969), 13, 14
women in film, 110–11, 136
women's emancipation, xxiv; *Discours d'Orientation Politique*, 72, 111, 190; female circumcision, 111; healthcare reforms, 112–13; marriage restrictions, 111; National Bureau for the UFB, 159; Plan of Action, 159; PPD programs, 103, 110–13, 133–34, 158–59; right to inherit property, 111; *Sarraounia* (Hondo), 135. *See also* patriarchy

World Bank: impact of PPD on environment, 102; loan conditions for Upper Volta, 19; PPD and requirements for assistance, 117–18; PQDP Five-Year Plan negotiations, 138–39, 141

Yaméogo, Maurice: declared emergency, 7–8; embraced Saye Zerbo's government, 25; MDV, 4; president of Upper Volta, 5–6; released, 53; return to power, 18–19; support for return to

presidency, 34
Yé, Arsène, 159
Young, Andrew, 114

Zerbo, Saye: charged at TPR, 90; coup, 24–31; deflationary policies of, 26–27; released, 53; sentenced reduced, 124. *See also* Sankara, Thomas (president)
Zongo, Henri: arrests, 30, 53; creation of underground military group, 3; execution, 185; exiled, 33; management of PQDP, 140; Marxist, xi; member of Coordonnateurs du Faso, 63, 97, 137, 173; minister in charge of state agencies, 66; no desire to succeed Sankara, 175; in OMR, 36; OMR's role in vanguard party, 168; organizing meetings, 170; refusal to denounce Jonas Somé, 179; restored to position, 31; ROC, 18, 34; Sankara, 17, 19; supervisor of textile mills, 160; surrender in Pô, 50. *See also* Somé, Valère